Digital Marketing for Public Dental Health:

Global Impact Strategies

Dachel Martínez Asanza
https://orcid.org/0000-0002-1830-7137

National School of Public Health, Cuba & University of Medical Sciences of Havana, Cuba

IGI Global
Scientific Publishing
Publishing Tomorrow's Research Today

Vice President of Editorial	Melissa Wagner
Director of Acquisitions	Mikaela Felty
Director of Book Development	Jocelynn Hessler
Production Manager	Mike Brehm
Cover Design	Jose Rosado

Published in the United States of America by
IGI Global Scientific Publishing
701 East Chocolate Avenue
Hershey, PA, 17033, USA
Tel: 717-533-8845 | Fax: 717-533-7115
Website: https://www.igi-global.com E-mail: cust@igi-global.com

Library of Congress Cataloging-in-Publication Data

LCCN: 2026011355 (CIP Data Pending)
ISBN13: 9798337388946
Isbn13Softcover: 9798337388953
EISBN13: 9798337388960
British Cataloguing in Publication Data
A Cataloguing in Publication record for this book is available from the British Library.

Table of Contents

Detailed Table of Contents

The aging of the global population presents a significant challenge to public health, demanding innovative and sustainable dental approaches. This integrative literature review synthesizes research on the intersection of Geriatric Dentistry, Gerodontology, and digital marketing and communication strategies in public health. Articles in English and Spanish were analyzed, published between January 2021 and December 2025. The search was conducted in the Google Scholar, PubMed/Medline, Wiley, and Scopus databases. The results reveal that integrating these fields improves patient-centered care, service accessibility, participation, and coordination through digital strategies. However, challenges persist, such as inadequate professional training, limited inclusion of interdisciplinary curricula, and insufficient public policy frameworks. To overcome these barriers, investment in interdisciplinary education and the strategic implementation of digital technologies is necessary to improve the oral health of older adults and ensure their overall well-being.

This chapter explores the role of digital marketing strategies in attracting new customers within health services, with a focus on how digital transformation reshapes patient acquisition processes. The purpose is to identify key strategies, determinants, challenges, and practical implications of digital marketing in healthcare contexts. A narrative literature review approach was adopted, synthesizing findings from recent empirical and theoretical studies in digital marketing, healthcare communication, and patient behavior. The results indicate that content marketing, social media engagement, and data-driven personalization significantly enhance trust, patient engagement, and service selection. However, effectiveness is influenced by regulatory constraints, digital health literacy, and concerns related to privacy and information credibility. The chapter concludes that successful customer acquisition in health services requires an integrated approach combining value-driven content, ethical communication, and technological capability to build trust and long-term patient relationships.

Alaa Abdulkareem Ghaleb Almado, Department of Business Administration, College of Administration and Economics, University of Baghdad, Iraq
Sarah Ali Saeed Alameri, Department of Business Administration, College of Administration and Economics, University of Baghdad, Iraq
Eshaq Youssef Hamdan, Department of Business Administration, College of Administration and Economics, University of Samarra, Iraq
Saadiyah Owaid Awni, Technical Institute of Management, Middle Technical University, Iraq
Sarab Jawad Mohammed Al-Obaidi, Department of Industrial Management, College of Administration and Economics, University of Baghdad, Iraq
Ahmed Abbas Hammadi, College of Administration and Economics, University of Fallujah, Iraq
Arafat Naser Jasim Alyousuf, University of Basrah, Iraq

This study examines the influence of AI-powered complaint management adoption on patient retention in dental healthcare settings. Specifically, the study investigates the effects of perceived efficiency, complaint resolution quality, trust in AI-powered complaint management, and perceived dehumanization of service on patient retention. A quantitative approach was employed using a self-administered questionnaire distributed to customers of dental clinics. A total of 165 valid responses were analyzed. The findings reveal that perceived efficiency, complaint resolution quality, and trust positively influence patient retention, whereas perceived dehumanization of service negatively affects retention intentions. Trust emerged as the strongest predictor of patient retention. The study contributes to the emerging literature on AI adoption in healthcare complaint management by highlighting both the opportunities and challenges associated with integrating AI into dental service recovery and patient relationship management.

This study investigates the impact of electronic customer relationship management (E-CRM) on the business performance of private dental clinics. It focuses on four dimensions: electronic patient data management, personalized electronic services, online appointment and scheduling systems, and electronic feedback and complaint management. A quantitative approach was used, with data collected from 95 employees in private dental clinics through a structured questionnaire. The results show that electronic patient data management, online appointment and scheduling systems, and electronic feedback and complaint management significantly enhance business performance, while personalized electronic services have no significant effect. Among all variables, online scheduling systems exert the strongest influence. The study contributes to the literature by extending E-CRM research to private dental clinics and provides practical implications for managers seeking to improve clinic performance through digital transformation.

This study examines the influence of digital health marketing on preventive oral health behavior among dental service customers in Algeria. A quantitative approach was employed using a structured questionnaire distributed to customers of dental services. A total of 196 valid responses were collected and analyzed using multiple regression analysis. The study investigated the effects of online oral health information quality, social media health engagement, personalized digital communication, and trust in digital health information on preventive oral health behavior. The findings revealed that all four dimensions significantly and positively influence preventive oral health behavior, with trust in digital health information emerging as the strongest predictor, followed by personalized digital communication. The model explained 61.2% of the variance in preventive oral health behavior. The study highlights the growing role of digital health marketing in encouraging preventive oral care and offers practical implications for dental clinics and healthcare policymakers.

Preface

The rapid evolution of digital technologies has fundamentally transformed the ways in which health information is communicated, accessed, and applied across diverse populations. As societies become increasingly interconnected through digital platforms, new opportunities have emerged to address longstanding public health challenges through innovative communication strategies. Among these challenges, oral health remains a critical yet often underrepresented component of global health promotion efforts. Despite significant advances in preventive dentistry and public health interventions, disparities in oral health awareness, access to care, and health outcomes continue to persist across regions and populations. In this context, digital marketing presents a powerful avenue for expanding the reach, effectiveness, and impact of public dental health initiatives worldwide.

Digital Marketing for Public Dental Health: Global Impact Strategies has been developed to address this timely and important need. This volume explores the intersection of public oral health, digital communication, and emerging technologies, providing a comprehensive examination of how digital marketing strategies can be leveraged to improve oral health promotion and education on a global scale. The book recognizes that effective health communication extends beyond the dissemination of information; it requires audience engagement, behavioral influence, cultural sensitivity, data-driven decision-making, and the strategic use of digital platforms to foster sustainable health outcomes.

The primary objective of this book is to equip researchers, practitioners, policymakers, and healthcare leaders with evidence-based approaches for utilizing digital marketing to enhance public oral health initiatives. Through the integration of contemporary research, practical applications, and strategic insights, the chapters presented in this volume demonstrate how digital tools can support more efficient, equitable, and impactful oral health interventions. By examining innovative communication models, social media engagement strategies, health informatics applications, digital campaign development, and emerging technological trends, this book offers valuable guidance for advancing oral health promotion in increasingly digital environments.

This volume serves a diverse and international audience. Academics and researchers in public health, dentistry, digital marketing, health informatics, healthcare management, and related disciplines will find a rich source of scholarly perspectives and emerging research directions. Dental professionals—including dentists, dental hygienists, clinic managers, and oral health educators—will benefit from practical frameworks that can enhance patient engagement and community outreach efforts. Policymakers, government officials, and public health administrators will gain insights into the development of scalable and evidence-informed digital health initiatives. Furthermore, postgraduate and undergraduate students, as well as entrepreneurs and innovators working in digital health and health technology sectors, will discover valuable perspectives on the future of oral health communication and service delivery.

The chapters within this book collectively emphasize the importance of interdisciplinary collaboration. Addressing global oral health challenges requires contributions from healthcare professionals, communication specialists, technology developers, data scientists, educators, and policymakers. By bringing together diverse viewpoints and expertise, this volume highlights how collaborative approaches can generate innovative solutions capable of reaching broader audiences and reducing oral health inequalities across different socioeconomic and geographic contexts.

As editor, I am grateful to the contributing authors whose expertise, research, and commitment have made this volume possible. Their contributions reflect the growing recognition that digital marketing is not merely a promotional tool but a strategic mechanism for advancing public health objectives and improving population well-being. I also extend my appreciation to the reviewers and publishing team whose efforts have helped ensure the quality and relevance of this work.

It is my hope that this book will serve as both a valuable reference and a catalyst for future innovation in public dental health communication. By embracing the opportunities afforded by digital technologies and evidence-based marketing strategies, healthcare professionals and researchers can contribute to a future in which oral health information is more accessible, interventions are more effective, and positive oral health outcomes are achieved for communities around the world.

ORGANIZATION OF THE BOOK

Chapter 1 examines the growing importance of integrating geriatric dentistry, gerodontology, and digital marketing within public health frameworks to address the oral health needs of an aging global population. Through an extensive review of recent literature, the chapter highlights how digital communication strategies can improve access to care, patient engagement, service coordination, and health outcomes among older adults. The discussion also identifies persistent barriers, including insufficient interdisciplinary training and limited policy support, while emphasizing the need for strategic investments in education and digital innovation to promote healthy aging and equitable oral healthcare.

Chapter 2 explores how digital marketing strategies are transforming patient acquisition in dental healthcare services. The chapter provides a comprehensive examination of contemporary approaches, including content marketing, social media engagement, and personalized communication, demonstrating their capacity to build trust and strengthen patient relationships. By addressing both opportunities and challenges associated with digital healthcare marketing, the chapter offers valuable insights into the ethical and strategic considerations necessary for attracting and retaining patients in an increasingly competitive digital environment.

Chapter 3 investigates the role of artificial intelligence in complaint management systems and its influence on patient retention within dental healthcare settings. The chapter demonstrates how AI-driven solutions can enhance service efficiency, improve complaint resolution, and foster patient trust, all of which contribute positively to long-term patient relationships. At the same time, it acknowledges concerns regarding the potential loss of human interaction and underscores the importance of balancing technological innovation with patient-centered care.

Chapter 4 focuses on the rapidly expanding field of international dental health tourism and examines how digital marketing adoption contributes to customer retention among patients seeking dental care abroad. The chapter highlights the significance of digital information quality, electronic service delivery, perceived value, and electronic word-of-mouth in shaping patient experiences and loyalty. Its findings reinforce the growing importance of strategic digital engagement in fostering trust and maintaining lasting relationships within the global dental tourism marketplace.

Chapter 5 evaluates the impact of electronic customer relationship management systems on the operational and business performance of private dental clinics. Emphasizing the role of digital patient data management, online scheduling platforms, and electronic feedback systems, the chapter demonstrates how technological integration can enhance organizational efficiency and service quality. The discussion provides practical guidance for dental clinic managers seeking to leverage digital transformation initiatives to strengthen both patient experiences and institutional performance.

Chapter 6 examines the relationship between digital health marketing and preventive oral health behaviors among dental service users. The chapter illustrates how high-quality online information, social media engagement, personalized digital communication, and trust in digital content can positively influence preventive health practices. By highlighting the central role of trust and targeted communication, the chapter underscores the potential of digital marketing strategies to support public health goals through behavioral change and proactive oral healthcare.

Chapter 7 provides a broad exploration of digital marketing tools and their capacity to encourage preventive health behaviors within dental public health initiatives. Drawing upon behavioral theories and contemporary communication technologies, the chapter discusses the use of mobile applications, wearable devices, artificial intelligence, and personalized messaging systems to enhance patient awareness and engagement. It also critically addresses ethical, regulatory, and equity-related challenges that must be considered when implementing digital interventions aimed at long-term health behavior change.

Chapter 8 presents a compelling reexamination of digital marketing as an essential component of oral health systems rather than merely a promotional activity. Introducing innovative conceptual frameworks and systems-based perspectives, the chapter positions digital marketing as a strategic mechanism for advancing prevention, public engagement, and health equity. By linking behavioral science, technological infrastructure, governance, and public value creation, the chapter offers a forward-looking vision for building more responsive and inclusive oral health systems in the digital age.

Chapter 9 explores the emerging role of TikTok and generative artificial intelligence in public dental health communication. Recognizing the influence of short-form video platforms on younger audiences, the chapter proposes innovative strategies for combating misinformation and promoting evidence-based oral health education. Through the integration of AI-generated content, audience-specific communication, and ethical digital care principles, the chapter demonstrates how modern technologies can expand the reach and effectiveness of dental public health campaigns.

Chapter 10 concludes the volume by examining global strategies for leveraging digital marketing and social media to advance public dental health promotion. Drawing upon a comprehensive review of recent scholarly literature, the chapter identifies major trends, opportunities, and challenges shaping the field. It highlights the growing role of digital platforms, influencer engagement, teledentistry, and digital infrastructure in improving patient education and access to care while advocating for inclusive, sustainable, and globally informed approaches to oral health promotion.

CONCLUSION

As the chapters in this volume collectively demonstrate, the future of public dental health will be shaped not only by advances in clinical knowledge and healthcare delivery but also by the strategic application of digital technologies and innovative communication practices. Digital marketing has evolved far beyond its traditional promotional role and now serves as a powerful mechanism for education, engagement, behavior change, service accessibility, and population health improvement.

The contributions presented in this book illustrate how digital tools can strengthen connections between dental professionals, healthcare systems, policymakers, and the communities they serve, creating new opportunities to address persistent oral health challenges on a global scale.

A recurring theme throughout this volume is the importance of trust, personalization, accessibility, and ethical responsibility in digital health communication. Whether through artificial intelligence, customer relationship management systems, social media platforms, digital health campaigns, teledentistry initiatives, or emerging technologies such as generative AI, the effectiveness of digital strategies ultimately depends on their ability to empower individuals with accurate information, foster meaningful engagement, and support informed health decisions. At the same time, the chapters remind us that technological innovation must be accompanied by careful consideration of privacy, equity, digital literacy, and regulatory frameworks to ensure that the benefits of digital transformation are shared broadly and responsibly.

This book also highlights the value of interdisciplinary collaboration in advancing public dental health. The convergence of dentistry, public health, marketing, information technology, behavioral science, and policy development offers a rich foundation for creating innovative and sustainable solutions to complex oral health issues. By bringing together diverse perspectives and experiences from different regions of the world, this volume contributes to a more comprehensive understanding of how digital strategies can be adapted to meet the needs of varied populations and healthcare systems.

It is my hope that this book will serve as both a scholarly reference and a practical guide for researchers, educators, practitioners, healthcare administrators, policymakers, and students seeking to navigate the evolving landscape of digital oral health promotion. The insights presented throughout these chapters not only reflect current developments in the field but also point toward future opportunities for innovation, research, and global collaboration.

As digital technologies continue to transform healthcare, the responsibility to harness these tools in ways that are ethical, inclusive, evidence-based, and patient-centered becomes increasingly important. By embracing this responsibility, the global oral health community can help create a future in which high-quality oral health information, preventive services, and patient support are more accessible than ever before, ultimately contributing to healthier individuals, stronger communities, and improved public health outcomes worldwide.

Chapter 1

Transforming Dental Care:
Integrating Geriatric Dentistry, Gerodontology, and Digital Marketing in Public Health

Dachel Martínez Asanza
http://orcid.org/0000-0002-1830-7137
National School of Public Health (ENSAP), Cuba & Havana Medical Sciences University, Cuba

Anuli Njoku
http://orcid.org/0009-0007-9158-5321
Southern Connecticut State University, USA

Snehal Baviskar
http://orcid.org/0009-0004-5597-0669
Southern Connecticut State University, USA

Farida Mouloudj
University of Medea, Algeria

ABSTRACT

The aging of the global population presents a significant challenge to public health, demanding innovative and sustainable dental approaches. This integrative literature review synthesizes research on the intersection of Geriatric Dentistry, Gerodontology, and digital marketing and communication strategies in public health. Articles in English and Spanish were analyzed, published between January 2021 and December 2025. The search was conducted in the Google Scholar, PubMed/Medline, Wiley, and

DOI: 10.4018/979-8-3373-8894-6.ch001

Scopus databases. The results reveal that integrating these fields improves patient-centered care, service accessibility, participation, and coordination through digital strategies. However, challenges persist, such as inadequate professional training, limited inclusion of interdisciplinary curricula, and insufficient public policy frameworks. To overcome these barriers, investment in interdisciplinary education and the strategic implementation of digital technologies is necessary to improve the oral health of older adults and ensure their overall well-being.

1. INTRODUCTION

In the 21st century the aging of the global population is one of the main challenges for public health, and demands innovative, technological, and sustainable solutions within the field of dentistry. It is estimated that by 2050, the population aged 60 and over will exceed 2.1 billion (Huenchuan, 2018). In response to this demographic transition, the United Nations and the World Health Organization (WHO, 2020) have designated the period 2021-2030 as the *Decade of Healthy Aging*, with the intent to encourage concerted action to promote longer, healthier lives.

Within this context, oral healthcare for the aging population symbolizes a critical challenge that necessitates an insightful understanding of the complexities inherent in this stage of life. Geriatric dentistry and Gerodontology are important, complementary disciplines within the context of a globally aging population. As highlighted by Martínez-Asanza et al. (2026), both fields are vital for addressing the specific oral health needs of older adults, playing a crucial role in both educational settings and the delivery of comprehensive care for this demographic.

The accelerated growth of the global older adult population has catalyzed a significant line of research, reflected in the works of Chávez et al. (2022), Janto et al. (2022), Leung & Chu (2023), Poudel et al. (2024), Lipsky et al. (2024), Patel and Gallagher (2024), and Tadjoedin et al. (2025) that positions oral health as a essential pillar of general well-being. This foundation utilizes a direct influence on the quality of life and functional capacity of senior individuals. In this sense, authors such as Chan et al. (2021), Deutsch & Jay (2021), and Janto et al. (2022) have argued that an effective clinical approach not only mitigates oral pathologies but also reduces the risk of systemic complications, thereby strengthening public health outcomes for this demographic group.

Public health initiatives remain vital for promoting access to high-quality, affordable oral healthcare services (da Mata & Alen, 2023; Bolukbasi & Dundar, 2024; Sidharthan et al., 2024; Srijaroen et al., 2025; Folorunsho et al., 2025; Hui et al., 2026). Maintaining good oral health is essential for general well-being and active societal participation (Martínez-Asanza et al., 2025[a]), underscoring the imperative to integrate oral healthcare into broader public health strategies to support active aging. To effectively bridge the gap between these public health goals and service accessibility, modern communication channels are essential.

Concurrently, digital marketing has materialized as a transformative force in dental practice (Piedra Andrade et al., 2024). In the clinical realm, digital marketing empowers professionals to optimize visibility, attract new patients, and foster retention through strategies such as Search Engine Optimization (SEO), social media engagement, and targeted content marketing (Nazely et al., 2023; Piedra-Andrade et al., 2024). These tools do more than enhance clinic profitability; they expand the reach of dental services, particularly for vulnerable or hard-to-reach populations, by disseminating educational information, promoting disease prevention, and ensuring timely, accessible specialized care.

This chapter presents a literature review synthesizing research on the intersection of Geriatric Dentistry, Gerodontology, and digital marketing and communication strategies within the context of public health. By identifying key barriers and highlighting promising digital and interdisciplinary approaches reported in the literature, this review seek address the following research question: How can the integration of Geriatric Dentistry, Gerodontology, and digital marketing strategies within a public health framework effectively overcome barriers and enhance access to oral health promotion and care coordination for older adults?

To conceptualize the integrative approach developed throughout this chapter, the following interrelationship model **(Figure 1)** is proposed, which articulates the pillars of geriatric dental care with digital innovations and public health.

Figure 1. Conceptual model of the Integration of strategic domains in geriatric dental care

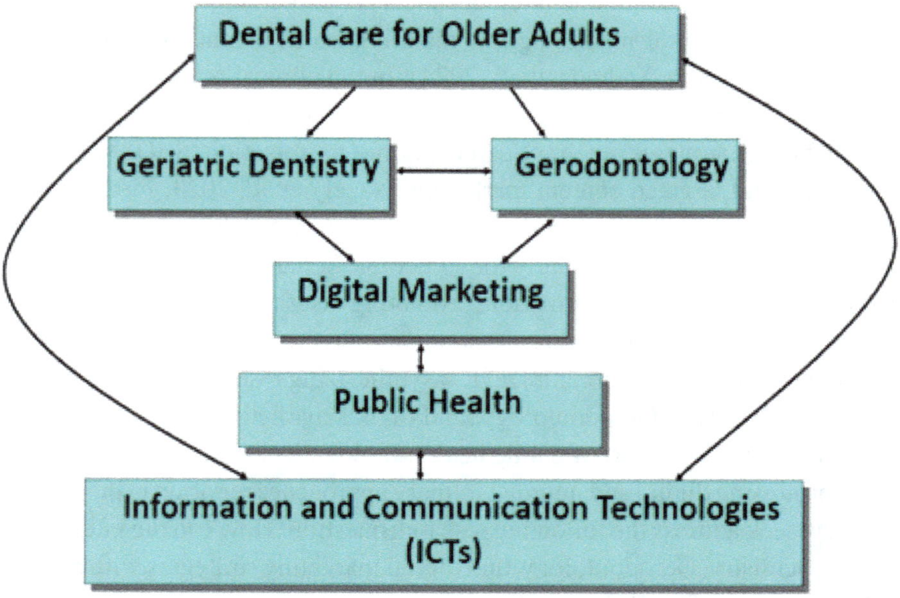

2. BACKGROUND

2.1. Introduction to Geriatric Dentistry and Gerodontology

Geriatric Dentistry emerged in the United States during 1960s, driven by oral health practitioners and scholars in the field (Chávez Reátegui et al., 2014). Often conflated with Gerodontology, this specialized branch of dentistry focuses on the clinical care of older adults. However, Martínez Asanza et al. (2025b) accentuate the importance of distinguishing between these terms to clarify their unique contributions to the clinical practice and public health.

"(…) Geriatric Dentistry involves the oral health care of individuals aged 60 or older, as well as adults of any age whose general health is significantly influenced by degenerative processes and diseases commonly associated with older adults (…)" (Chávez Reátegui et al., 2014). Geriatric Dentistry addresses the biological, systemic, and oral changes associated with aging to manage the etiology and pathophysiology of oral conditions linked to prevalent chronic diseases. Its interventions, restorative, rehabilitative, and palliative, are specifically tailored to the patient's physical and cognitive limitations (Martínez Asanza et al., 2026).

In contrast, Gerodontology emerged in Europe during the late 1970s (Chávez Reátegui et al., 2014). This discipline adopts a broader and more holistic approach that encompasses not only clinical oral care but also research and the development of public health policies tailored to the elderly population (Martínez Asanza et al., 2020a). Gerodontology is defined as:

"(...) the dental specialty that seeks to provide optimal oral care to older adults through the prevention, treatment, and rehabilitation of conditions inherent to aging, as well as the oral repercussions of chronic degenerative diseases associated with old age" (...). (Chávez Reátegui et al., 2014).

Gerodontology emphasizes the prevention and optimization of oral health in older adults, regardless of their health status, by holistically considering the scientific, biological, psychological, social, educational, economic, political, and demographic factors inherent to aging within each sociocultural context (Martínez Asanza et al., 2020b). By adopting a psychosocial, community-oriented, and multidisciplinary approach aligned with public health policies, this discipline transcends the traditional clinical-curative model to prioritize primary care, healthy aging, and the management of social determinants of health (Martínez Asanza et al., 2026). In this way, Gerodontology establishes itself as a comprehensive dental strategy that promotes health and self-care throughout the entire life cycle, aiming to substantially improve the quality of life of the older adult population. This distinction is vital for the integration of dental services into broader healthcare systems, moving toward a model that values healthy aging alongside clinical intervention.

The following is presented as Table 1. This table summarizes the key distinctions and similarities between Geriatric Dentistry and Gerodontology, highlighting their respective focuses on the oral care of older adults.

Table 1.

Feature	Geriatric Dentistry (Reactive)	Gerodontology (Proactive)
Concept	-Branch of dentistry focused on clinical treatment of the elderly, as well as adults of any age whose general health is significantly influenced by degenerative process.	-Focuses on the psychological, educational, social, economic and demographic aspects related to the oral health of older adults. -Branch of dentistry that emphasises the biopsychosocial prevention of oral health problems in this age group, whether they are healthy or ill. -Its purpose is to achieve optimal oral health and well-being within the sociocultural context.
Approach	-Biomedical and restorative.	-Biopsychosocial and preventive.
Patient Profile	-Older adults with established oral pathologies or systemic diseases.	-Healthy or ill individuals, focusing on maintaining functionality throughout life.
Intervention	-Remedial (fillings, extractions, prostheses).	-Strategic (promotion, education, early prevention).
Goal	-To treat the disease and rehabilitate the patient	-To ensure social dignity, quality of life, and functionality.

2.2. The Global Imperative of Geriatric Oral Health

The aging process implicates a multifaceted intervention of physiological, psychological, and social transitions that profoundly impact oral health outcomes (Patel & Gallagher, 2024; Lipsky et al., 2024; Sahab et al., 2025). Worldwide, the demographic shift toward older population, driven by unprecedented increased in life expectancy and medical advancements, has resulted in a higher prevalence of chronic diseases, physical disabilities, and cognitive impairments (Gianfredi et al., 2025; Callaway et al., 2025; Xi et al., 2025). These factors do not exist in isolation, rather, they directly dictate the complexity of oral healthcare requirements and necessitate a specialized highly adaptive professional response.

Moreover, poor oral health in older adults is increasingly recognized not merely as a localized concern but as a significant systemic risk factor. Compelling evidence link oral diseases to major general health conditions, including diabetes mellitus, cardiovascular diseases, and cerebrovascular disorders, often exacerbating the severity of these systemic ailments (Badewy et al., 2021; Janto et al., 2022). In this context, it is imperative for dental professionals to master the specific needs of the geriatric population. Preparation must extend beyond clinical proficiency to include a deep understanding of the systemic oral connection, enabling the delivery of high-quality, personalized care that supports the overall well-being of the aging population.

Despite this, the terms "Geriatric Dentistry" and "Gerodontology" are often used interchangeably in the literature, leading to confusion within the academic community. Researchers such as da Mata & Alen (2023)-and Dickie de Castillos & Rodríguez-Junior (2023) exemplify this trend, underscoring the need for terminological clarity in. Martínez –Asanza et al. (2025) advocate for a clear differentiation based on distinct approaches of each discipline, a perspective by earlier classifications from Jiménez-Herrero (1998) and Chávez-Reátegui et al. (2014). Adhering to these distinctions is essential for advancing oral healthcare for older adults.

Differentiating Geriatric Dentistry and Gerodontology enables for a more precise, effective responses to the oral health needs of older adults. While Geriatric Dentistry primarily focuses on individual clinical care, Gerodontology adopts a health-oriented approach that prioritizes. This distinction ensures comprehensive attention to both personal clinical requirements and public health policies, ultimately enhancing the quality of life and well-being of the elderly population.

The authors of the present study note that, although the terms "Geriatric Dentistry" and "Gerodontology" are sometimes used synonymously in the literature, each represents distinct health actions directed toward older adults, including health promotion, disease prevention, treatment, and rehabilitation. Integrating both approaches fosters more comprehensive oral healthcare for older adults.

Internationally, the field of dentistry should reflect this distinction within undergraduate and postgraduate curricula, akin to the approach in medicine. For example, in Cuba, the specialty is named *"Specialty of Geriatrics and Gerontology"*, as referenced by Martínez-Asanza et al. (2026), and is reflected in the name of the corresponding scientific society. Similarly, Spain hosts the prestigious *Revista Española de Geriatría y Gerontología* (*Spanish Journal of Geriatrics and Gerontology*), the oficial journal of the *Spanish Society of Geriatrics and Gerontology* (Jiménez-Herrero, 2003). Recognizing and differentiating these concepts enriches academic training, strengthens clinical practice, improves services planning, and contributes to a more ethical, humanistic approach to oral healthcare for older adults.

Nowadays, the influence of social media on oral health-related quality of life (OHRQL) and cognitive function in older adults can be positive, as suggested by Farzad et al. (2026). However, other researchers, including Rosales & Fernández-Ardèvol. (2020), Dickinson et al. (2024) and Beck Guimarães et al. (2025), highlight that many social media publications perpetuate ageism by reinforcing stereotypes of frailty associated with old age. These findings underscore the urgent need to raise awareness and implement educational initiatives that combat ageism and foster inclusive perspective on aging.

It is imperative to eradicate exclusionary stereotypes, commonly known as ageism, that now permeate the digital environment and social media platforms. It is essential to convey the message that aging is not synonymous with disease; on the contrary, healthy aging with a high quality of life is achievable. This is the commitment that the field of dentistry must lead: contributing to the construction of a sustainable and inclusive society where all individuals can age with general well-being and, specifically, with optimal oral health.

2.3. The Importance of Oral Health in Older Adults

The Global Oral Health Status Report (WHO, 2022) indicates that 3.5 billion people suffer from oral diseases, highlighting a critical global inequity in healthcare. The report emphasizes that this disease burden disproportionately impacts vulnerable populations, particularly older adults, who encounter significant barriers to access. Consequently, it is imperative to prioritize comprehensive care policies that ensure equitable oral health services to promote healthy and dignified aging.

Oral health is a fundamental component of overall well-being, particularly in older adults, as it not only reflects systemic health conditions but also directly impacts quality of life (Sahab et al., 2025; D'Aiuto et al., 2025; Hui et al., 2026). According to Glick et al. (2017), oral health is a multifaceted concept that encompasses the ability to speak, smile, chew, and express emotions confidently, free from pain or disease in the craniofacial complex. This definition, developed by the International Dental Federation (FDI), emphasizes that oral health extends beyond the absence of disease, incorporating physiological, psychological, and social dimensions essential for a high quality of life. The prevailing literature (Atanda et al., 2022; Michea et al., 2023; Slack-Smith et al., 2023) underscores that poor oral health and tooth loss are not inevitable consequences of aging, but rather the cumulative result of preventable pathological processes.

Maintaining good oral health in older adults is critical for preventing systemic diseases, enhancing nutrition, and supporting comprehensive well-being (Barranca-Enríquez & Romo-González, 2022; Tadjoedin et al., 2025). Achieving this requires more than proper oral hygiene and regular visits to the dentist; it also involves adopting healthy lifestyle habits, maintaining a balanced diet, and monitoring any changes in the oral cavity.

Common oral conditions in this population include dental caries, particularly root caries, periodontal disease, xerostomia (often exacerbated by polypharmacy), edentulism, prosthesis-related complications, oral cancer, and precancerous lesions. These conditions not only affect nutrition, masticatory ability, communication, and speech but also self-esteem and overall quality of life (Leung & Chu, 2023; Martínez Asanza et al., 2026).

Furthermore, oral health interacts bidirectionally with chronic diseases, such as diabetes mellitus and cardiovascular and cerebrovascular diseases, exacerbating their impact on general health (Chan et al., 2023; Lipsky et al., 2024).

Care for older adults must adopt a holistic approach that integrates the treatment of oral diseases with the psychosocial aspects of aging. This perspective aligns with the FDI's framework (Glick et al., 2017), which highlights the importance of addressing the complex interplay between oral health and overall well-being. By recognizing oral health as a key component of geriatric care, healthcare providers can improve the physical, mental, and emotional well-being of older adults, ensuring a healthier and more dignified aging process.

3. METHODOLOGY

This chapter provides a comprehensive literature review aimed at synthesizing current knowledge at the intersection of Geriatric Dentistry, Gerodontology, and digital marketing strategies within a public health framework.

3.1. Objective of the Review

The primary objective of this literature review is to synthesize existing literature on the intersection of Geriatric Dentistry, Gerodontology, and digital marketing and communication strategies within a public health framework.

3.2. Search Strategy

A comprehensive search was conducted across the following electronic databases: Google Scholar, PubMed/Medline, Wiley and Scopus.

The search were the organized into three main thematic areas, reflecting the current state of the art: (i) technological innovations in Geriatric Dentistry and Gerodontology, (ii) resource preparation for elderly care, and (iii) digital marketing communication in public health.

3.3. Keywords

A combination of keywords and Boolean operators (AND, OR) was used to refine the search strategy. The following MeSH terms were employed: "geriatric dentistry", "digital marketing", "public health", "older adults", "elderly", "health education", "telehealth", "teledentistry", and "three-dimensional"

3.4. Inclusion and Exclusion Criteria

3.4.1. Inclusion Criteria

Articles published between January 2021 and December 2025.
Studies available in English and Spanish.
Research addressing at least one of the key topics outlined in the review objective.

3.4.2. Exclusion Criteria

Studies that do not focus specifically on the elderly population. Case reports, letters, editorials, or commentary that lack facts were excluded from the review.

Articles unrelated to the core topics of interest (Geriatric Dentistry, Gerodontology, digital marketing, and public health).

3.5. Review Process

3.5.1. Data Collection

-Searches were systematically conducted using various combinations of the defined keywords across the selected databases.

-All retrieved references were exported to a citation management software (Mendeley) for efficient organization and deduplication.

3.5.2. Quality Assessment

-Each selected article was evaluated for relevance and contribution to review's objectives.

- The evaluation criteria included clarity of findings, methodological rigor, and direct applicability to the chapter's themes.

3.6. Analysis and Synthesis of Information

The collected information was systematically organized into matrices, categorizing studies by themes, methodologies, and key findings. To complement this synthesis and illustrate the prominence of resuming concepts across the literature, a word cloud was generated **(Figure 2)**, providing a visual snapshot of the most frequent themes identified in the selected research. This structured approach, combined with visual representation, facilitated the identification of patterns, emerging trends, and existing gaps with the current literature, forming the basis for the chapter's discussion and conclusions.

Figure 2. Word cloud

[Proposed by the authors, results using Edit word art - Wordart.com (2026). https://wordart.com/ create]

4. SYNTHESIS AND DISCUSSION OF EVIDENCE

The synthesis of evidence regarding the integration of Geriatric Dentistry, Gerodontology, and digital marketing within a public health framework reveals a fundamental transformation in the delivery of oral care for older adults. The findings of this review indicate a significant paradigm shift, moving from a traditional, reactive care-focused approach toward a systemic, comprehensive, and proactive model. This emerging framework is structured around three interdependent pillars: (a) Technological Innovation; (b) Resources Preparation and Restructuring Care Delivery for Older Adults; and (c) Digital Marketing and Communication Strategy in Public Health.

The first pillar of this transformation is technological innovation. Bellow, promising innovations in this area are presented.

4.1. Technological Innovations in Geriatric Dentistry and Gerodontology

The last decade has marked a structural transformation in Geriatric Dentistry and Gerodontology (Martínez- Asanza et al., 2024), driven by the convergence of technological innovations that have redefined oral care for the elderly population (Hartshorn & Nair, 2023). While these disciplines possess distinct approaches,

Geriatric Dentistry focusing on clinical intervention and rehabilitation, and Gerodontology oriented toward prevention and community well-being, their technological integration enables holistic, patient-centered care. This synergy optimizes clinical workflows and facilitates the adaptation of treatments to the intrinsic vulnerabilities of this demographic group. In this context, interdisciplinary collaboration stands as a fundamental pillar, integrating not only health professionals but also information technology specialists to ensure the effective implementation of the following advancements summarized in **Table 2.**

Table 2.

TECHNOLOGY	PRIMARY APPLICATION	KEY BENEFIT	CRITICAL CHALLENGE
Artificial Intelligence	Predictive Diagnosis	Precision, efficiency	Cost, data privacy
3D Printing	Custom-made Prosthetics	Personalization, speed	Cost specialized training
CAD/CAM	Dental Design and Manufacturing	Accuracy, error reduction	Initial investment, learning curve
Teledentistry	Remote Consultations	Accessibility, convenience	Digital divide, data security
Electronic Health Records (HER)	Comprehensive EHR Management	Centralization, improved care coordination	Interoperability, personal data protection

Source: own elaboration

4.1.1. Artificial Intelligence and Predictive Diagnostics in Geriatric Care

Artificial intelligence (AI) is emerging as a transformative force in Geriatric Dentistry and Gerodontology, offering significant possibilities, particularly in predictive diagnostics. Deep learning algorithms have demonstrated high precision in the analysis of radiographic images and clinical data, enabling the early identification of dental caries, periodontal disease, and various oral mucosal lesions (Khattak et al., 2025). By processing vast volumes of data, AI supports clinicians in robust, evidence-based decision-making, allowing for the anticipation of disease progression and the establishment of proactive treatment plans that substantially improve long-term prognosis (Moeini & Torabi, 2025; Patil et al., 2022).

Furthermore, AI is revolutionizing the detection and classification of oral mucosal lesions through the automated analysis of clinical photographs. A recent systematic review and meta-analysis by Rokhshad et al. (2024) illustrates how AI-driven algorithms can identify diverse oral lesions with high diagnostic accuracy, representing a significant milestone for early intervention and longitudinal monitoring. This technological approach complements traditional clinical evaluations, facilitating personalized, precise, and timely care for older patients who frequently present with multifaceted oral complications.

However, it is essential to highlight that despite these promising technological milestones, there is currently a notable scarcity of studies specifically designed for and applied to the older adult population (Javadi et al., 2025; Martínez-Asanza et al., 2025a). Most existing AI models in dentistry are trained on general adult datasets, which may not fully account for the unique physiological changes, systemic comorbidities, and anatomical variations inherent to the aging process. This gap in the literature underscores a critical need for future research to develop and validate AI tools specifically tailored to the geriatric demographic to ensure equitable and effective clinical outcomes.

4.1.2. Digital Manufacturing: CAD/CAM, 3D Printing, and Rapid Prototyping

In the field of rehabilitation, Computer-Aided Design and Manufacturing (CAD/CAM) technologies, alongside 3D printing, have revolutionized the production of prostheses (Borthakur, 2024; Alyami, 2024; Bełżek et al., 2025) and orthodontic devices (Bełżek et al., 2025; Ingle et al., 2025). These advanced tools facilitate the creation of highly customized prototypes with micrometric precision, significantly reducing production timelines. Almarshadi et al. (2025) argue that the enhanced anatomical adaptation of these devices not only improves functionality and aesthetics but also elevates patient comfort and satisfaction, thereby ensuring high-quality dental care. Furthermore, Ding et al. (2023) demonstrated that personalized 3D-printed micromist injection mouthguards are effective in reducing dental plaque, offering a particularly promising solution for older adults and individuals with disabilities.

For older adults, whose oral anatomy often presents complex challenges due to bone resorption or the loss of dental support, these digital solutions provide more efficient and less invasive rehabilitation options. By leveraging digital workflows, clinicians can address individual patient needs with greater accuracy, ensuring improved clinical outcomes and a higher quality of life (Alotaibi, 2025). Although evidence suggests that CAD/CAM and 3D printing technologies are beneficial for older adults (Srinivasan et al., 2021; Heikal et al., 2022; Alotaibi, 2025). In alignment with Alotaibi (2025), the authors of this study recognize the existence of a persistent research gap regarding the specific factors influencing patient satisfaction with digital dentures. It is essential to highlight that this deficit underscores the need for further research focused on clinical outcomes, economic feasibility, and patients' quality of life. This observation indicates that the field remains in a developmental stage, emphasizing the importance of continued exploration and optimization of digital technologies in the fabrication of dental prostheses.

4.1.3. Teledentistry and Virtual Consultation Ecosystems

Teledentistry has established itself as a strategic solution to mitigate the geographic and physical barriers that have historically limited access to oral health in geriatric populations (Ben-Omran et al. 2021; Gryglewska et al., 2022; Kallás et al., 2024; Fung, et al., 2024; Bhamra et al., 2024; Vieira et al., 2025; Beltrán et al., 2024). Beyond remote consultation, this modality facilitates continuous monitoring and real-time interdisciplinary collaboration, elevating the quality of preventive care. The ability to conduct longitudinal follow-ups without the need for frequent travel allows for the early detection of pathologies, optimizing the timeliness of intervention. This advancement proved critical during the COVID-19 pandemic, ensuring continuity of care for older adults with limited mobility or conditions of systemic frailty (Morón-Araújo. 2021; Sanzana-Luengo et al. 2022)

4.1.4. Digitalization and Comprehensive Health Data Management

Finally, it is crucial to underscore that the implementation of Electronic Health Records (EHR) has revolutionized clinical data management by enabling unprecedented interoperability across diverse healthcare settings (Ali et al., 2023). For geriatric patients, this digital transformation facilitates an integrated care approach, where systemic conditions, polypharmacy, and medical history are intrinsically incorporated into dental treatment planning (Schwendicke et al., 2025). While the immediate availability of accurate information enhances patient safety by mitigating the risk of drug interactions and personalizing therapeutic experiences, current literature reveals a critical gap in empirical evidence specific to the field of dentistry (Sravya et al., 2024). Consequently, it is imperative to develop new research initiatives that validate the clinical impact of these digital tools in the care of older adults.

In general terms, as highlighted by Hartshorn & Nair (2023) these technologies not only optimize prosthetic rehabilitation, orthodontics, and surgical planning but also have the potential to significantly improve the quality of life for older adults. However, their implementation faces critical barriers in terms of accessibility and equity, particularly in rural or underserved areas where a lack of infrastructure and limited professional training hinder widespread adoption (Janto et al., 2022; Folorunsho et al., 2025). It is essential to address these challenges to ensure that all older adults can benefit from technological advancements in oral health care.

4.2. Resources Preparation and Restructuring Care Delivery for Older Adults

The second pillar of this review focuses on resource preparation and the restructuring of care delivery for older adults. In this context, comprehensive oral health care for this population is an increasingly relevant topic at the international level (Janto et al., 2022; Bolukbasi & Dundar, 2024). Its successful implementation requires a well-structured interdisciplinary approach that considers several key elements.

In accordance with Jiang et al. (2021), the authors of this study argue that strategic planning is essential to ensure that human, material, and financial resources are utilized effectively to meet the specific oral health needs of this vulnerable population. Humanity is currently at a historic juncture with the presence of the longest-living generation to date; consequently, we all share a crucial role in supporting this transition toward healthy aging and improved quality of life."

The following areas are presented as susceptible to improvement in this regard.

4.2.1. Professional Training and Continuing Education

The foundation for providing adequate care lies in the comprehensive training of dental professionals. Internationally, academic programs must be designed to address the specific oral health needs of older adults by integrating Geriatric Dentistry and Gerodontology into both undergraduate and graduate dental curricula (Nilsson et al., 2021; Thompson et al., 2022; Prosser et al., 2022; Nitschke et al., 2022; Martínez-Asanza et al., 2024; León et al., 2024; Shigli et al., 2025; Chan et al., 2025). However, according to Nilsson et al. (2021), the format, length, and focus of geriatric dentistry content vary widely across universities. These authors also highlight the need for national and international guidelines to ensure the mandatory inclusion of sufficient and specific training to prepare graduates for a growing dentate, frail, and care-dependent population.

Furthermore, these programs should not only include content on the physical and biopsychosocial characteristics of the aging population but also emphasize the development of gerontogeriatric competencies (Stuck & Schimmel, 2022; Martínez-Asanza et al., 2025a). The authors of the present study also consider it essential to integrate Gerodontology and enhance the interpersonal skills necessary for delivering effective oral health care to older adults. This approach aims to develop the human resources required by healthcare systems to meet the needs of the aging population.

On an international scale, it is notable that Geriatric Dentistry has been incorporated into the curricula of numerous dental schools (Jiang et al., 2021; Martínez-Asanza et al., 2024). In countries such as Brazil and Chile, it has even been recognized as a specialty within dental sciences (Martínez-Asanza et al., 2025b). In other regions, it is offered through diploma programs and master's degrees (Jiang et al., 2021; León et al., 2024; Martínez-Asanza et al., 2024). However, most countries acknowledge the need for continuous improvements in these curricula to better prepare dental professionals for the challenges posed by an aging population (Nilsson et al., 2021; Thompson et al., 2022; Martínez-Asanza et al., 2024).

Additionally, an international study conducted by Chandel et al. (2022) highlights a limited number of adequately trained geriatric dentists, as well as a significant shortage of dental programs and curricula designed to equip professionals with the advanced competencies required to practice in rural settings. The authors emphasize the urgent need to expand the dental workforce and strengthen academic curricula and training, aiming to enhance the capacity of dentists to provide care for the elderly population in rural and remote areas.

In general, the academic literature reflects concerns among researchers about the inclusion of Geriatric Dentistry and Gerodontology content in dental school curricula, both at the undergraduate and postgraduate levels. These curricula must address the specific oral health needs of older adults. Furthermore, postgraduate education should be strengthened to address these gaps, ensuring that professionals are sensitized to the importance of improving the attitudes of older adults toward dental care, ultimately aiming to enhance their quality of life.

4.2.2. Interdisciplinary Approach

Dental care should be integrated into a holistic model that promotes interdisciplinary collaboration (Gaffar et al., 2022). To effectively address aging and its complexities from a biopsychosocial perspective, it is essential to have a multidisciplinary team coordinated by geriatricians and gerontologists. This team should include physicians, nurses, dentists, dental hygienist, social workers, psychologists, occupational therapists, and nutrionist, among other professionals (Jo et al., 2025; Shivakumar et al., 2026)

Health promotion and disease prevention through multidimensional interventions are essential priorities for ensuring healthy aging (Paoli et al., 2025). In this context, creating a safe, independent, and comfortable environment for older adults is a shared responsibility among multiple sectors.

The synergy among these disciplines is crucial, as it facilitates effective coordination in treatment, especially for patients with multiple comorbidities. Developing interdisciplinary modules not only improves health outcomes but also equips professionals to address the emotional and physical complexities of older adults (Alhumainy et al., 2024). Evidence supports the effectiveness of interdisciplinary approaches, such as training dental students in community health centers and implementing mobile dental units, which help mitigate the shortage of professionals in the field (Mara, 2023).

This comprehensive approach not only optimizes oral care but also contributes to a more humane and tailored model of care that meets the needs of the elderly population, thereby promoting dignified and healthy aging.

4.2.3. Public Policies and Resource Allocation

To ensure that all older adults have access to adequate oral care, it is essential to establish public policies that prioritize the role of these services in marginalized and rural communities (Anyikwa & Ogwo, 2025). Resource allocation should be based on epidemiological data that accurately reflect the needs of these communities. An ethical approach that considers justice and cost-effectiveness in treatment selection is also crucial (Jiang et al., 2021; Chávez et al., 2022; Davari et al., 2025).

Implementing alternatives such as home and community care can be an innovative solution to overcome access barriers (Beaven. & Marshman, 2024; Rani et al., 2025) The creation of personalized treatment protocols in Gerodontology is equally fundamental, as the elderly population is diverse and presents varying needs depending on their level of dependence and overall health (Nisizaki & Derregibus, 2014). Additionally, consistent with Ghezzi et al. (2023), leveraging emerging technologies is vital to making oral health services more accessible and sustainable.

This comprehensive strategy not only addresses the immediate dental care needs of older adults but also fosters a more equitable healthcare system that recognizes and responds to the unique challenges faced by this demographic.

4.2.4. Professional Competency and the Digital Transformation of Geriatric Care

The rapid digital transformation of oral healthcare necessitates a robust commitment to Continuous Professional Development (CPD) among dental professionals (Alauddin et al., 2021; de Ahumada Servant et al., 2025). To bridge the gap between technological potential and clinical efficacy, it is imperative that clinicians move beyond traditional paradigms and acquire advanced digital competencies (Surdu et al., 2025). As dental informatics continues to evolve, the systematic integration of these tools into daily practice is no longer optional but a fundamental requirement for ensuring high-quality, evidence-based geriatric care (Hirmas-Adauy et al., 2024) This educational evolution must address not only the technical mastery of hardware and software but also the ethical and clinical nuances of managing the geriatric patient within a digital ecosystem (Jutai et al., 2024).

In this context, teledentistry emerges as a cornerstone of global health equity, serving as a vital instrument for dismantling geographical and socioeconomic barriers to access. By facilitating remote diagnostic evaluations and longitudinal monitoring (Martínez-Asanza, 2025d), teledentistry provides a scalable solution for the specialized care of frail or homebound older adults (Vieira, et al., 2025; Kengne-Talla et al., 2025). To achieve a global impact, healthcare systems must prioritize the formalization of these digital workflows, ensuring that the next generation of dentists is equipped to provide precise, timely, and accessible interventions (de Ahumada-Servant et al., 2025). Ultimately, fostering a technologically proficient workforce is the only pathway to achieving a truly inclusive and modernized model of Geriatric Dentistry and Gerodontology that meets the complex demands of an aging global population.

4.3. Digital Marketing and Communication Strategy in Public Health

The second pillar of this review focuses on the communication in public health through digital marketing, acts as a catalyst connecting technological advances and care resources with the target population. Digital strategies, including social media, search SEO, and Pay-Per-Click (PPC) campaigns, have proven effective not only for increasing service visibility (Piedra-Andrade et al., 2024), but also for educating and empowering older adults and their caregivers.

Public health is fundamentally distinguished from clinical medicine by its approach. While the latter focuses on individual treatment, public health addresses population health as a collective effort to promote well-being and prevent diseases, both communicable and non-communicable, as well as disabilities. This field involves population surveillance, the regulation of social determinants of health (such as food security and sanitation), and the provision of services with a marked emphasis on prevention (Ng & Ruger, 2014).

Strategic communication in public health is a multidisciplinary field that integrates evidence, theory, strategy, and creativity to promote behaviors, policies, systems, and practices that improve the health and well-being of individuals and populations (Niederdeppe et al., 2025). Unlike the simple dissemination of information, this approach requires meticulous planning to design and execute plans adapted to the specific needs and characteristics of the target audience.

The World Health Organization (WHO, 2021), in its "Global Strategy on Digital Health (2020-2025)," establishes the global goal of strengthening health systems through the application of digital technologies. These tools aim to empower patients, improve service quality, and achieve a vision of health for all.

In this context, digital marketing has consolidated itself as an indispensable tool for oral health promotion and patient acquisition (Farrokhi et al., 2023; Nazeli et al., 2023; Yin et al., 2025), particularly in the fields of Geriatric Dentistry and Gerodontology. Beyond commercial promotion, these technologies act as an essential bridge connecting health professionals with the older adult population and their caregivers (Vrančić et al., 2024: Martínez Asanza et al., 2025c). They facilitate the dissemination of educational content, the resolution of queries, and the construction of a trust-based bond grounded in transparency and clinical results.

4.3.1. Inclusive Marketing and Combating Ageism

Inclusive marketing focuses on creating campaigns that authentically represent diverse audiences while avoiding stereotypes and ensuring accessibility (Verbytska et al., 2023; Upadhyay et al., 2024). Within the context of geriatric dentistry and gerodontology, this approach necessitates recognizing the specific needs of older adults and adapting communication and services to their unique circumstances. It is essential to acknowledge that older adults do not constitute a homogeneous group, as significant variations exist regarding health status, technological engagement, culture, and lifestyle (Győrffy et al., 2023; Emmesjö et al., 2025).

Ageism is defined as the stereotyping, prejudice, and discrimination directed against individuals based on their age (Brinkhof et al., 2023; Lau, 2023; Emmanuel et al., 2024; Ayalon, 2025). Concurrently, it is necessary to implement strategies that foster a positive perspective on aging. This includes training healthcare professionals to identify the effects of ageism and emphasizing the importance of delivering respectful, patient-centered care. Furthermore, campaigns must utilize inclusive and respectful language, complemented by imagery that reflects the diversity of ethnicities, genders, and physical or cognitive capabilities within the aging population (Palsgaard et al., 2022; Miranzadeh et al., 2025; Ugargol & D'Souza, 2025; Kim, 2025).

4.3.2. Overcoming the Digital Divide

The term "digital divide" refers to the challenges individuals encounter in accessing Information and Communication Technologies (ICT) due to socioeconomic disparities (Barreda-Gutiérrez et al., 2024). A primary challenge in the implementation of digital strategies is the divide affecting the older population (Mubarak & Suomi, 2022; Yang et al., 2024; Zhang et al., 2025). While technology offers significant potential, it is imperative to design intuitive interfaces and accessible content to ensure the meaningful inclusion of this demographic (Stamate et al., 2024; Walsh et al., 2025; Ghorbanian-Zolbin et al., 2025). Digital literacy for both patients and their caregivers is a prerequisite for bridging this gap and promoting active aging (Zainal et al., 2025; Flor et al., 2025

4.3.3. Impact and Future of Digital Marketing in Public Health

The integration of digital tools in public health significantly impacts two primary areas: enhanced health literacy and improved patient retention. The availability of reliable information in digital environments helps reduce misinformation, empowering older adults to make informed health decisions (Zhang et al., 2025). Strategies such as email marketing and digital postoperative follow-up not only enhance the user experience but also foster loyalty and ensure continuity in preventive care.

Digital marketing should be regarded not merely as a technological innovation but as a fundamental relational and educational infrastructure (Owhoeke et al., 2023; Yeoh & Oh, 2025; Zohriah et al., 2025). Tools such as teledentistry, electronic health records, and mobile applications expand communication channels and enhance patient engagement and satisfaction, thereby promoting continuity of care throughout the aging process (Ben-Omran et al., 2021; Emami et al., 2022; Surdu et al., 2025; Schierz et al., 2025).

The synergy between technological innovation, resource preparation, and the restructuring of care delivery for older adults, along with the implementation of digital marketing and communication strategies in public health, is essential for advancing towards a future where geriatric dental care is more accessible, preventive, personalized, and equitable (Ben-Omran et al., 2021; Emami et al., 2022). The effective integration of these elements constitutes the necessary pathway to consolidate a comprehensive care model that addresses the complex needs of the aging population.

To implement these strategies effectively, the digital ecosystem offers a suite of complementary tools. The strategic use of social media platforms such as Facebook, Instagram, TikTok, and YouTube facilitates direct communication channels, ideal for showcasing success stories and promoting preventive education (Farrokhi et al., 2023; Bashirian et al., 2023; Apel et al., 2024; Zhang et al., 2024). Concurrently, SEO and PPC campaigns, such as Google Ads, ensure that dental services are accessible to patients seeking specific solutions locally. This technical deployment not only increases clinical visibility and maximizes return on investment but also ensures that information reaches those who need it most (Nazeli et al., 2023; Miranda-Rosero et al., 2025)

Additionally, the creation of educational content, blogs, digital guides, and audiovisual materials positions clinics as leaders in dental care, fostering health literacy and empowering older adults through personalized awareness campaigns(Yu et al., 2024; Beltrán et al., 2024).

On the other hand, as referenced by Álvarez (2025), the concept of salutogenic marketing emphasizes promoting health and well-being rather than focusing solely on treating diseases. Its primary goal is to empower individuals and communities to make healthier choices and enhance their quality of life. In the context of Geriatric Dentistry and Gerodontology, this approach aligns seamlessly with the principles of salutogenic marketing. It leverages digital platforms and mobile applications as tools of empowerment, providing accessible resources that encourage patients to actively participate in maintaining optimal oral health. This strategy not only fosters well-being but also prioritizes disease prevention (Shmarina et al., 2021; Väyrynen et al., 2023).

Email marketing plays a crucial role in this landscape by maintaining regular contact with patients, providing valuable health tips, reminding them of appointments, and offering personalized communication that enhances patient engagement (Kulhánek et al., 2022; Usuemerai et al., 2024). Effective email campaigns can include welcome sequences for new patients, educational newsletters featuring seasonal health topics, and health awareness campaigns that promote preventive care. By prioritizing educational content and patient value, healthcare providers can build trust and encourage engagement, ultimately leading to improved patient retention and satisfaction (Hapsari & Asaari, 2025; Shah et al., 2025).

Finally, digital marketing should not be evaluated solely as a technological innovation, but as a fundamental relational and educational infrastructure. Tools such as teledentistry, electronic health records, and mobile applications not only expand communication channels but also enhance patient participation and satisfaction, thereby fostering continuity of care throughout the aging process (Fernández et al., 2021; Da Silva Mulder et al., 2024;).

The synergy between technological innovation, resource preparation, and the restructuring of care delivery for older adults, along with the implementation of digital marketing and communication strategies in public health, is essential for advancing towards a future where geriatric dental care is more accessible, preventive, personalized, and equitable (Ghezzi et al., 2023; Drafta et al., 2025). The effective integration of these elements constitutes the necessary pathway to consolidate a comprehensive care model that addresses the complex needs of the aging population.

5. LIMITATIONS AND FUTURE RESEARCH DIRECTIONS

Despite the significant promise of digital technologies in geriatric oral health care, their implementation and effectiveness are constrained by several substantial limitations. Digital solutions face considerable challenges across multiple dimensions. Firstly, the adoption of advanced technologies, such as AI and teledentistry, demands substantial investments in hardware, software, and robust connectivity infrastructure. This infrastructure often remains inaccessible, particularly in resource-limited regions, where inadequate foundational support and the absence of specialized training for dental health professionals represent critical barriers to effective technology integration.

A second significant challenge pertains to the pervasive digital literacy gap observed among both older adult patients and healthcare professionals. Persistent obstacles related to digital competency impede the effective integration of these tools into daily clinical practice. Older adults, in particular, present unique barriers that extend beyond simple access; these include psychological impediments such as fear and technophobia, a strong preference for human contact, and inherent difficulties in comprehending digital symbols and terminology. Addressing these limitations necessitates the development of user-centered designs and personalized support mechanisms that go beyond standard technological implementation.

Furthermore, the current regulatory landscape introduces additional complexities. The lack of clear regulations and standardized protocols generates significant uncertainty regarding the safe and ethical use of digital technologies, especially concerning patient data privacy and security. As digital solutions expand to serve older populations, strict compliance with robust privacy and security standards becomes paramount to prevent data misuse and ensure patient autonomy.

5.2. Future Research Directions

Future research in geriatric dental care should focus on evaluating and implementing technologies like teledentistry and mobile apps to improve access and oral health education, especially in underserved areas. It is important to assess the effectiveness of tailored prevention programs that address the specific needs of older adults, alongside developing quantitative measures linking biological aging with oral health. Identifying social and behavioral factors influencing oral health outcomes will deepen understanding of these complex interactions.

Research should also aim to produce actionable results for policymakers, including evidence-based guidelines, cost-effectiveness analyses, and clear access indicators. Given the diversity among older adults, solutions must be adaptable and economically feasible to ensure equitable care. Emphasizing interprofessional collaboration and integrating digital tools can further enhance preventive care and service delivery for this population.

6. CONCLUSIONS

The integration of Geriatric Dentistry, Gerodontology, and digital marketing within a public health framework remains an underexplored area in the existing body of literature. Nevertheless, this interdisciplinary approach holds significant potential to overcome barriers and improve access to oral health promotion, disease prevention, and coordinated care for older adults. By merging specialized clinical expertise with cutting-edge technologies and strategic communication methods, this integration aims to enhance health outcomes and overall well-being for the aging population. Digital tools like teledentistry and AI enhance personalized care, facilitate continuous monitoring, and expand access, especially in underserved areas.

Training dental professionals in geriatric-specific needs and digital competencies is essential to address the complex oral health challenges of aging populations. Collaborative, interdisciplinary approaches that integrate dental care into broader geriatric health services promote holistic well-being and healthy aging. Digital marketing strategies, including social media and SEO, increase awareness and engagement, supporting both patient education and service accessibility. Overall, this multidisciplinary model fosters equitable, preventive, and patient-centered oral healthcare for older adults within public health systems

REFERENCES

Alauddin, M. S., Baharuddin, A. S., & Mohd Ghazali, M. I. (2021). The Modern and Digital Transformation of Oral Health Care: A Mini Review. *Health Care*, *9*(2), 118. DOI: 10.3390/healthcare9020118 PMID: 33503807

Alhumainy, N., Alnajrani, T. M., Thobaiti, A. A. A., Alharthi, A. A. A., Alkhalide, H. M., Alghamdi, J. D. S., Alharthi, N. S., Alotaibi, A. A. G., Aldajani, H. M. H., & Al-Tarad, R. D. S. (2024). Enhancing primary care delivery: A comprehensive review of collaboration among multidisciplinary teams. *Journal of Posthumanism*, *4*(3), 2209–2223. DOI: 10.63332/joph.v4i3.3786

Ali, S. K., Khan, H., Shah, J., & Nadeem Ahmed, K. (2023). An electronic health record system implementation in a resource limited country-lessons learned. *Digital Health*, *9*, 20552076231203660. DOI: 10.1177/20552076231203660 PMID: 37744747

Almarshadi, R., Hamdi, S., Hadi, F., Alshehri, A., Alsahafi, R., Aljohani, N., Alyamani, R., Alhbchi, M., Alqahtani, N., Almutiri, R., Alqadi, T., Alhabardi, A., Abu Aziz, K., & Alshammeri, T. (2025). Redefining Digital Dentistry: Multidisciplinary Applications of 3D Printing for Personalized Dental Care. *Cureus*, *17*(6), e86791. DOI: 10.7759/cureus.86791 PMID: 40718273

Alotaibi, H. N. (2025). Patient Satisfaction with CAD/CAM 3D-Printed Complete Dentures: A Systematic *Analysis of the Clinical Studies. Health Care*, *13*(4), 388. DOI: 10.3390/healthcare13040388 PMID: 39997262

Álvarez, H. (2025). *Salutogenic Marketing*. Aim and Scope. Salud Uninorte., DOI: 10.14482/sun.41.01.001.245

Alyami, M. H. (2024). The Applications of 3D-Printing Technology in Prosthodontics: A Review of the Current Literature. *Cureus*, *16*(9), e68501. DOI: 10.7759/cureus.68501 PMID: 39364461

Anyikwa, C. L., & Ogwo, C. E. (2025). Enhancing oral health outcomes through public health policy reform. *Frontiers in Oral Health*, *6*, 1604465. DOI: 10.3389/froh.2025.1604465 PMID: 40551851

Apel, Z., Fagundes, N., Sharmin, N., Nassar, U., Gow, G., Apel, D., & Perez, A. (2024). Social Media in Oral Health Education: A Scoping Review. *European Journal of Dental Education : Official Journal of the Association for Dental Education in Europe*, *29*(1), 50–63. DOI: 10.1111/eje.13053 PMID: 39462438

Atanda, A. J., Livinski, A. A., London, S. D., Boroumand, S., Weatherspoon, D., Iafolla, T. J., & Dye, B. A. (2022). Tooth retention, health, and quality of life in older adults: A scoping review. *BMC Oral Health, 22*(1), 185. DOI: 10.1186/s12903-022-02210-5 PMID: 35585618

Ayalon, L. (2025). Toward an intragroup approach to alleviate ageism in the second half of life. *The Gerontologist, 65*(10), gnaf169. Advance online publication. DOI: 10.1093/geront/gnaf169 PMID: 40720236

Badewy, R., Singh, H., Quiñonez, C., & Singhal, S. (2021). Impact of Poor Oral Health on Community-Dwelling Seniors: A Scoping Review. *Health Services Insights, 14*, 1178632921989734. DOI: 10.1177/1178632921989734 PMID: 33597810

Barranca-Enríquez, A., & Romo-González, T. (2022). Your health is in your mouth: A comprehensive view to promote general wellness. *Frontiers in Oral Health, 3*, 971223. DOI: 10.3389/froh.2022.971223 PMID: 36186536

Barreda-Gutiérrez, M., Cantarero-Prieto, D., & Pascual Sáez, M. (2024). Age, Technology, and the Digital Divide: Are They Directly Related to Mental Health Problems? *Health Care, 12*(23), 2454. DOI: 10.3390/healthcare12232454 PMID: 39685075

Bashirian, S., Khoshravesh, S., Ayubi, E., Karimi-Shahanjarini, A., Shirahmadi, S., & Solaymani, P. (2023). The impact of health education interventions on oral health promotion among older people: A systematic review. *BMC Geriatrics, 23*(1), 548. Advance online publication. DOI: 10.1186/s12877-023-04259-5 PMID: 37697260

Beaven, A., & Marshman, Z. (2024). Barriers and facilitators to accessing oral healthcare for older people in the UK: A scoping review. *British Dental Journal*. Advance online publication. DOI: 10.1038/s41415-024-7740-x PMID: 39152268

Beck Guimarães, M., Vaz Machry, R., Fernandes de Carvalho, J. C., Machado Mota, M., Favero Bulgarelli, A., De Rezende Pinto, L., & Marchini, L. (2025). Ageism on geriatric dentistry Instagram posts. *PAJAR - Pan-American. Journal of Aging Research, 13*(1), e48238. DOI: 10.15448/2357-9641.2025.1.48238

Beltrán, V., Muñoz-Sepúlveda, F., Acevedo, C., Navarro, P., Venegas, B., Salgado, C., Uribe, P., & Engelke, W. (2024). A rural teledentistry care experience: A geriatric approach to assessing oral health status and treatment needs in older adults from Mapuche community in Chile. *Frontiers in Public Health, 12*, 1356622. DOI: 10.3389/fpubh.2024.1356622 PMID: 38903581

Bełżek, A., Żerebiec, M., Saj, N., Rupeć, Z., Kamiński, P., Kaczmarski, M., & Turżańska, K. (2025). Advances in 3D printed orthotics for rehabilitation. *Wiadomosci lekarskie (Warsaw, Poland)*: 1960), 78(3), 539–543. DOI: 10.36740/WLek/202602

Ben-Omran, M., Livinski, A., Kopycka-Kedzierawski, D., Boroumand, S., Williams, D., Weatherspoon, D., Iafolla, T., Fontelo, P., & Dye, B. (2021). The use of teledentistry in facilitating oral health for older adults: A scoping review. *The Journal of the American Dental Association, 152*(12), 998–1011.e17. Advance online publication. DOI: 10.1016/j.adaj.2021.06.005 PMID: 34521539

Bhamra, I. B., Gallagher, J. E., & Patel, R. (2024). Telehealth technologies in care homes: A gap for dentistry? *Journal of Public Health (Oxford, England), 46*(1), e106–e135. DOI: 10.1093/pubmed/fdad258 PMID: 38102945

Bolukbasi, G., & Dundar, N. (2024). Oral health in older adults: Current insights and tips. *Journal of Gerontology and Geriatrics, 72*(2), 96–107. DOI: 10.36150/2499-6564-N700

Borthakur, P. P. (2024). The Role and Future Directions of 3D Printing in Custom Prosthetic Design. *Engineering Proceedings, 81*(1), 10. DOI: 10.3390/engproc2024081010

Brinkhof, L. P., de Wit, S., Murre, J. M. J., & Ridderinkhof, K. R. (2023). Mitigating the Harmful Impact of Ageism among Older Individuals: The Buffering Role of Resilience Factors. *Geriatrics (Basel, Switzerland), 9*(1), 1. DOI: 10.3390/geriatrics9010001 PMID: 38392100

Callaway, J., Strozza, C., Christensen, K., Doblhammer, G., Rau, R., & Sogaard, J. (2025). Ageing populations: new challenges in longevity. *BMC public health challenges*, 25(1), 4395. DOI: 10.1186/s12889-025-25531

Chan, A. K. Y., Lin, C. P., Ijarogbe, O., Kateeb, E., Ogawa, H., Shah, S. M., Fernandez, F., Chen, T. C., Renn, T. Y., Chu, C. H., & Chang, W. J. (2025). Promoting Oral Health for Older Adults in the Asia-Pacific Region. *International dental journal*, 75 Suppl 2(Suppl 2), 100886. DOI: 10.1016/j.identj.2025.100886

Chan, A. K. Y., Tamrakar, M., Jiang, C. M., Lo, E. C. M., Leung, K. C. M., & Chu, C. H. (2021). Common Medical and Dental Problems of Older Adults: A Narrative Review. *Geriatrics (Basel, Switzerland), 6*(3), 76. DOI: 10.3390/geriatrics6030076 PMID: 34449647

Chávez, E. M., Kossioni, A., & Fukai, K. (2022). Policies supporting oral health in ageing populations are needed worldwide. *International Dental Journal, 72*(4, 4S), S27–S38. DOI: 10.1016/j.identj.2022.06.014 PMID: 36031323

D'Aiuto, F., Suvan, J., Siripaiboonpong, N., Gatzoulis, M. A., & D'Aiuto, F. (2025). The root of the matter: Linking oral health to chronic diseases prevention. *International Journal of Cardiology. Congenital Heart Disease, 19*(100574), 100574. DOI: 10.1016/j.ijcchd.2025.100574 PMID: 40066344

da Mata, C., & Allen, P. F. (2023). Providing Oral Healthcare to Older Patients—Do We Have What It Takes? *International Journal of Environmental Research and Public Health, 20*(13), 6234. DOI: 10.3390/ijerph20136234 PMID: 37444082

Da Silva Mulder, J., Pinto, M., Aníbal, I., Dornellas, A., Garrido, D., Huanca, C., Haddad, A., & Abdala, C. (2024). Teledentistry Applied to Health and Education Outcomes: Evidence Gap Map. *Journal of Medical Internet Research, 26*, e60590. Advance online publication. DOI: 10.2196/60590 PMID: 39602783

Davari, L. D., Morris, M., & Allison, P. J. (2025). Policy options to complement the new Canadian dental program enabling high quality care for people with disabilities and older adults. *Gerodontology, 42*(3), 307–320. DOI: 10.1111/ger.12813 PMID: 40163434

de Ahumada Servant, P., Martín-Martín, D., & Romero, I. (2025). Digital transformation of oral health care: Measuring the digitalization of dental clinics. *Social Indicators Research, 178*(3), 1145–1167. DOI: 10.1007/s11205-024-03366-z

Deutsch, A., & Jay, E. (2021). Optimising oral health in frail older people. *Australian Prescriber, 44*(5), 153–160. DOI: 10.18773/austprescr.2021.037 PMID: 34728880

Dickie de Castillos, E., & Rodriguez-Junior, S. A. (2023). Scientific production on Gerodontology as a dental specialty-Bibliometric literature review. *FisiSenectus, 11*(1), 11–22. DOI: 10.22298/rfs.2023.v11.n1.7593

Dickinson, R., Vahia, I., Singh, A., Gupta, S., Alkhatib, F., Handa, I., & Sekhon, H. (2024). Exploring digital ageism: A systematic literature review on social media and aging. *The American Journal of Geriatric Psychiatry : Official Journal of the American Association for Geriatric Psychiatry, 32*(4), S130–S131. DOI: 10.1016/j.jagp.2024.01.220

Ding, H., Zhang, M., Lo, B., Chan, K. K. F., Lo, E. C. M., & Tsoi, J. K. H. (2023). A Personalised 3D-Printed Dental Plaque Removal Mouthguard for Older Adults. *International Dental Journal, 73*(6), 828–833. DOI: 10.1016/j.identj.2023.04.005 PMID: 37202299

Drafta, S., Macris, A., & Petre, A. (2025). Innovations on the horizon: Teledentistry, artificial intelligence, and hybrid models to improve oral health for vulnerable communities. *Frontiers in Oral Health*, *6*, 1649715. Advance online publication. DOI: 10.3389/froh.2025.1649715 PMID: 40860795

Emami, E., Harnagea, H., Shrivastava, R., Ahmadi, M., & Giraudeau, N. (2022). Patient satisfaction with e-oral health care in rural and remote settings: A systematic review. *Systematic Reviews*, *11*(1), 234. Advance online publication. DOI: 10.1186/s13643-022-02103-2 PMID: 36309732

Emmanuel, A. K., Obasi, D. E., Gbadebo, A. J., Omolara, A. B., Emuobor, R. O., Oboite, D. U., Omoijate, A., & Karanji, C. (2024b). Impact of ageism on the social wellbeing of older adults: Evidence from a geriatric home in Lagos, Nigeria. *International Journal of Engineering and Management Research*, *14*(6), 46–54. DOI: 10.31033/ijemr.14.6.46-54

Emmesjö, L., Hallgren, J., & Gillsjö, C. (2025). Older adults' digital technology experiences: A qualitative study. *BMC Digital Health*, *3*(1), 24. Advance online publication. DOI: 10.1186/s44247-025-00163-7

Farrokhi, F., Ghorbani, Z., Farrokhi, F., Namdari, M., & Salavatian, S. (2023). Social media as a tool for oral health promotion: A systematic review. *PLoS One*, *18*(12), e0296102. DOI: 10.1371/journal.pone.0296102 PMID: 38113216

Farzad, M., Allahi, M. N., Hashemi, N., Mohammadi, M., & Zadeh, N. A. (2026). Influence of social media on the oral health-related quality of life and cognitive function in elderly individuals: A cross-sectional study. *Journal of Education and Health Promotion*, *15*(1), 34. DOI: 10.4103/jehp.jehp_1336_24 PMID: 41788952

Fernández, C., Maturana, C., Coloma, S. A. C., & Giacaman, R. (2021). Teledentistry and mHealth for Promotion and Prevention of Oral Health: A Systematic Review and Meta-analysis. *Journal of Dental Research*, *100*(9), 914–927. DOI: 10.1177/00220345211003828 PMID: 33769123

Flor, A., Ferreira, M. R., Oliveira, Ó., & Pereira, O. (2025). Cultivating continuing learning and active aging through digital literacy: A digital and social approach. Tec empresarial, 19(3), 98–119. DOI: 10.18845/te.v19i3.8137

Folorunsho, S., Ajayi, V., Sanmori, M., Suleiman, M., Abdullateef, R., & Abdulganiyu, A. (2025). Access to and utilization of dental care services by older adults in Nigeria: Barriers and facilitators. *Special Care in Dentistry : Official Publication of the American Association of Hospital Dentists, the Academy of Dentistry for the Handicapped, and the American Society for Geriatric Dentistry*, *45*(3), e70040. DOI: 10.1111/scd.70040 PMID: 40326488

Fung, C. K. C., Ha, D. H., Walsh, L. J., & Lopez Silva, C. P. (2024). A Pilot Study to Assess the Feasibility of Real-Time Teledentistry in Residential Aged Care Facilities. *Health Care*, *12*(22), 2216. DOI: 10.3390/healthcare12222216 PMID: 39595415

Gaffar, B., Farooqi, F. A., Nazir, M. A., Bakhurji, E., Al-Khalifa, K. S., Alhareky, M., & Virtanen, J. I. (2022). Oral health-related interdisciplinary practices among healthcare professionals in Saudi Arabia: Does integrated care exist? *BMC Oral Health*, *22*(1), 75. DOI: 10.1186/s12903-022-02113-5 PMID: 35300658

Ghezzi, E. M., Niessen, L. C., & Jones, J. A. (2023). Innovations in Geriatric Oral Health Care. *Clinics in Geriatric Medicine*, *39*(2), 343–357. DOI: 10.1016/j.cger.2023.01.005 PMID: 37045537

Ghorbanian- Zolbin, M., Kujala, S., Widén, G., Eriksson-Backa, K., & Huvila, I. (2025). Digital inclusion among older adults: Identifying potential solutions. Human Technology An Interdisciplinary. *Journal On Humans In ICT Environments*, 21(1), 51–72. DOI: 10.14254/1795-6889.2025.21-1.3

Gianfredi, V., Nucci, D., Pennisi, F., Veronesse, N., & Soysal, P. (2025). Aging, longevity, and healthy aging: The public health approach. *Aging Clinical and Experimental Research*, *37*(1), 125. DOI: 10.1007/s40520-025-03021-8 PMID: 40244306

Glick, M., Williams, D. M., Kleinman, D. V., Vujicic, M., Watt, R. G., & Weyant, R. J. (2017). A new definition for oral health developed by the FDI World Dental Federation opens the door to a universal definition of oral health. *American Journal of Orthodontics and Dentofacial Orthopedics*, *151*(2), 229–231. DOI: 10.1016/j.ajodo.2016.11.010 PMID: 28153139

Gryglewska, B., Perera, I., Klimek, E., Fedyk-Łukasik, M., Piotrowicz, K., Mocanu, I., Muntianu, L., & Gąsowski, J. (2022). Teledentistry and oral health in older adults - aspects for implementation of the "Patient centric solution for smart and sustainable healthcare *(ACESO)" project. Folia Medica Cracoviensia*, *62*(2), 5–16. DOI: 10.24425/fmc.2022.141697 PMID: 36256891

Győrffy, Z., Boros, J., Döbrössy, B., & Girasek, E. (2023). Older adults in the digital health era: Insights on the digital health related knowledge, habits and attitudes of the 65 year and older population. *BMC Geriatrics*, *23*(1), 779. DOI: 10.1186/s12877-023-04437-5 PMID: 38012565

Hapsari, A., & Asaari, A. (2025). *The Role of Personalized Marketing and Service Quality in Enhancing Patient Engagement in Health Care. JKBM*. JURNAL KONSEP BISNIS DAN MANAJEMEN., DOI: 10.31289/jkbm.v11i2.14678

Hartshorn, J. E., & Nair, R. U. (2023). Dental innovations which will influence the oral health care of baby boomers. *Special Care in Dentistry : Official Publication of the American Association of Hospital Dentists, the Academy of Dentistry for the Handicapped, and the American Society for Geriatric Dentistry, 43*(3), 359–369. DOI: 10.1111/scd.12835 PMID: 36782274

Heikal, M. M. A., Nabi, N. A., & Elkerdawy, M. W. (2022). A study comparing patient satisfaction and retention of CAD/CAM milled complete dentures and 3D printed CAD/CAM complete dentures versus conventional complete dentures: A randomized clinical trial. *Brazilian Dental Science, 25*(1), e2785. DOI: 10.4322/bds.2022.e2785

Hirmas-Adauy, M., Castillo-Laborde, C., Awad, C., Jasmen, A., Mattoli, M., Molina, X., Olea, A., Matute, I., Soto, F., Rubilar, P., Urrejola, O., Alfaro, T., Abusleme Lama, M. T., & Esnouf, S. (2024). Navigating Through Innovation in Elderly's Health: A Scoping Review of Digital Health Interventions. *Public Health Review, 45*, 1607756. DOI: 10.3389/phrs.2024.1607756 PMID: 39749218

Huenchuan, S. (Ed.). (2018). Envejecimiento, personas mayores y Agenda 2030 para el Desarrollo Sostenible: perspectiva regional y de derechos humanos, Libros de la CEPAL, No 154 (LC/PUB.2018/24-P), Santiago: Comisión Económica para América Latina y el Caribe (CEPAL); 2018. https://repositorio.cepal.org/handle/11362/44369 (accessed on 16 March 2026).[REMOVED HYPERLINK FIELD]

Hui, J. C. Y., Hu, L. L., Chan, A. K. Y., & Chu, C. H. (2026). Interdisciplinary Strategies for Improving Oral Health in Older Adults: A Comprehensive Review. *Geriatrics (Basel, Switzerland), 11*(1), 22. DOI: 10.3390/geriatrics11010022 PMID: 41744900

Ingle, N. A., Al-Hashimi, H., Alhammad, A. T., Aldajani, H. A., Alabsi, N. F., & Albuolayan, N. A. (2025). Impact of 3D printing and CAD/CAM technology on orthodontic treatment outcomes: A systematic review and meta-analysis. *Journal of Pharmacy & Bioallied Sciences, 17*(Suppl 1), S226–S228. DOI: 10.4103/jpbs.jpbs_639_25 PMID: 40510977

Janto, M., Iurcov, R., Daina, C. M., Neculoiu, D. C., Venter, A. C., Badau, D., Cotovanu, A., Negrau, M., Suteu, C. L., Sabau, M., & Daina, L. G. (2022). Oral Health among Elderly, Impact on Life Quality, Access of Elderly Patients to Oral Health Services and Methods to Improve Oral Health: A Narrative Review. *Journal of Personalized Medicine, 12*(3), 372. DOI: 10.3390/jpm12030372 PMID: 35330372

Javadi, S. K. H. S., Jamieson, L., Nouri, A., Sohn, W., & Rudman, A. (2025, December 10). (2025). Exploring Digital Health Technologies for Enhancing Oral Health: A Scoping Review of Interventions for Older Adults. *Gerodontology*, ger.70033. Advance online publication. DOI: 10.1111/ger.70033 PMID: 41368693

Jiang, C. M., Chu, C. H., Duangthip, D., Ettinger, R. L., Hugo, F. N., Kettratad-Pruksapong, M., Liu, J., Marchini, L., McKenna, G., Ono, T., Rong, W., Schimmel, M., Shah, N., Slack-Smith, L., Yang, S. X., & Lo, E. C. M. (2021). Global Perspectives of Oral Health Policies and Oral Healthcare Schemes for Older Adult Populations. *Frontiers in Oral Health*, *2*, 703526. DOI: 10.3389/froh.2021.703526 PMID: 35048040

Jiménez-Herrero, F. (1998). Gerodontología antaño, una disciplina descuidada: Revisión bibliográfica. *Revista Española de Geriatría y Gerontología*, *33*(91), 9148–9154.

Jiménez-Herrero, F. (2003). 25 años de la especialidad de Geriatría y Gerontología. *Revista Española de Geriatría y Gerontología*, *38*(6), 338–354. DOI: 10.1016/S0211-139X(03)74911-7

Jo, S.-R., Shin, B.-R., & Jang, J.-H. (2025). Multidisciplinary Professionals' Perceptions of Home-Visit Oral Care for Older Adults in Integrated Community Care: A Focus Group Interview Study. *Health Care*, *13*(18), 2365. DOI: 10.3390/healthcare13182365 PMID: 41008493

Jutai, J. W., Hatoum, F., Bhardwaj, D., & Hosseini, M. (2024). Implementation of digital health technologies for older adults: A scoping review. *Frontiers in Aging*, *5*, 1349520. DOI: 10.3389/fragi.2024.1349520 PMID: 38784681

Kallás, M. S., Guardeiro, B., Henrique, E. A., Silva, D. G., Takashi, D. A., & Marchini, L. (2024). Telehealth in geriatric dentistry: A comparative analysis of concordance between virtual and in-person examinations for hospitalized older patients. *Special Care in Dentistry : Official Publication of the American Association of Hospital Dentists, the Academy of Dentistry for the Handicapped, and the American Society for Geriatric Dentistry*, *44*(6), 1680–1687. DOI: 10.1111/scd.13036 PMID: 38984414

Kengne-Talla, P., Allison, P., Bussières, A., Rodrigues, A., Bergeron, F., Giraudeau, N., & Emami, E. (2025). Teledentistry for Improving Access To, and Quality of Oral Health Care: Overview of Systematic Reviews and Meta-Analyses. *Journal of Medical Internet Research*, *27*, e65211. https://www.jmir.org/2025/1/e65211. DOI: 10.2196/65211 PMID: 40737673

Khattak, O., Hashem, A. S., Alqarni, M. S., Almufarrij, R. A. S., Siddiqui, A. Y., Anis, R., Ahmad, S., Fareed, M. A., Alothmani, O. S., Alkhershawy, L. H. S., Al-abidin, W. W. Z., Issrani, R., & Agarwal, A. (2025). Deep Learning Applications in Dental Image-Based Diagnostics: A Systematic Review. *Health Care*, *13*(12), 1466. DOI: 10.3390/healthcare13121466 PMID: 40565492

Kim, J. (2025). Healthcare Professionals' Perceptions and Experiences of Ageism: A Qualitative Study. *International Journal of Environmental Research and Public Health*, *22*(3), 350. DOI: 10.3390/ijerph22030350 PMID: 40238402

Kulhánek, A., Lukavská, K., Gabrhelík, R., Burda, V., Holter, M., & Brendryen, H. (2022). Comparing Reminders Sent via SMS Text Messaging and Email for Improving Adherence to an Electronic Health Program: Randomized Controlled Trial. *JMIR mHealth and uHealth*, *10*(3), e31040. Advance online publication. DOI: 10.2196/31040 PMID: 35302945

Lau, M. H. M. (2023). Beyond Ageism: A Qualitative Study of Intersecting Forms of Prejudice towards Retired Older People. *Societies (Basel, Switzerland)*, *13*(1), 13. DOI: 10.3390/soc13010013

León, S., Giacaman, R. A., Araya-Bustos, F., Venegas, S., Saavedra, N., Hugo, F. N., De Marchi, R. J., Muñoz, M.-F., Salazar, C., Castrejón-Pérez, R. C., Bustillos, L., Fortanete, A., de López, A. C., Aredes, J. E., Marín-Zuluaga, D., & Elias-Boneta, A. (2024). Current status of geriatric dentistry education in selected dental schools in Latin America and the Caribbean. *Gerodontology*, *41*(3), 385–392. DOI: 10.1111/ger.12714 PMID: 37792411

Leung, K. C.-M., & Chu, C.-H. (2023). Dental Care for Older Adults. *International Journal of Environmental Research and Public Health*, *20*(1), 214. DOI: 10.3390/ijerph20010214 PMID: 36612536

Lipsky, M. S., Singh, T., Zakeri, G., & Hung, M. (2024). Oral Health and Older Adults: A Narrative Review. *Dentistry Journal*, *12*(2), 30. DOI: 10.3390/dj12020030 PMID: 38392234

Mara, M. (2023). Interdisciplinary education and health care in geriatric dental medicine. *Clinics in Geriatric Medicine*, *39*(2), 327–341. DOI: 10.1016/j.cger.2023.01.006 PMID: 37045536

Martínez-Asanza, D. (Ed.). (2024). *Geriatric Dentistry in the Age of Digital Technology*. IGI Global., DOI: 10.4018/979-8-3693-0260-6

Martínez-Asanza, D. Rojas- Herrera, I.A., Njoku, A., Reyes- Puig, A.C., Mouloudj, F., Gómez- Capote, I., et al. (2024). Study Plans and Programs Supporting Geriatric Dentistry Teaching in Cuba: An Update. In: Martínez- Asanza D, Editor. *Geriatric Dentistry in the Age of Digital Technology*. (pp. 174–191). IGI Global. DOI: 10.4018/979-8-3693-0260-6.ch007

Martínez-Asanza, D. (2025). Emerging Trends and Future Perspectives in Digital Dentistry for Rural Areas: An Update. In Martínez-Asanza, D. (Ed.), *Transforming Dental Health in Rural Communities: Digital Dentistry* (pp. 1–20). IGI Global., DOI: 10.4018/979-8-3693-7165-7.ch001

Martínez-Asanza, D., Álvarez Pérez, A., Guanche Martínez, A. S., & Gómez Capote, I. (2026). Gerodontology in Cuba as a strategic discipline for healthy aging. *Revista Cubana de Medicina Militar*, *55*(1), e026076903. https://revmedmilitar.sld.cu/index.php/mil/article/view/76903

Martínez-Asanza, D., Álvarez Pérez, A., & Rojas Herrera, I. A. (2025c). Dental education in gerontogeriatrics as a public health imperative for the Americas. *Revista Cubana de Medicina Militar*, *54*(3), e025076624. https://revmedmilitar.sld.cu/index.php/mil/article/view/76624

Martínez-Asanza, D., Gbenou-Morgan, Y., & Rosales-Reyes, S. Á. (2020b). Gerodontología: Introducción de un nuevo término en la asignatura Atención integral a la familia II. *Medicentro Electrónica, 24*(1), 149–158. http://scielo.sld.cu/scielo.php?script=sci_arttext&pid=S1029-30432020000100149&lng=es

Martínez-Asanza, D., Guanche-Martínez, A. S., & Reyes-Puig, A. C. (2020a). La odontogeriatría en la formación y superación de especialistas en Cuba. *Revista Cubana de Medicina Militar*, *49*(3), e502.

Martínez-Asanza, D., Njoku, A., Baviskar, S., Evans, M. A., & Mouloudj, K. (2025a). Oral Hygiene Care of Older Adults and Caregiver Education: A Systematic Review. *Hygiene*, *5*(4), 50. DOI: 10.3390/hygiene5040050

Martínez-Asanza, D., Rojas Herrera, I. A., & Rodríguez Washington, N. (2025b). Distinguishing between Gerodontology and Geriatric Dentistry: Key perspectives on oral health in older adults. *Gerodontology*, *42*(3), 434–435. DOI: 10.1111/ger.12820 PMID: 40470572

Michea, M. A., Barahona, P., Dreyer, E., Rojas, M., & Celis, A. (2023). Elderly, ageing and oral fragility. *Journal of Dental Health, Oral Disorders & Therapy*, *14*(2), 28–30. DOI: 10.15406/jdhodt.2023.14.00590

Miranda-Rosero, O., Sabando-Arteaga, J., & Castro-Freire, D. (2025). *Impacto de estrategias de marketing digital en odontología en la captación y fidelización de pacientes*. Revista Metropolitana de Ciencias Aplicadas., DOI: 10.62452/cf9cjr37

Miranzadeh, F., Sefidkar, R., & Rezaeipandari, H. (2025). Effectiveness of an educational intervention in modifying ageism among nurses in caring for older adults: A randomized controlled trial. *BMC Nursing*, *24*(1), 1132. DOI: 10.1186/s12912-025-03798-z PMID: 40890733

Moeini, A., & Torabi, S. (2025). The Role of Artificial Intelligence in Dental Diagnosis and Treatment Planning. *Journal of Oral and Dental Health Nexus*, *2*(1), 14–26. DOI: 10.61838/kman.jodhn.2.1.2

Mubarak, F., & Suomi, R. (2022). Elderly Forgotten? Digital Exclusion in the Information Age and the Rising Grey Digital Divide. *Inquiry : a Journal of Medical Care Organization, Provision and Financing*, *59*, 469580221096272. DOI: 10.1177/00469580221096272 PMID: 35471138

Nazeli, B., Sugiarto, Y., & Wahyudi, A. (2023). Digital Marketing Analysis in Dental Healthcare: The Role of Digital Marketing in Promoting Dental Health in the Community. *East Asian Journal of Multidisciplinary Research*, *2*(11), 4337–4360. DOI: 10.55927/eajmr.v2i11.6643

Ng, N. Y., & Ruger, J. P. (2014). Ethics and Social Value Judgments in Public Health. *Encyclopedia of Health Economics*, 287-291. DOI: 10.1016/B978-0-12-375678-7.00415-6

Niederdeppe, J., Boyd, A. D., King, A. J., & Rimal, R. N. (2025). Strategies for Effective Public Health Communication in a Complex Information Environment. *Annual Review of Public Health*, *46*(1), 411–431. DOI: 10.1146/annurev-publhealth-071723-120721 PMID: 39656948

Nilsson, A., Young, L., Glass, B., Lee, A., Nimmo, A., & Brumpton, K. (2021). Gerodontology in the dental School curriculum: A scoping. *Gerodontology*, *00*(4), 1–13. DOI: 10.1111/ger.12555 PMID: 33977554

Nisizaki & Derregibus. (2014). Protocolos de tratamiento y prevención en Gerodontología. *Odontoestomatología*, *16*(23), 44–53. http://www.scielo.edu.uy/scielo.php?pid=S1688-93392014000100006&script=sci_arttext&tlng=pt

Nitschke, S., Hahnel, S., Sobota, B. A. J., & Jockusch, J. (2022). Undergraduate Dental Education in Gerodontology in German between 2004 and 2019- A case for compulsory teaching? *European Journal of Dental Education : Official Journal of the Association for Dental Education in Europe*, *26*(523), 523–538. DOI: 10.1111/eje.12729 PMID: 34826171

Owhoeke, N., Oparaku, O., & Ordu, B. (2023). Digital Infrastructure and Sustainable Development of Marketing Education Curriculum in Tertiary Institutions in Nigeria. *International Journal of Research and Scientific Innovation*. .DOI: 10.51244/IJRSI.2023.101006

Palsgaard, P., Maino Vieytes, C. A., Peterson, N., Francis, S. L., Monroe-Lord, L., Sahyoun, N. R., Ventura-Marra, M., Weidauer, L., Xu, F., & Arthur, A. E. (2022). Healthcare Professionals' Views and Perspectives towards Aging. *International Journal of Environmental Research and Public Health*, *19*(23), 15870. DOI: 10.3390/ijerph192315870 PMID: 36497945

Paoli, A., Iaccarino, G., Lucidi, F., Pagnini, F., Boccuzzo, G., & Illario, M. (2025). Multidimensional determinants of active and healthy aging trajectories: A position paper from the Age-It Research Program. *The Journals of Gerontology. Series B, Psychological Sciences and Social Sciences*, *80*(Supplement_2), S145–S157. DOI: 10.1093/geronb/gbaf196 PMID: 41442760

Patel, R., & Gallagher, J. E. (2024). Healthy ageing and oral health: Priority, policy and public health. *BDJ Open*, *10*(1), 79. DOI: 10.1038/s41405-024-00262-z PMID: 39379352

Patil, S., Albogami, S., Hosmani, J., Mujoo, S., Kamil, M. A., Mansour, M. A., Abdul, H. N., Bhandi, S., & Ahmed, S. S. S. J. (2022). Artificial Intelligence in the Diagnosis of Oral Diseases: Applications and Pitfalls. *Diagnostics (Basel)*, *12*(5), 1029. DOI: 10.3390/diagnostics12051029 PMID: 35626185

Piedra-Andrade, M. N., Astudillo, P. A., Bravo, M. E., Cordero Coronel, M. I., & Bravo Calderón, M. E. (2024). Marketing and patient acquisition strategies in dental clinics: Development and implementation of digital marketing campaigns to attract new patients and effectiveness of social networks as a marketing tool for dental clinics. *Research. Social Development*, *13*(10), e101131047175. DOI: 10.33448/rsd-v13i10.47175

Poudel, P., Paudel, G., Acharya, R., George, A., Borgnakke, W. S., & Rawal, L. B. (2024). Oral health and healthy ageing: A scoping review. *BMC Geriatrics*, *24*(1), 33. DOI: 10.1186/s12877-023-04613-7 PMID: 38191307

Prosser, G. M., Louca, C., & Radford, D. R. (2022). Potential educational and workforce strategies to meet the oral health challenges of an increasingly older population: A qualitative study. *BDJ Open*, *8*(1), 6. DOI: 10.1038/s41405-022-00098-5 PMID: 35273157

Rani, H., Azizan, A. A., Walad, N. I. A., Hassan, S. A. A., Dom, T. N. M., Yeoh, D. S. H., Tay, J. W. C., Rosli, M. S. A., Aun, N. S. M., Aziz, A. F. A., Thwin, K. M., & Tew, I. M. (2025). Challenges and Recommendations for Oral Healthcare of Older Adults in a Long-Term Care Facility. *Health Care*, *13*(20), 2642. DOI: 10.3390/healthcare13202642 PMID: 41154320

Rokhshad, R., Mohammad-Rahimi, H., Price, J. B., Shoorgashti, R., Abbasiparashkouh, Z., Esmaeili, M., Sarfaraz, B., Rokhshad, A., Motamedian, S. R., Soltani, P., & Schwendicke, F. (2024). Artificial intelligence for classification and detection of oral mucosa lesions on photographs: A systematic review and meta-analysis. *Clinical Oral Investigations*, *28*(1), 88. DOI: 10.1007/s00784-023-05475-4 PMID: 38217733

Rosales, A., & Fernández-Ardèvol, M. (2020). Ageism in the era of digital platforms. *Convergence (London)*, *26*(5–6), 1074–1087. DOI: 10.1177/1354856520930905 PMID: 33239961

Sahab, L., Newton, J. T., & Sabbah, W. (2025). Oral Health and Healthy Aging: A Systematic Review of Longitudinal Studies. *Dentistry Journal*, *13*(7), 303. DOI: 10.3390/dj13070303 PMID: 40710148

Schwendicke, F., Uribe, S. E., Walji, M., Lam, W., & Tichy, A. (2025). Electronic Health Records in Dentistry: Relevance, Challenges and Policy Directions. *International Dental Journal*, *75*(6), 103964. DOI: 10.1016/j.identj.2025.103964 PMID: 41106216

Shah, A., Arman, M., & Khan, S. (2025). Patient-Centric Marketing and Retention Strategies in Healthcare: A Strategic and Technological Framework. *Journal of Business and Management Studies*. .DOI: 10.32996/jbms.2025.7.2.17

Shigli, K., Nayak, S., Lagali-Jirge, V., Nerali, J. T., Vadavi, D., Oginni, F. O., & Kusurkar, R. A. (2025). Dental teachers' perceptions about the status of geriatric dentistry in the dental curriculum: A qualitative exploration in the Indian context. *Gerodontology*, *42*(2), 256–268. DOI: 10.1111/ger.12793 PMID: 39428127

Shivakumar, A. T., Srinivas, S., Kalgeri, S. H., Kishor, M., & Avarebeel, S. (2026). A transformative interprofessional model for geriatric oral health care - A proposed working model. *Frontiers in Dental Medicine*, *7*, 1757007. DOI: 10.3389/fdmed.2026.1757007 PMID: 41867639

Shmarina, E., Ericson, D., Åkerman, S., & Axtelius, B. (2021). Salutogenic factors for oral health among older people: An integrative review connecting the theoretical frameworks of Antonovsky and Lalonde. *Acta Odontologica Scandinavica, 79*(3), 218–231. DOI: 10.1080/00016357.2020.1849790 PMID: 33596156

Sidharthan, S., Ramanarayanan, V., Karuveettil, V., & Ravindran, G. C. (2024). Utilization of dental health services and its associated factors among adult population in Ernakulam district, Kerala, India: A mixed-method analysis. *Journal of Oral Biology and Craniofacial Research, 14*(2), 133–142. DOI: 10.1016/j.jobcr.2024.01.010 PMID: 38352196

Slack-Smith, L., Arena, G., & See, L. (2023). Rapid Oral Health Deterioration in Older People-A Narrative Review from a Socio-Economic Perspective. *Journal of Clinical Medicine, 12*(6), 2396. DOI: 10.3390/jcm12062396 PMID: 36983395

Sravya, K., Movva, J. B., Sinha, R., Sharma, S., Patel, B. R., Thanneeru, D., & Tiwari, H. D. (2024). Electronic Health Records in Dentristry: A Systematic Review. *Journal of Contemporary Clinical Practice, 10*(1), 71–79. DOI: 10.18683/jccp.2024.1091

Srijaroen, W., Chuenjaichon, W., Tosasukul, J., Yamchuen, P., & Jongjitvimol, T. (2025). Factors associated with dental health care behaviors among elderly patients in lower northern Thailand: A case study of Mueang Phitsanulok Health Center. *Journal of Public Health Research, 14*(4), 22799036251388588. DOI: 10.1177/22799036251388588 PMID: 41211227

Srinivasan, M., Kalberer, N., Fankhauser, N., Naharro, M., Maniewicz, S., & Müller, F. (2021). CAD-CAM complete removable dental prostheses: A double-blind, randomized, crossover clinical trial evaluating milled and 3D-printed dentures. *Journal of Dentistry, 115*, 103842. DOI: 10.1016/j.jdent.2021.103842 PMID: 34637889

Stamate, A., Marzan, M. D., Velciu, M., Paul, C., & Spiru, L. (2024). Advancing user-centric design and technology adoption for aging populations: A multifaceted approach. *Frontiers in Public Health, 12*, 1469815. DOI: 10.3389/fpubh.2024.1469815 PMID: 39712308

Stuck, A. K., & Schimmel, M. (2022). A model for a geriatric teaching programme and its impact on self-rated and tested competencies of undergraduate dental students. *European Journal of Dental Education : Official Journal of the Association for Dental Education in Europe, 26*(1), 21–27. DOI: 10.1111/eje.12668 PMID: 33512016

Surdu, A., Foia, C. I., Luchian, I., Trifan, D., Budala, D. G., Scutariu, M. M., Ciupilan, C., Puha, B., & Tatarciuc, D. (2025). Telemedicine and Digital Tools in Dentistry: Enhancing Diagnosis and Remote Patient Care. *Medicina (Kaunas, Lithuania), 61*(5), 826. DOI: 10.3390/medicina61050826 PMID: 40428784

Tadjoedin, F. M., Adiatman, M., Lee, Y. Y. A., Banu, U. S., Tan, S. S. L., & Garg, V. (2025). Oral health and healthy aging: A multiregional review. *JAR Life*, *15*, 100057. DOI: 10.1016/j.jarlif.2025.100057 PMID: 41536749

Thompson, L. A., Kaplish, S., Park, S. E., & Chamut, S. (2022). Is dental education meeting the oral health needs of older adults? *Journal of Dental Education*, *86*(9), 1233–1241. DOI: 10.1002/jdd.13026 PMID: 36165248

Ugargol, A. P., & D'Souza, P. M. (2025). Addressing Ageism in Healthcare: Insights for an Age-Inclusive Longevity Society. In Rajan, S. I. (Ed.), *Handbook of Aging, Health and Public Policy*. Springer., DOI: 10.1007/978-981-99-7842-7_234

Upadhyay, S., Tuli, N., & Kumar, H. (2024). Crafting inclusive marketing campaigns: Insights and influential factors in the Indian context. *Australasian Marketing Journal*, *32*(3), 223–238. DOI: 10.1177/14413582241247328

Usuemerai, P., Ibikunle, O., Abass, L., Alemede, V., Nwankwo, E., & Mbata, A. (2024). *A conceptual framework for integrating digital transformation in healthcare marketing to boost patient engagement and compliance*. World Journal of Advanced Pharmaceutical and Medical Research., DOI: 10.53346/wjapmr.2024.7.2.0045

Väyrynen, E., Hakola, S., Keski-Salmi, A., Jämsä, H., Vainionpää, R., & Karki, S. (2023). The Use of Patient-Oriented Mobile Phone Apps in Oral Health: Scoping Review. *JMIR mHealth and uHealth*, *11*, e46143. Advance online publication. DOI: 10.2196/46143 PMID: 37672331

Verbytska, A., Lysenko, I., Babachenko, L., & Kraskivska, N. (2023). Inclusive social marketing: Representation and diversity in brand campaigns. *Marketing and Branding Research*, *10*, 45–58. DOI: 10.32038/mbr.2023.10.01.04

Vieira, A. R. R., Meurer, M. I., da Cruz, G. S., & Reses, M. de L. N., Castilhos, E. D. de, & Mello, A. L. S. F. de. (2025). Older adults' oral health follow-up in primary care: A teledentistry feasibility exploratory study. *Saúde em Debate*, 49(spe1). DOI: 10.1590/2358-28982025e19901i

Vrančić, A., Zadravec, H., & Orehovački, T. (2024). The Role of Smart Homes in Providing Care for Older Adults: A Systematic Literature Review from 2010 to 2023. *Smart Cities*, *7*(4), 1502–1550. DOI: 10.3390/smartcities7040062

Walsh, K., Joseph, P., Herbert, A., O'Neill, M., & Vogel, C. (2025). Digital technology design in ageing and engaged societies: Challenges in inclusion and context. *Behaviour & Information Technology*, •••, 1–19. DOI: 10.1080/0144929X.2025.2584205

World Health Organization. WHO. (2020). Decade of Healthy Ageing; WHO: Geneva, Switzerland. Available online: https://www.who.int/initiatives/decadeof-healthy-ageing (accessed on 16 March 2026).

World Health Organization. WHO. (2021). Global strategy on digital health 2020-2025, 1–44. https://www.who.int/publications/i/item/9789240020924 (accessed March 2026).

World Health Organization. WHO. (2022). WHO highlights oral health neglect affecting nearly half of the world's population. 18 November 2022. Available at: https://www.who.int/news/item/18-11-2022-who-highlights-oral-health-neglect-affecting-nearly-half-of-the-world-s-population (accessed March 2026).

Xi, J. Y., Liang, B. H., Zhang, W. J., Yan, B., Dong, H., Chen, Y.-Y., Lin, X., Gu, J., & Hao, Y.-T. (2025). Effects of population aging on quality of life and disease burden: A population-based study. *Global Health Research and Policy*, *10*(2), 2. Advance online publication. DOI: 10.1186/s41256-024-00393-8 PMID: 39810282

Yang, R., Gao, S., & Jiang, Y. (2024). Digital divide as a determinant of health in the U.S. older adults: Prevalence, trends, and risk factors. *BMC Geriatrics*, *24*(1), 1027. DOI: 10.1186/s12877-024-05612-y PMID: 39709341

Yeoh, C. W., & Oh, Z. J. (2025). Integrating AI-Powered Digital Marketing Strategies for Enhancing Educational Communication and Technopreneurship. *International Journal of Academic Research in Business & Social Sciences*, *15*(2), 1159–1176. DOI: 10.6007/IJARBSS/v15-i2/24835

Yin, Q., Chai, Z., Tao, B., Liu, P., Luo, Y., Zhao, Q., & Yang, B. (2025). The Impact of Online Interactive Platform Services on Oral Health Behaviors in Older Adults with Mild Cognitive Impairment: Protocol for a Randomized Controlled Trial. *Journal of Multidisciplinary Healthcare*, *18*, 663–674. DOI: 10.2147/JMDH.S508247 PMID: 39935432

Yu, S., Huang, S., Song, S., Lin, J., & Liu, F. (2024). Impact of oral health literacy on oral health behaviors and outcomes among the older adults: A scoping review. *BMC Geriatrics*, *24*(1), 858. Advance online publication. DOI: 10.1186/s12877-024-05469-1 PMID: 39438807

Zainal, H., Xiaohui, X., Thumboo, J., Seah, S. J., Leng, L. L., & Kok Yong, F. (2025). Exploring caregiver challenges, digital health technologies, and healthcare support: A qualitative study. *Frontiers in Digital Health*, *7*, 1587162. DOI: 10.3389/fdgth.2025.1587162 PMID: 40547053

Zhang, C., Mohamad, E., Azlan, A., Wu, A. Y., & Qi, Y. (2024). Social Media and eHealth Literacy Among Older Adults: Systematic Literature Review. *Journal of Medical Internet Research*, *27*, e66058. Advance online publication. DOI: 10.2196/66058 PMID: 40138684

Zhang, K., Cheng, X., Li, D., & Meng, X. (2025). The digital divide of older people in communities: Urban-rural, gender, and health disparities and inequities. *Health & Social Care in the Community*, 2025(1). DOI: 10.1155/hsc/1361214

Zohriah, A., Muin, A., Rohimat, S., & Faqih, S. (2025). The Dynamics of Educational Services Marketing in the Digital Era. International *Journal of Education, Social Studies, and Management*. .DOI: 10.52121/ijessm.v5i3.871

KEY TERMS AND DEFINITIONS

Artificial Intelligence (AI): Refers to the ability of machines and computer systems to implement tasks that typically require human intelligence, such as learning, perception, reasoning, problem-solving, and decision-making.

Digital Health: A multidisciplinary field that integrates information and communication technologies (ICTs) in to healthcare delivery to manage illnesses, mitigate health risks, and improve patient well-being. This ecosystem encompasses tools such as telemedicine, mobile health (mHealth), data analytics, and AI, aimed at optimizing healthcare efficiency, empowering patients, and facilitating more precise, personalized, and accessible care.

Email Marketing: A digital marketing strategy that uses email as a means to send commercial, promotional, or informational messages to a specific group of people, aiming to foster customer loyalty, generate sales, and maintain effective relationships between businesses and consumers. This practice includes the use of segmentation, personalization, and automation, personalization, and automation techniques, as well as the analysis of metrics to evaluate campaign performance.

PPC Campaigns (Pay Per Click): A digital advertising model in which advertisers pay a fee each time one of their ads is clicked. Essentially, it is a method of buying targeted traffic to a website rather than attempting to earn those visits organically. It is widely used in search engines (SEM) and social media platforms.

Salutogenic Marketing: A branch of social marketing that focuses its actions on the promotion and preservation of individual and collective health and well-being, empowering people to make healthy decisions.

SEO (Search Engine Optimization): A set of strategies and techniques aimed at improving the visibility and ranking of a website in the organic search results of search engines, through the optimization of content, site structure, and other relevant factors.

Social Ads: Paid advertisements on platforms such as Facebook, LinkedIn, Instagram, or Tik Tok that leverage user data for precise targeting and native interface integration.

Social Marketing: The application of marketing principles and techniques to influence individual and collective behaviors that benefit society as a whole and individuals, promoting social causes, public well-being, or health, without seeking profit for the promoter.

Teledentistry: Is a way of providing dental services remotely, using digital technology such as video conferencing, online image and data sharing. It allows patients to receive dental evaluations, diagnoses, and treatments without the need to physically visit a dentist.

Telehealth: The use of information and communication technologies (ICTs) to facilitate the delivery of clinical health care, health-related education, health administration, and public health, effectively overcoming geographical barriers between patients and health care providers.

Chapter 2
Leveraging Digital Marketing Strategies to Attract New Customers in Dental Health Services

Najat Dakhil Oufi Alnaemat
http://orcid.org/0009-0001-2173-6442
University of Basrah, Iraq

ABSTRACT

This chapter explores the role of digital marketing strategies in attracting new customers within health services, with a focus on how digital transformation reshapes patient acquisition processes. The purpose is to identify key strategies, determinants, challenges, and practical implications of digital marketing in healthcare contexts. A narrative literature review approach was adopted, synthesizing findings from recent empirical and theoretical studies in digital marketing, healthcare communication, and patient behavior. The results indicate that content marketing, social media engagement, and data-driven personalization significantly enhance trust, patient engagement, and service selection. However, effectiveness is influenced by regulatory constraints, digital health literacy, and concerns related to privacy and information credibility. The chapter concludes that successful customer acquisition in health services requires an integrated approach combining value-driven content, ethical communication, and technological capability to build trust and long-term patient relationships.

DOI: 10.4018/979-8-3373-8894-6.ch002

INTRODUCTION

Over the past decade, the health services sector has undergone a profound transformation driven by digital technologies (Mouloudj et al., 2025). What was once a predominantly face-to-face, institution-centered system is increasingly becoming a hybrid ecosystem where digital platforms, online communication, and data-driven decision-making play a central role. This shift is not merely technological; rather, it reflects broader changes in how individuals search for, evaluate, and ultimately choose health service providers. In this evolving landscape, digital marketing has emerged as a strategic lever for attracting new customers, enhancing visibility, and strengthening competitive positioning (ALKasassbeh et al., 2025; Al-Gasawneh et al., 2025).

At the organizational level, digital transformation is now widely recognized as a prerequisite for sustaining competitiveness (Alnaemat & Saleem, 2026). Recent research emphasizes the importance of assessing digital maturity within healthcare organizations as a foundation for planning and implementing effective strategies (de Ahumada Servant et al., 2025). The development of measurement tools such as composite digitalization indices highlights the growing need for systematic evaluation of digital progress across healthcare settings. Importantly, digitalization extends beyond operational improvements to encompass communication, service promotion, and customer engagement (Alameri et al., 2026; Malik et al., 2024; Tsai et al., 2024).

At the same time, the integration of digital tools into health services has reshaped customer expectations (Mouloudj et al., 2025). Patients are no longer passive recipients of care; instead, they actively seek information, compare alternatives, and engage with providers through digital channels. Social media platforms, in particular, have become influential environments where health-related information is shared and evaluated. Empirical evidence shows that online content, especially images and treatment outcomes, can significantly influence perceptions of professional credibility and willingness to choose a provider (Meira et al., 2021). Similarly, exposure to social media content has been found to affect patients' decisions to select or change healthcare providers (Freire et al., 2023; Alqabbani et al., 2025). However, the adoption of digital marketing in health services is not without complexity. Unlike traditional consumer markets, healthcare operates within a highly regulated and ethically sensitive environment. For example, healthcare professionals often express concerns regarding legal risks and professional boundaries when using social media for marketing purposes (Değirmencioğlu & Kılıçoğlu, 2024). In many contexts, restrictions on advertising limit the extent to which providers can directly promote their services, requiring more subtle and compliant communication strategies. These constraints highlight the need to balance marketing effectiveness with ethical responsibility.

Despite these challenges, digital marketing offers substantial opportunities for enhancing customer engagement and influencing behavior (Malik et al., 2024). The rapid growth of interactive content, particularly short-form videos, has transformed how information is consumed online. Studies based on behavioral frameworks such as the "Stimulus–Organism–Response" (S-O-R) model demonstrate that digital content can shape attitudes, build trust, and influence behavioral intentions (Luo et al., 2025; Shen & Wang, 2024). Elements such as perceived usefulness, entertainment, and ease of use contribute to positive user experiences, while trust plays a central mediating role in driving decision-making outcomes (Mouloudj et al., 2023; Zheng, 2023). Moreover, emotional engagement and flow experiences generated by digital content have been shown to significantly affect individuals' willingness to adopt behaviors or engage with specific activities (Zeng et al., 2025).

Beyond customer acquisition, digital marketing also plays a critical role in promoting healthier behaviors. Social marketing approaches emphasize the use of targeted communication strategies to influence attitudes and behavioral intentions. Empirical findings indicate that psychosocial factors such as attitudes, subjective norms, and perceived behavioral control significantly shape preventive health behaviors (Mouloudj et al., 2026). Additionally, health literacy has been identified as a key determinant that strengthens individuals' intentions to adopt healthier practices, highlighting the importance of informative and accessible digital content.

From a strategic perspective, the effectiveness of digital marketing lies in its ability to deliver personalized, interactive, and data-driven experiences. Contemporary research consistently demonstrates that digital marketing strategies enhance customer engagement, improve brand promotion, and contribute to organizational performance (Kamyabi et al., 2025; Malik et al., 2024). Systematic reviews further indicate that tools such as social media marketing, search engine optimization, and email marketing play a central role in improving customer experience and satisfaction (Nuseir et al., 2023). In addition, digital platforms enable organizations to reach broader audiences at lower cost while maintaining continuous interaction with customers, thereby strengthening loyalty and long-term relationships (López García et al., 2019).

The importance of digital marketing has become even more evident in recent years, particularly during periods of global disruption such as the COVID-19 pandemic. During this time, healthcare organizations increasingly relied on digital channels to communicate with patients, promote services, and maintain continuity of care. Evidence suggests that digital marketing contributed to increased patient engagement, improved trust, and greater utilization of health services (Pasaribu et al., 2022). Furthermore, the use of analytics tools allows organizations to monitor performance, understand customer behavior, and continuously refine their strategies, ultimately enhancing effectiveness and efficiency (ALKasassbeh et al., 2025).

Nevertheless, the implementation of digital marketing strategies in health services requires careful planning and continuous evaluation. The selection of appropriate channels, alignment with organizational objectives, and monitoring of outcomes are essential steps in ensuring success. At the same time, challenges such as data privacy concerns, digital inequality, and resource limitations must be addressed to achieve sustainable impact (Alameri et al., 2026).

Based on the above, the objective of this chapter is to examine how digital marketing strategies can be effectively leveraged to attract new customers in health services by identifying key approaches, determinants, challenges, and practical implications. In particular, it seeks to synthesize existing knowledge on content marketing, social media engagement, and data-driven targeting in shaping patient acquisition and decision-making processes. Methodologically, the chapter adopts a narrative literature review approach, drawing on recent empirical and theoretical studies in digital marketing and healthcare services. The selected literature was systematically analyzed and thematically organized to develop an integrated understanding of how digital transformation influences customer attraction in contemporary health service environments.

DEVELOPMENT OF DIGITAL HEALTH

Evolution of Digital Health Technologies

The evolution of digital health technologies reflects a gradual yet transformative shift in how healthcare systems operate, communicate, and deliver value to patients (Bouarar et al., 2024). Initially, digitalization in healthcare was limited to basic information systems, primarily focused on administrative efficiency and data storage (Martínez Asanza, 2025). Early applications such as "electronic health records" (EHRs) and hospital information systems marked the first step toward digitizing healthcare processes (Almokdad et al., 2026). However, over time, these foundational tools have expanded into a much broader and more complex digital ecosystem that integrates clinical care, patient engagement, and health communication (Lam et al., 2026).

This transition from simple digitization to comprehensive digital transformation has been neither linear nor uniform across contexts (Alnaemat & Saleem, 2026). In some healthcare systems, policy-driven initiatives, such as national e-health strategies, telematics infrastructures, and electronic patient records, have accelerated adoption (Martínez Asanza, 2025). Yet, despite technological progress, challenges such as fragmented governance, privacy concerns, and limited public trust continue to hinder full implementation (Perez Guzman & Ajami, 2026). These barriers highlight that the evolution of digital health is not solely a technological issue but also an institutional and cultural one.

At the clinical level, the scope of digital health technologies has expanded significantly in recent years. The emergence of telemedicine, remote patient monitoring, and mobile health applications has redefined the boundaries of healthcare delivery, allowing services to extend beyond traditional clinical settings (Martínez Asanza et al., 2024). In particular, digital technologies have demonstrated measurable improvements in patient outcomes, especially in areas such as cardiovascular care, where remote monitoring and digital interventions contribute to better disease management and reduced morbidity (Bouarar et al., 2024; Zwack et al., 2023). This shift toward decentralized care models illustrates how digital tools are enabling more continuous and personalized healthcare experiences (Almokdad et al., 2026). More recently, the integration of advanced technologies, such as "artificial intelligence" (AI) and wearable devices, has further accelerated the evolution of digital health. These innovations allow for real-time health monitoring, early disease detection, and highly personalized treatment approaches (Martínez Asanza et al., 2024). AI-driven diagnostics, for example, can analyze large volumes of data to support clinical decision-making, while wearable technologies provide continuous insights into patients' health status (Bahadori et al., 2025). Together, these developments are contributing to a transition from reactive to proactive healthcare, where prevention and early intervention are increasingly prioritized.

The COVID-19 pandemic represents a critical turning point in the trajectory of digital health. Faced with unprecedented challenges, healthcare systems worldwide rapidly adopted digital solutions to ensure continuity of care and communication. Teleconsultations, digital platforms, and online health communication tools became essential components of service delivery almost overnight (Bouarar et al., 2024). This period not only accelerated technological adoption but also reshaped both provider and patient attitudes toward digital health solutions (Dettori & Castiglia, 2022; Pasaribu et al., 2022). As a result, many of these practices have persisted beyond the pandemic, becoming integral to modern healthcare systems.

Another important dimension of digital health evolution concerns the role of communication technologies. The shift from traditional health communication methods, such as printed materials and mass media, to interactive digital platforms has fundamentally changed how health information is disseminated and consumed. Websites, mobile applications, and social media platforms now serve as key channels for delivering health information, enabling more accessible, timely, and user-centered communication (Dettori & Castiglia, 2022). This transformation has direct implications for digital marketing in health services, as communication and promotion are increasingly intertwined within the same digital environments.

Despite these advancements, the effectiveness of digital health technologies depends heavily on users' ability to engage with them. Digital health literacy has therefore emerged as a critical factor influencing the success of digital transformation initiatives. Research shows that disparities in digital health literacy can lead to unequal access to digital services and, consequently, to health inequalities (Madsen et al., 2025). Healthcare professionals also play a key role in this process, as their ability to assess and support patients' digital competencies directly affects the adoption and utilization of digital tools (Almokdad et al., 2026). Furthermore, the evolution of digital health technologies is closely linked to broader developments in digital marketing and consumer behavior. As patients increasingly rely on digital platforms to seek information and evaluate providers, the integration of digital health technologies with marketing strategies becomes essential (Martínez Asanza et al., 2024). The use of online platforms, social media, and interactive content not only facilitates service delivery but also enhances visibility and customer engagement (Nuseir et al., 2023; Luo et al., 2025). In this sense, digital health technologies are not merely operational tools; they are strategic assets that support both healthcare delivery and customer acquisition (Bouarar et al., 2024).

In summary, the evolution of digital health technologies reflects a multidimensional transformation encompassing technological innovation, organizational change, and shifts in user behavior (Martínez Asanza, 2025). From basic digitization to advanced AI-driven systems, digital health has redefined how services are delivered and experienced. However, its continued development depends on addressing key challenges related to governance, literacy, trust, and equity. Understanding this evolution is essential for designing effective digital marketing strategies that align with the realities of modern health services and the expectations of digitally empowered customers.

Implications for Customer Acquisition

The evolution of digital health technologies has profound implications for how health service providers attract new customers. As healthcare systems increasingly integrate digital platforms into service delivery and communication, customer acquisition is no longer limited to traditional referral networks or geographic proximity (Malik et al., 2024). Instead, it has become a dynamic, data-driven process shaped by digital visibility, user experience, and continuous engagement across multiple channels. One of the most important implications is the growing interdependence between customer acquisition and retention. In service industries, these two dimensions are closely linked, as efforts to attract new customers can influence existing customers' perceptions and behaviors (Furman et al., 2021; King et al., 2016). In health services, this relationship is particularly critical because perceived service quality, accessibility, and trust directly affect both initial choice and long-term loyalty. For instance, digital appointment systems, teleconsultations, and responsive communication channels not only attract new customers but also reinforce satisfaction among existing ones, creating a virtuous cycle of engagement.

From a strategic perspective, effective customer acquisition in health services requires careful allocation of resources between attracting new customers and maintaining existing relationships. Analytical models suggest that organizations should initially invest more heavily in acquisition when their customer base is limited, gradually shifting toward retention as the base expands (King et al., 2016). However, in digital environments, this balance becomes more complex, as online campaigns targeting new customers are often visible to existing users, potentially influencing their expectations and satisfaction (Lhoest-Snoeck et al., 2014). Therefore, healthcare providers must design acquisition strategies that are not only attractive but also perceived as fair and consistent across all customer groups.

Another key implication concerns the role of service access quality in shaping customer acquisition outcomes. Research highlights that customer decisions are strongly influenced by their ability to access services in a timely and convenient manner (Afeche et al., 2017; Malik et al., 2024). Digital health technologies directly enhance this dimension by reducing waiting times, enabling remote consultations, and providing 24/7 access to information. Consequently, organizations that leverage digital tools to improve accessibility are more likely to attract new customers, particularly in competitive environments where convenience is a decisive factor (Odoom & Agyeman, 2019). In addition, the rise of data-driven decision-making has transformed customer acquisition strategies. Big data analytics allows organizations to analyze large volumes of user information, identify patterns, and predict customer behavior (Kaur & Bala, 2024). In the context of health services, this capability enables providers to segment their audience more precisely, personalize communication, and deliver targeted marketing campaigns. For example, digital platforms can track user interactions, search behavior, and engagement levels, providing insights that support more effective acquisition strategies (Malik et al., 2024). At the same time, these approaches must be carefully managed to address privacy and security concerns, which remain critical in healthcare settings.

Digital marketing channels also play a central role in shaping customer acquisition. Social media platforms, websites, and mobile applications serve as primary touchpoints where potential customers form their first impressions of health service providers (Bouarar et al., 2024). Empirical evidence shows that online content, such as treatment outcomes, patient testimonials, and educational materials, significantly influences customer decisions (Meira et al., 2021; Alqabbani et al., 2025). Moreover, the interactive nature of digital platforms allows users to engage directly with providers, ask questions, and compare alternatives, thereby enhancing transparency and trust (Alameri et al., 2026). These factors collectively contribute to more informed and confident decision-making among potential customers.

Another important dimension is the influence of market competition and positioning on acquisition strategies. In highly competitive service markets, organizations must continuously adapt their marketing efforts to maintain visibility and attract new customers. Research indicates that acquisition costs and effectiveness are closely linked to market dynamics, including competition intensity and market share (Min et al., 2016). In the health services sector, this is evident in the increasing use of promotional tools, such as digital campaigns and targeted incentives, to differentiate services and attract new patients. For example, in pharmaceutical markets, pricing strategies and incentives can be used to encourage initial adoption and subsequently build customer loyalty (Gibbons et al., 2025).

At the same time, customer acquisition in health services is influenced by perceived service quality and trust, which are critical determinants of decision-making. Digital platforms can enhance these perceptions by providing transparent information, showcasing professional expertise, and facilitating communication (Almokdad et al., 2026). However, they also expose organizations to greater scrutiny, as negative experiences or service failures can quickly spread online. Studies show that effective service recovery and perceived fairness play a significant role in maintaining customer trust and loyalty, even after service failures (Choi et al., 2023). This highlights the importance of integrating customer experience management into acquisition strategies.

Furthermore, the integration of digital health technologies with marketing strategies enables a more holistic approach to customer acquisition. Digital tools not only facilitate service delivery but also support continuous engagement throughout the customer journey—from awareness and consideration to decision and post-service interaction (Odoom & Agyeman, 2019). This aligns with broader findings that digital marketing enhances customer engagement, improves satisfaction, and strengthens brand positioning (Kamyabi et al., 2025; Nuseir et al., 2023). In this sense, customer acquisition should not be viewed as a one-time event but as part of an ongoing relationship-building process. Therefore, the implications of digital health for customer acquisition are multifaceted. They involve a shift toward integrated, data-driven strategies that balance acquisition and retention, prioritize accessibility and user experience, and leverage digital channels to enhance visibility and trust. While these developments create significant opportunities for health service providers, they also require careful management of ethical, regulatory, and operational challenges. Understanding such implications is essential for designing effective digital marketing strategies that can successfully attract and engage customers in an increasingly competitive and digitalized healthcare environment.

ATTRACTING TARGET CUSTOMERS IN HEALTH SERVICES

Understanding Customer Needs and Behavior

Understanding customer needs and behavior is a fundamental prerequisite for attracting target customers in the services sector (Alameri et al., 2026). Unlike many other service sectors, healthcare decisions are often complex, high-involvement, and influenced by both rational evaluations and emotional considerations. Patients do not simply "purchase" services; rather, they seek trust, reassurance, accessibility, and perceived quality (Bouarar et al., 2024). Consequently, effective customer acquisition strategies must be grounded in a comprehensive understanding of how individuals search for information, evaluate alternatives, and make healthcare decisions.

In the digital era, customer behavior has become increasingly information-driven and interactive. Patients actively use online platforms to explore symptoms, compare providers, read reviews, and assess service quality before making decisions (Martínez Asanza et al., 2024). Social media, in particular, plays a critical role in shaping perceptions and influencing choices. Empirical evidence shows that digital content, such as before-and-after treatment images, educational posts, and professional credentials, significantly affects perceived credibility and willingness to choose a provider (Meira et al., 2021; Alqabbani et al., 2025). Moreover, engagement with healthcare providers' social media accounts has been linked to decisions to switch providers, highlighting the growing importance of digital touchpoints in the customer journey (Freire et al., 2023; Odoom & Agyeman, 2019). At the same time, trust emerges as a central determinant of customer behavior in health services. Unlike traditional consumer goods, healthcare decisions involve higher perceived risks, making trust a key mediating factor between information exposure and behavioral intention. Research based on behavioral models such as the "technology acceptance model" (TAM) framework demonstrates that certain triggers, such as content quality, perceived risk, usefulness, ease of use, and interactivity, shape internal psychological states, particularly trust, which in turn influence decision-making (Alameri et al., 2026; Luo et al., 2025; Shen & Wang, 2024). This implies that digital marketing strategies must not only inform but also build confidence and credibility.

Another important aspect of customer behavior is the role of experience and engagement. Digital environments enable immersive and engaging experiences that can influence attitudes and intentions. For example, studies on short-form video content highlight how emotional stimulation and flow experiences can significantly affect individuals' willingness to engage with activities or services (Zeng et al., 2025; Zheng, 2023). In the context of health services, this suggests that engaging and well-designed digital content can enhance customer interest and motivate action, particularly when it simplifies complex health information and presents it in an accessible manner (Mouloudj et al., 2023).

Customer behavior is also shaped by socio-demographic and psychological factors. Variables such as age, education, health literacy, and cultural background influence how individuals perceive and use digital health information. For instance, higher levels of health literacy are associated with stronger intentions to adopt preventive health behaviors (Mouloudj et al., 2026). Conversely, limited digital or health literacy can act as a barrier to engagement, reducing the effectiveness of digital marketing efforts (Martínez Asanza et al., 2024). This highlights the importance of tailoring communication strategies to different audience segments to ensure inclusivity and accessibility.

Furthermore, service accessibility and convenience play a decisive role in customer choice. Digital health technologies, such as telemedicine, online appointment systems, and mobile applications, reduce barriers to access and enhance user convenience, making services more attractive to potential customers (Lam et al., 2026; Tsai et al., 2024). Research in service operations also emphasizes that timely access to services significantly influences customer acquisition and retention (Afeche et al., 2017). Therefore, understanding customer expectations regarding accessibility is essential for designing effective acquisition strategies.

In addition to individual-level factors, market dynamics and competitive environments influence customer behavior. In highly competitive health service markets, customers are more likely to compare multiple providers and base their decisions on perceived value, service quality, and digital presence. Digital marketing strategies that enhance visibility, provide transparent information, and facilitate interaction can therefore create a competitive advantage (Kamyabi et al., 2025; Nuseir et al., 2023). At the same time, organizations must ensure consistency between their online communication and actual service delivery, as discrepancies can negatively impact trust and satisfaction.

To synthesize these determinants, Table 1 summarizes the key factors influencing customer needs and behavior in health services.

Table 1. Key determinants of customer needs and behavior in health services

Determinant	Description	Implications for Digital Marketing
Trust and Credibility	Confidence in provider competence and reliability	Use transparent, evidence-based content and testimonials
Information Seeking Behavior	Active search for health-related information online	Optimize websites, SEO, and educational content
Social Media Influence	Impact of online interactions and peer opinions	Leverage engaging and interactive social media strategies

continued on following page

Table 1. Continued

Determinant	Description	Implications for Digital Marketing
Health Literacy	Ability to understand and use health information	Simplify content and ensure accessibility
Service Accessibility	Ease of accessing healthcare services	Promote telemedicine and online booking systems
Emotional Engagement	Influence of feelings and experiences	Use visual and interactive content (e.g., videos)
Perceived Value and Quality	Evaluation of benefits relative to cost	Highlight service outcomes and patient satisfaction

As shown in Table 1, customer behavior in health services is shaped by a combination of cognitive, emotional, and contextual factors. These determinants are interconnected and must be considered holistically when designing digital marketing strategies. For example, providing high-quality information may enhance trust, but without accessibility and user-friendly design, it may not lead to actual engagement.

Based on the above, attracting target customers in health services requires a deep understanding of evolving customer behavior in the digital age. Patients are increasingly informed, engaged, and selective, relying on digital platforms to guide their decisions (Odoom & Agyeman, 2019). Therefore, healthcare providers must adopt a customer-centric approach that integrates trust-building, personalization, accessibility, and engagement. By aligning digital marketing strategies with these behavioral insights, organizations can more effectively attract and retain customers in an increasingly competitive and digitalized healthcare environment.

Segmentation and Targeting Strategies

Effective customer acquisition in health services depends not only on understanding customer behavior but also on the ability to segment and target distinct groups with precision. In increasingly competitive and digitalized environments, treating patients as a homogeneous group is no longer viable (Mouloudj et al., 2023). Instead, healthcare organizations must adopt structured segmentation approaches that reflect differences in needs, preferences, health conditions, and digital engagement patterns. A key development in this area is the shift toward needs-based population segmentation, which groups individuals according to their healthcare requirements rather than solely demographic characteristics. This approach has gained strong support in the literature, as it enables more accurate planning of services and targeted interventions (Chong et al., 2019). Rather than relying on broad categories such as age or gender, needs-based segmentation considers factors such as disease burden, risk levels, and expected healthcare utilization. Empirical evidence further shows that such segmentation models can effectively predict outcomes such as service use, mortality, and quality of life, making them highly relevant for strategic decision-making (Chong et al., 2020).

In parallel, data-driven segmentation approaches have become increasingly important with the rise of digital health technologies. The availability of large-scale datasets, including "electronic health records, insurance claims, and digital interaction data", allows healthcare providers to identify patterns and classify customers into meaningful segments. For example, clustering techniques based on utilization patterns, morbidity, and demographic variables can reveal distinct groups with significantly different service needs and cost profiles (Pioch et al., 2023). These insights enable organizations to allocate resources more efficiently and design targeted marketing strategies that align with the specific characteristics of each segment.

Beyond clinical and utilization-based segmentation, digital behavior and engagement patterns are also critical in defining target customers. As patients increasingly interact with healthcare providers through digital channels, their online behavior, such as search activity, social media engagement, and content consumption, provides valuable signals for segmentation. Studies show that digital marketing effectiveness is enhanced when strategies are tailored to specific audience segments, particularly through personalized communication and interactive content (Bovsh et al., 2024; Nuseir et al., 2023; Luo et al., 2025). For instance, younger, digitally active users may respond more positively to short-form video content, while older populations may prefer more structured and informational communication formats.

Another important dimension is the integration of technology into segmentation and targeting processes. Healthcare organizations that effectively combine technological tools, such as "mHealth applications, telemedicine platforms, and social media", with strategic planning are better positioned to reach and engage target customers (Odoom & Agyeman, 2019). However, this requires moving beyond a purely technical perspective and recognizing technology as part of a broader system that includes information management, organizational processes, and service delivery (Alnaemat & Saleem, 2026). When these elements are aligned, digital technologies can significantly enhance access, personalization, and overall customer experience.

Importantly, segmentation must be directly linked to targeting strategies that guide how organizations communicate with and attract specific customer groups. Targeting involves selecting the most relevant segments and designing tailored value propositions for each group. In health services, this may include promoting preventive care programs to low-risk populations, chronic disease management services to high-risk patients, or specialized treatments to niche segments. The effectiveness of these strategies depends on the alignment between customer needs, service offerings, and communication channels.

To support this process, Table 2 outlines a structured framework for identifying and targeting customer segments in health services.

Table 2. Steps to identify and target customer segments in health services

Step	Description	Strategic Implication
Data Collection	Gather demographic, clinical, and behavioral data	Enables evidence-based segmentation
Segmentation	Classify customers into homogeneous groups (e.g., needs-based, behavioral)	Improves understanding of target groups
Profiling	Develop detailed profiles for each segment (needs, preferences, risks)	Supports personalized marketing strategies
Targeting	Select priority segments based on strategic goals and resource capacity	Enhances efficiency of marketing efforts
Strategy Design	Tailor communication channels and messages for each segment	Increases engagement and conversion rates
Evaluation	Monitor outcomes and refine segmentation and targeting strategies	Ensures continuous improvement

As shown in Table 2, segmentation and targeting are iterative processes that rely on continuous data analysis and refinement. Digital tools and analytics platforms play a crucial role in this cycle, enabling real-time monitoring of customer responses and facilitating adaptive strategies. However, several challenges must be considered. First, data availability and quality can limit the effectiveness of segmentation, particularly in contexts where digital infrastructure is underdeveloped. Second, privacy and ethical considerations are especially critical in healthcare, requiring strict adherence to data protection regulations. Third, digital inequalities may lead to the exclusion of certain population groups, highlighting the need for inclusive and accessible strategies (Madsen et al., 2025). Therefore, segmentation and targeting strategies are central to attracting customers in health services. By leveraging needs-based, data-driven, and behavior-oriented approaches, healthcare organizations can design more precise and effective marketing strategies. When combined with digital technologies and personalized communication, these strategies not only improve customer acquisition but also contribute to better alignment between service provision and population needs.

DIGITAL MARKETING STRATEGIES FOR CUSTOMER ACQUISITION IN HEALTH SERVICES

Content Marketing for Customer Attraction and Health Awareness

Content marketing has become a central pillar in attracting new customers within health services, particularly as patients increasingly rely on digital platforms to search for information and evaluate providers. Unlike traditional promotion, content marketing emphasizes the creation of relevant, informative, and trustworthy material that supports both awareness and decision-making (Bovsh et al., 2024; Hur et al., 2025). This is especially important in healthcare, where trust and credibility directly influence service selection (Hollebeek & Macky, 2019).

Empirical evidence shows that high-quality digital content, whether educational articles, videos, or patient testimonials, enhances engagement and fosters positive perceptions of service providers. For instance, informative, entertaining, and socially valuable content contributes significantly to users' experiential evaluations and, ultimately, loyalty (Bovsh et al., 2024; Bui et al., 2023). In health contexts, this aligns with findings that patients are influenced by online images, treatment explanations, and before–after cases when choosing providers (Meira et al., 2021; Alqabbani et al., 2025). Thus, content not only informs but also reduces uncertainty and perceived risk, which are critical barriers in healthcare decision-making. Moreover, content marketing plays a key role in shaping "brand health," measured through indicators such as engagement, repeat visits, and online interactions (Ahmad et al., 2016; Bovsh et al., 2024). When patients perceive content as credible and useful, they are more likely to develop trust, which mediates behavioral intentions (Luo et al., 2025). This is consistent with broader digital marketing research emphasizing that value-driven content fosters long-term relationships rather than immediate transactions (Hollebeek & Macky, 2019; Hur et al., 2025).

From a strategic perspective, healthcare organizations should align content with patient needs, health literacy levels, and cultural context. Integrating preventive health messaging, such as those identified in social marketing research (Mouloudj et al., 2026), can simultaneously promote healthier behaviors and attract new patients. In this sense, content marketing operates at the intersection of education, engagement, and acquisition, making it a powerful tool for sustainable growth in health services.

Social Media Marketing and Customer Engagement Strategies

Social media marketing represents one of the most dynamic channels for acquiring new customers in health services, offering opportunities for real-time interaction, personalized communication, and broad audience reach. Platforms such as Instagram, Facebook, and short-video applications have transformed how patients discover, evaluate, and engage with healthcare providers (Freire et al., 2023; Luo et al., 2025). A key advantage of social media lies in its ability to facilitate two-way communication, enabling healthcare organizations to move beyond passive information delivery toward active engagement. Research indicates that social media content, particularly when visually rich and emotionally appealing, can significantly influence perceptions of credibility and willingness to become a client (Meira et al., 2021). Similarly, influencer marketing and user-generated content enhance trust when messages are perceived as authentic, informative, and relatable (Lou & Yuan, 2019).

Effective social media strategies depend not only on content but also on how content is delivered and managed. Studies highlight that multimedia formats, creative storytelling, and consistent posting schedules increase engagement levels (Ashley & Tuten, 2015; Drossos et al., 2024). In addition, responsive communication strategies, such as timely replies and interactive dialogue, strengthen customer relationships and improve digital engagement outcomes (Liu et al., 2021). These interactions contribute to building trust, which is a critical determinant of customer acquisition in healthcare settings. However, healthcare organizations must also navigate regulatory and ethical constraints, particularly regarding advertising and patient confidentiality (Değirmencioğlu & Kılıçoğlu, 2024). Despite these challenges, social media remains a powerful tool when used strategically, allowing providers to showcase expertise, share patient success stories, and differentiate their services in competitive markets.

Ultimately, social media marketing supports the transition from awareness to engagement and conversion by creating meaningful connections with potential patients. When integrated with broader digital strategies, it enhances visibility, strengthens trust, and drives customer acquisition in health services.

Determinants of Effective Digital Marketing Strategies

The effectiveness of digital marketing strategies in health services is shaped by a set of interrelated determinants that influence how potential patients perceive, evaluate, and engage with digital content. Foremost among these is trust, which plays a decisive role in healthcare contexts characterized by high perceived risk and information asymmetry. Empirical evidence shows that trust is strengthened through credible, transparent, and informative digital content, and acts as a mediator between digital stimuli (e.g., social media content, short videos) and behavioral intentions such as service selection (Luo et al., 2025; Lou & Yuan, 2019). In addition, content that reflects professional competence, such as treatment explanations or before–after cases, enhances perceived credibility and willingness to become a client (Meira et al., 2021; Alqabbani et al., 2025).

A second determinant is the perceived value of digital content, including its informational, emotional, and social dimensions. Content that is relevant, engaging, and tailored to user needs improves experiential evaluations and fosters positive attitudes toward healthcare providers (Bui et al., 2023). This aligns with the broader logic of digital content marketing, which emphasizes value creation and relationship building rather than direct persuasion (Hollebeek & Macky, 2019). In health services, such value is further reinforced when content contributes to health awareness and literacy, thereby supporting both individual decision-making and preventive behaviors (Mouloudj et al., 2026).

Customer engagement represents another critical determinant, reflecting the depth of interaction between users and digital platforms. Engagement is driven by creative strategies such as multimedia content, storytelling, and interactive communication, which have been shown to increase participation and strengthen relationships (Ashley & Tuten, 2015; Drossos et al., 2024). Moreover, responsive communication strategies, such as timely replies and personalized interactions, enhance cognitive and emotional engagement, ultimately improving customer acquisition outcomes (Liu et al., 2021).

From a strategic standpoint, data-driven capabilities significantly enhance marketing effectiveness. The use of big data analytics enables healthcare organizations to understand patient preferences, personalize communication, and optimize targeting strategies (Kaur & Bala, 2024). This is particularly important in competitive environments where efficient allocation of resources between acquisition and retention activities is required (Min et al., 2016; King et al., 2016).

Finally, contextual and regulatory factors shape the implementation of digital marketing in health services. Legal restrictions on advertising and concerns about privacy and data protection may limit the use of certain promotional practices (Değirmencioğlu & Kılıçoğlu, 2024). Additionally, variations in digital health literacy influence how patients interpret and use online information, highlighting the need for accessible and user-centered communication (Madsen et al., 2025; Mouloudj et al., 2023). Together, these determinants underscore that effective digital marketing in healthcare requires an integrated approach that balances technological capabilities, user engagement, and ethical responsibility. Table 3 provides a structured summary of the main factors influencing the effectiveness of digital marketing strategies in health services, along with their corresponding implications.

Table 3. Determinants of effective digital marketing strategies in health services

Determinant	Description	Key Supporting Insights
Trust and Credibility	The extent to which patients perceive digital content and providers as reliable and professional	Trust mediates the relationship between digital content and behavioral intentions; credibility enhances patient choice (Luo et al., 2025; Meira et al., 2021)
Perceived Content Value	Informational, emotional, and social benefits derived from digital content	Valuable content improves engagement, attitudes, and loyalty (Bui et al., 2023; Hollebeek & Macky, 2019)
Customer Engagement	Level of cognitive, emotional, and behavioral interaction with digital platforms	Multimedia and interactive strategies increase engagement and acquisition potential (Ashley & Tuten, 2015; Liu et al., 2021)
Data-Driven Personalization	Use of analytics and big data to tailor marketing strategies and messages	Enables targeted communication and improves decision-making (Kaur & Bala, 2024)
Service Quality and Experience Signals	Online representation of service quality (e.g., testimonials, images, outcomes)	Influences credibility and willingness to choose providers (Alqabbani et al., 2025)
Regulatory and Ethical Constraints	Legal restrictions, privacy concerns, and professional guidelines	May limit promotional practices but ensure ethical compliance (Değirmencioğlu & Kılıçoğlu, 2024)
Digital Health Literacy	Patients' ability to access, understand, and use digital health information	Affects how marketing messages are interpreted and acted upon (Madsen et al., 2025)

CHALLENGES OF DIGITAL MARKETING IN HEALTH SERVICES

Despite the increasing adoption of digital marketing in health services, several challenges constrain its effective implementation. One of the most critical issues relates to regulatory and ethical constraints. Healthcare marketing is subject to strict professional guidelines that limit advertising practices and patient communication. For instance, many healthcare professionals express concerns about legal risks associated with social media interactions, particularly regarding patient confidentiality and professional boundaries (Değirmencioğlu & Kılıçoğlu, 2024). These restrictions often reduce the flexibility of digital campaigns and discourage proactive engagement, even when such engagement could enhance patient acquisition.

Another major challenge is data privacy and security. Digital marketing strategies rely heavily on data analytics and personalization, yet the use of patient data raises concerns about confidentiality and cybersecurity. While big data analytics can improve targeting and decision-making, it also introduces vulnerabilities related to data breaches and misuse, requiring organizations to implement strict governance mechanisms (Kaur & Bala, 2024). These concerns are further intensified in healthcare due to the sensitive nature of personal health information.

A third barrier involves digital health literacy and unequal access to technology. Not all patients are equally equipped to navigate digital platforms or interpret health-related content. Limited digital literacy can reduce the effectiveness of online communication and may lead to disparities in access to healthcare services. Research highlights that improving digital health literacy among both patients and professionals is essential to ensure equitable access and meaningful engagement (Madsen et al., 2025). In developing contexts, these challenges are often exacerbated by infrastructural limitations and uneven access to digital tools.

Additionally, content credibility and information overload pose significant risks. The vast amount of health information available online makes it difficult for patients to distinguish between reliable and misleading content. Since trust is a key determinant of patient decision-making, any perceived lack of credibility can negatively affect engagement and acquisition outcomes (Luo et al., 2025). Healthcare providers must therefore invest in producing accurate, evidence-based, and user-friendly content to maintain credibility and avoid misinformation.

Finally, organizational and resource constraints remain a persistent challenge. Many healthcare institutions lack the financial resources, technological infrastructure, or skilled personnel required to design and implement effective digital marketing strategies. Moreover, integrating digital tools into healthcare systems often requires overcoming cultural resistance and ensuring alignment with broader organizational objectives (Perez Guzman & Ajami, 2026). These limitations can slow down digital transformation efforts and reduce the overall impact of marketing initiatives.

Table 4 summarizes the key challenges affecting the implementation of digital marketing strategies in health services and their implications.

Table 4. Challenges of digital marketing in health services

Challenge	Description	Key Supporting Insights
Regulatory and Ethical Constraints	Restrictions on advertising, patient communication, and professional conduct	Legal concerns limit social media use and interactive marketing (Değirmencioğlu & Kılıçoğlu, 2024)
Data Privacy and Security Risks	Risks associated with collecting, storing, and analyzing patient data	Big data enhances targeting but increases privacy and security concerns (Kaur & Bala, 2024)
Digital Health Literacy Gaps	Limited ability of patients to access and understand digital health information	Low literacy reduces engagement and increases inequalities (Madsen et al., 2025)

continued on following page

Table 4. Continued

Challenge	Description	Key Supporting Insights
Information Overload and Credibility Issues	Difficulty distinguishing reliable from misleading online health content	Trust is critical for influencing patient decisions (Luo et al., 2025)
Technological and Infrastructure Limitations	Unequal access to digital tools and platforms across populations	Digital divide affects reach and effectiveness of marketing strategies
Organizational and Resource Constraints	Lack of expertise, funding, and strategic alignment	Slows adoption and limits effectiveness of digital transformation (Perez Guzman & Ajami, 2026)

PRACTICAL IMPLICATIONS

The findings of this chapter offer several practical implications for healthcare managers, policymakers, and digital marketing practitioners. First, healthcare organizations should prioritize trust-building strategies by delivering accurate, transparent, and patient-centered digital content. Given the strong influence of credibility on patient decisions, incorporating educational materials, real patient experiences, and evidence-based information can enhance confidence and attract new customers (Meira et al., 2021; Luo et al., 2025).

Second, organizations are encouraged to adopt a data-driven marketing approach. Leveraging analytics tools enables providers to better understand patient preferences, segment target audiences, and personalize communication strategies. This not only improves marketing efficiency but also enhances patient engagement and satisfaction (Kaur & Bala, 2024). However, such practices must be aligned with strict data privacy and ethical standards.

Third, healthcare providers should invest in multi-channel digital strategies, integrating websites, social media, and mobile platforms to ensure consistent and accessible communication. Social media, in particular, can be used to foster interaction, respond to patient inquiries, and strengthen long-term relationships (Freire et al., 2023).

Finally, improving digital health literacy among both patients and professionals is essential. Training programs and simplified communication can help bridge the digital divide and maximize the effectiveness of digital marketing initiatives (Madsen et al., 2025). Overall, a balanced approach that combines technological innovation with ethical responsibility is key to achieving sustainable customer acquisition in health services.

LIMITATIONS AND FUTURE RESEARCH

This chapter provides a conceptual synthesis of digital marketing strategies for customer acquisition in health services; however, several limitations should be acknowledged. First, the discussion relies primarily on existing literature rather than primary empirical data, which may limit the generalizability of the conclusions across different healthcare systems and cultural contexts. Digital marketing practices and regulatory environments vary considerably between countries, potentially influencing the applicability of the proposed insights. Second, the rapid evolution of digital technologies, particularly "social media platforms, AI, and data analytics", means that some findings may become outdated as new tools and practices emerge. Third, while the chapter integrates perspectives from marketing and healthcare, it does not empirically test specific models or frameworks, such as the role of trust or engagement in driving actual patient acquisition.

Future research should focus on empirical validation of the proposed relationships using quantitative and mixed-method approaches. empirical studies could provide deeper insights into how digital marketing strategies influence patient behavior. Additionally, further research is needed to explore the role of emerging technologies, such as AI-driven personalization and predictive analytics, in enhancing marketing effectiveness. Finally, studies examining digital health literacy and ethical concerns across diverse populations would contribute to more inclusive and sustainable digital marketing practices.

CONCLUSION

This chapter has examined the growing role of digital marketing strategies in attracting new customers within health services, highlighting the shift toward more patient-centered, technology-driven approaches. As healthcare systems continue to digitalize, tools such as content marketing, social media engagement, and data-driven targeting have become essential for enhancing visibility and building relationships with potential patients. The findings emphasize that effective digital marketing is not solely about promotion, but rather about creating value, fostering trust, and supporting informed decision-making. At the same time, the chapter underscores the importance of addressing key determinants, such as engagement, personalization, and digital literacy, while navigating challenges related to regulation, privacy, and resource constraints. Ultimately, healthcare organizations that successfully integrate ethical considerations with innovative digital strategies are better positioned to improve patient acquisition and long-term sustainability in an increasingly competitive environment.

REFERENCES

Afeche, P., Araghi, M., & Baron, O. (2017). Customer acquisition, retention, and service access quality: Optimal advertising, capacity level, and capacity allocation. *Manufacturing & Service Operations Management, 19*(4), 674–691. DOI: 10.1287/msom.2017.0635

Ahmad, N. S., Musa, R., & Harun, M. H. M. (2016). The impact of social media content marketing (SMCM) towards brand health. *Procedia Economics and Finance, 37*, 331–336. DOI: 10.1016/S2212-5671(16)30133-2

Al-Gasawneh, J. A., Alghizzawi, M., & Al Attyia, N. F. Y. (2025). The Influence Factor of Digital Marketing on Customer Satisfaction. In Alzoubi, H. M., Al-Gasaymeh, A. S., & Vasudevan, S. (Eds.), *Bridging Digital Innovation and Technology for Business Transformation—ICTIM* (pp. 125–130). Springer., DOI: 10.1007/978-3-031-90558-2_16

Alameri, S. A., Mahmoud, B. I., Almado, A. A., Jasim, Z. A., Jahlool, I. H., & Alyousuf, A. N. (2026). Consumer Acceptance of AI-Supported Circular Fashion Services: A Technology Acceptance Perspective. In Mouloudj, K., & Arantes, L. (Eds.), *Ethical Consumption and Responsible Innovation in Fashion through AI* (pp. 35–58). IGI Global., DOI: 10.4018/979-8-3373-7200-6.ch002

ALKasassbeh. H., Alghizzawi, M., Abu-AlSondos, I.A., Yaseen, S.G., Almuhaisen, O., Al-Daoud, K.I. (2025). Digital Marketing and Consumer Satisfaction. In S.G. Yaseen (Eds.), *Applied Artificial Intelligence in Business* (pp. 349–360), Springer. DOI: 10.1007/978-3-031-90271-0_25

Almokdad, E., Mouloudj, K., Njoku, A., Bouarar, A. C., Evans, M. A., Asanza, D. M., & Mouloudj, S. (2026). Exploring healthcare workers' intentions to volunteer in digital healthcare services for underserved communities: An extended TAM-based study. *Electronic Journal of General Medicine, 23*(1), em714. DOI: 10.29333/ejgm/17915

Alnaemat, N. D., & Saleem, S. A. (2026). Integrating Digital Technologies into Fashion Management: Opportunities and Challenges. In Mouloudj, K., & Arantes, L. (Eds.), *Ethical Consumption and Responsible Innovation in Fashion through AI* (pp. 145–168). IGI Global., DOI: 10.4018/979-8-3373-7200-6.ch006

Alqabbani, Y. N., Alfhaed, N. K., Almasaad, K. F., Mahanshi, R. Y., Farooqi, F., Al-Khalifa, K. S., & Gaffar, B. O. (2025). The impact of dental photography in social media platforms on patients' selection of dentists and type of treatment. *BMC Oral Health, 25*(1), 111. DOI: 10.1186/s12903-025-05483-8 PMID: 39838400

Ashley, C., & Tuten, T. (2015). Creative strategies in social media marketing: An exploratory study of branded social content and consumer engagement. *Psychology and Marketing*, *32*(1), 15–27. DOI: 10.1002/mar.20761

Bahadori, S., Buckle, P., Ascensao, T. S., Ghafur, S., & Kierkegaard, P. (2025). Evolving digital health technologies: Aligning with and enhancing the national institute for health and care excellence evidence standards framework. *JMIR mHealth and uHealth*, *13*, e67435. DOI: 10.2196/67435 PMID: 40845677

Bouarar, A. C., Asanza, D. M., Mouloudj, S., Bouarar, A., Mouloudj, K., & Bozorgi, M. (2024). Elderly's Intention to Use Teledentistry Services: Antecedents and Challenges. In Martínez Asanza, D. (Ed.), *Geriatric Dentistry in the Age of Digital Technology* (pp. 101–116). IGI Global., DOI: 10.4018/979-8-3693-0260-6.ch004

Bovsh, A. L., Mouloudj, K., Rasulova, A. M., & Tkachuk, T. M. (2024). Viral Content in Event Management of Hospitality and Socio-Cultural Activities. In S. Kulshreshtha & C. Webster (Eds.), *New Technologies in Virtual and Hybrid Events* (pp. 229-258). IGI Global. DOI: 10.4018/979-8-3693-2272-7.ch012

Bui, T. T., Tran, Q. T., Alang, T., & Le, T. D. (2023). Examining the relationship between digital content marketing perceived value and brand loyalty: Insights from Vietnam. *Cogent Social Sciences*, *9*(1), 2225835. DOI: 10.1080/23311886.2023.2225835

Choi, H.-K., Kim, S.-S., & Kim, B.-S. (2023). Perceived justice and customer loyalty in the situation of beauty service failure. *SAGE Open*, *13*(4), 1–14. DOI: 10.1177/21582440231217729

Chong, J. L., Lim, K. K., & Matchar, D. B. (2019). Population segmentation based on healthcare needs: A systematic review. *Systematic Reviews*, *8*(1), 202. DOI: 10.1186/s13643-019-1105-6 PMID: 31409423

Chong, J. L., Low, L. L., Matchar, D. B., Malhotra, R., Lee, K. H., Thumboo, J., & Chan, A. W. M. (2020). Do healthcare needs-based population segments predict outcomes among the elderly? Findings from a prospective cohort study in an urbanized low-income community. *BMC Geriatrics*, *20*(1), 78. DOI: 10.1186/s12877-020-1480-9 PMID: 32103728

de Ahumada Servant, P., Martín-Martín, D., & Romero, I. (2025). Digital transformation of oral health care: Measuring the digitalization of dental clinics. *Social Indicators Research*, *178*(3), 1145–1167. DOI: 10.1007/s11205-024-03366-z

Değirmencioğlu, E., & Kılıçoğlu, H. (2024). Evaluating the impact of social media marketing from the perspective of orthodontists. *BMC Oral Health*, *24*(1), 779. DOI: 10.1186/s12903-024-04558-2 PMID: 38992712

Dettori, M., & Castiglia, P. (2022). COVID-19 and Digital Health: Evolution, Perspectives and Opportunities. *International Journal of Environmental Research and Public Health, 19*(14), 8519. DOI: 10.3390/ijerph19148519 PMID: 35886366

Drossos, D., Coursaris, C., & Kagiouli, E. (2024). Social media marketing content strategy: A comprehensive framework and empirically supported guidelines for brand posts on Facebook pages. *Journal of Consumer Behaviour, 23*(3), 1175–1192. DOI: 10.1002/cb.2269

Freire, Y., Sánchez, M. G., Suárez, A., Joves, G., Nowak, M., & Díaz-Flores García, V. (2023). Influence of the use of social media on patients changing dental practice: A web-based questionnaire study. *BMC Oral Health, 23*(1), 365. DOI: 10.1186/s12903-023-03078-9 PMID: 37277765

Furman, E., Diamant, A., & Kristal, M. (2021). Customer acquisition and retention: A fluid approach for staffing. *Production and Operations Management, 30*(11), 4236–4257. DOI: 10.1111/poms.13520

Gibbons, J. B., Hermosilla, M., & Trujillo, A. (2025). On the motivation for pharmaceutical manufacturer coupons: Brand loyalty or customer acquisition? *Health Services Research, 60*(2), e14379. DOI: 10.1111/1475-6773.14379 PMID: 39219365

Hollebeek, L. D., & Macky, K. (2019). Digital content marketing's role in fostering consumer engagement, trust, and value: Framework, fundamental propositions, and implications. *Journal of Interactive Marketing, 45*(1), 27–41. DOI: 10.1016/j.intmar.2018.07.003

Hur, W. M., Chung, J., & Park, H. (2025). Beyond Hallyu celebrity appeal: Understanding celebrity attractiveness and content creativity as strategic marketing resources in Taiwan. *Asia Pacific Business Review*, •••, 1–26. DOI: 10.1080/13602381.2025.2512815

Kamyabi, M., Özgit, H., & Ahmed, J. N. (2025). Sustaining digital marketing strategies to enhance customer engagement and brand promotion: Position as a moderator. *Sustainability (Basel), 17*(7), 3270. DOI: 10.3390/su17073270

Kaur, A., & Bala, R. (2024). Role of Big Data in Customer Acquisition and Retention. In Malik, R., Sharma, A., & Chaudhary, P. (Eds.), *Augmenting Customer Retention Through Big Data Analytics* (pp. 263–276). Apple Academic Press., DOI: 10.1201/9781003538486-16

King, G. J., Chao, X., & Duenyas, I. (2016). Dynamic customer acquisition and retention management. *Production and Operations Management, 25*(8), 1332–1343. DOI: 10.1111/poms.12559

Lam, L., Ng, F., Fung, C., Poon, W., & Smith, G. D. (2026). Digital Health and Technology Adoption. In: Fong, B.Y.F. (Eds.), *The Handbook of Public Health in the Asia-Pacific* (pp. 1–13), *Handbooks in Asian Studies*, Springer. DOI: 10.1007/978-981-97-1788-0_6-1

Lhoest-Snoeck, S., van Nierop, E., & Verhoef, P. C. (2014). For new customers only: A study on the effect of acquisition campaigns on a service company's existing customers' CLV. *Journal of Interactive Marketing*, *28*(3), 210–224. DOI: 10.1016/j.intmar.2014.02.004

Liu, Y., Liu, X., Wang, M., & Wen, D. (2021). How to catch customers' attention? A study on the effectiveness of brand social media strategies in digital customer engagement. *Frontiers in Psychology*, *12*, 800766. DOI: 10.3389/fpsyg.2021.800766 PMID: 34975700

López García, J. J., Lizcano, D., Ramos, C. M., & Matos, N. (2019). Digital marketing actions that achieve a better attraction and loyalty of users: An analytical study. *Future Internet*, *11*(6), 130. DOI: 10.3390/fi11060130

Lou, C., & Yuan, S. (2019). Influencer marketing: How message value and credibility affect consumer trust of branded content on social media. *Journal of Interactive Advertising*, *19*(1), 58–73. DOI: 10.1080/15252019.2018.1533501

Luo, C., Hasan, N. A. M., Zamri bin Ahmad, A. M., & Lei, G. (2025). Influence of short video content on consumers purchase intentions on social media platforms with trust as a mediator. *Scientific Reports*, *15*(1), 16605. DOI: 10.1038/s41598-025-94994-z PMID: 40360752

Madsen, J. Ø., Guldbæk, R. S., Hæsum, L. K. E., & Thorup, C. B. (2025). Health care professionals´ knowledge of and ability to identify citizens' digital health literacy from a shared perspective of education, practice, policy and politics. *Health and Technology*, *15*(4), 769–776. DOI: 10.1007/s12553-025-00994-4

Malik, R., Sharma, A., & Chaudhary, P. (Eds.). (2024). *Augmenting Customer Retention Through Big Data Analytics* (1st ed.). Apple Academic Press., DOI: 10.1201/9781003538486

Martínez Asanza, D. (Ed.). (2025). *Transforming Dental Health in Rural Communities: Digital Dentistry*. IGI Global., DOI: 10.4018/979-8-3693-7165-7

Martínez Asanza, D., Rojas Herrera, I. A., Mouloudj, K., Amable, O. G., & Muzzamil, M. (2024). Impact of Digital Innovations in Preventive Dentistry: A Narrative Review. In Asanza, D. (Ed.), *Leveraging Digital Technology for Preventive Dentistry* (pp. 55–84). IGI Global., DOI: 10.4018/979-8-3693-3872-8.ch003

Meira, T. M., Prestes, J., Gasparello, G. G., Antelo, O. M., Pithon, M. M., & Tanaka, O. M. (2021). The effects of images posted to social media by orthodontists on public perception of professional credibility and willingness to become a client. *Progress in Orthodontics*, *22*(1), 7. DOI: 10.1186/s40510-021-00353-9 PMID: 33682012

Min, S., Zhang, X., Kim, N., & Srivastava, R. K. (2016). Customer Acquisition and Retention Spending: An Analytical Model and Empirical Investigation in Wireless Telecommunications Markets. *JMR, Journal of Marketing Research*, *53*(5), 728–744. DOI: 10.1509/jmr.14.0170

Mouloudj, K., Alameri, S. A. S., Evans, M. A., Almado, A. A. G., Mahmoud, B. I., & Asanza, D. M. (2026). Social marketing for health equity: Promoting preventive health behavior among women in rural communities. *International Journal of Environmental Research and Public Health*, *23*(5), 584. DOI: 10.3390/ijerph23050584 PMID: 42196677

Mouloudj, K., Bouarar, A. C., Martínez Asanza, D., Saadaoui, L., Mouloudj, S., Njoku, A. U., Evans, M. A., & Bouarar, A. (2023). Factors Influencing the Adoption of Digital Health Apps: An Extended Technology Acceptance Model (TAM). In Bouarar, A., Mouloudj, K., & Martínez Asanza, D. (Eds.), *Integrating Digital Health Strategies for Effective Administration* (pp. 116–132). IGI Global., DOI: 10.4018/978-1-6684-8337-4.ch007

Mouloudj, K., Bouarar, A. C., Martínez Asanza, D. A., & Dimitrova, M. (2025). Understanding Customers' Intentions to Use Digital Dental Health Services: An Expanded Technology Acceptance Model. In Martínez Asanza, D. (Ed.), *Transforming Dental Health in Rural Communities: Digital Dentistry* (pp. 189–210). IGI Global., DOI: 10.4018/979-8-3693-7165-7.ch007

Nuseir, M. T., El Refae, G. A., Aljumah, A., Alshurideh, M., Urabi, S., & Kurdi, B. A. (2023). Digital Marketing Strategies and the Impact on Customer Experience: A Systematic Review. In Alshurideh, M., Al Kurdi, B. H., Masa'deh, R., Alzoubi, H. M., & Salloum, S. (Eds.), *The Effect of Information Technology on Business and Marketing Intelligence Systems* (pp. 21–44). Springer., DOI: 10.1007/978-3-031-12382-5_2

Odoom, R., & Agyeman, D. O. (2019). Technology and Social Media in Healthcare Delivery. In Hinson, R., Osei-Frimpong, K., Adeola, O., & Aziato, L. (Eds.), *Health Service Marketing Management in Africa* (pp. 267–279). Productivity Press., DOI: 10.4324/9780429400858-21

Pasaribu, S. B., Novitasari, D., Goestjahjanti, F. S., & Hendratono, T. (2022). The impact and challenges of digital marketing in the health care industry during the digital era and the COVID-19 pandemic. *Frontiers in Public Health, 10*, 969523. DOI: 10.3389/fpubh.2022.969523 PMID: 35968423

Perez Guzman, S., & Ajami, D. S. (2026). Evolution of Digital Technologies in Healthcare. In Scholz, S., Wüchner-Fuchs, M., & Höller, K. (Eds.), *Advancements in Digital Health and Care* (pp. 3–10). Springer., DOI: 10.1007/978-3-032-16837-5_1

Pioch, C., Henschke, C., Lantzsch, H., Busse, R., & Vogt, V. (2023). Applying a data-driven population segmentation approach in German claims data. *BMC Health Services Research, 23*(1), 591. DOI: 10.1186/s12913-023-09620-3 PMID: 37286993

Shen, X., & Wang, J. (2024). How short video marketing influences purchase intention in social commerce: The role of users' persona perception, shared values, and individual-level factors. *Humanities & Social Sciences Communications, 11*(1), 290. DOI: 10.1057/s41599-024-02808-w

Tsai, I. C., Wei, H. C., & Chen, P. T. (2024). User Preferences for Medical Digital Transformation: A Case Study of Orthodontic Services. *Human Behavior and Emerging Technologies, 2024*(1), 7476097. DOI: 10.1155/2024/7476097

Zeng, H., Yao, G., & Ma, X. (2025). The impact of short videos on young people's willingness to engage in martial arts: Establishing and testing a conditional process model. *Humanities & Social Sciences Communications, 12*(1), 624. DOI: 10.1057/s41599-025-04963-0

Zheng, C. (2023). Research on the flow experience and social influences of users of short online videos. A case study of DouYin. *Scientific Reports, 13*(1), 3312. DOI: 10.1038/s41598-023-30525-y PMID: 36849531

Zwack, C. C., Haghani, M., Hollings, M., Zhang, L., Gauci, S., Gallagher, R., & Redfern, J. (2023). The evolution of digital health technologies in cardiovascular disease research. *NPJ Digital Medicine, 6*(1), 1. DOI: 10.1038/s41746-022-00734-2 PMID: 36596833

KEY TERMS AND DEFINITIONS

Content Marketing: The creation and distribution of valuable, relevant, and informative digital content designed to attract and engage potential patients while supporting informed healthcare decision-making and building trust in health services.

Customer Acquisition: The process of attracting and converting potential individuals into new patients or service users through targeted marketing strategies and communication activities in health service settings.

Digital Marketing: The use of digital channels such as websites, social media, search engines, and mobile platforms to promote health services, communicate with patients, and support service visibility and engagement.

Health Services: Organized systems of medical, preventive, and supportive care delivered by healthcare providers to meet the physical and psychological needs of individuals and communities.

Patient Engagement: The degree of active involvement, interaction, and participation of patients with healthcare providers and digital platforms, influencing awareness, trust, and health-related decisions.

Social Media Marketing: The use of social networking platforms to share content, interact with users, and promote health services in order to increase visibility, engagement, and patient acquisition.

Chapter 3
AI-Powered Complaint Management Adoption and Its Influence on Patient Retention in Dental Healthcare Settings

Alaa Abdulkareem Ghaleb Almado
http://orcid.org/0009-0004-9524-3642
Department of Business Administration, College of Administration and Economics, University of Baghdad, Iraq

Sarah Ali Saeed Alameri
http://orcid.org/0000-0002-6587-6527
Department of Business Administration, College of Administration and Economics, University of Baghdad, Iraq

Eshaq Youssef Hamdan
Department of Business Administration, College of Administration and Economics, University of Samarra, Iraq

Saadiyah Owaid Awni
Technical Institute of Management, Middle Technical University, Iraq

Sarab Jawad Mohammed Al-Obaidi
http://orcid.org/0009-0005-2168-7491
Department of Industrial Management, College of Administration and Economics, University of Baghdad, Iraq

Ahmed Abbas Hammadi
http://orcid.org/0000-0003-3767-3420
College of Administration and Economics, University of Fallujah, Iraq

Arafat Naser Jasim Alyousuf
http://orcid.org/0000-0003-1153-8618
University of Basrah, Iraq

DOI: 10.4018/979-8-3373-8894-6.ch003

ABSTRACT

This study examines the influence of AI-powered complaint management adoption on patient retention in dental healthcare settings. Specifically, the study investigates the effects of perceived efficiency, complaint resolution quality, trust in AI-powered complaint management, and perceived dehumanization of service on patient retention. A quantitative approach was employed using a self-administered questionnaire distributed to customers of dental clinics. A total of 165 valid responses were analyzed. The findings reveal that perceived efficiency, complaint resolution quality, and trust positively influence patient retention, whereas perceived dehumanization of service negatively affects retention intentions. Trust emerged as the strongest predictor of patient retention. The study contributes to the emerging literature on AI adoption in healthcare complaint management by highlighting both the opportunities and challenges associated with integrating AI into dental service recovery and patient relationship management.

INTRODUCTION

The increasing integration of artificial intelligence (AI) into service industries is reshaping how organizations interact with customers, respond to problems, and maintain long-term relationships (Alameri et al., 2026; Fan et al., 2025). In healthcare, where service quality and patient experience are closely linked to organizational success, the management of patient complaints has emerged as an increasingly important issue. Complaints are not merely expressions of dissatisfaction; they provide valuable information about service shortcomings, unmet expectations, and areas requiring immediate attention. Scholars have long argued that effective complaint management can transform dissatisfied customers into loyal ones by restoring trust and improving perceptions of fairness and responsiveness (Fierro et al., 2014; Istanbulluoglu & Sakman, 2024; Kamran & Attiq, 2011). In healthcare settings, where emotions and vulnerability often accompany service encounters, the consequences of unresolved complaints may be even more significant, influencing both patient trust and continuity of care.

Healthcare organizations are increasingly recognizing patient complaints as a valuable source of feedback for quality improvement. In this context, Teymourifar (2026) points out that "complaints serve as multidimensional organizational assets that can reveal systemic weaknesses, cultural blind spots, and latent safety risks". Patient feedback can reveal inefficiencies in communication, service delivery, responsiveness, and administrative processes that might otherwise remain unnoticed by healthcare professionals (Wong et al., 2020). More importantly, complaints have been identified as an essential mechanism for improving patient-centered care, helping organizations refine both clinical and non-clinical aspects of service delivery. Yet, despite their importance, complaint handling in many healthcare settings continues to rely heavily on traditional manual procedures that are often slow, fragmented, and inconsistent (Teymourifar, 2026). Such limitations may negatively affect patient perceptions of fairness and responsiveness, ultimately weakening patient retention and loyalty.

Recent technological developments have introduced new opportunities to modernize complaint management systems through AI-powered solutions (Alyahya et al., 2026). Advances in machine learning, natural language processing, and large language models have enabled organizations to automate the classification, prioritization, and analysis of complaints with greater speed and accuracy (Anagun et al., 2022; Esperança et al., 2025; Koh et al., 2025). In healthcare contexts, AI systems have shown promising potential in categorizing patient complaints and identifying recurrent service problems more efficiently than conventional methods (Li et al., 2025; Koh et al., 2025). Similarly, AI-supported complaint systems can facilitate proactive service recovery by detecting recurring dissatisfaction patterns, accelerating response times, and enabling healthcare providers to intervene before dissatisfaction escalates into patient attrition.

The value of efficient complaint handling has already been emphasized across several service sectors. Prior studies consistently demonstrate that complaint management quality contributes positively to customer satisfaction, loyalty, and retention (Ogbeide et al., 2017; Etemad-Sajadi & Bohrer, 2019). In particular, promptness, effective resolution, and fairness in complaint handling have been associated with stronger intentions to continue relationships with service providers. Complaint resolution quality appears especially important, as customers are more likely to remain loyal when they perceive that their concerns have been handled fairly, transparently, and effectively (Choi et al., 2023). Likewise, trust plays a central role in shaping post-complaint behavior, particularly in healthcare environments where privacy, professional credibility, and emotional reassurance strongly influence patient decisions.

At the same time, the increasing use of AI in service encounters has raised concerns regarding the possible dehumanization of services (Almokdad et al., 2025; Sun et al., 2023; Xu et al., 2025). While AI can improve efficiency and consistency (Alnaemat & Saleem, 2026), healthcare remains fundamentally relational and emotionally sensitive. Customers often expect empathy, reassurance, and human understanding when expressing dissatisfaction (Chen et al., 2025; Gip et al., 2023; Liu et al., 2024), particularly in settings such as healthcare where anxiety and discomfort may already exist. Scholars have argued that excessive dependence on technology can reduce perceived warmth and interpersonal connection, potentially leading customers to feel neglected or emotionally disconnected from healthcare providers (Bambauer-Sachse & Stuhldreier, 2026; Kim & McGill, 2025). Thus, although AI-powered complaint management may improve responsiveness and service efficiency (Alyahya et al., 2026), it may simultaneously create perceptions of impersonal treatment that negatively affect patient retention.

Despite growing scholarly attention to AI applications in healthcare, research examining AI-powered complaint management remains limited. Existing studies have largely focused on technical aspects such as complaint classification accuracy, automated triaging, and semantic analysis systems (Elmessiry et al., 2017; Esperança et al., 2025). Comparatively less attention has been directed toward understanding how patients perceive the adoption of AI-powered complaint management and whether such perceptions influence their willingness to continue receiving healthcare services. This gap is particularly noticeable in dental healthcare, where complaint management plays an important role in maintaining patient relationships, trust, and treatment continuity.

Furthermore, empirical evidence from developing healthcare contexts remains scarce. In Iraq, dental healthcare providers continue to face growing patient expectations, service quality concerns, and increasing competition, yet complaint management practices are often underdeveloped and heavily dependent on manual interactions. The limited adoption of AI technologies in complaint management creates an important opportunity to investigate how patients perceive the potential implementation of such systems and whether these perceptions shape their retention intentions.

In this context, the present study aims to examine the influence of AI-powered complaint management adoption on patient retention in dental healthcare settings. Specifically, the study investigates the effects of perceived efficiency, complaint resolution quality, and trust as positive determinants of patient retention, while also examining the negative role of perceived dehumanization of service. By focusing on dental service customers in Iraq, this study contributes to the emerging literature on AI-enabled healthcare management and extends current knowledge on complaint management in underexplored healthcare environments. Accordingly, this study seeks to answer the following research questions: (1) Does perceived efficiency of AI-powered complaint management adoption influence patient retention? (2) Does complaint resolution quality affect patient retention? (3) Does trust in AI-powered complaint management shape patients' retention intentions? and (4) Does perceived dehumanization of service negatively influence patient retention? To address these questions, the study pursues four objectives: (1) to examine the influence of perceived efficiency on patient retention; (2) to assess the effect of complaint resolution quality on patient retention; (3) to investigate the role of trust in shaping patient retention; and (4) to analyze whether perceived dehumanization of service negatively affects patient retention in dental healthcare settings.

LITERATURE REVIEW AND HYPOTHESES DEVELOPMENT

Customers Retention in Dental Healthcare Settings

Customer retention in healthcare refers to customers' willingness to continue receiving services from the same service provider over time, despite the availability of alternative options (Mahmoud et al., 2018; Narteh et al., 2013). Within dental healthcare settings, patient retention is particularly important because dental treatment frequently requires repeated visits, long-term monitoring, preventive care, and sustained professional relationships. Unlike one-time service encounters, dental care often involves continuous interaction between patients and providers, making trust, satisfaction, and service experience critical determinants of retention (Mouloudj et al., 2025). Retaining existing patients is also strategically beneficial for dental clinics, as acquiring new patients are often more costly than maintaining long-term relationships with current ones. Previous studies suggest that positive healthcare experiences, perceived treatment quality, effective communication, and responsiveness to patient concerns significantly enhance patients' intentions to revisit and recommend healthcare providers (Teymourifar, 2026; Wong et al., 2020). Consequently, patient retention has become an important indicator of healthcare quality, organizational performance, and service sustainability in competitive healthcare markets.

In dental healthcare settings, complaint management represents an often-overlooked yet highly influential factor shaping patient retention. Patients who experience dissatisfaction due to appointment delays, communication problems, administrative inefficiencies, or perceived treatment issues may decide to discontinue treatment if their concerns are not appropriately addressed (Antonopoulou et al., 2024; Teymourifar, 2026). Research on service recovery demonstrates that effective complaint handling, fairness, responsiveness, and problem resolution can restore customer confidence and reduce switching intentions (Choi et al., 2023; Lal & Kashyap, 2024). More importantly, the way complaints are managed may significantly shape patients' emotional responses and long-term perceptions of care quality (Antonopoulou et al., 2024). Since dental visits can already be associated with fear, discomfort, or anxiety, empathetic and efficient responses to complaints may strengthen patients' confidence in healthcare providers. Therefore, understanding the factors that influence customer retention remains essential for dental healthcare organizations seeking to improve patient loyalty and continuity of care.

AI-powered Complaint Management

AI-powered complaint management refers to the use of artificial intelligence technologies to automate, analyze, prioritize, and improve the handling of customer or patient complaints (Alyahya et al., 2026). Teymourifar (2026) argues that "patient complaints represent a significant yet sometimes underutilized source of organisational learning in hospitals". Unlike traditional complaint management systems, which frequently depend on manual processes and human judgment, AI-powered systems employ technologies such as "machine learning" (ML), "natural language processing" (NLP), speech recognition, and "large language models" (LLMs) to process complaints more efficiently and accurately (Anagun et al., 2022; Esperança et al., 2025; Koh et al., 2025). These systems can identify complaint categories, detect emotional tone, recognize recurring service issues, and support faster response mechanisms. As organizations increasingly pursue digital transformation (Alnaemat & Saleem, 2026), AI-powered complaint management is gaining attention as an innovative approach to improving service responsiveness, complaint resolution quality, and customer experience (Alyahya et al., 2026; Esperança et al., 2025). In healthcare settings, where patient feedback is highly valuable for improving care quality, AI-powered systems may offer opportunities to transform complaint handling from a reactive process into a proactive quality improvement mechanism.

The growing importance of AI in complaint management is particularly evident in healthcare organizations facing high complaint volumes and limited administrative resources. Recent studies demonstrate that AI-based systems can effectively classify and triage customer complaints, reducing delays associated with traditional manual processing (Alyahya et al., 2026; Anagun et al., 2022). For instance, Li et al. (2025) developed an NLP-based complaint classification system that demonstrated strong predictive performance in categorizing healthcare complaints, thereby enhancing the efficiency of patient feedback management. Similarly, Koh et al. (2025) found that AI-powered large language models showed promising accuracy in classifying patient complaints and identifying key service concerns, such as waiting times, staff attitudes, and appointment-related problems. Earlier evidence by Elmessiry et al. (2017) also highlighted the effectiveness of machine learning techniques in automatically identifying complaints requiring urgent medical attention, emphasizing the scalability and responsiveness of AI-supported systems.

Despite these advantages, the adoption of AI-powered complaint management in healthcare remains relatively limited, particularly in developing contexts and specialized healthcare services such as dental care. Concerns surrounding data privacy, system reliability, ethical governance, and reduced human interaction continue to challenge adoption efforts. Importantly, healthcare complaint management differs from other service sectors because patient complaints often involve emotional vulnerability, anxiety, and expectations for empathy (Antonopoulou et al., 2024). While AI may improve efficiency, speed, and consistency in complaint handling, excessive reliance on automated systems may create perceptions of impersonal service and diminished emotional support (Bambauer-Sachse & Stuhldreier, 2026). Therefore, understanding patient perceptions of AI-powered complaint management adoption is essential, as positive evaluations may enhance patient trust and retention, whereas concerns regarding service dehumanization may discourage long-term engagement with healthcare providers.

Hypotheses Development

Perceived Efficiency of AI Complaint Management and Patient Retention

Perceived efficiency of AI complaint management refers to the extent to which patients believe AI-powered systems can handle complaints quickly, accurately, and with minimal delays. Efficiency is considered one of the primary advantages of AI-supported services because automated systems can process large volumes of information, provide immediate responses, and reduce waiting times associated with traditional manual complaint handling (Alyahya et al., 2026). In healthcare environments, delays in responding to patient concerns may negatively influence perceptions of service quality and continuity of care. Previous research consistently suggests that effective complaint handling procedures, particularly those emphasizing promptness and responsiveness, contribute positively to customer satisfaction, loyalty, and intention to return (Antonopoulou et al., 2024; Ogbeide et al., 2017; Etemad-Sajadi & Bohrer, 2019). Similarly, AI-enabled complaint systems have demonstrated strong potential in improving the efficiency of complaint classification and triaging processes in healthcare settings (Anagun et al., 2022; Li et al., 2025; Elmessiry et al., 2017). When patients perceive complaint management systems as efficient and responsive, they are more likely to develop confidence in the healthcare provider and continue using its services (Mirzoev & Kane, 2018). Therefore, we propose the following hypothesis:

H1: Perceived efficiency of AI-powered complaint management adoption positively influences patient retention in dental healthcare settings.

Complaint Resolution Quality and Patient Retention

Complaint resolution quality refers to patients' perceptions regarding the fairness, accuracy, effectiveness, and overall adequacy of solutions provided in response to their complaints. In the service settings, complaint resolution extends beyond merely responding to dissatisfaction; it involves restoring customer confidence and ensuring that concerns are addressed in a transparent and satisfactory manner (Homburg et al., 2010). Service recovery literature consistently highlights the importance of justice and quality in complaint resolution for maintaining customer satisfaction and loyalty

(Istanbulluoglu & Sakman, 2024; Lu et al., 2018). For example, studies have shown that fair treatment, appropriate corrective actions, and effective service recovery significantly improve customer trust, satisfaction, and retention intentions (Kamran & Attiq, 2011; Choi et al., 2023; Singh et al., 2016). Likewise, Lal and Kashyap (2024) found that positive complaint-handling experiences contribute directly to retention and repurchase intentions. Within AI-powered complaint systems, higher complaint resolution quality may result from improved consistency, accurate categorization, and better prioritization of complaints (Anagun et al., 2022), thereby strengthening patients' trust in healthcare providers. Therefore, when patients perceive complaint outcomes as fair and effective, they are more likely to maintain long-term relationships with healthcare providers (Antonopoulou et al., 2024; Mirzoev & Kane, 2018). Therefore, we propose the following hypothesis:

H2: Complaint resolution quality of AI-powered complaint management adoption positively influences patient retention in dental healthcare settings.

Trust in AI Complaint Management and Patient Retention

Trust in AI complaint management refers to patients' confidence in the reliability, competence, fairness, and security of AI-powered systems used to manage complaints. In the services industry, trust is particularly important because customers often disclose personal information and expect organizations to manage their concerns responsibly and ethically (Gelibolu & Mouloudj, 2025). The adoption of AI technologies in complaint management may improve consistency and responsiveness (Alyahya et al., 2026); however, patients must first trust that these systems can accurately understand and appropriately resolve their concerns. Existing literature demonstrates that trust significantly shapes post-complaint behavioral responses and long-term customer relationships (Istanbulluoglu & Sakman, 2024). Effective complaint handling processes that are perceived as fair and responsive often strengthen confidence and loyalty toward service providers (Choi et al., 2023; Fierro et al., 2014; Singh et al., 2016). Moreover, recent AI studies suggest that automated complaint systems can support proactive problem identification and improve service responsiveness, potentially increasing patient confidence in healthcare delivery (Koh et al., 2025; Esperança et al., 2025). In dental healthcare settings, greater trust in AI-powered complaint management may encourage patients to continue receiving treatment from the same provider. Therefore, we propose the following hypothesis:

H3: Trust in AI-powered complaint management adoption positively influences patient retention in dental healthcare settings.

Dehumanization of Service and Patient Retention

Perceived dehumanization of service refers to customers' perceptions that service interactions become impersonal, emotionally distant, and lacking in empathy due to excessive reliance on technology (Almokdad et al., 2025). Although AI-powered complaint management may improve efficiency and consistency, healthcare services remain highly relational and emotionally sensitive. Customers often expect empathy, reassurance, and individualized attention when raising complaints, particularly in services sector where anxiety and emotional discomfort are common (Golossenko et al., 2023; Fan et al., 2025). Prior studies suggest that reduced interpersonal interaction and excessive technological mediation may increase feelings of service dehumanization, ultimately weakening emotional connections with service providers (Almokdad et al., 2025; Chen et al., 2025; Kim & McGill, 2025). Similarly, research indicates that diminished human contact can negatively affect psychological well-being, service recovery experiences, and perceptions of care quality (Gip et al., 2023; Liu et al., 2024; Xu et al., 2025). While some service situations may encourage mechanistic interactions (Sun et al., 2023), healthcare complaints frequently require emotional understanding and compassionate communication. Consequently, when patients perceive AI-powered complaint systems as replacing meaningful human interaction, they may become less willing to continue relationships with dental providers. Therefore, we propose the following hypothesis:

H4: Perceived dehumanization of service resulting from AI-powered complaint management adoption negatively influences patient retention in dental healthcare settings.

METHOD

Sampling and Procedures

The target population of this study consisted of customers of dental clinics in Iraq. Given the exploratory nature of the study and the limited adoption of AI-powered complaint management systems in Iraqi dental healthcare settings, a non-probability convenience sampling approach was employed to recruit respondents. Data were collected from customers visiting dental clinics in three major Iraqi cities, Baghdad, Mosul, and Basra, which were selected due to their large populations, concentration of healthcare facilities, and diversity of dental service providers. Both public and private dental clinics were included to ensure broader representation of customers with different service experiences and healthcare preferences. A total of 220 questionnaires were distributed to customers who had prior experience receiving dental care services and were willing to participate in the study.

A self-administered paper-based questionnaire was used as the primary data collection instrument. The data collection process took place between December 2025 and the end of January 2026. To facilitate access to respondents, questionnaires were distributed in waiting areas of participating dental clinics with the assistance of reception staff, which helped identify eligible participants and briefly explain the purpose of the study. Participants completed the questionnaire voluntarily while waiting for appointments or after receiving treatment. Prior to participation, respondents were informed about the objectives of the study, the academic purpose of the research, and the voluntary nature of participation. They were also assured that all responses would remain confidential and anonymous, that participation involved no risks, and that they could withdraw from the study at any stage without consequences. Verbal informed consent was obtained from all participants before questionnaire administration. Of the 220 questionnaires distributed, 172 were returned, yielding a response rate of approximately 78.2%. Following a screening process, seven questionnaires were excluded due to incomplete responses and substantial missing data. Consequently, 165 valid questionnaires were retained for statistical analysis. The final sample size was considered adequate for examining the proposed relationships between AI-powered complaint management adoption variables and patient retention in dental healthcare settings, particularly given the exploratory nature of the study.

Measurement Tool Development

The questionnaire used in this study consisted of two sections. The first section collected respondents' demographic information, including gender, age group, educational level, and frequency of dental visits during the past year. The second section focused on measuring the study constructs. All measurement items were adapted from previous studies and modified to suit the context of AI-powered complaint management adoption in dental healthcare settings. More specifically, the measurement items for perceived efficiency of AI-powered complaint management were developed by the authors to reflect the emerging nature of AI-supported complaint systems in dental healthcare. The items for complaint resolution quality were adapted from the works of Homburg et al. (2010) and Lu et al. (2018). Trust in AI-powered complaint management was measured using adapted items derived from Gelibolu and Mouloudj (2025), Mahmoud et al. (2018), and Mouloudj et al. (2023). The items for perceived dehumanization of service were adapted from

Almokdad et al. (2025) and Golossenko et al. (2023), while patient retention was measured using items adapted from Mahmoud et al. (2018) and Narteh et al. (2013).

The questionnaire was initially developed in English and subsequently translated into Arabic using the back-translation technique to ensure linguistic accuracy and conceptual equivalence between the two versions. A language specialist fluent in both English and Arabic conducted the translation process to minimize interpretation inconsistencies and preserve the meaning of the original measurement items. After the questionnaire was developed, two experts in complaint management within the healthcare sector were invited to evaluate the content validity, clarity, relevance, and contextual appropriateness of the measurement items. Their feedback contributed to refining wording, improving clarity, and ensuring alignment with the dental healthcare context.

All items were measured using a five-point Likert scale, ranging from 1 = "strongly disagree" to 5 = "strongly agree". Prior to the main data collection process, a pilot study involving 20 respondents was conducted to assess the clarity, readability, and overall comprehensibility of the questionnaire. Minor wording adjustments were made based on participant feedback to improve item clarity and ensure respondents could easily understand the questions before administering the final survey instrument. Table 1 presents the measurement items used in this study.

Table 1. Measurement items

Constructs and Items
Perceived Efficiency of AI-Powered Complaint Management (EFF)
EFF1: AI-powered complaint management would help dental clinics handle complaints more quickly.
EFF2: AI-powered complaint management would reduce delays in responding to patient complaints.
EFF3: AI-powered complaint management would make complaint handling more efficient in dental clinics.
Complaint Resolution Quality (CRQ)
CRQ1: AI-powered complaint management would improve the quality of complaint resolution in dental clinics.
CRQ2: AI-powered complaint management would help provide fair solutions to patient complaints.
CRQ3: AI-powered complaint management would improve the accuracy of handling patient complaints.
Trust in AI-Powered Complaint Management (TRU)
TRU1: I would trust an AI-powered system to manage complaints in dental clinics.
TRU2: I believe AI-powered complaint management would handle patient complaints reliably.
TRU3: I would feel confident using a dental clinic that adopts AI-powered complaint management.
Perceived Dehumanization of Service (DEH)

continued on following page

Table 1. Continued

Constructs and Items
DEH1: AI-powered complaint management may reduce personal interaction between patients and clinic staff.
DEH2: Using AI to manage complaints may make dental services feel less personal.
DEH3: AI-powered complaint management may reduce empathy when handling patient complaints.
Patient Retention (RET)
RET1: I would continue visiting a dental clinic that adopts AI-powered complaint management.
RET2: I would prefer to return to a dental clinic that uses AI-powered complaint management if it improves service quality.
RET3: I would remain loyal to a dental clinic that effectively adopts AI-powered complaint management.

RESULTS

Table 2 shows that female respondents represented the majority of the sample (56.97%), while male respondents accounted for 43.03%. Regarding age distribution, participants aged 35–44 years constituted the largest group (28.49%), followed by those aged 45–54 years (25.81%) and 25–34 years (24.73%), whereas respondents aged 55 years and above represented the smallest proportion (9.68%). In terms of educational level, most respondents held a bachelor's degree (36.36%), followed by diploma holders (27.27%), high school education or below (23.03%), and postgraduate degree holders (13.34%). Concerning the frequency of dental visits during the past year, the majority of respondents reported visiting dental clinics two to three times (44.85%), followed by one visit (23.64%), four to five visits (21.21%), and more than five visits (10.30%).

Table 2. Sample characteristics (N = 165)

Demographic profile	Characteristics	Frequency	Percent (%)
Gender	Male	71	43.03
	Female	94	56.97
Age Group	Less than 25 years	22	11.79
	25–34 years	46	24.73
	35–44 years	53	28.49
	45–54 years	48	25.81
	55 years and above	18	09.68

continued on following page

Table 2. Continued

Demographic profile	Characteristics	Frequency	Percent (%)
Educational Level	High school or below	38	23.03
	Diploma	45	27.27
	Bachelor's degree	60	36.36
	Postgraduate degree	22	13.34
Frequency of Dental Visits in the Past Year	Once	39	23.64
	2-3 times	74	44.85
	4-5 times	35	21.21
	More than 5 times	17	10.30

Table 3 presents the descriptive statistics, reliability, and normality assessment of the study constructs. Trust in AI-powered complaint management recorded the highest mean score (M = 3.96), followed by complaint resolution quality (M = 3.84), patient retention (M = 3.72), and perceived efficiency (M = 3.52), whereas perceived dehumanization of service showed the lowest mean score (M = 2.94). The Cronbach's alpha values ranged from 0.851 to 0.946, indicating satisfactory to excellent internal consistency reliability for all constructs, as all values exceeded the recommended threshold of 0.70 (Alyousuf et al., 2026). Regarding normality, skewness values ranged from −1.316 to 0.424, while kurtosis values ranged from −0.314 to 2.502. Since all skewness and kurtosis values fell within acceptable ranges (Alameri et al., 2026), the data were considered normally distributed and suitable for statistical analyses.

Table 3. Descriptive statistics and reliability

Constructs	Mean	Cronbach's α	Skewness	Kurtosis
Perceived Efficiency	3.52	0.946	-0.926	1.373
Complaint Resolution Quality	3.84	0.882	-1.303	1.886
Trust in AI-Powered Complaint Management	3.96	0.851	-1.316	2.502
Perceived Dehumanization of Service	2.94	0.907	0.424	-0.314
Patient Retention	3.72	0.890	-0.935	1.044

Table 4 presents the hypothesis testing results and multicollinearity diagnostics. The findings indicate that perceived efficiency had a positive and statistically significant influence on patient retention (β = 0.180, t = 2.933, p = 0.004), thereby supporting H1. Similarly, complaint resolution quality demonstrated a positive and significant effect on patient retention (β = 0.197, t = 2.669, p = 0.008), providing support for H2. Trust in AI-powered complaint management showed the strongest positive influence on patient retention (β = 0.516, t = 5.898, p = 0.000), confirming H3. In contrast, perceived dehumanization of service exerted a negative and statistically significant effect on patient retention (β = −0.207, t = −2.496, p = 0.014), thus supporting H4. Regarding multicollinearity, the "variance inflation factor" (VIF) values ranged from 1.560 to 3.013, indicating no multicollinearity concerns, as all values remained below the recommended threshold of 5.0 (Alyousuf et al., 2026; Mouloudj et al., 2023).

Table 4. Hypothesis testing results and VIF diagnostics

Hypothesis	Path	β	t	Sig.	VIF
H1	Perceived Efficiency → Patient Retention	0.180	2.933	0.004	1.704
H2	Resolution Quality → Patient Retention	0.197	2.669	0.008	2.507
H3	Trust → Patient Retention	0.516	5.898	0.000	3.013
H4	Dehumanization → Patient Retention	-0.207	-2.496	0.014	1.560

DISCUSSION

The primary objective of this study was to examine the influence of AI-powered complaint management adoption on patient retention in dental healthcare settings. Specifically, the study investigated how perceived efficiency, complaint resolution quality, and trust in AI-powered complaint management positively influence patient retention, while also examining the negative effect of perceived dehumanization of service. Conducted within the context of Iraqi dental healthcare, the study contributes to the emerging literature on AI-enabled service management by exploring patients' perceptions toward adopting AI-powered complaint handling systems in a setting where such technologies remain relatively limited. The findings provide important insights into the opportunities and challenges associated with integrating AI into patient complaint management and its implications for sustaining long-term patient relationships.

The findings support H1, confirming that perceived efficiency positively influences patient retention in dental healthcare settings. This result suggests that patients are more likely to continue visiting dental clinics when they perceive AI-powered complaint systems as capable of responding quickly, reducing waiting time, and improving the efficiency of complaint handling. In healthcare environments, delays in resolving concerns may intensify dissatisfaction and weaken trust in providers, particularly in dental services where anxiety and repeated visits are common. Thus, efficient complaint management can reassure patients that their concerns will be addressed in a timely and organized manner (Antonopoulou et al., 2024). This finding aligns with previous studies emphasizing the importance of responsiveness and promptness in complaint management and service recovery (Alyahya et al., 2026). For example, Ogbeide et al. (2017) found that prompt complaint handling significantly contributes to customer loyalty and intention to return in service settings. Similarly, Etemad-Sajadi and Bohrer (2019) reported that efficient service recovery processes positively influence customer satisfaction and loyalty. The present study extends this understanding to AI adoption in dental healthcare, suggesting that efficiency-related benefits may encourage patients to maintain relationships with healthcare providers.

The results also support H2, indicating that complaint resolution quality positively influences patient retention. This finding demonstrates that patients value not only the speed of complaint handling but also the fairness, accuracy, and effectiveness of solutions offered in response to service problems (Antonopoulou et al., 2024; Homburg et al., 2010). In dental healthcare settings, where trust and perceived care quality strongly influence patient decisions, effective complaint resolution may restore confidence following negative experiences and reduce switching intentions (Mouloudj et al., 2025). Customers who believe that complaints are resolved fairly and professionally may become more willing to continue treatment and maintain long-term engagement with service providers (Istanbulluoglu & Sakman, 2024; Lu et al., 2018; Singh et al., 2016). This finding is consistent with earlier research emphasizing the importance of justice and quality in complaint management (Mirzoev & Kane, 2018). Kamran and Attiq (2011) found that distributive, procedural, and interactional justice significantly improve customer satisfaction following service failures. Likewise, Choi et al. (2023) reported that perceived service recovery justice enhances customer loyalty through satisfaction mechanisms. Lal and Kashyap (2024) further confirmed that positive complaint experiences improve customer retention intentions. Therefore, AI-powered complaint management systems capable of providing consistent and high-quality resolutions may play a valuable role in strengthening customer loyalty (Alyahya et al., 2026).

Regarding H3, the findings reveal that trust in AI-powered complaint management exerts the strongest positive influence on patient retention, highlighting trust as a critical determinant of patient willingness to remain with dental providers. This result indicates that patients are more inclined to continue receiving services from clinics when they trust AI systems to handle complaints reliably, fairly, and securely. In the services sector, trust remains especially important because customers often share personal information and expect ethical handling of sensitive concerns (Gelibolu & Mouloudj, 2025; Istanbulluoglu & Sakman, 2024; Singh et al., 2016). Since AI-powered complaint systems remain relatively unfamiliar in dental settings, trust may reduce uncertainty surrounding technology adoption and increase patient confidence in service quality. This finding is consistent with prior literature emphasizing the importance of trust in post-complaint behavioral responses and customer relationships (e.g., Alyahya et al., 2026). Fierro et al. (2014) demonstrated that effective service recovery strengthens customer commitment and loyalty when organizations are perceived as making fair efforts to resolve dissatisfaction. Additionally, Koh et al. (2025) and Li et al. (2025) highlighted the capability of AI systems to improve complaint management efficiency and responsiveness, potentially enhancing patient confidence in healthcare services. The strong effect observed in this study suggests that trust may be the most influential factor shaping patients' acceptance of AI-supported complaint management.

Finally, the findings confirm H4, demonstrating that perceived dehumanization of service negatively influences patient retention. This result suggests that although AI-powered complaint systems may improve efficiency and consistency, excessive reliance on technology may create perceptions of impersonal service, emotional distance, and reduced empathy. In dental healthcare contexts, patients frequently expect reassurance, understanding, and personalized interaction when communicating dissatisfaction, particularly given the emotional sensitivity often associated with dental treatment. Consequently, patients who perceive complaint management as overly mechanistic may become less willing to maintain long-term relationships with healthcare providers. This finding aligns with emerging research on service dehumanization in technology-mediated environments (Chen et al., 2025). Almokdad et al. (2025) found that reduced human interaction and empathy in self-service technologies increase perceptions of service dehumanization and diminish emotional value. Similarly, Gip et al. (2023) reported that dehumanization negatively affects service recovery outcomes by weakening psychological well-being and performance quality. Although Sun et al. (2023) suggested that mechanistic interactions may sometimes be preferred in sensitive situations, the present findings indicate that complaint management in dental healthcare still requires an element of human empathy to sustain patient retention.

Practical Suggestions

The findings of this study provide several practical implications for dental healthcare providers seeking to improve patient retention through the adoption of AI-powered complaint management systems. First, dental clinics should prioritize the implementation of AI technologies that enhance efficiency in complaint handling without creating unnecessary complexity for patients. Since perceived efficiency positively influenced patient retention, clinics should adopt user-friendly systems capable of providing rapid responses, automated complaint tracking, appointment-related updates, and timely follow-up notifications. AI-powered chatbots or complaint portals may help reduce waiting times and improve responsiveness, particularly in busy healthcare environments where administrative delays can negatively affect patient satisfaction.

Second, clinics should focus on improving the quality of complaint resolution, rather than merely increasing response speed. AI systems should be designed to support fair, transparent, and accurate complaint handling by categorizing complaints appropriately and ensuring that unresolved or high-priority cases are escalated to experienced human staff. Standardized complaint procedures supported by AI may also help reduce inconsistencies in decision-making and strengthen patients' confidence in service fairness. Since complaint resolution quality significantly influences patient retention, clinics should regularly assess patient feedback to refine complaint management practices and improve service recovery outcomes.

Third, healthcare managers should actively build trust in AI-powered complaint systems. Patients may initially hesitate to rely on AI due to concerns regarding privacy, accuracy, and the ethical handling of sensitive information. To address these concerns, dental clinics should clearly communicate how patient data are protected, explain the role of AI in supporting, not replacing, staff, and ensure transparency regarding complaint-handling processes. Staff training is also essential so employees can confidently assist patients in using AI-supported systems.

Finally, clinics should avoid excessive automation that may contribute to the dehumanization of service. Rather than fully replacing human interaction, AI-powered complaint systems should complement human support through hybrid models that preserve empathy and personalized communication. Allowing patients the option to speak directly with staff during sensitive complaint situations may reduce emotional distance and strengthen long-term patient relationships.

FUTURE RESEARCH DIRECTIONS

This study offers several opportunities for future research on AI-powered complaint management and patient retention in healthcare settings. First, future studies may expand the proposed framework by incorporating additional explanatory variables that may influence customers' evaluations of AI-powered complaint management. Factors such as perceived usefulness, perceived ease of use, perceived responsiveness, service recovery satisfaction, perceived empathy, privacy concerns, technology anxiety, and perceived fairness (justice) may provide a deeper understanding of customer reactions to AI-supported complaint systems. Likewise, healthcare-specific variables such as perceived care quality, patient satisfaction, and perceived service transparency could further enrich the explanatory power of future models.

Second, future researchers may benefit from adopting alternative theoretical perspectives to explain customer responses toward AI-powered complaint management. While the present study primarily focused on direct relationships, future work may integrate theories such as the "Technology Acceptance Model", "Unified Theory of Acceptance and Use of Technology", Justice Theory, or the "Stimulus-Organism-Response Model" to better explain the psychological and behavioral mechanisms underlying AI adoption in complaint handling. Future studies may also examine mediating factors, such as customer satisfaction, emotional reassurance, service recovery perceptions, or trust, to explain how AI-powered complaint management influences customers retention. Additionally, moderating variables such as age, educational level, prior experience with digital healthcare services, or frequency of dental visits may help clarify differences in customer perceptions across demographic groups.

Future research should also broaden the scope of participants and research settings. Instead of focusing exclusively on dental clinic customers, researchers may include complaint management staff, reception employees, healthcare administrators, and dentists to gain a more comprehensive understanding of the operational and organizational dimensions of AI-powered complaint management. Comparative studies involving both customers and healthcare employees may provide valuable insights into differences between service expectations and implementation realities. Furthermore, future research may extend beyond dental healthcare to examine AI-powered complaint management in other service sectors, including hospitality, tourism, hotels, restaurants, and retail, where complaint handling and customer retention are equally important. Cross-sector comparisons may help identify context-specific factors and improve the generalizability of findings regarding AI-supported complaint management systems.

CONCLUSION

This study examined the influence of AI-powered complaint management adoption on patient retention in dental healthcare settings, with a particular focus on customers of dental clinics in Iraq. Specifically, the study investigated the effects of perceived efficiency, complaint resolution quality, trust in AI-powered complaint management, and perceived dehumanization of service on patient retention. The findings revealed that perceived efficiency, complaint resolution quality, and trust positively influence patient retention, whereas perceived dehumanization of service negatively affects patients' intentions to continue receiving care from the same dental provider. Among the examined factors, trust emerged as the strongest predictor of patient retention, highlighting the importance of confidence in AI-supported complaint systems within healthcare contexts. The study contributes to the growing literature on AI adoption in healthcare service management by extending complaint management research into the underexplored context of dental healthcare. The findings suggest that while AI-powered complaint systems may improve responsiveness and service quality, maintaining a balance between technological efficiency and human empathy remains essential. Ultimately, successful adoption of AI-supported complaint management may help dental clinics strengthen patient relationships and improve long-term retention outcomes.

REFERENCES

Alameri, S. A., Mahmoud, B. I., Almado, A. A., Jasim, Z. A., Jahlool, I. H., & Alyousuf, A. N. (2026). Consumer Acceptance of AI-Supported Circular Fashion Services: A Technology Acceptance Perspective. In Mouloudj, K., & Arantes, L. (Eds.), *Ethical Consumption and Responsible Innovation in Fashion through AI* (pp. 35–58). IGI Global., DOI: 10.4018/979-8-3373-7200-6.ch002

Almokdad, E., Mouloudj, K., & Lee, C. H. (2025). Rehumanizing AI-Driven Service: How Employee Presence Shapes Consumer Perceptions in Digital Hospitality Settings. *Journal of Theoretical and Applied Electronic Commerce Research*, *20*(3), 209. DOI: 10.3390/jtaer20030209

Alnaemat, N. D., & Saleem, S. A. (2026). Integrating Digital Technologies Into Fashion Management: Opportunities and Challenges. In Mouloudj, K., & Arantes, L. (Eds.), *Ethical Consumption and Responsible Innovation in Fashion through AI* (pp. 145–168). IGI Global., DOI: 10.4018/979-8-3373-7200-6.ch006

Alyahya, M., Agag, G., & Abdelwahab, M. (2026). AI-enabled complaint handling and customer recommendation: A quasi-experimental difference-in-differences (DiD) perspective. *Journal of Retailing and Consumer Services*, *92*, 104803. DOI: 10.1016/j.jretconser.2026.104803

Alyousuf, A. N., Sabeeh, A. O., Alnaemat, N. D., Mouloudj, K., & Hussein, S. A. (2026). Understanding Gen Z's Adoption of AI Technologies in Green Product Purchases: An Extension of the Technology Acceptance Model. In Mouloudj, K., & Bouarar, A. (Eds.), *Insights on Consumer Psychology in the Digital Landscape* (pp. 369–392). IGI Global., DOI: 10.4018/979-8-3373-2424-1.ch013

Anagun, Y., Bolel, N. S., Isik, S., & Ozkan, S. E. (2022). Deep Learning-based customer complaint management. *Journal of Organizational Computing and Electronic Commerce*, *32*(3–4), 217–231. DOI: 10.1080/10919392.2023.2210049

Antonopoulou, V., Meyer, C., Chadwick, P., Gibson, B., Sniehotta, F. F., Vlaev, I., Vassova, A., Goffe, L., Lorencatto, F., McKinlay, A., & Chater, A. M. (2024). Understanding healthcare professionals' responses to patient complaints in secondary and tertiary care in the UK: A systematic review and behavioural analysis using the Theoretical Domains Framework. *Health Research Policy and Systems*, *22*(1), 137. DOI: 10.1186/s12961-024-01209-4 PMID: 39354470

Bambauer-Sachse, S., & Stuhldreier, S. M. (2026). Effective complaint management on social networks: The impact of response strategy, type and account on consumer reactions. *Journal of Services Marketing*, *40*(10), 1–21. DOI: 10.1108/JSM-03-2025-0215

Chen, Q., Gong, Y., Lu, Y., & Luo, X. (2025). The golden zone of AI's emotional expression in frontline chatbot service failures. *Internet Research*, *35*(3), 1065–1103. DOI: 10.1108/INTR-07-2023-0551

Choi, H.-K., Kim, S.-S., & Kim, B.-S. (2023). Perceived justice and customer loyalty in the situation of beauty service failure. *SAGE Open*, *13*(4), 1–14. DOI: 10.1177/21582440231217729

Elmessiry, A., Cooper, W. O., Catron, T. F., Karrass, J., Zhang, Z., & Singh, M. P. (2017). Triaging patient complaints: Monte Carlo cross-validation of six machine learning classifiers. *JMIR Medical Informatics*, *5*(3), e19. DOI: 10.2196/medinform.7140 PMID: 28760726

Esperança, M., Freitas, D., Paixão, P. V., Marcos, T. A., Martins, R. A., & Ferreira, J. C. (2025). Proactive complaint management in public sector informatics using AI: A semantic pattern recognition framework. *Applied Sciences (Basel, Switzerland)*, *15*(12), 6673. DOI: 10.3390/app15126673

Etemad-Sajadi, R., & Bohrer, L. (2019). The impact of service recovery output/process on customer satisfaction and loyalty: The case of the airline industry. *Tourism and Hospitality Research*, *19*(2), 259–266. DOI: 10.1177/1467358417743080

Fan, Y., Wu, L. Z., Lyu, Y., & Kwan, H. K. (2025). Don't expect robots to be creative: Why and when organizational dehumanization is a creativity killer. *International Journal of Hospitality Management*, *130*, 104229. DOI: 10.1016/j.ijhm.2025.104229

Fierro, J. C., Polo, I. M., & Oliván, F. J. S. (2014). From Dissatisfied Customers to Evangelists of the Firm: A Study of the Spanish Mobile Service Sector. *Business Research Quarterly*, *17*(3), 191–204. DOI: 10.1016/j.cede.2013.10.001

Gelibolu, M., & Mouloudj, K. (2025). Motivators and demotivators of consumers' smart voice assistant usage for online shopping. *Journal of Theoretical and Applied Electronic Commerce Research*, *20*(3), 152. DOI: 10.3390/jtaer20030152

Gip, H., Guchait, P., Paşamehmetoğlu, A., & Khoa, D. T. (2023). How organizational dehumanization impacts hospitality employees service recovery performance and sabotage behaviors: The role of psychological well-being and tenure. *International Journal of Contemporary Hospitality Management*, *35*(1), 64–91. DOI: 10.1108/IJCHM-02-2022-0155

Golossenko, A., Palumbo, H., Mathai, M., & Tran, H. A. (2023). Am I being dehumanized? Development and validation of the experience of dehumanization measurement. *The British Journal of Social Psychology*, *62*(3), 1285–1329. DOI: 10.1111/bjso.12633 PMID: 36861855

Homburg, C., Fürst, A., & Koschate, N. (2010). On the importance of complaint handling design: A multi-level analysis of the impact in specific complaint situations. *Journal of the Academy of Marketing Science*, *38*(3), 265–287. DOI: 10.1007/s11747-009-0172-y

Istanbulluoglu, D., & Sakman, E. (2024). Successful complaint handling on social media predicts increased repurchase intention: The roles of trust in company and propensity to trust. *European Management Journal*, *42*(1), 11–22. DOI: 10.1016/j.emj.2022.06.004

Kamran, S., & Attiq, M. (2011). Value recovery with customer dissatisfaction: A study of restaurant services in Pakistan. *Tourism and Hospitality Research*, *11*(3), 169–180. DOI: 10.1177/1467358411415088

Kim, H. Y., & McGill, A. L. (2025). AI-induced dehumanization. *Journal of Consumer Psychology*, *35*(3), 363–381. DOI: 10.1002/jcpy.1441

Koh, S. W. C., Wong, E. R. N., Tan, J. C. M., van der Lubbe, S. C., Goh, J. C., Ching, E. S. Y., Chia, I. W. Y., Low, S. H., Ang, P. Y., Quek, Q., Motani, M., & Valderas, J. M. (2025). Classifying patient complaints using artificial intelligence–powered large language models: Cross-sectional study. *Journal of Medical Internet Research*, *27*, e74231. DOI: 10.2196/74231 PMID: 40768757

Lal, M., & Kashyap, H. (2024). Consumer complaint satisfaction and customer retention: A study of complaint satisfaction in electronic industry. *Jindal Journal of Business Research*, *13*(1), 82–99. DOI: 10.1177/22786821231183745

Li, X., Shu, Q., Kong, C., Wang, J., Li, G., Fang, X., Lou, X., & Yu, G. (2025). An intelligent system for classifying patient complaints using machine learning and natural language processing: Development and validation study. *Journal of Medical Internet Research*, *27*, e55721. DOI: 10.2196/55721 PMID: 39778195

Liu, J., Zhou, L., Yang, L., & Liu, D. (2024). The dehumanization of service robots influences hospitality consumption emotion. *International Journal of Hospitality Management*, *119*, 103707. DOI: 10.1016/j.ijhm.2024.103707

Lu, L., Gursoy, D., Chi, C. G.-Q., & Xiao, G. (2018). Developing a consumer complaining and recovery effort scale. *Journal of Hospitality & Tourism Research (Washington, D.C.)*, *42*(5), 686–715. DOI: 10.1177/1096348015597033

Mahmoud, M. A., Hinson, R. E., & Adika, M. K. (2018). The effect of trust, commitment, and conflict handling on customer retention: The mediating role of customer satisfaction. *Journal of Relationship Marketing, 17*(4), 257–276. DOI: 10.1080/15332667.2018.1440146

Mirzoev, T., & Kane, S. (2018). Key strategies to improve systems for managing patient complaints within health facilities – what can we learn from the existing literature? *Global Health Action, 11*(1), 1458938. DOI: 10.1080/16549716.2018.1458938 PMID: 29658393

Mouloudj, K., Bouarar, A. C., Martínez Asanza, D., & Dimitrova, M. (2025). Understanding Customers' Intentions to Use Digital Dental Health Services: An Expanded Technology Acceptance Model. In Martínez Asanza, D. (Ed.), *Transforming Dental Health in Rural Communities: Digital Dentistry* (pp. 189–210). IGI Global., DOI: 10.4018/979-8-3693-7165-7.ch007

Mouloudj, K., Bouarar, A. C., Martínez Asanza, D., Saadaoui, L., Mouloudj, S., Njoku, A. U., Evans, M. A., & Bouarar, A. (2023). Factors Influencing the Adoption of Digital Health Apps: An Extended Technology Acceptance Model (TAM). In Bouarar, A., Mouloudj, K., & Martínez Asanza, D. (Eds.), *Integrating Digital Health Strategies for Effective Administration* (pp. 116–132). IGI Global., DOI: 10.4018/978-1-6684-8337-4.ch007

Narteh, B., Agbemabiese, G. C., Kodua, P., & Braimah, M. (2013). Relationship marketing and customer loyalty: Evidence from the Ghanaian luxury hotel industry. *Journal of Hospitality Marketing & Management, 22*(4), 407–436. DOI: 10.1080/19368623.2012.660564

Ogbeide, G.-C. A., Böser, S., Harrinton, R. J., & Ottenbacher, M. C. (2017). Complaint management in hospitality organizations: The role of empowerment and other service recovery attributes impacting loyalty and satisfaction. *Tourism and Hospitality Research, 17*(2), 204–216. DOI: 10.1177/1467358415613409

Singh, V., Jain, A., & Choraria, S. (2016). Exploring the role of complaint handling among complaining consumers. *Vision: The Journal of Business Perspective, 20*(4), 331–344. DOI: 10.1177/0972262916668739

Sun, Y., Wang, X., Hoegg, J., & Dahl, D. W. (2023). How consumers respond to embarrassing service encounters: A dehumanization perspective. *JMR, Journal of Marketing Research, 60*(4), 646–664. DOI: 10.1177/00222437221130721

Teymourifar, A. (2026). Defining an integrative multidimensional framework for patient complaint management systems. *Frontiers in Health Services, 6*, 1767605. DOI: 10.3389/frhs.2026.1767605 PMID: 41982510

Wong, E., Mavondo, F., & Fisher, J. (2020). Patient feedback to improve quality of patient-centred care in public hospitals: A systematic review of the evidence. *BMC Health Services Research, 20*(1), 530. DOI: 10.1186/s12913-020-05383-3 PMID: 32527314

Xu, T., Zheng, Y. H., Zhang, J., & Wang, Z. (2025). "They" threaten my work: How AI service robots negatively impact frontline hotel employees through organizational dehumanization. *International Journal of Hospitality Management, 128*, 104162. DOI: 10.1016/j.ijhm.2025.104162

KEY TERMS AND DEFINITIONS

AI-Powered Complaint Management: The use of artificial intelligence technologies, such as machine learning and automated systems, to receive, analyze, classify, and respond to customer or patient complaints in a faster and more efficient manner.

Dental Healthcare: A branch of healthcare focused on the prevention, diagnosis, treatment, and management of oral health conditions through professional dental services provided in clinics or healthcare facilities.

Patient Retention: The ability of a healthcare provider or clinic to maintain long-term relationships with patients and encourage their continued use of healthcare services over time.

Service Dehumanization: A perception that service interactions have become impersonal, emotionally distant, or lacking in empathy due to excessive reliance on technology or reduced human involvement.

Trust: A patient's confidence in the reliability, fairness, competence, and security of a service provider or technology used to deliver healthcare-related services.

Chapter 4

Investigating the Impact of Digital Marketing Adoption on Customer Retention in Dental Health Tourism

Rosa Saeed Abed AlHadi
http://orcid.org/0009-0009-5675-0517
Al-Bayan University, Iraq

Raghad Mohamed Najm
Al Hikma University College, Iraq

Khatab Mohamed Fadel
Al Hikma University College, Iraq

Shamael Abd Al Karim Ibrahim
Al Hikma University College, Iraq

Ayman Raed Abd
http://orcid.org/0009-0009-8178-8891
Al Hikma University College, Iraq

Najat Dakhil Oufi Alnaemat
http://orcid.org/0009-0001-2173-6442
University of Basrah, Iraq

ABSTRACT

This study investigates the impact of digital marketing adoption on customer retention in international dental health tourism, focusing on Iraqi customers seeking dental treatment abroad. Specifically, the study examines the influence of digital information quality, electronic service quality, perceived value, and electronic word-of-mouth (eWOM) on customer retention. A quantitative approach was employed using a structured questionnaire distributed to actual/former and potential international dental tourists. Using convenience sampling, 125 valid responses were obtained for analysis. Multiple regression analysis revealed that all four variables significantly and positively influence customer retention. Perceived value emerged as the strongest

DOI: 10.4018/979-8-3373-8894-6.ch004

predictor, followed by electronic service quality, eWOM, and digital information quality. The findings highlight the importance of effective digital marketing strategies in enhancing long-term relationships with international dental tourists and improving retention intentions in cross-border dental healthcare settings.

INTRODUCTION

The healthcare tourism industry has experienced significant transformation over the past decade, driven by globalization, increasing healthcare costs, technological advancement, and the growing accessibility of digital communication channels (Fengmin et al., 2022). Among the various forms of medical tourism, dental health tourism has emerged as one of the fastest-growing segments due to the relatively high costs of dental procedures in many developed countries and the availability of affordable yet quality treatment options in emerging destinations (Velmurugan et al., 2026; Adams et al., 2018). Dental health tourism refers to patients traveling across geographic boundaries to receive dental treatments, including implants, cosmetic dentistry, orthodontics, veneers, and restorative procedures, often combined with tourism-related experiences (Ramos & Cuamea, 2023). In this increasingly competitive environment, attracting and retaining customers has become a strategic priority for dental clinics and health tourism providers.

The growing digitalization of healthcare services has profoundly altered how patients search for information, evaluate treatment alternatives, and select dental providers. Unlike traditional healthcare consumption patterns, dental tourists frequently rely on digital platforms to gather information due to limited opportunities for face-to-face consultation before treatment (Velmurugan et al., 2026). The Internet, social media platforms, online reviews, organization websites, and digital content have therefore become influential mechanisms shaping costumer decisions and expectations (Alyousuf et al., 2026; Horsfall et al., 2013). Potential dental tourists increasingly depend on websites, search engines, social media, and online recommendations to compare clinics, assess treatment quality, estimate costs, and build confidence before making travel decisions (Kopmaz et al., 2019).

The emergence of digital marketing has consequently transformed the way healthcare providers interact with prospective patients. Digital marketing enables healthcare organizations in general and dental clinics in particular to communicate treatment information, showcase expertise, improve service accessibility, and establish credibility through online interactions (Hollebeek & Macky, 2019; Mouloudj et al., 2026). Research suggests that digital content marketing significantly strengthens consumer trust, engagement, and value perceptions, which ultimately influence behavioral intentions and loyalty (Bui et al., 2023; Hollebeek & Macky, 2019).

Similarly, short-form digital content and social media interactions have demonstrated strong effects on consumers' trust and behavioral intentions in online environments (Luo et al., 2025; Shen & Wang, 2024). In healthcare settings, social media has become particularly relevant because patients increasingly evaluate providers based on digital presence, professional communication, and online credibility (Meira et al., 2021; Alqabbani et al., 2025).

In the context of dental health tourism, digital marketing adoption is particularly important because healthcare services involve high levels of uncertainty, perceived risk, and trust concerns. Prospective patients often seek extensive online information before selecting a clinic, making the quality of digital information a critical determinant of healthcare decisions (Horsfall et al., 2013). Prior studies have highlighted that dental websites and digital communication channels play a substantial role in patient decision-making, especially when websites provide accessible information, foreign language options, transparent communication, and user-friendly layouts (Kopmaz et al., 2019). However, concerns remain regarding incomplete or misleading digital information, which may negatively influence trust and decision-making processes among healthcare tourists (Horsfall et al., 2013).

In addition to information quality, electronic service quality has become increasingly important in enhancing customer experiences (Fengmin et al., 2022). Digital service quality refers to the efficiency, responsiveness, accessibility, and convenience of online interactions between customers and service providers (Alyousuf et al., 2026). In healthcare and tourism sectors, high service quality has been consistently associated with patient satisfaction, loyalty, and revisit intention (Han & Hwang, 2018; Almodawer et al., 2025a). Features such as online appointment systems, rapid responses, virtual consultations, and accessible communication channels contribute to more positive experiences and may encourage patients to maintain long-term relationships with healthcare providers (Modha, 2023).

Furthermore, perceived value represents an important predictor of customer retention in both healthcare and tourism industries (Tuncer et al., 2021). Customers generally evaluate healthcare services based on the balance between perceived benefits and sacrifices, including treatment quality, affordability, convenience, and overall experience (Gan et al., 2023; Nguyen Huu et al., 2024). In dental tourism, perceived value becomes especially relevant because patients often travel to obtain affordable treatment without compromising quality (Adams et al., 2018). Previous studies have consistently demonstrated that higher perceived value positively influences satisfaction, loyalty, and revisit intentions among tourists and healthcare costumers (Cham et al., 2021; Habibi, & Rasoolimanesh, 2021; Nguyen Huu et al., 2024).

Another important factor shaping customer retention is "electronic word-of-mouth" (eWOM), which includes online reviews, testimonials, social media discussions, and digital recommendations shared by previous customers (Alameri et al., 2026;

Hennig-Thurau et al., 2004; Jalilvand & Heidari, 2017). Healthcare customers increasingly rely on online reviews because they are perceived as authentic and informative sources of information (Ponathil et al., 2021). Positive eWOM can strengthen trust, improve destination image, and encourage revisit intentions in tourism contexts (Farrukh et al., 2022; Bouarar et al., 2025). Similarly, responsiveness to online reviews and interactive digital communication have been found to improve patient trust and future behavioral intentions toward dental clinics (Vafeiadis, 2023).

Despite the growing significance of digital marketing in healthcare tourism, limited empirical studies have specifically investigated how digital marketing adoption contributes to customer retention in dental health tourism, particularly within developing healthcare contexts such as Iraq. Existing studies have mainly focused on medical tourism satisfaction, revisit intention, and destination image in countries such as Malaysia, Mexico, China, and South Korea (Cham et al., 2021; Han & Hwang, 2018; Ramos & Cuamea, 2023). Moreover, prior research has largely emphasized travel intentions and destination attractiveness rather than the influence of digital marketing-related factors on customer retention in dental tourism services. This indicates an important research gap requiring empirical investigation.

Accordingly, this chapter seeks to investigate the impact of digital marketing adoption on customer retention in dental health tourism by examining the influence of digital information quality, electronic service quality, perceived value, and eWOM. Understanding these relationships may provide practical insights for dental clinics and healthcare tourism providers seeking to improve customer retention strategies through effective digital engagement.

Therefore, this investigation addresses the following questions:

- Does digital information quality significantly influence customer retention in dental health tourism?
- Does electronic service quality significantly influence customer retention in dental health tourism?
- Does perceived value significantly influence customer retention in dental health tourism?
- Does eWOM significantly influence customer retention in dental health tourism?

Consequently, this study seeks to achieve four objectives: (1) To examine the effect of digital information quality on customer retention in dental health tourism; (2) To investigate the influence of electronic service quality on customer retention in dental health tourism; (3) To assess the impact of perceived value on customer retention in dental health tourism; and (4) To analyze the influence of eWOM on customer retention in dental health tourism.

LITERATURE REVIEW

Dental Health Tourism

Dental health tourism has emerged as an important segment within the broader medical tourism industry, reflecting the increasing mobility of patients seeking affordable, high-quality, and timely dental care beyond their local healthcare systems (Gan et al., 2023; Han & Hyun, 2015). The concept generally refers to individuals traveling to another city or country to obtain dental treatment while often combining healthcare services with leisure or tourism activities. Treatments sought through dental health tourism commonly include cosmetic dentistry, dental implants, orthodontics, veneers, oral surgery, and restorative procedures that may be prohibitively expensive or inaccessible in patients' home locations (Velmurugan et al., 2026; Ramos & Cuamea, 2023).

The growing popularity of health tourism can be attributed to several interconnected factors (Han & Hyun, 2015). Cost savings remain one of the strongest drivers, particularly for patients from regions where dental care expenses are relatively high. However, affordability alone does not explain the expansion of this sector (Gan et al., 2023; Habibi, & Rasoolimanesh, 2021). Patients are increasingly motivated by the desire to access better-quality services, shorter waiting times, advanced treatment technologies, and specialized expertise unavailable in their home healthcare systems (Adams et al., 2018). In many cases, dental tourists actively compare destinations based on treatment quality, service reputation, convenience, and overall patient experience before making travel decisions (Cham et al., 2021).

Over the last decade, digital transformation has fundamentally reshaped how many organizations operate (Alnaemat & Saleem, 2026). Unlike conventional healthcare consumption, dental tourists often make decisions without prior physical interaction with providers. Consequently, digital channels have become central to information gathering and decision-making processes (Alyousuf et al., 2026). Prospective patients frequently rely on websites, social media, online reviews, and digital testimonials to evaluate clinics and reduce uncertainty surrounding treatment outcomes (Horsfall et al., 2013). The internet has therefore become more than a communication medium; it now serves as an influential marketplace where organizations compete for visibility, trust, and credibility (Alnaemat & Saleem, 2026).

The role of digital communication is especially pronounced in dental tourism because healthcare services involve relatively high levels of perceived risk. Customers must often make decisions based on information available online, including treatment explanations, before-and-after cases, pricing transparency, and previous patient experiences (Jalilvand & Heidari, 2017). Research has shown that professionally designed dental websites with accessible information, multilingual options, and user-friendly layouts are more attractive to potential health tourists and may positively shape perceptions of credibility (Kopmaz et al., 2019). Similarly, social media platforms increasingly influence healthcare choices, as patients evaluate dentists and clinics based on digital presence, online professionalism, and visible treatment outcomes (Meira et al., 2021; Alqabbani et al., 2025).

At the same time, the rapid growth of dental tourism has intensified competition among healthcare providers, making effective marketing and patient relationship management increasingly important. Contemporary dental clinics are no longer competing solely on treatment quality or price but also on their ability to communicate value, maintain online engagement, and build long-term patient trust through digital channels (Modha, 2023). This shift highlights the growing importance of understanding how digital marketing practices shape patient experiences and influence retention within dental health tourism settings.

Customers Retention in Dental Health Tourism

Customer and employee retention has become an increasingly important objective in the healthcare and tourism sectors (Jasim et al., 2026), particularly in dental health tourism, where attracting new patients often requires substantial financial and marketing investments (Gan et al., 2023; Han & Hyun, 2015). In general, customer retention refers to an organization's ability to maintain long-term relationships with customers and encourage them to revisit or continue using its services over time (Fengmin et al., 2022). Within dental health tourism, customer retention reflects patients' willingness to return to the same dental provider for future treatments and to maintain an ongoing relationship with the clinic despite the availability of competing alternatives (Han & Hwang, 2018).

Retaining patients in dental health tourism is particularly challenging because healthcare consumers typically face a wide range of choices across destinations, clinics, and treatment providers. Patients may compare service quality, treatment affordability, convenience, communication, and overall healthcare experiences before deciding whether to revisit a clinic (Ramos & Cuamea, 2023). In this context, retaining existing customers is often more sustainable than continuously attracting new ones, as repeat patients tend to exhibit stronger trust, lower perceived risk, and greater familiarity with healthcare providers.

Prior research in medical and health tourism has consistently highlighted the importance of service-related experiences in fostering retention intentions. For example, perceived healthcare quality, communication effectiveness, and post-treatment experiences have been found to positively influence satisfaction and revisit intentions among medical tourists (Han & Hwang, 2018; Almodawer et al., 2025a). Likewise, customer satisfaction has been recognized as a central mechanism linking healthcare experiences to loyalty and repeat visitation behaviors (Dar & Kashyap, 2025). Positive healthcare experiences can strengthen trust and encourage patients to return to the same provider for additional procedures or long-term care (Sousa & Alves, 2019).

In the context of health tourism, customer retention may also be shaped by digital interactions. Since patients frequently rely on online communication, reviews, and digital information before treatment, healthcare providers that effectively manage digital engagement may strengthen patient confidence and improve retention outcomes. Consequently, understanding the factors that encourage patients to remain loyal to dental providers has become increasingly important in today's digitally driven healthcare environment.

Hypothesis Development

Digital Information Quality and Customer Retention

Digital information quality refers to the extent to which online information provided by service organizations is accurate, complete, relevant, understandable, and useful for consumers' decision-making. In the context of international dental health tourism, digital information quality is particularly important because prospective patients often make treatment decisions without prior physical interaction with healthcare providers (Fengmin et al., 2022; Ramos & Cuamea, 2023). Since customers travel outside their home country to receive dental treatment, they frequently depend on digital sources such as clinic websites, social media pages, treatment descriptions, pricing information, patient testimonials, and virtual consultations to evaluate available alternatives and reduce uncertainty (Horsfall et al., 2013; Sousa & Alves, 2019).

The quality of online information can substantially shape customers' perceptions of credibility and trust toward service providers (Qalati et al., 2021). Previous studies have shown that professionally designed dental websites offering transparent, detailed, and accessible information positively influence healthcare-related decision-making among international patients (Kopmaz et al., 2019). Similarly, digital content that is informative and useful enhances consumer trust and value perceptions, ultimately influencing behavioral intentions and loyalty (Hollebeek & Macky, 2019; Bui et al., 2023). Research in medical tourism also suggests that access to reliable information strengthens destination image and revisit intentions among international healthcare travelers (de la Hoz-Correa & Muñoz-Leiva, 2019). Furthermore, quality information has been identified as an important predictor of revisit behavior among dental tourists (Ramos & Cuamea, 2023). Therefore, we develop the following hypothesis:

H1: Digital information quality positively influences customer retention in dental health tourism.

Electronic Service Quality and Customer Retention

Electronic service quality refers to the effectiveness and efficiency of digital service delivery through online platforms and electronic communication channels (Qalati et al., 2021). In dental health tourism, electronic service quality may include website usability, responsiveness to inquiries, online appointment scheduling, virtual consultations, communication efficiency, and post-treatment online support (Almodawer et al., 2025a). Because international dental tourists are geographically distant from healthcare providers, electronic interactions often become essential touchpoints throughout the customer journey, beginning from information search and continuing beyond treatment completion (Modha, 2023). High-quality electronic services can improve convenience, reduce uncertainty, and foster positive healthcare experiences (Qalati et al., 2021; Sousa & Alves, 2019). Prior studies have consistently demonstrated that service quality plays a critical role in strengthening satisfaction and revisit intentions in healthcare tourism settings (Fengmin et al., 2022; Han & Hyun, 2015; Han & Hwang, 2018; Marković et al., 2014). Similarly, research on Arab medical tourists in Malaysia found that healthcare service quality, particularly post-treatment support, significantly enhances satisfaction and loyalty intentions (Almodawer et al., 2025a). Effective digital communication and responsiveness can also strengthen trust and improve behavioral intentions among prospective healthcare customers (Vafeiadis, 2023). Since international patients often rely on digital support before traveling and after treatment, superior electronic service quality may increase their confidence and willingness to revisit the same dental provider. Therefore, we propose the following hypothesis:

H2: Electronic service quality positively influences customer retention in dental health tourism.

Perceived Value and Customer Retention

Perceived value refers to customers' overall assessment of the benefits received relative to the sacrifices incurred when purchasing or consuming a service (Nguyen et al., 2021; Tuncer et al., 2021). In international dental health tourism, perceived value reflects how patients evaluate treatment quality, affordability, convenience, travel effort, and overall healthcare experience in relation to the financial and psychological costs involved (Cham et al., 2021; Habibi, & Rasoolimanesh, 2021). Since many dental tourists seek treatment abroad primarily for cost advantages without compromising quality, perceived value represents a critical determinant of post-treatment evaluations and behavioral intentions (Adams et al., 2018). Previous literature has repeatedly emphasized the importance of perceived value in influencing customer loyalty and revisit behavior across tourism and healthcare sectors (Fengmin et al., 2022; Nguyen et al., 2021; Tuncer et al., 2021). For example, studies on medical tourism destinations found that perceived value significantly contributes to revisit intentions among international healthcare travelers (Cham et al., 2021; Gan et al., 2023). Similarly, research in tourism settings demonstrated that perceived value positively affects tourist satisfaction, which subsequently strengthens intentions to revisit destinations (Nguyen Huu et al., 2024). Digital marketing practices that effectively communicate treatment quality, affordability, and expected outcomes may further strengthen value perceptions among dental tourists (Velmurugan et al., 2026). When international patients perceive that dental services abroad offer superior value, they are more likely to maintain relationships with providers and seek repeat treatment. Therefore, we propose the following hypothesis:

H3: Perceived value positively influences customer retention in dental health tourism.

Electronic Word-of-Mouth (eWOM) and Customer Retention

eWOM refers to "any positive or negative statement made by potential, actual, or former customers about a product or company which is made available to a multitude of the people and institutes via the Internet" (Hennig-Thurau et al., 2004, p. 39). In other words, it is defined as online opinions, recommendations, reviews, ratings, and experiences shared by consumers through digital platforms (Alameri et al., 2026; Bouarar et al., 2025). In international dental health tourism, eWOM represents an influential source of information because prospective patients often rely on the experiences of previous customers to evaluate treatment quality, trustworthiness, and provider credibility before traveling abroad for healthcare services. Compared to traditional advertising, online reviews and testimonials are often perceived as more authentic and less commercially biased, making them especially influential in healthcare decision-making (Ponathil et al., 2021). The significance of eWOM becomes even greater in cross-border healthcare contexts, where patients face higher levels of uncertainty and perceived risk. Prior studies have shown that positive eWOM significantly influences travel intentions in medical tourism by enhancing destination image and reducing concerns about treatment outcomes (Farrukh et al., 2022). Similarly, positive online recommendations have been found to strengthen tourists' behavioral intentions and destination attractiveness (Bouarar et al., 2025; Jalilvand & Heidari, 2017). In dentistry, online interactions and review responsiveness have also been linked to stronger trust and favorable patient behavioral intentions toward healthcare providers (Vafeiadis, 2023). Consequently, favorable eWOM may encourage international dental tourists to return to the same provider and recommend the clinic to others. Therefore, we propose the following hypothesis:

H4: eWOM positively influences customer retention in international dental health tourism.

METHODS

3.1 Research instrument

Data for this study were collected using a structured questionnaire designed to examine the impact of digital marketing adoption on customer retention in international dental health tourism. The questionnaire consisted of two sections. The first section gathered demographic information about respondents, including gender, age group, educational level, and previous experience with international dental tourism. The second section included items designed to measure the study variables, namely digital information quality, electronic service quality, perceived value, eWOM, and customer retention. The measurement items were adapted from prior studies and refined to suit the context of international dental health tourism, particularly among customers seeking or considering dental treatment abroad. Specifically, items measuring digital information quality were developed by the authors based on the work of Qalati et al. (2021). Electronic service quality items were adapted from Han and Hyun (2015) and Marković et al. (2014). The measurement of perceived value was adapted from Gan et al. (2023) and Nguyen et al. (2021), whereas eWOM items were adapted from Bouarar et al. (2025), Jalilvand and Heidari (2017), and Nguyen et al. (2021). Finally, items assessing customer retention were adapted from Han and Hyun (2015). As shown in Table 1, each construct was measured using three items to ensure concise yet reliable measurement.

To improve the suitability of the questionnaire for the Iraqi context, the instrument was initially prepared in English and then translated into Arabic using a back-translation procedure performed by two bilingual experts to ensure linguistic accuracy and conceptual equivalence. Furthermore, two specialists in medical tourism were invited to review the questionnaire content and evaluate the appropriateness, clarity, and relevance of the items to the study objectives. Their feedback contributed to minor wording refinements to improve contextual relevance. Before the full-scale data collection process, a pilot study involving ten respondents was conducted to assess the clarity and comprehensibility of the questionnaire. The pilot sample consisted of five former international dental tourists and five potential dental tourists, representing the target population of the study. Based on participant feedback, minor modifications were introduced to improve item clarity and readability. All study variables were measured using a five-point Likert scale, ranging from 1 = "Strongly Disagree" to 5 = "Strongly Agree".

Table 1. Measurement and questionnaire items

Constructs	Coding	Item
Digital Information Quality (DIQ)	DIQ1	The online information provided by the dental clinic was clear and easy to understand.
	DIQ2	The dental clinic provided complete and useful information about treatments, prices, and procedures through digital platforms.
	DIQ3	I found the online information about the dental clinic to be accurate and reliable.
Electronic Service Quality (ESQ)	ESQ1	The dental clinic responded promptly to my online inquiries and requests.
	ESQ2	The dental clinic's online services (e.g., appointments, communication, consultation) were efficient and easy to use.
	ESQ3	I was satisfied with the quality of electronic communication provided by the dental clinic.
Perceived Value (PV)	PV1	Receiving dental treatment from this clinic was worth the money and effort spent.
	PV2	Compared with other alternatives, this dental clinic offered good value for the services received.
	PV3	Overall, I believe the dental treatment experience provided good value for me.
Electronic Word-of-Mouth (EWOM)	EWOM1	Positive online reviews influenced my decision to choose this dental clinic.
	EWOM2	Recommendations and experiences shared online increased my confidence in this dental clinic.
	EWOM3	I consider online reviews and ratings important when selecting dental healthcare services abroad.
Customer Retention (CR)	CR1	I intend to return to this dental clinic for future dental treatment if needed.
	CR2	I would prefer this dental clinic over other clinics for future dental care abroad.
	CR3	I would continue using this dental clinic's services in the future.

Source: Authors' own creation

Data Collection

Data for this study were collected using a structured questionnaire administered to actual/former and potential international tourists of dental tourism services from various Iraqi governorates who were aged 18 years and above. Since the study focuses on international dental tourism, respondents included individuals who had either previously traveled abroad to receive dental treatment or had intentions to do so in the future. Due to the absence of an accessible sampling frame for international dental tourists in Iraq, a convenience sampling technique was employed to recruit participants. This approach was considered appropriate given the exploratory nature of the study and the challenges associated with identifying individuals with direct or potential experience in international dental tourism. The questionnaire was distributed through multiple channels to improve accessibility and participation, including travel agencies, private dental clinics, email invitations, and various social media platforms such as Facebook and WhatsApp, which are widely used communication tools.

The data collection process took place over a two-month period, from October 1, 2025, to November 30, 2025. During this period, a total of 170 questionnaires were distributed to eligible respondents. Of these, 129 completed questionnaires were returned, representing a satisfactory response rate. Following the screening process, four questionnaires were excluded due to incomplete responses or inconsistencies, resulting in 125 valid questionnaires retained for final analysis. Before participation, respondents were informed about the purpose of the study and provided verbal consent to participate voluntarily. They were also assured that participation was entirely voluntary, responses would remain anonymous, and the collected information would be used solely for academic research purposes. In accordance with applicable local legislation and institutional practices, anonymous questionnaire-based surveys that do not involve sensitive personal data do not require formal ethical committee approval. Consequently, no formal ethics approval was necessary for conducting this study.

RESULTS

Respondents' Demographic Profile

As shown in Table 2, the respondents consisted of 68 males (54.40%) and 57 females (45.60%), indicating a relatively balanced gender distribution with a slight predominance of male participants. Regarding age, the majority of respondents were between 41–50 years (41.60%), followed by those aged 31–40 years (27.20%), while respondents aged 51 years and above (20.00%) and 18–30 years (11.20%) represented smaller proportions. In terms of educational attainment, most participants held a Bachelor's degree (36.00%), followed by Postgraduate degrees (24.80%), Diplomas (20.80%), and Secondary school education or below (18.40%), reflecting a relatively educated sample. Concerning previous experience with international dental tourism, the majority of respondents reported no prior experience (85.60%), whereas only 14.40% indicated that they had previously traveled abroad to receive dental healthcare services. This distribution suggests that the sample includes both experienced and prospective international dental tourists, which is relevant to the objectives of the present study.

Table 2. Demographic characteristics

Characteristics	Category	Frequency	%
Gender	Male	68	54.40
	Female	57	45.60
Age Group	18–30 years	14	11.20
	31–40 years	34	27.20
	41–50 years	52	41.60
	51 years and above	25	20.00
Educational Level	Secondary school or below	23	18.40
	Diploma	26	20.80
	Bachelor's degree	45	36.00
	Postgraduate degree	31	24.80
Previous Experience with International Dental Tourism	Yes	18	14.40
	No	107	85.60

Reliability and Descriptive Statistics

Table 3 presents the descriptive statistics, internal consistency reliability, and normality indicators for the study variables. The mean values indicate that customer retention recorded the highest average score (M = 3.997), followed by electronic service quality (M = 3.882), digital information quality (M = 3.648), and eWOM (M = 3.570). In contrast, perceived value reported the lowest mean (M = 2.834), suggesting comparatively lower perceptions among respondents.

Regarding reliability, all constructs demonstrated satisfactory internal consistency, as reflected by Cronbach's alpha values exceeding the recommended threshold of 0.70 (Mouloudj et al., 2026). Specifically, alpha values ranged from 0.745 for customer retention to 0.935 for Perceived Value, confirming the reliability of the measurement scales used in this study. The skewness and kurtosis statistics further indicate that the data are approximately normally distributed. Skewness values ranged from −1.259 to −0.311, while kurtosis values varied between −0.645 and 1.847. Since these values fall within acceptable ranges commonly suggested in social science research (Alyousuf et al., 2026), the data were considered suitable for subsequent statistical analyses.

Table 3. Reliability analysis and descriptive statistics of the study constructs

Constructs	Mean	Cronbach's α	Skewness	Kurtosis
Digital Information Quality	3.648	0.913	-1.097	1.031
Electronic Service Quality	3.882	0.850	-1.259	1.847
Perceived Value	2.834	0.935	-0.464	-0.126
Electronic Word-of-Mouth (eWOM)	3.570	0.856	-0.311	-0.645
Customer Retention	3.997	0.745	-0.652	-0.222

Correlation Analysis among Study Variables

As illustrated in Table 4, the correlation analysis reveals statistically significant positive relationships among all study variables. Customer retention demonstrated positive correlations with all independent variables, indicating that higher levels of digital marketing-related factors are associated with stronger retention intentions among international dental tourism customers. Among these relationships, electronic service quality showed the strongest correlation with customer retention ($r = 0.687$, $p < 0.005$), followed by perceived value ($r = 0.640$, $p < 0.005$), digital information quality ($r = 0.602$, $p < 0.005$), and eWOM ($r = 0.542$, $p < 0.005$). A closer look at the intercorrelations among the independent variables also indicates moderate positive associations. For instance, digital information quality was positively correlated with electronic service quality ($r = 0.607$, $p < 0.005$) and eWOM ($r = 0.459$, $p < 0.005$). Likewise, perceived value displayed a notable relationship with electronic service quality ($r = 0.603$, $p < 0.005$). Overall, the correlation coefficients remained below commonly accepted multicollinearity concern thresholds, suggesting that the constructs are related yet sufficiently distinct to be included simultaneously in the regression analysis.

Table 4. Correlation matrix of the study constructs

Constructs	1	2	3	4
1. Digital Information Quality				
2. Electronic Service Quality	0.607**			
3. Perceived Value	0.399**	0.603**		
4. eWOM	0.459**	0.482**	0.369**	
5. Customer Retention	0.602**	0.687**	0.640**	0.542**

Note: ** ($p < 0.005$)

Hypotheses Testing

The results of the multiple regression analysis are reported in Table 5, which examines the impact of digital information quality, electronic service quality, perceived value, and eWOM on customer retention in international dental health tourism. The overall regression model was statistically significant (F = 50.367, p < 0.001), indicating that the selected independent variables collectively explain variations in customer retention. Furthermore, the model achieved an Adjusted R^2 value of 0.614, suggesting that approximately 61.4% of the variance in customer retention is explained by the four predictors included in the model.

The findings reveal that digital information quality exerts a positive and statistically significant influence on customer retention (β = 0.175, t = 3.121, p = 0.002), thereby supporting H1. Likewise, electronic service quality demonstrated a significant positive effect (β = 0.205, t = 3.203, p = 0.002), providing support for H2. Perceived value emerged as the strongest predictor of customer retention (β = 0.282, t = 4.529, p < 0.001), confirming H3. In addition, eWOM significantly influenced customer retention (β = 0.193, t = 2.935, p = 0.004), supporting H4.

Table 5. Results of multiple regression analysis for customer retention

Model	β	t	Sig.	Tolerance	VIF	Result
Constant	1.188	5.372	0.000			-
Digital Information Quality	0.175	3.121	0.002	0.595	1.680	Supported
Electronic Service Quality	0.205	3.203	0.002	0.456	2.194	Supported
Perceived Value	0.282	4.529	0.000	0.628	1.594	Supported
Electronic Word-of-Mouth	0.193	2.935	0.004	0.716	1.396	Supported
F = 50.367 ($p < 0.001$)			Adjusted R^2= 0.614			

Concerning multicollinearity diagnostics, the Tolerance values ranged from 0.456 to 0.716, while Variance Inflation Factor (VIF) values ranged from 1.396 to 2.194, remaining well below the recommended threshold of 5 (Alyousuf et al., 2026; Jasim et al., 2026). These findings indicate the absence of multicollinearity concerns, confirming that the independent variables were sufficiently distinct and suitable for inclusion in the regression model.

DISCUSSION AND MANAGERIAL IMPLICATIONS

Discussion

The primary purpose of this study was to investigate the impact of digital marketing adoption on customer retention in international dental health tourism within the Iraqi context. More specifically, the study examined the effects of digital information quality, electronic service quality, perceived value, and eWOM on customers' retention intentions among actual, former, and potential Iraqi dental tourists seeking treatment abroad. The findings demonstrate that all four dimensions exert significant positive effects on customer retention, highlighting the increasingly influential role of digital marketing practices in shaping long-term behavioral intentions in cross-border dental healthcare.

The findings confirmed that digital information quality positively influences customer retention, supporting H1. This result suggests that international dental tourists are more likely to maintain relationships with dental providers when they perceive the online information offered by clinics as clear, reliable, detailed, and useful. In the context of international healthcare travel, where patients cannot physically inspect clinics before treatment, high-quality digital information appears to reduce uncertainty and strengthen confidence in healthcare providers (Marković et al., 2014; Sousa & Alves, 2019). Dental tourists may particularly depend on websites, social media pages, treatment explanations, pricing transparency, and online consultations when evaluating foreign clinics. This finding aligns with earlier research emphasizing the importance of online healthcare information in shaping patient trust and behavioral decisions. For example, Horsfall et al. (2013) highlighted that internet-based medical tourism information plays a critical role in patient decision-making, although information quality remains an ongoing concern. Similarly, Kopmaz et al. (2019) found that well-designed dental websites with comprehensive information positively support dental tourism communication and patient attraction. The present finding is also consistent with de la Hoz-Correa and Muñoz-Leiva (2019), who demonstrated that information sources significantly influence medical tourism intentions. These results reinforce the argument that providing accurate and transparent digital information is not merely promotional but strategically important for sustaining long-term patient relationships.

The study also revealed that electronic service quality has a significant positive impact on customer retention, supporting H2. This indicates that efficient online interactions, responsive communication, digital appointment systems, and accessible electronic services contribute meaningfully to customers' willingness to revisit dental providers abroad. Given the geographical distance involved in international dental tourism, electronic interactions often substitute for face-to-face communication before and after treatment. Consequently, patients may interpret fast responses, effective virtual support, and smooth digital experiences as indicators of professionalism and care quality (Fengmin et al., 2022; Habibi, & Rasoolimanesh, 2021; Sousa & Alves, 2019). The current finding is consistent with Han and Hwang (2018), who reported that service quality and effective communication are critical drivers of revisit intention in medical tourism contexts. Likewise, Almodawer et al. (2025a) emphasized that healthcare quality and post-treatment support significantly improve medical tourists' satisfaction and revisit intentions. Moreover, the findings echo Vafeiadis (2023), who found that digital responsiveness and interactive communication strengthen trust and positive behavioral intentions in dental healthcare settings. This result highlights the practical importance of investing in digitally enabled customer service systems to maintain international patient loyalty.

Regarding perceived value, the findings showed that it exerts the strongest influence on customer retention, thereby supporting H3. This result implies that dental tourists are particularly concerned with the overall value gained from treatment abroad, including affordability, treatment quality, convenience, and expected outcomes relative to financial and non-financial sacrifices (Fengmin et al., 2022; Habibi, & Rasoolimanesh, 2021; Nguyen et al., 2021). Since dental tourism is often motivated by cost savings without compromising service quality, customers are likely to revisit providers when they perceive the benefits received to outweigh the costs incurred (Gan et al., 2023). The strong influence of perceived value observed in this study is unsurprising, especially in a healthcare tourism setting where financial considerations are central to decision-making (Tuncer et al., 2021). This finding corresponds with Cham et al. (2021), who found that perceived value significantly enhances revisit intentions among medical tourists in Malaysia. Similarly, Nguyen Huu et al. (2024) reported that perceived value positively affects satisfaction and return intentions in tourism settings. The present result also resonates with Velmurugan et al. (2026), who emphasized affordability and trust-building as essential factors in attracting and retaining dental tourists. The prominence of perceived value in this study suggests that foreign dental providers seeking to attract international customers should focus on delivering a strong balance between cost-effectiveness and service excellence.

Finally, the study found that eWOM significantly and positively influences customer retention, supporting H4. This finding indicates that online reviews, patient testimonials, recommendations, and shared treatment experiences play an important role in shaping loyalty intentions in international dental tourism. Since healthcare decisions involve high perceived risk, especially when treatment occurs abroad, prospective patients often seek reassurance from the experiences of previous customers. Positive eWOM appears to enhance trust and reduce uncertainty, thereby strengthening intentions to revisit the same provider (Hennig-Thurau et al., 2004;

Jalilvand & Heidari, 2017). This finding is consistent with Farrukh et al. (2022), who reported that eWOM positively affects travel intentions in medical tourism through destination image formation. Similarly, Bouarar et al. (2025) found that positive eWOM significantly enhances tourists' behavioral intentions. In dental healthcare specifically, Ponathil et al. (2021) demonstrated that online reviews substantially influence provider selection decisions, while Vafeiadis (2023) showed that digital engagement surrounding reviews positively shapes patient behavioral intentions. These findings suggest that dental clinics targeting international patients should actively manage online reputation, encourage satisfied patients to share experiences, and maintain transparent communication across digital platforms to strengthen customer retention.

Managerial Implications

The findings of this study provide several practical implications for dental clinics, health tourism facilitators, and digital marketers seeking to attract and retain international dental tourists. First, given the positive influence of digital information quality, dental healthcare providers should prioritize delivering clear, transparent, and comprehensive information through their websites and social media platforms. Information related to treatment procedures, expected outcomes, pricing, travel arrangements, qualifications of dentists, and post-treatment care should be presented in a detailed yet understandable manner. Since international patients often make decisions remotely, high-quality digital information can reduce uncertainty and foster trust before travel.

Second, the significant role of electronic service quality suggests that clinics should invest in responsive digital communication systems. Online appointment scheduling, prompt replies to inquiries, virtual consultations, multilingual customer support, and efficient follow-up communication may substantially improve customer experiences. Because international patients are geographically distant, professional and timely digital interactions can strengthen perceptions of reliability and care quality. The findings further highlight the importance of Perceived Value, which emerged as the strongest predictor of customer retention. Managers should therefore ensure that treatment quality justifies the financial and non-financial costs incurred by international patients. Offering transparent pricing packages, personalized treatment plans, travel assistance, and value-added services may improve patients' perceptions of overall value and encourage repeat visits.

Finally, since eWOM significantly influences retention, dental providers should actively manage their online reputation. Encouraging satisfied patients to share testimonials, responding professionally to online reviews, and maintaining an engaging social media presence may strengthen credibility and positively influence future retention intentions. Collectively, these strategies can help dental tourism providers build sustainable relationships with international patients and maintain a competitive advantage in an increasingly digital healthcare market.

LIMITATIONS AND FUTURE RESEARCH

Despite its contributions, this study has several limitations that should be acknowledged and may offer useful directions for future research. First, the study focused on four digital marketing-related predictors to explain customer retention in international dental health tourism. Future studies may expand the model by incorporating additional variables that are particularly relevant to cross-border healthcare contexts. For example, trust in travel agencies, trust in dental service providers, destination image, perceived risk, treatment affordability, service recovery quality, and patient satisfaction may provide deeper insights into retention behavior among international dental tourists. Future scholars may also benefit from integrating established theoretical frameworks to strengthen explanatory power. For instance, the theory of planned behavior, stimulus–organism–response model, or the technology acceptance model could be extended to better explain how digital interactions shape retention intentions in medical tourism settings. In addition, future research may examine the mediating role of trust, satisfaction, or attitude, while also exploring moderating effects such as previous dental tourism experience, income level, or perceived risk. Another valuable direction would involve investigating specific dental tourism destinations frequently visited by Iraqi patients, such as Turkey, Lebanon, Jordan, or Iran. Conducting destination-specific studies may reveal contextual differences in service expectations, digital marketing effectiveness, and customer retention drivers across international healthcare markets.

CONCLUSION

This study investigated the impact of digital marketing adoption on customer retention in international dental health tourism, focusing on Iraqi customers who had prior experience with or intentions to seek dental treatment abroad. Specifically, the study examined the influence of digital information quality, electronic service quality, perceived value, and eWOM on customer retention intentions. The findings revealed that all four variables significantly and positively affect customer retention, highlighting the growing importance of digital marketing practices in shaping long-term patient relationships in cross-border dental healthcare. Among the examined predictors, perceived value emerged as the strongest determinant of customer retention, indicating that international dental tourists place considerable emphasis on obtaining high-quality treatment at reasonable costs. In addition, electronic service quality and digital information quality were found to positively strengthen retention intentions, suggesting that efficient online interactions and reliable digital information are essential in reducing uncertainty and fostering confidence among international patients. Likewise, eWOM significantly contributed to customer retention, emphasizing the importance of online reviews and patient recommendations in influencing healthcare-related decisions.

Overall, the study contributes to the growing literature on dental health tourism by demonstrating how digital marketing dimensions shape retention behavior in an international healthcare setting. The findings underscore the need for dental clinics and health tourism providers to adopt patient-centered digital strategies that strengthen trust, improve perceived value, and encourage lasting relationships with international customers.

REFERENCES

Adams, K., Snyder, J., Crooks, V. A., & Berry, N. S. (2018). A critical examination of empowerment discourse in medical tourism: The case of the dental tourism industry in Los Algodones, Mexico. *Globalization and Health*, *14*(1), 70. DOI: 10.1186/s12992-018-0392-3

Alameri, S. A., Mahmoud, B. I., Almado, A. A., Jasim, Z. A., Jahlool, I. H., & Alyousuf, A. N. (2026). Consumer Acceptance of AI-Supported Circular Fashion Services: A Technology Acceptance Perspective. In Mouloudj, K., & Arantes, L. (Eds.), *Ethical Consumption and Responsible Innovation in Fashion through AI* (pp. 35–58). IGI Global., DOI: 10.4018/979-8-3373-7200-6.ch002

Almodawer, Y., Alam, S. S., Sinniah, S., & Ali, M. H. (2025a). Health tourism in Malaysia: Understanding the drivers of satisfaction and revisit intention. *Tourism Recreation Research*, *50*(5), 1088–1109. DOI: 10.1080/02508281.2024.2379686

Alnaemat, N. D., & Saleem, S. A. (2026). Integrating Digital Technologies into Fashion Management: Opportunities and Challenges. In Mouloudj, K., & Arantes, L. (Eds.), *Ethical Consumption and Responsible Innovation in Fashion through AI* (pp. 145–168). IGI Global., DOI: 10.4018/979-8-3373-7200-6.ch006

Alqabbani, Y. N., Alfhaed, N. K., Almasaad, K. F., Mahanshi, R. Y., Farooqi, F., Al-Khalifa, K. S., & Gaffar, B. O. (2025). The impact of dental photography in social media platforms on patients' selection of dentists and type of treatment. *BMC Oral Health*, *25*(1), 111. DOI: 10.1186/s12903-025-05483-8

Alyousuf, A. N., Sabeeh, A. O., Alnaemat, N. D., Mouloudj, K., & Hussein, S. A. (2026). Understanding Gen Z's Adoption of AI Technologies in Green Product Purchases: An Extension of the Technology Acceptance Model. In Mouloudj, K., & Bouarar, A. (Eds.), *Insights on Consumer Psychology in the Digital Landscape* (pp. 369–392). IGI Global., DOI: 10.4018/979-8-3373-2424-1.ch013

Bouarar, A. C., Mouloudj, K., Čaušević, A., & Mouloudj, S. (2025). Investigating intentions to visit Sarajevo city: Expanding the theory of planned behavior. *Tourism and Hospitality Management*, *31*(3), 371–383. DOI: 10.20867/thm.31.3.4

Bui, T. T., Tran, Q. T., Alang, T., & Le, T. D. (2023). Examining the relationship between digital content marketing perceived value and brand loyalty: Insights from Vietnam. *Cogent Social Sciences*, *9*(1), 2225835. DOI: 10.1080/23311886.2023.2225835

Cham, T. H., Lim, Y. M., Sia, B. C., Cheah, J. H., & Ting, H. (2021). Medical tourism destination image and its relationship with the intention to revisit: A study of Chinese Medical tourists in Malaysia. *Journal of China Tourism Research, 17*(2), 163–191. DOI: 10.1080/19388160.2020.1734514

Dar, H., & Kashyap, K. (2025). Structural equation modeling (SEM) approach for envisaging the connotation among medical tourists' satisfaction, attitude and loyalty: A case of Delhi-NCR, India. *International Journal of Spa and Wellness*, *8*(2), 246–264. DOI: 10.1080/24721735.2025.2455867

de la Hoz-Correa, A., & Muñoz-Leiva, F. (2019). The role of information sources and image on the intention to visit a medical tourism destination: A cross-cultural analysis. *Journal of Travel & Tourism Marketing*, *36*(2), 204–219. DOI: 10.1080/10548408.2018.1507865

Farrukh, M., Shahzad, I. A., Sajid, M., Sheikh, M. F., & Alam, I. (2022). Revisiting the intention to travel framework in the perspective of medical tourism: The role of eWord-of-mouth and destination image. *International Journal of Healthcare Management*, *15*(1), 28–35. DOI: 10.1080/20479700.2020.1836733

Fengmin, Z., Baijun, W., Jiangtao, B., Li, L., & Patwary, A. K. (2022). Investigating revisit intention of medical tourists in China through nutritional knowledge, perceived medical quality, and trust in the physiologist: A recommendation on health tourism policy measures. *Frontiers in Public Health*, *10*, 893497. DOI: 10.3389/fpubh.2022.893497

Gan, T., Zheng, J., Li, W., Li, J., & Shen, J. (2023). Health and wellness tourists' motivation and behavior intention: The role of perceived value. *International Journal of Environmental Research and Public Health*, *20*(5), 4339. DOI: 10.3390/ijerph20054339

Habibi, A., & Rasoolimanesh, S. M. (2021). Experience and service quality on perceived value and behavioral intention: Moderating effect of perceived risk and fee. *Journal of Quality Assurance in Hospitality & Tourism*, *22*(6), 711–737. DOI: 10.1080/1528008X.2020.1837050

Han, H., & Hwang, J. (2018). Growing competition in the healthcare tourism market and customer retention in medical clinics: New and experienced travellers. *Current Issues in Tourism*, *21*(6), 680–702. DOI: 10.1080/13683500.2015.1104292

Han, H., & Hyun, S. S. (2015). Customer retention in the medical tourism industry: Impact of quality, satisfaction, trust, and price reasonableness. *Tourism Management*, *46*, 20–29. DOI: 10.1016/j.tourman.2014.06.003

Hennig-Thurau, T., Gwinner, K. P., Walsh, G., & Gremler, D. D. (2004). Electronic word of-mouth via consumer-opinion platforms: What motivates consumers to articulate themselves on the Internet? *Journal of Interactive Marketing*, *18*(1), 38–52. DOI: 10.1002/dir.10073

Hollebeek, L. D., & Macky, K. (2019). Digital Content Marketing's Role in Fostering Consumer Engagement, Trust, and Value: Framework, Fundamental Propositions, and Implications. *Journal of Interactive Marketing*, *45*(1), 27–41. DOI: 10.1016/j.intmar.2018.07.003

Horsfall, D., Lunt, N., King, H., Hanefeld, J., & Smith, R. D. (2013). The Impact of the Internet on Medical Tourism. In Botterill, D., Pennings, G., & Mainil, T. (Eds.), *Medical Tourism and Transnational Health Care* (pp. 223–239). Palgrave Macmillan., DOI: 10.1057/9781137338495_14

Jalilvand, M. R., & Heidari, A. (2017). Comparing face-to-face and electronic word-of-mouth in destination image formation: The case of Iran. *Information Technology & People*, *30*(4), 710–735. DOI: 10.1108/ITP-09-2016-0204

Jasim, Z. A., Alameri, S. A., Almado, A. A., Abdulrahman, F. Y., & Alyousuf, A. N. (2026). Investigating the Impact of Ethical Organizational Culture on Employee Retention. In Rodrigues, R., Mohanty, V., & Figueiredo, P. (Eds.), *Organizational Culture and Employee Experience in the AI-Driven Organization* (pp. 85–110). IGI Global., DOI: 10.4018/979-8-2600-0610-8.ch004

Kopmaz, B., Kitapci, N. S., Kitapci, O. C., Bulu, S. B., Aksu, P. K., Koksal, L., & Mumcu, G. (2019). Dental websites as new media tools for patients in dental health tourism. *Acta Informatica Medica*, *27*(2), 128–132. DOI: 10.5455/aim.2019.27.128-132

Luo, C., Hasan, N. A. M., Zamri bin Ahmad, A. M., & Lei, G. (2025). Influence of short video content on consumers purchase intentions on social media platforms with trust as a mediator. *Scientific Reports*, *15*(1), 16605. DOI: 10.1038/s41598-025-94994-z

Marković, S., Lončarić, D., & Lončarić, D. (2014). Service quality and customer satisfaction in the health care industry-towards health tourism market. *Tourism and Hospitality Management*, *20*(2), 155–170. DOI: 10.20867/thm.20.2.1

Meira, T. M., Prestes, J., Gasparello, G. G., Antelo, O. M., Pithon, M. M., & Tanaka, O. M. (2021). The effects of images posted to social media by orthodontists on public perception of professional credibility and willingness to become a client. *Progress in Orthodontics*, *22*(1), 7. DOI: 10.1186/s40510-021-00353-9

Modha, B. (2023). Exploring customer journeys in the context of dentistry: A case study. *Dentistry Journal*, *11*(3), 75. DOI: 10.3390/dj11030075

Mouloudj, K., Alameri, S. A. S., Evans, M. A., Almado, A. A. G., Mahmoud, B. I., & Asanza, D. M. (2026). Social marketing for health equity: Promoting preventive health behavior among women in rural communities. *International Journal of Environmental Research and Public Health*, *23*(5), 584. DOI: 10.3390/ijerph23050584

Nguyen, N. X., Tran, K., & Nguyen, T. A. (2021). Impact of service quality on in-patients' satisfaction, perceived value, and customer loyalty: A mixed-methods study from a developing country. *Patient Preference and Adherence*, *15*, 2523–2538. DOI: 10.2147/PPA.S333586

Nguyen Huu, T., Nguyen Ngoc, H., Nguyen Dai, L., Nguyen Thi Thu, D., Truc, L. N., & Nguyen Trong, L. (2024). Effect of tourist satisfaction on revisit intention in Can Tho City, Vietnam. *Cogent Business & Management*, *11*(1), 2322779. DOI: 10.1080/23311975.2024.2322779

Ponathil, A., Khasawneh, A., Byrne, K., & Chalil Madathil, K. (2021). Factors affecting the choice of a dental care provider by older adults based on online consumer reviews. *IISE Transactions on Healthcare Systems Engineering*, *11*(1), 51–69. DOI: 10.1080/24725579.2020.1854394

Qalati, S. A., Vela, E. G., Li, W., Dakhan, S. A., Hong Thuy, T. T., & Merani, S. H. (2021). Effects of perceived service quality, website quality, and reputation on purchase intention: The mediating and moderating roles of trust and perceived risk in online shopping. *Cogent Business & Management*, *8*(1), 1869363. DOI: 10.1080/23311975.2020.1869363

Ramos, K., & Cuamea, O. (2023). Dental tourism: Factors influencing travelers' revisit intention to the Mexican border. *International Journal of Tourism Cities*, *9*(3), 806–831. DOI: 10.1108/IJTC-03-2023-0046

Shen, X., & Wang, J. (2024). How short video marketing influences purchase intention in social commerce: The role of users' persona perception, shared values, and individual-level factors. *Humanities & Social Sciences Communications*, *11*(1), 290. DOI: 10.1057/s41599-024-02808-w

Sousa, B. M., & Alves, G. M. (2019). The role of relationship marketing in behavioural intentions of medical tourism services and guest experiences. *Journal of Hospitality and Tourism Insights*, *2*(3), 224–240. DOI: 10.1108/JHTI-05-2018-0032

Tuncer, I., Unusan, C., & Cobanoglu, C. (2021). Service quality, perceived value and customer satisfaction on behavioral intention in restaurants: An integrated structural model. *Journal of Quality Assurance in Hospitality & Tourism*, *22*(4), 447–475. DOI: 10.1080/1528008X.2020.1802390

Vafeiadis, M. (2023). Message interactivity and source credibility in online dental practice reviews: Responding to reviews triggers positive consumer reactions regardless of review valence. *Health Communication*, *38*(1), 80–90. DOI: 10.1080/10410236.2021.1935538

Velmurugan, R., Bhuvaneswari, R., & Thirumalaisamy, R. (2026). Dental Tourism Marketing: Attracting International Patient Strategies for Dental Clinics and Health Tourism Operators. In Şarkbay, Ö., & Kaya, A. (Eds.), *Next-Generation Treatment Methods and Destinations in Dental Health Tourism* (pp. 97–118). IGI Global., DOI: 10.4018/979-8-3373-4114-9.ch005

KEY TERMS AND DEFINITIONS

Customer Retention: The ability of a service provider to maintain long-term relationships with customers by encouraging repeat use of services and continued loyalty over time.

Dental Health Tourism: A form of medical tourism in which individuals travel to another country to obtain dental treatments, often motivated by factors such as affordability, quality of care, or service availability.

Digital Information Quality: The degree to which online information provided through digital platforms is accurate, reliable, complete, relevant, and useful for supporting customer decision-making.

Electronic Service Quality: The effectiveness and efficiency of services delivered through digital channels, including online communication, responsiveness, appointment systems, and virtual support.

Perceived Value: A customer's overall evaluation of the benefits received from a service in comparison with the financial, time, and effort-related costs involved.

Chapter 5

Assessing the Impact of Electronic Customer Relationship Management on the Business Performance of Private Dental Clinics

Sarah Ali Saeed Alameri
http://orcid.org/0000-0002-6587-6527
College of Administration and Economics, University of Baghdad, Iraq

Alaa Abdulkareem Ghaleb Almado
http://orcid.org/0009-0004-9524-3642
College of Administration and Economics, University of Baghdad, Iraq

Saadiyah Owaid Awni
Technical Institute of Management, Middle Technical University, Iraq

Yasmin Khudair Abbas Doori
Department of Business Administration, College of Administration and Economics, University of Baghdad, Iraq

Maryam Salim Jabbar
Department of Management Information Systems, College of Administration and Economics, University of Basrah, Iraq

Ahmed Abbas Hammadi
http://orcid.org/0000-0003-3767-3420
College of administration and economics, University of Fallujah, Iraq

Arafat Naser Jasim Alyousuf
http://orcid.org/0000-0003-1153-8618
University of Basrah, Iraq

DOI: 10.4018/979-8-3373-8894-6.ch005

ABSTRACT

This study investigates the impact of electronic customer relationship management (E-CRM) on the business performance of private dental clinics. It focuses on four dimensions: electronic patient data management, personalized electronic services, online appointment and scheduling systems, and electronic feedback and complaint management. A quantitative approach was used, with data collected from 95 employees in private dental clinics through a structured questionnaire. The results show that electronic patient data management, online appointment and scheduling systems, and electronic feedback and complaint management significantly enhance business performance, while personalized electronic services have no significant effect. Among all variables, online scheduling systems exert the strongest influence. The study contributes to the literature by extending E-CRM research to private dental clinics and provides practical implications for managers seeking to improve clinic performance through digital transformation.

INTRODUCTION

The growing digital transformation of business activities has significantly changed the way organizations interact with customers, manage information, and improve operational performance (Alnaemat et al., 2026; Alyousuf et al., 2026; Lin et al., 2025). In highly competitive service sectors, organizations increasingly rely on electronic customer relationship management (E-CRM) systems to strengthen customer relationships, improve service quality, and enhance organizational outcomes. CRM has evolved from a traditional administrative function into a strategic capability that integrates technology, people, and processes to create long-term customer value (Haislip & Richardson, 2017; Thai et al., 2024). This transformation has become particularly important in service industries where customer interaction, responsiveness, and information management directly influence organizational success (Jayapal, 2025).

The importance of CRM was emphasized early by Reinartz et al. (2004), who conceptualized CRM as a comprehensive organizational process consisting of customer initiation, maintenance, and termination activities. Their study demonstrated that effective CRM implementation is positively associated with both perceptual and objective organizational performance. Since then, CRM has increasingly been recognized as a strategic resource capable of improving customer retention, organizational efficiency, and competitive advantage (Heileman et al., 2026). Recent developments in digital technologies have accelerated the evolution of CRM into electronic and AI-driven systems. Modern E-CRM systems allow organizations to manage customer data electronically, automate communication processes, provide personalized services, and monitor customer feedback in real time. According to Soltani et al. (2018), CRM success is strongly influenced by information technology usage, customer orientation, organizational capability, and customer knowledge management. Their findings confirmed that organizations capable of integrating technological capabilities with customer-focused strategies achieve higher levels of organizational performance.

The integration of digital technologies into CRM activities has become increasingly important in environments characterized by intense competition and changing customer expectations (Thai et al., 2024). Wang and Kim (2017) argued that social media technologies and social CRM capabilities help organizations improve customer engagement and firm performance through dynamic marketing capabilities. Similarly, Jayachandran et al. (2005) emphasized that relational information processes and CRM technologies play a critical role in enhancing customer relationship performance. Their work highlighted that technology alone is insufficient unless accompanied by effective organizational routines and information-sharing processes. The relationship between CRM and organizational performance has also been widely supported in the strategic management literature. Coltman et al. (2011) demonstrated that superior CRM capability positively influences firm performance when organizations successfully combine IT infrastructure with organizational capabilities such as human analytics and business architecture. Their findings suggested that CRM initiatives emphasizing both customer intimacy and operational efficiency achieve better outcomes than narrowly focused strategies.

In recent years, artificial intelligence and data analytics have further expanded the capabilities of E-CRM systems. AI-driven CRM technologies can automate routine tasks, analyze large customer databases, predict customer preferences, and support managerial decision-making processes (Jayapal, 2025). Roba and Maric (2023) emphasized that AI-supported CRM systems improve customer analysis and strengthen long-term customer relationships through collaborative and analytical CRM functions. Likewise, Leelavathi et al. (2024) noted that AI-driven CRM systems enhance customer segmentation, personalized marketing strategies, chatbot communication, and predictive analytics, which collectively improve customer satisfaction and organizational success.

Artificial intelligence integration has also become increasingly important in improving organizational sustainability and decision-making efficiency (Alnaemat et al., 2026; Martínez Asanza et al., 2024). Chatterjee and Chaudhuri (2022) argued that AI-integrated CRM systems help organizations overcome challenges associated with analyzing large volumes of customer data while improving consistent decision-making and operational sustainability. Furthermore, Chatterjee and Chaudhuri (2023) explained that AI-CRM technologies contribute to organizational growth by automating routine activities, improving process efficiency, and supporting digital transformation in sales, marketing, and operational functions.

The increasing importance of data analytics in CRM systems has further enhanced organizations' ability to process and utilize customer information effectively (Heileman et al., 2026). Raj (2024) highlighted that modern CRM systems collect substantial customer information from multiple digital channels, including websites, social media, live chat, and marketing platforms. The study emphasized that data mining and artificial intelligence techniques significantly improve the efficiency of handling large customer databases and support customer retention and revenue generation.

Despite the growing importance of E-CRM across industries, its implementation within healthcare organizations remains relatively underexplored, particularly in developing countries and private healthcare contexts. Healthcare institutions increasingly operate in competitive environments where patient satisfaction, service quality, and operational efficiency determine organizational sustainability (Al-Hassan et al., 2026; Alyousuf et al., 2026; Bouarar et al., 2024; Keeling et al., 2025; Tubaishat, 2019). In this regard, CRM systems can provide healthcare providers with opportunities to strengthen patient relationships, improve communication, and optimize service delivery processes.

Private dental clinics represent an important segment of the healthcare industry where patient trust, personalized care, and timely service are essential for maintaining competitiveness (Martínez Asanza, 2025; Mouloudj et al., 2025). Healthcare organizations, including dental clinics, rely heavily on continuous patient interaction, accurate patient records, appointment scheduling, and follow-up communication (Adane et al., 2019; Douma et al., 2024; Lin et al., 2025). Consequently, the successful implementation of E-CRM systems may help clinics improve business performance through enhanced operational efficiency, stronger patient loyalty, and improved service quality.

Several studies conducted in service-related sectors support this assumption. For instance, Ofori and Appiah-Nimo (2022) found that customer relationship management contributes positively to competitive advantage in the hotel industry, which subsequently improves operational performance. Similarly, Ernst et al. (2011) demonstrated that CRM positively affects new product performance and company performance by improving the utilization of customer information within organizations. Additional evidence was provided by Valmohammadi (2017), who found that CRM practices positively influence organizational performance and innovation capability. Chang et al. (2014) also reported that effective CRM relational information processes enhance customer satisfaction, positive word-of-mouth, and profitability. Likewise, Das and Hassan (2022) confirmed that CRM significantly contributes to organizational performance alongside sustainable supply chain management practices.

More recent studies have reinforced the strategic importance of CRM in improving organizational competitiveness and customer loyalty (Haislip & Richardson, 2017; Heileman et al., 2026). Attia (2023) demonstrated that CRM positively influences competitive advantage and organizational performance in the Egyptian textile industry. Similarly, Khan et al. (2022) found that CRM significantly improves customer loyalty through the mediating role of customer satisfaction and company reputation.

Within hospitality and healthcare contexts, CRM implementation has become increasingly relevant in enhancing organizational outcomes. Hat et al. (2025) showed that digital marketing capabilities strengthen the relationship between CRM and hospitality business performance. In the healthcare sector, Sharma et al. (2025) emphasized the importance of integrated digital care pathways, national health identity systems, and health literacy in supporting CRM adoption within public healthcare systems.

Recent literature also indicates that personalized electronic services, online appointment management systems, electronic patient data management, and electronic feedback systems are among the most influential dimensions of E-CRM. These dimensions improve responsiveness, service accessibility, and customer experience while simultaneously supporting organizational efficiency and competitiveness. Furthermore, Ozay et al. (2024) concluded that AI-based CRM systems significantly improve customer engagement and operational efficiency through data-driven CRM strategies and customer experience management.

Although prior studies have extensively examined CRM in manufacturing, hospitality, retail, and supply chain sectors, limited empirical research has focused on the effect of E-CRM practices on the business performance of private dental clinics. This gap is particularly evident in emerging economies where healthcare digitalization remains in a developmental stage. Therefore, this study seeks to assess the impact of electronic customer relationship management on the business performance of private dental clinics by focusing on four major dimensions: electronic patient data management, personalized electronic services, online appointment and scheduling systems, and electronic feedback and complaint management.

The study contributes to the growing E-CRM literature by extending CRM research into the private dental healthcare context and by providing empirical evidence regarding the role of digital customer relationship practices in improving organizational performance. It also offers practical insights for clinic managers seeking to enhance competitiveness and service quality through digital transformation initiatives.

LITERATURE REVIEW AND HYPOTHESES DEVELOPMENT

Business Performance

Business performance is considered one of the most important indicators used to evaluate the success and sustainability of organizations in competitive environments. It reflects the extent to which organizations achieve their strategic objectives through the efficient utilization of resources, effective operational processes, and the delivery of high-quality services. In service industries such as healthcare and tourism, business performance is not limited to financial outcomes alone, but also includes operational efficiency, customer satisfaction, service quality, competitiveness, employee and customer retention (Al-Hassan et al., 2026; Jasim et al., 2026; Lin et al., 2025). For private dental clinics, maintaining strong business performance is essential due to increasing competition, rising patient expectations, and the growing dependence on digital technologies (Bouarar et al., 2024; Mouloudj et al., 2025).

Previous studies have emphasized that business performance is multidimensional and influenced by both organizational and technological capabilities. Reinartz et al. (2004) found that effective customer relationship management contributes positively to organizational performance through improved customer interactions and retention. Similarly, Coltman et al. (2011) argued that superior CRM capability enhances firm performance when supported by organizational competencies and technological infrastructure. Their findings highlighted that organizations capable of integrating customer-focused strategies with operational processes achieve stronger performance outcomes.

In service-oriented organizations, performance improvement is often linked to customer satisfaction, safety, operational efficiency, and green practices (Al-Hassan et al., 2026; Douma et al., 2024; Tubaishat, 2019). Chang et al. (2014) reported that effective CRM relational information processes improve customer satisfaction and profitability by enhancing customer acquisition and retention activities. Likewise, Das and Hassan (2022) confirmed that CRM practices significantly improve organizational performance by strengthening customer-oriented operations and managerial efficiency.

In the healthcare sector, business performance is closely associated with service responsiveness, patient trust, and the quality of healthcare delivery. Private dental clinics particularly depend on maintaining positive patient experiences because patient loyalty and word-of-mouth recommendations strongly influence long-term sustainability (Mouloudj et al., 2025). Efficient appointment systems, personalized communication, and rapid complaint handling can contribute directly to clinic productivity and competitiveness (Martínez Asanza et al., 2024).

Furthermore, digital transformation has reshaped the measurement of business performance by emphasizing customer-centered indicators. Studies such as Hat et al. (2025) and Sharma et al. (2025) highlighted the growing importance of digital capabilities in improving organizational responsiveness and service effectiveness. Consequently, organizations increasingly evaluate performance through both financial and non-financial indicators, including service quality, operational efficiency, patient satisfaction, and competitive advantage.

In this study, business performance refers to the extent to which private dental clinics achieve operational efficiency, service effectiveness, competitiveness, and overall organizational improvement through the implementation of E-CRM practices. Table 1 summarizes the major dimensions and perspectives of business performance identified in previous studies and highlights their relevance within service-oriented organizations such as private dental clinics.

Table 1. Summary of the main dimensions and perspectives of business performance

Dimension	Description	References
Operational Efficiency	Refers to improving internal processes, reducing delays, and enhancing workflow efficiency.	Haislip and Richardson (2017); Das & Hassan (2022)
Service Quality	Represents the clinic's ability to provide reliable, responsive, and high-quality healthcare services.	Chang et al. (2014); Sharma et al. (2025)
Customer/Patient Satisfaction	Reflects patients' positive evaluation of services and their overall healthcare experience.	Khan et al. (2022); Reinartz et al. (2004)
Customer Retention and Loyalty	Indicates the clinic's ability to maintain long-term relationships with patients and encourage repeated visits.	Ernst et al. (2011); Thai et al. (2024)
Competitive Advantage	Refers to the clinic's ability to differentiate itself from competitors through superior services and digital capabilities.	Ofori and Appiah-Nimo (2022); Attia (2023)
Financial and Organizational Outcomes	Includes profitability, growth, service effectiveness, and organizational sustainability.	Valmohammadi (2017); Coltman et al. (2011)

Source: Authors' own work

Electronic Customer Relationship Management (E-CRM)

E-CRM refers to the use of digital technologies, internet-based systems, and electronic communication tools to manage and strengthen relationships between organizations and customers. Unlike traditional CRM systems, E-CRM integrates information technology into customer interaction processes, enabling organizations to collect, analyze, and utilize customer information more efficiently. E-CRM systems support organizations in improving communication, personalizing services, managing customer data, and enhancing customer satisfaction and loyalty.

The development of E-CRM has been strongly associated with the rapid advancement of information technology and digital transformation. Soltani et al. (2018) described CRM as a strategic business approach that utilizes customer information to improve relationships and organizational performance. The authors emphasized that information technology use, customer orientation, and organizational capability are among the key determinants of successful CRM implementation.

Modern E-CRM systems rely heavily on digital communication channels, electronic databases, and automated customer service tools. Wang and Kim (2017) argued that social CRM capabilities enable organizations to improve customer engagement and business performance through social media integration and dynamic marketing capabilities. Similarly, Jayachandran et al. (2005) highlighted the importance of relational information processes in improving customer relationship performance and organizational responsiveness.

The increasing integration of artificial intelligence and data analytics has further enhanced E-CRM capabilities. Roba and Maric (2023) explained that AI-supported CRM systems improve customer analysis, automate communication processes, and facilitate long-term customer relationship management. Leelavathi et al. (2024) also noted that AI-driven CRM technologies improve personalized marketing, predictive analytics, and customer interaction efficiency. These technologies help organizations better understand customer preferences and provide more tailored services.

In healthcare organizations, E-CRM systems play a crucial role in improving patient-centered services. Healthcare providers increasingly use electronic systems for appointment scheduling, patient record management, follow-up communication, and complaint handling (Dubovitskaya et al., 2020; Keeling et al., 2025). Sharma et al. (2025) emphasized that digitalized healthcare systems and integrated patient information systems are essential for improving healthcare responsiveness and service quality.

For private dental clinics, E-CRM systems can improve operational efficiency and strengthen patient relationships by facilitating electronic patient data management, personalized communication, online scheduling, and electronic feedback management. These practices contribute to improving patient experiences while supporting the clinic's overall business performance and competitiveness. Table 2 presents the major dimensions and functions of E-CRM identified in the literature and demonstrate how these dimensions contribute to improving organizational performance and customer relationships.

Table 2. Summary of the main dimensions and functions of E-CRM

E-CRM Dimension	Description	References
Electronic Patient Data Management	Involves storing, organizing, and accessing patient information electronically for efficient service delivery.	Soltani et al. (2018); Raj (2024)
Personalized Electronic Services	Refers to customized communication and tailored services based on patient preferences and needs.	Leelavathi et al. (2024); Jayapal (2025)
Online Appointment and Scheduling Systems	Enables patients to book appointments electronically and improves scheduling efficiency.	Sharma et al. (2025); Wang and Kim (2017)
Electronic Feedback and Complaint Management	Facilitates the collection and management of patient feedback and complaints through digital platforms.	Chang et al. (2014); Khan et al. (2022)
AI and Data Analytics Integration	Uses AI technologies and predictive analytics to improve customer insights and decision-making.	Roba and Maric (2023); Ozay et al. (2024)
Customer Engagement and Communication	Enhances interaction between organizations and customers through digital communication channels.	Jayachandran et al. (2005); Wang and Kim (2017)

Source: Authors' own work

Hypotheses Development

Electronic Patient Data Management and Business Performance

Electronic patient data management refers to the use of digital systems to collect, organize, store, and retrieve patient information accurately and efficiently. In health care management, patient data management is particularly important because clinics depend heavily on maintaining detailed records related to patient medical histories, treatment plans, appointments, and follow-up services (Keeling et al., 2025; Lin et al., 2025; Tapuria et al., 2021). Effective electronic management of patient information helps clinics reduce administrative errors, improve service speed, and enhance communication among healthcare staff (Abdolkhani et al., 2019; Adane et al., 2019; Damen et al., 2022). Compared to traditional paper-based systems, electronic databases (e.g., "blockchain-based electronic health record data management ") facilitate faster access to patient records and support more efficient decision-making processes (Dubovitskaya et al., 2020; Martínez Asanza et al., 2024). Previous studies have emphasized the importance of information management within CRM systems for improving organizational performance. Reinartz et al. (2004) argued that effective CRM processes improve organizational outcomes by enhancing customer information management and relationship maintenance. Similarly, Soltani et al. (2018) found that information technology use and customer knowledge management significantly contribute to CRM success and organizational performance. Raj (2024) further explained that modern CRM systems rely on efficient data collection and processing capabilities to improve customer interaction and operational efficiency.

Within healthcare environments, accurate and accessible patient information contributes directly to service quality, responsiveness, and operational efficiency (Damen et al., 2022; Douma et al., 2024; Tapuria et al., 2021; Tubaishat, 2019; Yu & Qian, 2018). Electronic patient data systems also help reduce delays and improve coordination among clinic employees, which can positively influence patient satisfaction and clinic productivity (Dubovitskaya et al., 2020; Keeling et al., 2025; Lin et al., 2025). Therefore, private dental clinics that effectively manage patient data electronically are expected to achieve stronger business performance outcomes. Consequently, the following hypothesis has been proposed:

H1. Electronic patient data management has a positive impact on the business performance of private dental clinics.

Personalized Electronic Services and Business Performance

Personalized electronic services refer to the ability of organizations to provide customized digital interactions and tailored services based on customer preferences, needs, and previous experiences. In the context of the services sector, personalized electronic services may include customized appointment reminders, individualized treatment follow-ups, tailored communication, and personalized healthcare recommendations (Krishnaraju et al., 2016; Maksimova et al., 2021). These services contribute to improving patient experiences by making communication more responsive, interactive, and patient-centered (Douma et al., 2024). The relationship marketing literature suggests that personalization is a critical component of successful customer relationship management because it strengthens customer trust, engagement, and satisfaction (Mouloudj et al., 2025). Wang and Kim (2017) argued that social CRM capabilities and digital interaction tools enhance customer engagement and organizational performance by facilitating personalized communication strategies. Similarly, Leelavathi et al. (2024) emphasized that AI-driven CRM systems improve customer satisfaction through personalized marketing, predictive analytics, and customized interactions. Jayapal (2025) also found that AI-driven personalization positively influences customer loyalty through increased trust, engagement, and perceived value.

In healthcare settings, personalized electronic communication can improve patient confidence and strengthen long-term relationships between clinics and patients. Dental clinics that provide customized digital services are more likely to improve patient retention and increase service effectiveness. Furthermore, personalized services can enhance operational performance by improving communication efficiency and reducing misunderstandings between service providers and customers (Krishnaraju et al., 2016; Maksimova et al., 2021). Consequently, personalized electronic services may contribute positively to the overall business performance of private dental clinics. Accordingly, the following hypothesis has been developed:

H2. Personalized electronic services have a positive impact on the business performance of private dental clinics.

Online Appointment and Scheduling Systems and Business Performance

Online appointment and scheduling systems refer to digital platforms that enable patients to book, modify, and manage appointments electronically. These systems represent one of the most widely used E-CRM applications in healthcare organizations because they improve service accessibility and reduce administrative burdens. In private dental clinics, appointment scheduling efficiency is essential for managing patient flow, minimizing waiting times, and improving resource utilization. Electronic scheduling systems also help clinics optimize staff coordination and reduce appointment conflicts or cancellations. Previous research has highlighted the role of digital technologies in improving customer relationship processes and organizational efficiency. Jayachandran et al. (2005) emphasized that CRM technologies enhance customer relationship performance when integrated with effective organizational processes. Likewise, Haislip and Richardson (2017) found that CRM system implementation improves operational efficiency and organizational performance through better management processes and improved operational outcomes. Wang and Kim (2017) further explained that digital technologies and social CRM systems improve organizational responsiveness and customer engagement.

Within healthcare contexts, efficient scheduling systems contribute significantly to patient satisfaction because long waiting times and poor appointment management negatively affect service experiences. Sharma et al. (2025) stressed the importance of integrated digital healthcare systems in improving service delivery and healthcare responsiveness. In private dental clinics, online scheduling systems can improve operational efficiency by facilitating appointment organization, reducing administrative workload, and enhancing patient convenience. These improvements are likely to contribute positively to the clinic's business performance and competitiveness. Therefore, the following hypothesis has been formulated:

H3. Online appointment and scheduling systems have a positive impact on the business performance of private dental clinics.

Electronic Feedback and Complaint Management and Business Performance

Electronic feedback and complaint management refers to the use of digital platforms and communication technologies to collect, monitor, and respond to customer feedback and complaints efficiently. In private dental clinics, patient feedback plays a crucial role in evaluating service quality, identifying operational weaknesses, and improving healthcare delivery. Electronic feedback systems enable clinics to interact with patients more quickly and transparently, while digital complaint management systems facilitate timely problem resolution and strengthen patient trust.

CRM literature consistently emphasizes the importance of customer interaction and responsiveness in improving organizational performance. Chang et al. (2014) found that effective CRM relational information processes positively influence customer satisfaction, positive word-of-mouth communication, and profitability. Similarly, Khan et al. (2022) reported that CRM practices significantly improve customer loyalty through enhanced customer satisfaction and company reputation. The ability to respond effectively to customer concerns helps organizations maintain stronger customer relationships and improve long-term competitiveness.

In healthcare organizations, rapid complaint resolution and active patient feedback management contribute significantly to service improvement and patient retention. Customers are more likely to trust organizations that demonstrate responsiveness and willingness to address concerns professionally (Breitsohl et al., 2010). Furthermore, electronic feedback systems provide clinics with valuable information that can support continuous service improvement and operational decision-making (Nuansi & Ngamcharoenmongkol, 2021). Consequently, private dental clinics that effectively manage patient feedback and complaints electronically are expected to achieve stronger business performance outcomes. Hence, the following hypothesis has been suggested:

H4. Electronic feedback and complaint management positively influences the business performance of private dental clinics.

METHODOLOGY

Questionnaire Design

This study adopted a quantitative research methodology to investigate the impact of E-CRM on the business performance of private dental clinics in Iraq. A structured questionnaire was used as the primary instrument for data collection. The questionnaire consisted of two main sections comprising 15 items designed to measure the four independent variables and one dependent variable included in the research model. The first section collected demographic information related to the respondents, including gender, age, educational level, years of experience, and type of clinic. These variables were included to provide a clearer understanding of the characteristics of the study sample and to support the interpretation of the findings.

The second section measured the key constructs of the study, namely electronic patient data management, personalized electronic services, online appointment and scheduling systems, electronic feedback and complaint management, and business performance. Each construct was measured using three items evaluated on a five-point Likert scale ranging from "strongly disagree" (1) to "strongly agree" (5). The measurement items were adapted from previous studies and modified to suit the context of private dental clinics. Specifically, the items for electronic patient data management were adapted from Yu and Qian (2018), while the personalized electronic services items were adapted from Krishnaraju et al. (2016). The measurement items related to online appointment and scheduling systems were developed by the authors based on the objectives of the study and the operational characteristics of private dental clinics. In addition, the electronic feedback and complaint management items were adapted from Nuansi and Ngamcharoenmongkol (2021). Finally, the business performance scale was adapted from Reinartz et al. (2004) and Hat et al. (2025).

The questionnaire was originally developed in English and subsequently translated into Arabic, which represents the primary language of the respondents. To ensure translation accuracy and conceptual consistency, a back-translation procedure was performed by two independent experts specializing in business and management studies. Furthermore, three experts in customer relationship management and healthcare management were invited to review the questionnaire and evaluate the clarity, relevance, and suitability of the measurement items. Based on their feedback, several revisions and wording improvements were introduced to enhance content validity. Before conducting the final survey, the authors carried out a pilot study involving ten participants working in private dental clinics to assess the clarity and initial reliability of the questionnaire. Feedback obtained from the pilot study led to minor modifications, including simplifying several statements and improving item wording to ensure better respondent understanding.

Additionally, several procedural measures were implemented to minimize the potential risk of common method bias. The anonymity and confidentiality of respondents were fully ensured to encourage honest responses. The questionnaire items were organized systematically according to construct categories, and all questions were written using simple, neutral, and non-leading language to reduce response bias and improve data quality. Table 3 presents the final measurement items used in this study.

Table 3. Constructs and items description

Constructs	Items
Electronic Patient Data Management (EPDM)	EPDM1. Our clinic maintains accurate electronic records for patients. EPDM2.Patient information can be accessed quickly through the electronic system. EPDM3. Electronic systems help organize patient data efficiently.
Personalized Electronic Services (PES)	PES1. The clinic provides personalized electronic communication with patients. PES2. Electronic systems help deliver customized follow-up services to patients. PES3. The clinic uses digital platforms to better understand patient needs and preferences.
Online Appointment and Scheduling Systems (OASS)	OASS1. The online appointment system makes booking easier for patients. OASS2. Electronic scheduling systems help reduce patient waiting times. OASS3. Online scheduling improves the efficiency of clinic operations.
Electronic Feedback and Complaint Management (EFCM)	EFCM1. The clinic effectively collects patient feedback through electronic channels. EFCM2. Electronic systems help address patient complaints quickly. EFCM3. Online feedback systems contribute to improving service quality in the clinic.
Business Performance (BP)	BP1. Electronic systems have improved the overall performance of our clinic. BP2. The clinic has achieved higher operational efficiency through E-CRM practices. BP3. E-CRM applications contribute to enhancing the clinic's competitiveness and service quality.

Source: Authors' own work

Data Collection Procedure

The data collection process was conducted using a convenience sampling technique due to the accessibility and availability of respondents working in private dental clinics. Through a network of friends, professional contacts, and colleagues, the questionnaires were distributed to employees working in different private dental clinics. A total of 160 questionnaires were sent to potential participants who were over the age of 18 and actively involved in the daily operations of dental clinics. This criterion ensured that respondents possessed sufficient knowledge and practical experience regarding E-CRM practices and clinic performance.

Participants were invited to voluntarily complete the paper-based questionnaire. Before participation, respondents were informed about the purpose of the study and assured that their responses would remain anonymous and confidential. They were also informed that there were no right or wrong answers and that participation was entirely voluntary. Furthermore, participants were advised that they could withdraw from the study at any stage without any consequences. Verbal consent was obtained from all participants prior to data collection. The data collection process was carried out over a two-month period, from November to December 2025. At the end of the collection period, 104 completed questionnaires were returned. After careful screening and data verification, 9 questionnaires were excluded due to incomplete or inconsistent responses. Consequently, the final valid sample consisted of 95 questionnaires, which were considered suitable for statistical analysis and hypothesis testing.

RESULTS

Demographic Profile of Respondents

Table 4 presents the demographic characteristics of the respondents participating in the study. The sample consisted of 95 employees working in private dental clinics. Regarding gender, male respondents represented 52.63% of the sample, while females accounted for 47.37%, indicating a relatively balanced distribution between male and female participants. With respect to age, the largest proportion of respondents belonged to the 41–50 years category (32.63%), followed by the 30–40 years category (26.32%). Respondents aged 51 years and above represented 24.21% of the sample, while employees younger than 30 years accounted for 16.84%. In terms of educational level, bachelor's degree holders represented the highest percentage (38.95%), followed by respondents with master's degrees or above (29.47%). Diploma holders accounted for 25.26%, whereas respondents with secondary education or below represented only 6.32% of the sample. Regarding years of experience, employees with 11–15 years of experience represented the largest group (35.79%), followed by those with 5–10 years of experience (33.68%). Respondents with more than 15 years of experience accounted for 18.95%, while employees with less than 5 years of experience represented 11.58%. Finally, medium-sized clinics constituted the largest proportion of the sample (56.84%), followed by large clinics (25.26%) and small clinics (17.89%).

Table 4. Profile of respondents (N = 95)

Variables	Category	Responses	Percentage
Gender	Male	50	52.36
	Female	45	47.37
Age (years)	Less than 30 years	16	16.84
	30–40 years	25	26.32
	41–50 years	31	32.63
	51 years and above	23	24.21
Educational Background	Secondary education or below	06	06.32
	Diploma	24	25.26
	Bachelor's degree	37	38.95
	Master's degree or above	28	29.47
Years of Experience	Less than 5 years	11	11.58
	5–10 years	32	33.68
	11–15 years	34	35.79
	More than 15 years	18	18.95
Type of Clinic	Small clinic	17	17.89
	Medium-sized clinic	54	56.84
	Large clinic	24	25.26

Descriptive Statistics, Reliability, and Correlation Analysis

Table 5 presents the descriptive statistics, reliability analysis, and correlation coefficients among the study variables. The mean values ranged from 3.14 to 4.04, indicating generally positive perceptions among respondents toward the implementation of E-CRM practices and business performance in private dental clinics. Business performance recorded the highest mean value (M = 4.04), followed by online appointment and scheduling systems (M = 3.87) and electronic patient data management (M = 3.86). Personalized electronic services achieved a mean score of 3.58, while electronic feedback and complaint management reported the lowest mean value (M = 3.14). These findings suggest that respondents perceived online scheduling systems and electronic patient data management practices more positively than feedback and complaint management practices.

The reliability analysis demonstrated satisfactory internal consistency for all study constructs. Cronbach's alpha values ranged from 0.758 to 0.901, exceeding the recommended threshold of 0.70 (Jasim et al., 2026). Online appointment and scheduling systems reported the highest reliability coefficient ($\alpha = 0.901$), followed by personalized electronic services ($\alpha = 0.872$) and electronic patient data management ($\alpha = 0.870$). Business performance achieved a reliability coefficient of 0.827, while electronic feedback and complaint management recorded the lowest but still acceptable reliability value ($\alpha = 0.758$). These results confirm the adequacy and consistency of the measurement scales used in the study.

Regarding correlation analysis, the results revealed significant positive relationships among all variables at the 0.01 significance level. Business performance showed the strongest positive correlation with online appointment and scheduling systems ($r = 0.832$, $p < 0.01$), followed by electronic patient data management ($r = 0.757$, $p < 0.01$). Electronic feedback and complaint management also demonstrated a positive relationship with Business Performance ($r = 0.609$, $p < 0.01$), while personalized electronic services showed a moderate positive correlation with business performance ($r = 0.581$, $p < 0.01$).

Table 5. Descriptive statistics and correlation analysis

Constructs	1	2	3	4	5
1. EPDM	-				
2. Personalized Electronic Services	0.612**	-			
3. OASS	0.706**	0.560**	-		
4. EFCM	0.523**	0.332**	0.558**	-	
5. Business Performance	0.757**	0.581**	0.832**	0.609**	-
Mean	3.86	3.58	3.87	3.14	4.04
Cronbach's alpha (α)	0.870	0.872	0.901	0.758	0.827

Note: Electronic Patient Data Management (EPDM); Online Appointment and Scheduling Systems (OASS); Electronic Feedback and Complaint Management (EFCM). **. Correlation is significant at the 0.01 level (2-tailed).

Hypotheses Testing Results

Table 6 presents the results of the multiple regression analysis conducted to examine the impact of electronic customer relationship management dimensions on the business performance of private dental clinics. The overall regression model was statistically significant ($F = 74.705$, $p < 0.001$). The adjusted R^2 value of 0.758 demonstrates that approximately 75.8% of the variation in business performance is explained by the four E-CRM dimensions included in the model, suggesting strong explanatory power.

The results revealed that electronic patient data management had a positive and significant effect on business performance ($\beta = 0.219$, $t = 3.328$, $p = 0.001$). Therefore, H1 was supported. This finding indicates that efficient electronic management of patient information contributes positively to operational effectiveness and overall clinic performance. Similarly, online appointment and scheduling systems showed the strongest positive effect on business performance ($\beta = 0.471$, $t = 6.604$, $p < 0.001$). Accordingly, H3 was supported. This result suggests that effective online scheduling systems play a critical role in improving operational efficiency, patient convenience, and service delivery within private dental clinics. Electronic feedback and complaint management also demonstrated a positive and statistically significant relationship with business performance ($\beta = 0.216$, $t = 2.535$, $p = 0.013$). Thus, H4 was supported. The finding implies that digital feedback systems and effective complaint handling mechanisms contribute to enhancing organizational performance and patient satisfaction.

However, personalized electronic services did not show a statistically significant impact on Business Performance ($\beta = 0.086$, $t = 1.215$, $p = 0.228$). Therefore, H2 was not supported. This result may indicate that personalized electronic services are still insufficiently developed or not fully integrated into operational activities within private dental clinics.

Furthermore, the "variance inflation factor" (VIF) values ranged between 1.532 and 2.431, remaining well below the recommended threshold of 5.0, which confirms the absence of multicollinearity issues among the independent variables (Alyousuf et al., 2026).

Table 6. Hypotheses tests

Hypotheses	Path	β	t	Sig.	VIF	Decision
H1	EPDM→ BP	0.219	3.328	0.001	2.431	Accepted
H2	PES → BP	0.086	1.215	0.228	1.693	Rejected
H3	OASS→ BP	0.471	6.604	0.000	2.339	Accepted
H4	EFCM→ BP	0.216	2.535	0.013	1.532	Accepted

Note: Electronic Patient Data Management (EPDM); Personalized Electronic Services (PES); Online Appointment and Scheduling Systems (OASS); Electronic Feedback and Complaint Management (EFCM); Business Performance (BP); Adjusted R2= 0.758; F = 74.705 (p<0.001)

DISCUSSION

The findings of this study revealed that electronic patient data management has a significant positive impact on the business performance of private dental clinics. This result indicates that clinics capable of organizing, storing, and retrieving patient information efficiently are more likely to achieve better operational outcomes and service effectiveness (Douma et al., 2024; Dubovitskaya et al., 2020; Lin et al., 2025; Tapuria et al., 2021; Tubaishat, 2019). In healthcare settings, patient information represents a strategic resource that directly influences service speed, treatment coordination, and decision-making quality (Abdolkhani et al., 2019; Damen et al., 2022; Keeling et al., 2025; Yu & Qian, 2018). The result suggests that electronic systems help reduce administrative inefficiencies and improve workflow management within dental clinics. Adane et al. (2019) stated that "poor medical data processing systems are the key reasons for medical errors". This finding is consistent with the study by Reinartz et al. (2004), which emphasized that CRM processes improve organizational performance through effective customer information management. The result also aligns with Soltani et al. (2018), who found that information technology usage and customer knowledge management are major determinants of CRM success. In the context of private clinics, accurate patient data management may also improve communication among staff and reduce service delays, ultimately contributing to stronger organizational performance and patient satisfaction (Dubovitskaya et al., 2020; Keeling et al., 2025; Lin et al., 2025).

The results also demonstrated that personalized electronic services do not significantly influence business performance in private dental clinics. Although personalized communication and tailored services are widely recognized as important dimensions of modern electronic services (Krishnaraju et al., 2016; Maksimova et al., 2021), their effect was statistically insignificant in the present study. One possible explanation is that many private dental clinics may still rely on basic digital systems that focus primarily on operational activities rather than advanced personalization features. In addition, patients visiting dental clinics may prioritize treatment quality, appointment availability, and professional competence more than personalized digital interactions. This finding partially differs from previous studies such as Wang and Kim (2017), who argued that personalized digital engagement strengthens customer relationships and enhances organizational performance. It also contrasts with the findings of Leelavathi et al. (2024) and Jayapal (2025), which highlighted the importance of AI-driven personalization in improving customer satisfaction and loyalty. However, the insignificant result may reflect the relatively early stage of digital transformation in private healthcare clinics, where personalized E-CRM practices are not yet fully integrated into daily operations.

Among all examined variables, online appointment and scheduling systems showed the strongest positive influence on business performance. This result highlights the central role of scheduling efficiency in healthcare organizations, particularly in private dental clinics where patient flow management and time coordination are essential for operational success. Efficient online scheduling systems appear to improve clinic productivity by reducing waiting times, minimizing appointment conflicts, and facilitating smoother communication between patients and clinic staff (Mouloudj et al., 2025). In practical terms, digital appointment systems may also contribute to better resource allocation and improved patient experiences, which can strengthen clinic competitiveness (Martínez Asanza, 2025). The result strongly supports prior research emphasizing the importance of CRM technologies in enhancing organizational efficiency. For example, Haislip and Richardson (2017) found that CRM implementation contributes positively to operational performance and efficiency improvements. Likewise, Sharma et al. (2025) emphasized the importance of integrated digital healthcare systems in improving service responsiveness. The strong effect observed in this study suggests that scheduling-related digital services represent one of the most visible and impactful E-CRM practices within private dental clinics.

The findings further revealed that electronic feedback and complaint management positively influences business performance. This result reflects the importance of maintaining open digital communication channels with customers (i.e., patients) and responding effectively to their concerns (Breitsohl et al., 2010). In healthcare environments, patient feedback serves as an important source of information for identifying service weaknesses and improving the quality of care. Organizations that actively manage customers' complaints through electronic systems may build stronger trust relationships with customers while simultaneously improving service quality and organizational responsiveness (Nuansi & Ngamcharoenmongkol, 2021). Unlike traditional complaint procedures, digital feedback systems allow clinics to address issues more rapidly and systematically, which may enhance patient perceptions and loyalty. This finding is consistent with Chang et al. (2014), who reported that CRM relational information processes improve customer satisfaction and profitability through better customer interaction. The result also agrees with Khan et al. (2022), who found that CRM practices positively influence customer loyalty and organizational reputation. In the context of private dental clinics, effective electronic feedback management may therefore contribute not only to patient retention but also to long-term organizational sustainability and competitive advantage.

MANAGERIAL IMPLICATIONS

The findings of this study offer several important managerial implications for administrators and decision-makers in private dental clinics. First, the strong impact of electronic patient data management and online appointment and scheduling systems highlights the necessity of prioritizing core operational digital tools within E-CRM strategies. Clinic managers should invest in integrated patient information systems that ensure accuracy, accessibility, and real-time updates of patient records.

This not only improves internal coordination among staff but also enhances service efficiency and reduces waiting times. Similarly, the significant role of online scheduling systems suggests that clinics should adopt user-friendly digital platforms that allow patients to book, modify, and confirm appointments easily, thereby improving patient flow management and overall service productivity.

In addition, the positive influence of electronic feedback and complaint management emphasizes the importance of maintaining continuous communication channels with patients. Managers should implement structured digital feedback systems that enable patients to express concerns and receive timely responses. This can strengthen patient trust, improve service quality, and support continuous improvement initiatives within clinics. Although personalized electronic services did not show a significant impact, managers should not overlook their long-term strategic value. Instead, they may consider gradually enhancing personalization features as digital maturity increases. Overall, the study suggests that successful E-CRM implementation in private dental clinics requires a balanced focus on operational efficiency, patient engagement, and responsive communication systems to achieve sustainable business performance.

LIMITATIONS AND FUTURE RESEARCH

Despite its valuable findings, this study has several limitations that should be acknowledged. First, the research relied on a relatively small sample of 95 employees from private dental clinics, which may limit the generalizability of the results to other healthcare settings or larger populations. Second, the study adopted a cross-sectional design, which captures perceptions at a single point in time and does not allow for the examination of changes in E-CRM implementation or business performance over time. Third, the data were collected using self-reported questionnaires, which may introduce common method bias and subjective interpretation of responses. Finally, the study focused on four specific dimensions of E-CRM, while other potentially relevant factors such as organizational culture, technological readiness, and management support were not included in the model.

Future research is encouraged to address these limitations by using larger and more diverse samples, including clinics from different regions and healthcare systems. Longitudinal research designs could also be applied to better understand how E-CRM implementation influences business performance over time. In addition, future studies may extend the current model by incorporating mediating or moderating variables such as customer satisfaction, employee digital competence, or organizational support. Comparative studies between public and private healthcare institutions could also provide deeper insights into the effectiveness of E-CRM systems across different contexts. Finally, qualitative or mixed-method approaches may enrich understanding by exploring how E-CRM is actually implemented in practice within dental clinics and how employees perceive its benefits and challenges.

CONCLUSION

This study examined the impact of E-CRM on the business performance of private dental clinics by focusing on four key dimensions: electronic patient data management, personalized electronic services, online appointment and scheduling systems, and electronic feedback and complaint management. The empirical results demonstrated that three dimensions "electronic patient data management, online appointment and scheduling systems, and electronic feedback and complaint management" have a significant positive influence on business performance, highlighting their essential role in improving operational efficiency, service quality, and patient-centered care. However, personalized electronic services were found to have no significant effect, suggesting that such practices may still be underdeveloped or not fully integrated into clinic operations. Overall, the study confirms that E-CRM is a critical strategic tool for enhancing the performance of private dental clinics in an increasingly digital healthcare environment. It also emphasizes that clinics should prioritize the development of functional digital systems that directly support operational processes and patient interaction. The findings contribute to the growing body of literature on E-CRM in healthcare and provide practical guidance for clinic managers aiming to strengthen competitiveness and sustainability through digital transformation.

REFERENCES

Abdolkhani, R., Gray, K., Borda, A., & DeSouza, R. (2019). Patient-generated health data management and quality challenges in remote patient monitoring. *JAMIA Open*, *2*(4), 471–478. DOI: 10.1093/jamiaopen/ooz036 PMID: 32025644

Adane, K., Gizachew, M., & Kendie, S. (2019). The role of medical data in efficient patient care delivery: A review. *Risk Management and Healthcare Policy*, *12*, 67–73. DOI: 10.2147/RMHP.S179259 PMID: 31114410

Al-Hassan, R. A., Dirawi, W. M., Almosafri, W. H., Alabduladheem, M. F., Jahloul, I. H., & Alyousuf, A. N. (2026). Green HRM in Hospitals as a Strategic Approach to Promoting Employees' Pro-Environmental Behavior and Achieving Organizational Sustainability. In Rodrigues, R., Mohanty, V., & Figueiredo, P. (Eds.), *Organizational Culture and Employee Experience in the AI-Driven Organization* (pp. 269–308). IGI Global., DOI: 10.4018/979-8-2600-0610-8.ch010

Alnaemat, N. D., Alradhi, A. I., & Saleem, S. A. (2026). The Impact of Artificial Intelligence on Strategic Decision-Making and the Enhancement of Ethical Leadership in the Fashion Industry. In Mouloudj, K., & Arantes, L. (Eds.), *Ethical Consumption and Responsible Innovation in Fashion through AI* (pp. 205–228). IGI Global., DOI: 10.4018/979-8-3373-7200-6.ch008

Alyousuf, A. N., Sabeeh, A. O., Alnaemat, N. D., Mouloudj, K., & Hussein, S. A. (2026). Understanding Gen Z's Adoption of AI Technologies in Green Product Purchases: An Extension of the Technology Acceptance Model. In Mouloudj, K., & Bouarar, A. (Eds.), *Insights on Consumer Psychology in the Digital Landscape* (pp. 369–392). IGI Global., DOI: 10.4018/979-8-3373-2424-1.ch013

Attia, A. (2023). Effect of sustainable supply chain management and customer relationship management on organizational performance in the context of the Egyptian textile industry. *Sustainability (Basel)*, *15*(5), 4072. DOI: 10.3390/su15054072

Bouarar, A. C., Asanza, D. M., Mouloudj, S., Bouarar, A., Mouloudj, K., & Bozorgi, M. (2024). Elderly's Intention to Use Teledentistry Services: Antecedents and Challenges. In Martínez Asanza, D. (Ed.), *Geriatric Dentistry in the Age of Digital Technology* (pp. 101–116). IGI Global., DOI: 10.4018/979-8-3693-0260-6.ch004

Breitsohl, J., Khammash, M., & Griffiths, G. (2010). E-business complaint management: Perceptions and perspectives of online credibility. *Journal of Enterprise Information Management*, *23*(5), 653–660. DOI: 10.1108/17410391011083083

Chang, H. H., Wong, K. H., & Fang, P. W. (2014). The effects of customer relationship management relational information processes on customer-based performance. *Decision Support Systems*, *66*, 146–159. DOI: 10.1016/j.dss.2014.06.010

Chatterjee, S., & Chaudhuri, R. (2022). Adoption of Artificial Intelligence Integrated Customer Relationship Management in Organizations for Sustainability. In Vrontis, D., Thrassou, A., Weber, Y., Shams, S. M. R., Tsoukatos, E., & Efthymiou, L. (Eds.), *Business under Crisis* (Vol. III, pp. 137–156). Palgrave Studies in Cross-disciplinary Business Research. Palgrave Macmillan., DOI: 10.1007/978-3-030-76583-5_6

Chatterjee, S., & Chaudhuri, R. (2023). Customer relationship management in the digital era of artificial intelligence. In S.S. Kamble, R.S. Mor, A. Belhadi (Eds.), *Digital Transformation and Industry 4.0 for Sustainable Supply Chain Performance* (pp. 175–190). *EAI/Springer Innovations in Communication and Computing*, Springer. https://doi.org/DOI: 10.1007/978-3-031-19711-6_8

Coltman, T., Devinney, T. M., & Midgley, D. F. (2011). Customer relationship management and firm performance. *Journal of Information Technology*, *26*(3), 205–219. DOI: 10.1057/jit.2010.39

Damen, D. J., Schoonman, G. G., Maat, B., Habibović, M., Krahmer, E., & Pauws, S. (2022). Patients managing their medical data in personal electronic health records: Scoping review. *Journal of Medical Internet Research*, *24*(12), e37783. DOI: 10.2196/37783 PMID: 36574275

Das, S., & Hassan, H. K. (2022). Impact of sustainable supply chain management and customer relationship management on organizational performance. *International Journal of Productivity and Performance Management*, *71*(6), 2140–2160. DOI: 10.1108/IJPPM-08-2020-0441

Douma, M. C., Rejeb, M. B., Zardoub, N., Braham, A., Chouchene, H., Bouallegue, O., & Latiri, H. S. (2024). Impact of implementing electronic nursing records on quality and safety indicators in care. *The Libyan Journal of Medicine*, *19*(1), 2421625. DOI: 10.1080/19932820.2024.2421625 PMID: 39570988

Dubovitskaya, A., Baig, F., Xu, Z., Shukla, R., Zambani, P. S., Swaminathan, A., Jahangir, M. M., Chowdhry, K., Lachhani, R., Idnani, N., Schumacher, M., Aberer, K., Stoller, S. D., Ryu, S., & Wang, F. (2020). ACTION-EHR: Patient-centric blockchain-based electronic health record data management for cancer care. *Journal of Medical Internet Research*, *22*(8), e13598. DOI: 10.2196/13598 PMID: 32821064

Ernst, H., Hoyer, W. D., Krafft, M., & Krieger, K. (2011). Customer relationship management and company performance—The mediating role of new product performance. *Journal of the Academy of Marketing Science*, *39*(2), 290–306. DOI: 10.1007/s11747-010-0194-5

Haislip, J. Z., & Richardson, V. J. (2017). The effect of customer relationship management systems on firm performance. *International Journal of Accounting Information Systems*, *27*, 16–29. DOI: 10.1016/j.accinf.2017.09.003

Hat, N. D., Tan, K. L., Ngoc Vi, N. L., Phu, N. A., & Ting, H. (2025). The influence of customer relationship management in enhancing hospitality business performance: The conditional mediation of digital marketing capabilities. *International Journal of Hospitality & Tourism Administration*, *26*(3), 520–546. DOI: 10.1080/15256480.2024.2346142

Heileman, M. D., Kodzi, E. T.Jr, & Pett, T. L. (2026). The choice of customer relationship management approach in the supply chain: Examining small business performance. *Vision: The Journal of Business Perspective*, *30*(2), 213–228. DOI: 10.1177/09722629221092091

Jasim, Z. A., Alameri, S. A., Almado, A. A., Abdulrahman, F. Y., & Alyousuf, A. N. (2026). Investigating the Impact of Ethical Organizational Culture on Employee Retention. In Rodrigues, R., Mohanty, V., & Figueiredo, P. (Eds.), *Organizational Culture and Employee Experience in the AI-Driven Organization* (pp. 85–110). IGI Global., DOI: 10.4018/979-8-2600-0610-8.ch004

Jayachandran, S., Sharma, S., Kaufman, P., & Raman, P. (2005). The role of relational information processes and technology use in customer relationship management. *Journal of Marketing*, *69*(4), 177–192. DOI: 10.1509/jmkg.2005.69.4.177

Jayapal, J. (2025). Unveiling the impact of AI-driven personalization on customer loyalty in online shopping: The moderating effects of privacy concerns. *Journal of Promotion Management*, *31*(5), 865–894. DOI: 10.1080/10496491.2025.2525099

Keeling, A., Downey, J., Halkes, M., & Wei, Y. (2025). The impact of patient-generated health data from mobile health technologies on health care management and clinical decision-making: Narrative scoping review. *Journal of Medical Internet Research*, *27*, e77359. DOI: 10.2196/77359 PMID: 41417964

Khan, R. U., Salamzadeh, Y., Iqbal, Q., & Yang, S. (2022). The Impact of customer relationship management and company reputation on customer loyalty: The mediating role of customer satisfaction. *Journal of Relationship Marketing*, *21*(1), 1–26. DOI: 10.1080/15332667.2020.1840904

Krishnaraju, V., Mathew, S. K., & Sugumaran, V. (2016). Web personalization for user acceptance of technology: An empirical investigation of E-government services. *Information Systems Frontiers*, *18*(3), 579–595. DOI: 10.1007/s10796-015-9550-9

Leelavathi, R., Philip, B., Madhusudhanan, R., Sony, N., & Mukthar, K. P. J. (2024). AI-Driven Customer Relationship Management (CRM): A Review of Implementation Strategies. In El Khoury, R. (Eds.), *Anticipating Future Business Trends: Navigating Artificial Intelligence Innovations* (pp. 283–295). Studies in Systems, Decision and Control, Vol. 536. Springer. https://doi.org/DOI: 10.1007/978-3-031-63402-4_22

Lin, J., Bates, S. M., Allen, L. N., Wright, M., Mao, L., & Kidd, M. (2025). Integrating mobile health app data into electronic medical or health record systems and its impact on health care delivery and patient health outcomes: Scoping review. *JMIR mHealth and uHealth*, *13*(1), e66650. DOI: 10.2196/66650 PMID: 40549960

Maksimova, M., Solvak, M., & Krimmer, R. (2021). Data-Driven Personalized E-Government Services: Literature Review and Case Study. In Edelmann, N. (Eds.), *Electronic Participation* (Vol. 12849, pp. 151–165). Springer., DOI: 10.1007/978-3-030-82824-0_12

Martínez Asanza, D. (2025). Emerging Trends and Future Perspectives in Digital Dentistry for Rural Areas: An Update. In Martínez Asanza, D. (Ed.), *Transforming Dental Health in Rural Communities: Digital Dentistry* (pp. 1–36). IGI Global., DOI: 10.4018/979-8-3693-7165-7.ch001

Martínez Asanza, D., Rojas Herrera, I. A., Mouloudj, K., Amable, O. G., & Muzzamil, M. (2024). Impact of Digital Innovations in Preventive Dentistry: A Narrative Review. In Martínez Asanza, D. (Ed.), *Leveraging Digital Technology for Preventive Dentistry* (pp. 55–84). IGI Global., DOI: 10.4018/979-8-3693-3872-8.ch003

Mouloudj, K., Bouarar, A. C., Martínez Asanza, D. A., & Dimitrova, M. (2025). Understanding Customers' Intentions to Use Digital Dental Health Services: An Expanded Technology Acceptance Model. In Martínez Asanza, D. (Ed.), *Transforming Dental Health in Rural Communities: Digital Dentistry* (pp. 189–210). IGI Global., DOI: 10.4018/979-8-3693-7165-7.ch007

Nuansi, P., & Ngamcharoenmongkol, P. (2021). Proactive complaint management: Effects of customer voice initiation on perceived justices, satisfaction, and negative word-of-mouth. *SAGE Open*, *11*(3), 1–17. DOI: 10.1177/21582440211040788

Ofori, D., & Appiah-Nimo, C. (2022). Relationship management, competitive advantage and performance of hotels: A resource-based view. *Journal of African Business*, *23*(3), 712–730. DOI: 10.1080/15228916.2021.1924573

Ozay, D., Jahanbakht, M., Shoomal, A., & Wang, S. (2024). Artificial Intelligence (AI)-based Customer Relationship Management (CRM): A comprehensive bibliometric and systematic literature review with outlook on future research. *Enterprise Information Systems*, *18*(7), 2351869. DOI: 10.1080/17517575.2024.2351869

Raj, E. F. I. (2024). Applications of Data Science and Artificial Intelligence Methodologies in Customer Relationship Management. In Kautish, S., Chatterjee, P., Pamucar, D., Pradeep, N., & Singh, D. (Eds.), *Computational Intelligence for Modern Business Systems. Disruptive Technologies and Digital Transformations for Society 5.0* (pp. 227–242). Springer., DOI: 10.1007/978-981-99-5354-7_12

Reinartz, W., Krafft, M., & Hoyer, W. D. (2004). The customer relationship management process: Its measurement and impact on performance. *JMR, Journal of Marketing Research*, *41*(3), 293–305. DOI: 10.1509/jmkr.41.3.293.35991

Roba, G. B., & Maric, P. (2023). AI in Customer Relationship Management. In Kryvinska, N., Greguš, M., Fedushko, S. (Eds.), *Developments in Information and Knowledge Management Systems for Business Applications* (pp. 469–487). Studies in Systems, Decision and Control, Vol. 462. Springer. https://doi.org/DOI: 10.1007/978-3-031-25695-0_21

Sharma, V. K., Sharma, V., & Kumar, D. (2025). Customer relationship management in healthcare: Strategies for adoption in a public health system. *Journal of Marketing Theory and Practice*, *33*(4), 560–585. DOI: 10.1080/10696679.2024.2394485

Soltani, Z., Zareie, B., Milani, F. S., & Navimipour, N. J. (2018). The impact of the customer relationship management on the organization performance. *The Journal of High Technology Management Research*, *29*(2), 237–246. DOI: 10.1016/j.hitech.2018.10.001

Tapuria, A., Porat, T., Kalra, D., Dsouza, G., Xiaohui, S., & Curcin, V. (2021). Impact of patient access to their electronic health record: Systematic review. *Informatics for Health & Social Care*, *46*(2), 194–206. DOI: 10.1080/17538157.2021.1879810 PMID: 33840342

Thai, N. V., Trang, B. T. Q., Quy, N. L. D., Huong, N. T. Q., & Huyen, V. T. T. (2024). Factors affecting the successful implementation of customer relationship management in 3-to-5-star hotels in Viet Nam. *Cogent Social Sciences*, *10*(1), 2316062. DOI: 10.1080/23311886.2024.2316062

Tubaishat, A. (2019). The effect of electronic health records on patient safety: A qualitative exploratory study. *Informatics for Health & Social Care*, *44*(1), 79–91. DOI: 10.1080/17538157.2017.1398753 PMID: 29239662

Valmohammadi, C. (2017). Customer relationship management: Innovation and performance. *International Journal of Innovation Science*, *9*(4), 374–395. DOI: 10.1108/IJIS-02-2017-0011

Wang, Z., & Kim, H. G. (2017). Can Social Media Marketing Improve Customer Relationship Capabilities and Firm Performance? Dynamic Capability Perspective. *Journal of Interactive Marketing*, *39*(1), 15–26. DOI: 10.1016/j.intmar.2017.02.004

Yu, P., & Qian, S. (2018). Developing a theoretical model and questionnaire survey instrument to measure the success of electronic health records in residential aged care. *PLoS One*, *13*(1), e0190749. DOI: 10.1371/journal.pone.0190749 PMID: 29315323

KEY TERMS AND DEFINITIONS

Business Performance: The extent to which an organization achieves its operational, financial, and strategic objectives through effective management and service delivery.

Electronic Customer Relationship Management (E-CRM): The use of digital technologies and electronic communication systems to manage, maintain, and strengthen relationships between organizations and customers.

Feedback Management: The process of collecting, monitoring, and responding to customer opinions, suggestions, and complaints to improve service quality and organizational performance.

Online Appointment Systems: Digital platforms that enable customers or patients to schedule, modify, and manage appointments electronically.

Patient Data Management: The electronic collection, storage, organization, and retrieval of patient information to support efficient healthcare services and decision-making.

Personalized Services: Customized interactions and service offerings designed to meet the specific needs, preferences, and expectations of individual customers or patients.

Chapter 6
Digital Health Marketing and Preventive Oral Health Behavior:
Evidence From Dental Service Customers

Zaid khawam Mahmood
http://orcid.org/0009-0007-5409-3117
College of Administration and Economics, University of Fallujah, Iraq

Eshaq Youssef Hamdan Ahmed
Department of Business Administration, College of Administration and Economics, University of Samarra, Iraq

Layla Laftah Ali
Basra Management Technical College, Southern Technical University, Iraq

Kamel Mouloudj
http://orcid.org/0000-0001-7617-8313
Department of Commercial Sciences, College of Economics, University of Medea, Algeria

Dachel Martínez Asanza
http://orcid.org/0000-0002-1830-7137
National School of Public Health (ENSAP), Cuba & Havana Medical Sciences University, Cuba

DOI: 10.4018/979-8-3373-8894-6.ch006

ABSTRACT

This study examines the influence of digital health marketing on preventive oral health behavior among dental service customers in Algeria. A quantitative approach was employed using a structured questionnaire distributed to customers of dental services. A total of 196 valid responses were collected and analyzed using multiple regression analysis. The study investigated the effects of online oral health information quality, social media health engagement, personalized digital communication, and trust in digital health information on preventive oral health behavior. The findings revealed that all four dimensions significantly and positively influence preventive oral health behavior, with trust in digital health information emerging as the strongest predictor, followed by personalized digital communication. The model explained 61.2% of the variance in preventive oral health behavior. The study highlights the growing role of digital health marketing in encouraging preventive oral care and offers practical implications for dental clinics and healthcare policymakers.

INTRODUCTION

Oral health is increasingly recognized as an essential component of overall health and well-being, influencing not only physical functioning but also psychological confidence, quality of life, and broader health outcomes (Martínez Asanza et al., 2024). Despite considerable advances in preventive dentistry, oral diseases continue to affect a substantial proportion of the global population, with many of these conditions remaining largely preventable through appropriate hygiene practices, regular dental visits, and early health awareness (Sharma et al., 2022; Goldberg et al., 2022). Yet, preventive oral health behavior remains inconsistent across many populations, particularly in developing contexts where awareness, access to information, and preventive engagement are often uneven. Recent evidence suggests that many individuals still rely on emergency-based dental care rather than routine preventive practices, reflecting persistent gaps in oral health awareness and behavior (Asiri et al., 2024; Martínez Asanza, 2025).

In response to these challenges, health systems have increasingly turned toward digital technologies and marketing-oriented approaches to improve preventive outcomes (Martínez Asanza et al., 2024). The growing digitalization of healthcare has transformed the ways health information is communicated, accessed, and consumed (Bouarar et al., 2024). Digital health promotion now encompasses a broad range of tools, including social media platforms, mobile applications, online educational materials, personalized digital communication, and telehealth systems, all designed to encourage healthier behaviors and improve access to preventive information

(Stark et al., 2022; Willis et al., 2022). Unlike traditional health communication, digital health marketing allows healthcare providers and policymakers to interact with audiences in more accessible, immediate, and personalized ways, creating new opportunities to influence preventive decision-making (Martínez Asanza, 2025).

The importance of health marketing in encouraging behavior change has received increasing scholarly attention in recent years. Health marketing extends beyond merely disseminating information; it seeks to bridge the gap between professional health expertise and community understanding by improving health literacy and motivating positive behavioral outcomes (Parkinson & Davey, 2023). Through carefully designed communication strategies, health marketing can shape attitudes, increase awareness, and support the adoption of healthier lifestyles and preventive practices. Evidence suggests that health marketing interventions are particularly effective when they focus on audience needs, employ tailored communication, and emphasize long-term behavioral change rather than short-term information delivery (Nejad et al., 2021; Roger et al., 2023).

Social marketing approaches, in particular, have demonstrated considerable promise in promoting preventive health behaviors across diverse healthcare contexts. Research has shown that social marketing interventions can substantially improve preventive screening uptake, health knowledge, and behavioral intentions among different populations (Maleki et al., 2025; Olubodun et al., 2022). Likewise, findings from Algeria indicate that psychosocial and informational factors can significantly shape preventive health intentions, underscoring the importance of targeted health communication strategies in encouraging healthier behavior (Mouloudj et al., 2026). As healthcare increasingly embraces patient-centered approaches, understanding how digital communication influences preventive behavior has become an important research priority (Swenson et al., 2018).

Within oral healthcare, digital media has emerged as a particularly promising avenue for promoting preventive practices and improving oral health literacy (Martínez Asanza et al., 2024). A growing body of evidence suggests that digital interventions, including "social media, educational videos, text messaging systems, mobile health applications, and teledentistry platforms", can positively influence oral health knowledge, attitudes, and hygiene behaviors (Sharma et al., 2022; Fernández et al., 2021). Systematic reviews further indicate that online social networks such as WhatsApp, YouTube, and Instagram may contribute to behavioral improvements and enhanced oral health awareness, particularly among younger populations (de Oliveira Júnior et al., 2023). Similarly, social media–based oral health interventions have shown encouraging, albeit modest, improvements in oral hygiene practices and preventive behaviors (Calderon et al., 2023; Sanghavi et al., 2025).

Nevertheless, the growing reliance on digital health communication also introduces several challenges. The quality, credibility, and trustworthiness of online health information remain critical concerns. Although social media facilitates broad information accessibility and interaction, it also exposes individuals to misinformation, inconsistent content quality, and misleading health claims (Ghalavand et al., 2025). Studies indicate that trust in online health information plays a central role in determining whether individuals translate digital exposure into actual preventive action (Jayasinghe et al., 2024). Furthermore, digital health interventions appear to be most effective when information is perceived as relevant, understandable, and tailored to users' needs (Katusiime et al., 2022).

In the Algerian context, interest in digital health services has grown substantially, particularly within dental care. Emerging evidence demonstrates that customers' intentions to adopt digital dental health services are shaped not only by perceptions of technological usefulness and ease of use but also by social media influence and attitudinal factors (Mouloudj et al., 2025). Despite these developments, empirical research examining how digital health marketing contributes specifically to preventive oral health behavior remains limited, particularly among dental service customers in developing countries such as Algeria. Existing research has largely focused on technology adoption, oral health literacy, or clinical outcomes, leaving a noticeable gap regarding the behavioral implications of digital marketing strategies in preventive oral care.

Based on the above, the present study seeks to examine the role of digital health marketing in promoting preventive oral health behavior among dental service customers. More specifically, the study investigates whether online oral health information quality, social media health engagement, personalized digital communication, and trust in digital health information positively influence preventive oral health behavior. By focusing on customers of dental services in Algeria, this study aims to contribute to the growing discussion on digital health promotion while offering practical insights for dental practitioners and policymakers seeking to encourage preventive oral health practices through more effective digital engagement strategies.

THEORETICAL FRAMEWORK

Preventive Oral Health Behavior

Preventive oral health behavior refers to the set of actions individuals undertake to maintain oral hygiene, reduce the risk of dental diseases, and preserve long-term oral health outcomes (Martínez Asanza et al., 2025). These behaviors commonly include regular tooth brushing, flossing, reduced sugar consumption, routine dental check-ups, adherence to professional recommendations, and early treatment-seeking before oral problems worsen (Asiri et al., 2024; Nazari et al., 2025). Preventive oral health behavior is increasingly viewed not merely as an individual habit but as a multidimensional health practice shaped by awareness, attitudes, access to care, and exposure to health-related information. Since many oral diseases are preventable, encouraging preventive practices has become a priority for healthcare systems and public health professionals worldwide (Goldberg et al., 2022). In fact, the literature consistently suggests that preventive oral behaviors contribute to lower rates of oral disease progression, improved oral-health-related quality of life, and reduced long-term treatment costs (Sharma et al., 2022; Fernández et al., 2021).

Despite the recognized importance of preventive oral healthcare, adherence to recommended oral hygiene behaviors remains inconsistent across different population groups. Evidence indicates that many individuals continue to seek dental care only when symptoms become severe, reflecting a treatment-oriented rather than prevention-oriented approach to oral healthcare (Asiri et al., 2024). Several factors may shape preventive oral health behavior, including oral health literacy, trust in health information, social influence, communication quality, and access to educational resources (Jayasinghe et al., 2024; Ghalavand et al., 2025). Theory-based health promotion interventions have demonstrated positive effects on oral-health-related knowledge, attitudes, self-efficacy, and behavioral adoption, suggesting that preventive behaviors can be strengthened through effective educational and communication strategies (Nazari et al., 2025). As digital technologies increasingly mediate health information access, understanding the factors that encourage preventive oral health behavior has become an important area of inquiry in contemporary dental healthcare research.

Digital Health Marketing

Digital health marketing refers to the strategic use of digital communication technologies and marketing practices to inform, educate, and influence individuals toward healthier decisions and behaviors. Unlike conventional health communication, digital health marketing employs interactive channels such as websites, social media platforms, mobile applications, online campaigns, email communication, and telehealth systems to deliver health-related content in a timely and personalized manner (Parkinson & Davey, 2023; Stark et al., 2022). Its primary objective extends beyond information dissemination to actively encouraging behavioral change, improving health literacy, and facilitating access to preventive healthcare services (Butt et al., 2019). In recent years, digital health marketing has gained increased relevance as healthcare systems seek more patient-centered and scalable approaches to health promotion. Scholars emphasize that effective health marketing bridges the divide between medical expertise and public understanding by translating professional knowledge into accessible and actionable information that supports healthier lifestyles and preventive decision-making (Parkinson & Naidu, 2024; Nejad et al., 2021).

The growing integration of digital technologies into healthcare has significantly expanded the role of digital health marketing in preventive health promotion (Martínez Asanza, 2025). Evidence suggests that digital interventions, including social media engagement, mobile health applications, personalized reminders, and targeted educational campaigns, can positively influence health awareness and encourage preventive practices (Willis et al., 2022; Katusiime et al., 2022; Mouloudj et al., 2023). Within oral healthcare specifically, digital media platforms have shown promise in improving oral health literacy, strengthening preventive knowledge, and encouraging healthier oral hygiene behaviors (Sharma et al., 2022; Fernández et al., 2021). Nevertheless, the effectiveness of digital health marketing depends on several conditions, including the quality and credibility of health information, users' trust in digital content, and the degree of personalization in communication (Jayasinghe et al., 2024; Ghalavand et al., 2025). Consequently, understanding how digital health marketing influences preventive oral health behavior remains increasingly important for healthcare practitioners and policymakers.

Hypothesis Development

Online Oral Health Information Quality and Preventive Oral Health Behavior

Online oral health information quality refers to individuals' perceptions regarding the accuracy, relevance, clarity, completeness, and usefulness of oral health information obtained through digital channels such as websites, social media platforms, online videos, and mobile applications. In digital healthcare environments, information quality plays a central role in shaping individuals' understanding of health risks and preventive practices (Bouarar et al., 2024; Martínez Asanza, 2025; Mouloudj et al., 2023). Research suggests that digital health promotion becomes more effective when information is perceived as understandable, relevant, and evidence-based (Parkinson & Davey, 2023; Passos et al., 2020; Willis et al., 2022). Within oral healthcare, high-quality digital content has been shown to improve oral health literacy, knowledge, and preventive awareness (Sharma et al., 2022; Sanghavi et al., 2025). Conversely, poor-quality or misleading online information may discourage healthy decision-making and create confusion among healthcare users (Ghalavand et al., 2025). Since preventive oral health behavior relies heavily on informed decisions, access to reliable and comprehensible oral health information may positively influence individuals' willingness to adopt preventive practices. Therefore, the following hypothesis is proposed:

H1: Online oral health information quality positively influences preventive oral health behavior among dental service customers.

Social Media Health Engagement and Preventive Oral Health Behavior

Social media health engagement refers to the extent to which individuals interact with, consume, share, or participate in health-related content through social media platforms such as "Facebook, Instagram, WhatsApp, YouTube, and TikTok". Increasingly, social media platforms are becoming influential channels for disseminating health information and encouraging preventive behaviors (Mouloudj et al., 2025). Studies suggest that engagement with digital health content may improve health awareness and motivate behavioral change by increasing exposure to educational messages and peer influence (Katusiime et al., 2022; Mouloudj et al., 2023; Stark et al., 2022). In oral healthcare, online social networks have shown promising outcomes in promoting oral health literacy, reducing gingival problems, and enhancing preventive knowledge through educational interventions (de Oliveira Júnior et al., 2023). Similarly, social media interventions and digital campaigns have demonstrated positive, although sometimes moderate, effects on oral hygiene behavior and preventive awareness (Calderon et al., 2023; Jayasinghe et al., 2024). Given the growing role of social media in health communication, active engagement with oral health content may strengthen preventive oral health behavior. Based on the above discussion, the following hypothesis is proposed:

H2: Social media health engagement positively influences preventive oral health behavior among dental service customers.

Personalized Digital Communication and Preventive Oral Health Behavior

Personalized digital communication refers to tailored health-related messages, reminders, recommendations, and interactions delivered to individuals through digital platforms based on their specific needs, preferences, or health conditions. In healthcare settings, personalization is increasingly recognized as an effective approach for strengthening patient engagement and encouraging preventive behavior. Digital communication strategies such as personalized reminders, text messaging systems, and customized educational content can improve health awareness by delivering timely and relevant information to users (Bouarar et al., 2024; Willis et al., 2022). Evidence from preventive healthcare suggests that targeted interventions are more effective in influencing attitudes and behavioral intentions because they address users' unique concerns and barriers (Nejad et al., 2021; Roger et al., 2023). Within oral healthcare, teledentistry interventions and mobile health applications have demonstrated promising effects on improving oral hygiene behavior and preventive outcomes through individualized communication and monitoring (Fernández et al., 2021; Tiffany et al., 2018). As such, personalized digital communication may encourage greater adherence to preventive oral health practices. Therefore, we propose the following hypothesis:

H3: Personalized digital communication positively influences preventive oral health behavior among dental service customers.

Trust in Digital Health Information and Preventive Oral Health Behavior

Trust in digital health information refers to the degree to which individuals perceive health information obtained through digital channels as credible, reliable, and dependable for making healthcare decisions. Trust is particularly important in digital environments where users encounter large volumes of information with varying levels of quality and accuracy. Existing literature suggests that individuals are more likely to adopt health recommendations and preventive behaviors when they believe the source of information is trustworthy (Parkinson & Davey, 2023). In the oral health context, studies indicate that perceptions of reliability significantly influence users' acceptance and use of digital oral health information (Mouloudj et al., 2025; Jayasinghe et al., 2024). However, Mouloudj et al. (2023) found that behavioral intentions for using digital health apps in Algeria were not significantly affected by trust in the "digital health system". At the same time, concerns about misinformation, misleading advertising, and content credibility remain important barriers to effective digital health promotion (Ghalavand et al., 2025; Sanghavi et al., 2025). Because preventive oral health behavior often depends on informed and confident decision-making, trust in digital health information may enhance individuals' likelihood of engaging in preventive oral care practices. Based on the preceding discussion, the following hypothesis is proposed:

H4: Trust in digital health information positively influences preventive oral health behavior among dental service customers.

MATERIALS AND METHODS

Research Design

This study adopted a quantitative research approach to examine the influence of digital health marketing on preventive oral health behavior among dental service customers in Algeria. A cross-sectional survey design was employed, as it enables the collection of standardized data from a relatively large number of respondents within a specific period and facilitates the examination of relationships between variables. Quantitative methods are particularly appropriate for testing theoretically derived hypotheses and assessing the strength and direction of relationships among constructs using statistical techniques.

Data were collected using a structured self-administered questionnaire developed based on previously validated measurement scales. The questionnaire consisted of three sections. The first section gathered respondents' demographic information, including gender, age group, educational level, and marital status. These variables were included to provide an overview of the sample characteristics and better understand the profile of dental service customers participating in the study. The second section focused on measuring the four independent variables related to digital health marketing. Specifically, online oral health information quality, social media health engagement, personalized digital communication, and trust in digital health information were each measured using four items. The third section included four items measuring the dependent variable, namely preventive oral health behavior. All questionnaire items were adapted from previous studies to ensure content validity and conceptual consistency. The items measuring online oral health information quality were adapted from Passos et al. (2020), while social media health engagement was adapted from Mouloudj et al. (2025). The scale for personalized digital communication was developed by the authors to align with the context of digital dental health communication in Algeria. Furthermore, trust in digital health information was adapted from Mouloudj et al. (2023), whereas preventive oral health behavior items were adapted from Mouloudj et al. (2026).

The questionnaire was initially developed in English and subsequently translated into Arabic using the back-translation method to ensure linguistic accuracy and conceptual equivalence between the two versions. A language specialist and an academic expert reviewed the translation process to minimize ambiguity and maintain item consistency. Following questionnaire development, two experts in digital marketing and health communication were invited to assess the content validity, clarity, wording, and contextual appropriateness of the instrument. Their comments contributed to refining several statements to improve readability and measurement precision. Before launching the final survey, a pilot study involving 20 respondents was conducted to assess the clarity, reliability, and comprehensibility of the questionnaire items. Feedback obtained from the pilot participants indicated that the questionnaire was easy to understand and complete, with only minor wording modifications required. The pilot phase also helped estimate the average completion time and identify potential response issues before the main data collection process.

A five-point Likert scale was used to measure all study constructs, ranging from 1 = "strongly disagree" to 5 = "strongly agree". The use of a Likert scale is widely recommended in behavioral and health-related research because it facilitates respondents' evaluation of perceptions, attitudes, and behavioral tendencies while improving consistency in statistical analysis. The final questionnaire items used in this study are presented in Table 1.

Table 1. Measurement items of the final questionnaire

Construct	Code	Measurement Item
Online Oral Health Information Quality	OHIQ1	The oral health information I find online is clear and understandable.
	OHIQ2	Online oral health information is accurate and reliable.
	OHIQ3	The online oral health information I access is useful for maintaining oral health.
	OHIQ4	Online oral health information helps me make informed dental health decisions.
Social Media Health Engagement	SMHE1	I frequently engage with oral health information shared on social media.
	SMHE2	Social media platforms increase my awareness of preventive oral healthcare.
	SMHE3	I pay attention to oral health advice shared through social media.
	SMHE4	Social media encourages me to improve my oral health habits.
Personalized Digital Communication	PDC1	I value personalized digital reminders related to dental care.
	PDC2	Personalized oral health messages motivate me to take better care of my oral health.
	PDC3	Tailored digital communication helps me follow preventive oral health recommendations.
	PDC4	I prefer receiving oral health guidance customized to my personal needs.
Trust in Digital Health Information	TDHI1	I trust oral health information obtained through digital platforms.
	TDHI2	Digital oral health information is dependable for preventive decisions.
	TDHI3	I believe reliable online oral health information improves preventive care.
	TDHI4	I feel confident using digital oral health information to guide my behavior.

continued on following page

Table 1. Continued

Construct	Code	Measurement Item
Preventive Oral Health Behavior	POHB1	I regularly practice recommended oral hygiene behaviors.
	POHB2	I seek preventive dental care before oral problems become severe.
	POHB3	I follow professional recommendations to maintain oral health.
	POHB4	I actively try to prevent oral health problems through healthy practices.

Data Collection

The target population of this study consisted of customers of dental services in Algeria, as they represent an appropriate group for examining how digital health marketing may influence preventive oral health behavior. Since the study focuses on perceptions and behaviors related to oral health information, social media engagement, personalized digital communication, and trust in digital health information, individuals with prior experience in using dental services were considered the most suitable respondents.

A non-probability convenience sampling technique was employed to recruit participants. This sampling method was considered appropriate due to the exploratory nature of the study and the practical challenges associated with accessing a comprehensive sampling frame of dental service customers. A total of 300 questionnaires were distributed between February and March 2026. Of these, 205 questionnaires were returned, resulting in a satisfactory response rate. After a screening process to identify incomplete questionnaires and responses with substantial missing data or patterned answering, 196 questionnaires remained valid and suitable for statistical analysis. The final sample size was considered adequate for examining the proposed relationships among the study variables.

The questionnaire was distributed across several healthcare-related locations to increase respondent diversity and accessibility. Specifically, data collection took place in private dental clinics, medical analysis centers, and pharmacies, where potential respondents were approached with the assistance of staff members working at these locations. Their cooperation facilitated access to participants who had previous or ongoing interactions with dental and healthcare services. Respondents completed the questionnaire in person, and the average time required for completion was approximately ten minutes, making participation manageable and minimizing respondent fatigue.

Before completing the questionnaire, participants were informed about the purpose of the study, emphasizing that participation was entirely voluntary, anonymous, and intended solely for academic research purposes. Respondents were assured that their personal information would remain confidential and that no identifying information would be collected. Verbal consent was obtained from all respondents prior to participation. In accordance with local regulations and institutional requirements, formal ethics committee approval was not required, as the study relied exclusively on an anonymous questionnaire, involved no medical intervention, and posed no foreseeable risk to participants.

The demographic characteristics of the respondents are presented in Table 2.

Table 2. Demographic characteristics of respondents (N = 196)

Variable	Category	Frequency	Percentage (%)
Gender	Male	85	43.37
	Female	111	56.63
Age Group	Less than 25 years	34	17.35
	25–34 years	47	23.98
	35–44 years	65	33.16
	45 years and above	50	25.51
Educational Level	Secondary school or below	58	29.59
	Diploma	35	17.86
	Bachelor's degree	78	39.80
	Postgraduate degree	25	12.75
Marital Status	Single	81	41.33
	Married	102	52.04
	Other (divorced, widowed)	13	6.63

As shown in Table 2, the sample comprised 196 respondents, with females representing the majority (56.63%) compared to males (43.37%). In terms of age distribution, respondents aged 35–44 years constituted the largest group (33.16%), followed by those aged 45 years and above (25.51%), 25–34 years (23.98%), and less than 25 years (17.35%). Regarding educational level, the majority of participants held a bachelor's degree (39.80%), followed by respondents with secondary school education or below (29.59%), diplomas (17.86%), and postgraduate degrees (12.75%). Concerning marital status, most respondents were married (52.04%), while 41.33% were single, and 6.63% belonged to the category of other (divorced or widowed).

RESULTS

Reliability and Descriptive Statistics of Study Constructs

Table 3 presents the descriptive statistics, reliability coefficients, and normality assessment of the study constructs. The findings indicate acceptable levels of internal consistency reliability, as all Cronbach's alpha values exceeded the recommended threshold of 0.70 (Alameri et al., 2026), ranging from 0.756 to 0.861, confirming satisfactory reliability of the measurement scales. Among the constructs, social media health engagement recorded the highest mean score (M = 3.635), suggesting relatively stronger respondent agreement, whereas trust in digital health information reported the lowest mean (M = 3.197). The remaining constructs demonstrated moderate mean values, including preventive oral health behavior (M = 3.348), personalized digital communication (M = 3.293), and online oral health information quality (M = 3.220). Regarding data normality, the values of skewness ranged from 0.415 to 1.283, while kurtosis values ranged from −0.667 to 2.345. Since all values fall within the commonly accepted thresholds (±2 for skewness and ±7 for kurtosis) (Alameri et al., 2026), the data can be considered adequately normally distributed for subsequent statistical analyses.

Table 3. Reliability, descriptive statistics, and normality assessment of study constructs

Constructs	Mean	Cronbach's α	Skewness	Kurtosis
Online Oral Health Information Quality	3.220	0.778	1.119	1.525
Social Media Health Engagement	3.635	0.793	0.415	-0.667
Personalized Digital Communication	3.293	0.756	1.283	2.345
Trust in Digital Health Information	3.197	0.766	0.818	1.357
Preventive Oral Health Behavior	3.348	0.861	0.977	0.931

Hypothesis Testing Results

Table 4 presents the results of the multiple regression analysis examining the effects of digital health marketing dimensions on preventive oral health behavior. The overall regression model was statistically significant ($F = 77.867$, $p < 0.001$), indicating that the independent variables collectively explain variations in preventive oral health behavior. The model demonstrated substantial explanatory power, with an Adjusted R^2 of 0.612, suggesting that approximately 61.2% of the variance in preventive oral health behavior was explained by the four predictors. Furthermore, the Durbin–Watson value (1.678) indicates no serious autocorrelation issue in the regression model. Additionally, the Tolerance and VIF values indicate the absence of multicollinearity concerns, as all tolerance values exceeded 0.20 and all VIF values remained well below the threshold of 5 (Al Ameri et al., 2026).

Table 4. Multiple regression results for the effects of digital health marketing dimensions

Model	β	t	Sig.	Tolerance	VIF	Decision
Online Oral Health Information Quality	0.168	2.785	0.006	0.543	1.842	Supported
Social Media Health Engagement	0.127	3.041	0.003	0.929	1.077	Supported
Personalized Digital Communication	0.346	5.247	0.000	0.552	1.813	Supported
Trust in Digital Health Information	0.463	7.121	0.000	0.659	1.518	Supported

Note: F = 77.867 ($p < 0.001$); Adjusted R^2= 0.612; Durbin-Watson = 1.678

Regarding the hypotheses, the findings revealed that online oral health information quality had a significant positive effect on preventive oral health behavior (β = 0.168, t = 2.785, p = 0.006), supporting H1. Similarly, social media health engagement positively influenced preventive oral health behavior (β = 0.127, t = 3.041, p = 0.003), supporting H2. Personalized digital communication demonstrated a stronger positive effect (β = 0.346, t = 5.247, p < 0.001), confirming H3. The strongest predictor was trust in digital health information, which exerted a significant positive influence on preventive oral health behavior (β = 0.463, t = 7.121, p < 0.001), thereby supporting H4.

DISCUSSION

The findings confirmed that online oral health information quality has a significant positive effect on preventive oral health behavior, supporting H1. This result suggests that when dental service customers perceive online oral health information as accurate, clear, relevant, and useful, they are more likely to adopt preventive oral health practices such as regular brushing, reducing sugar intake, preventive dental visits, and adherence to oral hygiene recommendations. One plausible explanation is that high-quality information reduces uncertainty and increases individuals' confidence in making informed oral health decisions (Bouarar et al., 2024). In the context of Algeria, where many individuals increasingly seek health-related information online before consulting professionals, the quality of available digital information may shape awareness and behavioral choices. This finding aligns with prior studies emphasizing the role of digital health communication in encouraging preventive behaviors (Stark et al., 2022; Willis et al., 2022). It is also consistent with the systematic review of Sharma et al. (2022), which concluded that digital media interventions contribute positively to oral health literacy, knowledge, and health practices. Likewise, Goldberg et al. (2022) found that oral health campaigns delivered through digital and mass communication channels improved oral health knowledge and preventive behaviors. Therefore, the present result reinforces the argument that credible and understandable online oral health information can serve as an important catalyst for preventive oral health behavior.

The results also demonstrated a positive and significant relationship between social media health engagement and preventive oral health behavior, thereby supporting H2. Although the effect size was comparatively smaller than other predictors, the findings suggest that active engagement with oral health-related content on social media platforms may encourage healthier oral practices among dental service customers. This relationship may be explained by the interactive nature of social media, where users are exposed to educational videos, dentists' advice, peer experiences, and preventive oral care recommendations in accessible and engaging formats (Bouarar et al., 2024). Such exposure may strengthen awareness and normalize preventive habits over time. The finding corresponds with de Oliveira Júnior et al. (2023), whose systematic review highlighted the effectiveness of online social networks in improving oral health knowledge and reducing negative oral health indicators among young populations. Similarly, Sanghavi et al. (2025) concluded that social media platforms can modestly improve oral health behaviors and knowledge, despite concerns regarding misinformation. Moreover, Jayasinghe et al. (2024) reported that a substantial proportion of adults changed their oral health behaviors after accessing oral health information through social media. Taken together, these studies support the notion that digital engagement through social media can play a meaningful role in promoting preventive oral health behavior.

A stronger effect emerged for personalized digital communication, which significantly influenced preventive oral health behavior and supported H3. This finding indicates that tailored digital messages, reminders, recommendations, and individualized communication strategies can effectively motivate customers to engage in preventive oral health activities. Unlike general health messages, personalized communication may feel more relevant and actionable because it addresses individuals' specific needs, preferences, or oral health conditions. In practice, reminders for dental checkups, customized oral hygiene advice, or personalized educational messages may encourage individuals to become more proactive in maintaining oral health. This result resonates with previous health marketing literature emphasizing the value of customer-centered communication in promoting behavior change (Parkinson & Davey, 2023). It also reflects evidence from preventive health studies showing that targeted digital interventions improve health-related intentions and preventive practices (Maleki et al., 2025; Olubodun et al., 2022). Furthermore, the findings parallel Fernández et al. (2021), who observed that mHealth interventions and teledentistry approaches, including personalized digital messages, enhanced oral health outcomes and preventive practices. Thus, personalization appears to strengthen the persuasive power of digital health marketing efforts in the oral healthcare context.

Among all predictors, trust in digital health information emerged as the strongest determinant of preventive oral health behavior, lending strong support to H4. This finding underscores the central importance of trust in shaping individuals' willingness to follow oral health guidance encountered through digital channels. Even when information is accessible and engaging, customers may hesitate to act upon it if they question its credibility or accuracy. In other words, trust seems to function as the foundation upon which digital health marketing efforts become behaviorally influential (Bouarar et al., 2024). In Algeria, concerns regarding misinformation and inconsistent health content across digital platforms may explain why trust plays such a decisive role. The result is consistent with Ghalavand et al. (2025), who identified trustworthiness and information quality as essential factors influencing the usability of social media for oral health literacy. Similarly, Katusiime et al. (2022) emphasized that trust significantly affects the adoption of mHealth technologies for preventive health purposes. The finding also complements the conclusions of Parkinson and Naidu (2024), who argued that successful health marketing initiatives depend on public confidence in health communication to generate meaningful behavioral and social outcomes. Consequently, fostering trust in digital oral health information should be viewed as a strategic priority for practitioners and policymakers seeking to improve preventive oral health behavior.

MANAGERIAL IMPLICATIONS

The findings of this study provide several practical implications for dental clinic managers, healthcare marketers, and public health authorities seeking to promote preventive oral health behavior. First, the significant effects of online oral health information quality and trust in digital health information suggest that dental service providers should prioritize the development of accurate, understandable, and evidence-based digital content. Dental clinics can improve their websites and social media pages by offering preventive oral health guidance in simple language, using short educational videos, infographics, and frequently asked questions addressing common oral health concerns. Collaborating with licensed dentists and oral health professionals to validate shared information may further strengthen public trust and reduce skepticism toward digital health messages. Since trust emerged as the strongest predictor, managers should also ensure consistency, transparency, and credibility in all digital communications to encourage patients to adopt preventive oral health behaviors.

Furthermore, the positive influence of social media health engagement and personalized digital communication highlights the importance of interactive and patient-centered digital marketing strategies. Dental clinics may benefit from actively engaging with patients through platforms such as Facebook, Instagram, WhatsApp, and TikTok by sharing oral health tips, responding to questions, and promoting preventive campaigns tailored to different age groups. Personalized communication tools, including appointment reminders, oral hygiene recommendations, and customized follow-up messages, can strengthen patient involvement and encourage long-term preventive habits. Public health institutions may also partner with dental clinics to design culturally appropriate digital awareness campaigns that target specific population groups and emphasize the importance of routine oral care, early prevention, and healthy oral hygiene practices.

FUTURE RESEARCH DIRECTIONS

Although this study contributes to understanding the relationship between digital health marketing and preventive oral health behavior among dental service customers, several avenues remain open for future investigation. First, future studies may broaden the conceptual model by incorporating additional psychological, cultural, and lifestyle-related variables that could shape preventive oral health behavior. For example, perceptions of healthy eating, awareness of sugar consumption risks, oral health literacy, perceived susceptibility to oral diseases, self-efficacy, and health consciousness may offer valuable explanatory insights. In the Algerian and broader Arab context, Islamic religious values may also represent a meaningful predictor, particularly given the emphasis placed on cleanliness, personal hygiene, and practices such as oral care through miswak. Similarly, variables such as family influence, preventive health orientation, digital health anxiety, or perceived credibility of healthcare institutions may enrich understanding of oral health behavior formation.

Future research could also benefit from adopting alternative theoretical perspectives to explain preventive oral health behavior more comprehensively. For instance, the "Health Belief Model" may help explain how perceived susceptibility, severity, benefits, and barriers shape preventive oral health practices. Likewise, the "Information Acceptance Model" may provide additional insight into how individuals evaluate and accept oral health information encountered through digital platforms. Researchers may also consider integrating models such as the "Theory of Planned Behavior" or the Technology Acceptance Model to examine the combined effects of attitudinal, technological, and social determinants. Additionally, introducing mediating variables, such as oral health literacy, attitudes toward preventive oral care, or trust in healthcare providers, may clarify the underlying mechanisms linking digital health marketing to behavior. Potential moderating variables, including age, gender, education level, digital literacy, rural–urban differences, or prior dental experiences, may also reveal important variations in the strength of these relationships across different population segments.

CONCLUSION

This study examined the influence of digital health marketing on preventive oral health behavior among dental service customers by focusing on four key dimensions: online oral health information quality, social media health engagement, personalized digital communication, and trust in digital health information. The findings revealed that all proposed factors exerted significant positive effects on preventive oral health behavior, with trust in digital health information emerging as the strongest predictor. These results underscore the growing importance of digital communication channels in shaping health-related awareness and encouraging preventive oral care practices. The study contributes to the expanding literature on digital health marketing by extending its application to oral healthcare within a developing-country context, where empirical evidence remains limited. Practically, the findings emphasize the need for dental clinics and health authorities to invest in credible, engaging, and personalized digital communication strategies to enhance preventive oral health awareness and behaviors among the public. Ultimately, strengthening digital health marketing efforts may represent a valuable pathway toward improving oral health outcomes and supporting preventive healthcare practices in many countries with similar contexts.

REFERENCES

Al Ameri, A. A., Qaddouri, N. G., Alradhi, A. I., & Mouloudj, S. (2026). AI-Driven Sustainability Accounting and Auditing for Enhancing Ethical Practices in Fashion Manufacturing Companies. In Mouloudj, K., & Arantes, L. (Eds.), *Ethical Consumption and Responsible Innovation in Fashion through AI* (pp. 419–448). IGI Global., DOI: 10.4018/979-8-3373-7200-6.ch014

Alameri, S. A., Mahmoud, B. I., Almado, A. A., Jasim, Z. A., Jahlool, I. H., & Alyousuf, A. N. (2026). Consumer Acceptance of AI-Supported Circular Fashion Services: A Technology Acceptance Perspective. In Mouloudj, K., & Arantes, L. (Eds.), *Ethical Consumption and Responsible Innovation in Fashion through AI* (pp. 35–58). IGI Global., DOI: 10.4018/979-8-3373-7200-6.ch002

Asiri, F. Y. I., Tennant, M., & Kruger, E. (2024). Oral health behaviour, care utilisation, and barriers among students with disabilities: A parental perspective. *Health Care*, *12*(19), 1955. DOI: 10.3390/healthcare12191955 PMID: 39408135

Bouarar, A. C., Asanza, D. M., Mouloudj, S., Bouarar, A., Mouloudj, K., & Bozorgi, M. (2024). Elderly's Intention to Use Teledentistry Services: Antecedents and Challenges. In Martínez Asanza, D. (Ed.), *Geriatric Dentistry in the Age of Digital Technology* (pp. 101–116). IGI Global., DOI: 10.4018/979-8-3693-0260-6.ch004

Butt, I., Iqbal, T., & Zohaib, S. (2019). Healthcare marketing: A review of the literature based on citation analysis. *Health Marketing Quarterly*, *36*(4), 271–290. DOI: 10.1080/07359683.2019.1680120 PMID: 31646959

Calderon, S. J., Comnick, C. L., Villhauer, A., Marshall, T., Dahl, J.-U., Banas, J. A., & Drake, D. R. (2023). A social media intervention for promoting oral health behaviors in adolescents: A non-randomized pilot clinical trial. *Oral*, *3*(2), 203–214. DOI: 10.3390/oral3020018 PMID: 38162993

de Oliveira Júnior, A. J., Oliveira, J. M., Bretz, Y. P., & Mialhe, F. L. (2023). Online social networks for prevention and promotion of oral health: A systematic review. *Canadian Journal of Dental Hygiene : CJDH = Journal Canadien de l'Hygiène Dentaire : JCHD*, *57*(2), 83. PMID: 37464997

Fernández, C. E., Maturana, C. A., Coloma, S. I., Carrasco-Labra, A., & Giacaman, R. A. (2021). Teledentistry and mHealth for promotion and prevention of oral health: A systematic review and meta-analysis. *Journal of Dental Research*, *100*(9), 914–927. DOI: 10.1177/00220345211003828 PMID: 33769123

Ghalavand, H., Panahi, S., & Nouri, M. (2025). Opportunities and challenges of social media for oral health literacy improvement: A qualitative investigation based on Iranian dentists' perspectives. *BMC Health Services Research, 25*(1), 673. DOI: 10.1186/s12913-025-12845-z PMID: 40346510

Goldberg, E., Eberhard, J., Bauman, A., & Smith, B. J. (2022). Mass media campaigns for the promotion of oral health: A scoping review. *BMC Oral Health, 22*(1), 182. DOI: 10.1186/s12903-022-02212-3 PMID: 35568896

Jayasinghe, Y. A., Kanmodi, K. K., Jayasinghe, R. M., & Jayasinghe, R. D. (2024). Assessment of patterns and related factors in using social media platforms to access health and oral health information among Sri Lankan adults, with special emphasis on promoting oral health awareness. *BMC Public Health, 24*(1), 1472. DOI: 10.1186/s12889-024-19008-5 PMID: 38824505

Katusiime, J., Tumuhimbise, W., Rwambuka Mugyenyi, G., Kobutungi, P., Mugaba, A., Zender, R., Pinkwart, N., & Musiimenta, A. (2022). The role of mobile health technologies in promoting COVID-19 prevention: A narrative review of intervention effectiveness and adoption. *Digital Health, 8*, 1–12. DOI: 10.1177/20552076221131146 PMID: 36276182

Maleki, A., Ahadinezhad, B., Alizadeh, A., & Khosravizadeh, O. (2025). Using a social marketing approach to increase the pap-smear test uptake: Randomized controlled trial among women residing in urban region. *BMC Women's Health, 25*(1), 114. DOI: 10.1186/s12905-025-03642-1 PMID: 40082980

Martínez Asanza, D. (2025). Emerging Trends and Future Perspectives in Digital Dentistry for Rural Areas: An Update. In Martínez Asanza, D. (Ed.), *Transforming Dental Health in Rural Communities: Digital Dentistry* (pp. 1–36). IGI Global., DOI: 10.4018/979-8-3693-7165-7.ch001

Martínez Asanza, D., Rojas Herrera, I. A., Mouloudj, K., Amable, O. G., & Muzzamil, M. (2024). Impact of Digital Innovations in Preventive Dentistry: A Narrative Review. In Martínez Asanza, D. (Ed.), *Leveraging Digital Technology for Preventive Dentistry* (pp. 55–84). IGI Global., DOI: 10.4018/979-8-3693-3872-8.ch003

Mouloudj, K., Alameri, S. A. S., Evans, M. A., Almado, A. A. G., Mahmoud, B. I., & Asanza, D. M. (2026). Social marketing for health equity: Promoting preventive health behavior among women in rural communities. *International Journal of Environmental Research and Public Health, 23*(5), 584. DOI: 10.3390/ijerph23050584 PMID: 42196677

Mouloudj, K., Bouarar, A. C., Martínez Asanza, D., & Dimitrova, M. (2025). Understanding Customers' Intentions to Use Digital Dental Health Services: An Expanded Technology Acceptance Model. In Martínez Asanza, D. (Ed.), *Transforming Dental Health in Rural Communities: Digital Dentistry* (pp. 189–210). IGI Global., DOI: 10.4018/979-8-3693-7165-7.ch007

Mouloudj, K., Bouarar, A. C., Martínez Asanza, D., Saadaoui, L., Mouloudj, S., Njoku, A. U., Evans, M. A., & Bouarar, A. (2023). Factors Influencing the Adoption of Digital Health Apps: An Extended Technology Acceptance Model (TAM). In Bouarar, A., Mouloudj, K., & Martínez Asanza, D. (Eds.), *Integrating Digital Health Strategies for Effective Administration* (pp. 116–132). IGI Global., DOI: 10.4018/978-1-6684-8337-4.ch007

Nazari, A., Hajihashemi, M., Safavi, S. R., Ataei, R., & Hosseinnia, M. (2025). Health promotion theory-based educational interventions for improving oral health in children and adolescents: A systematic review and meta-analysis. *BMC Oral Health*, *25*(1), 1153. DOI: 10.1186/s12903-025-06549-3 PMID: 40653471

Nejad, M. S., Harooni, J., Charkazi, A., Shams, M., & Latifi, M. (2021). Using social marketing to promote preventive behaviors related to COVID-19. *Journal of Lifestyle Medicine*, *11*(2), 52–56. DOI: 10.15280/jlm.2021.11.2.52 PMID: 34549026

Olubodun, T., Balogun, M. R., Odeyemi, K. A., Osibogun, A., Odukoya, O. O., Banjo, A. A., Sonusi, S. E., Olubodun, A. B., Ogundele, O. O. P., & Dolapo, D. C. (2022). Effect of social marketing on the knowledge, attitude, and uptake of pap smear among women residing in an urban slum in Lagos, Nigeria. *BMC Women's Health*, *22*(1), 42. DOI: 10.1186/s12905-022-01620-5 PMID: 35164717

Parkinson, J., & Davey, J. (2023). The importance of health marketing and a research agenda. *Health Marketing Quarterly*, *40*(4), 347–351. DOI: 10.1080/07359683.2024.2271780 PMID: 37897233

Parkinson, J., & Naidu, J. (2024). Driving and evaluating social impact in health marketing. *Health Marketing Quarterly*, *41*(2), 113–129. DOI: 10.1080/07359683.2024.2363568 PMID: 39010695

Passos, K. K. M., da Silva Leonel, A. C. L., Bonan, P. R. F., de Castro, J. F. L., dos Anjos Pontual, M. L., de Moraes Ramos-Perez, F. M., & da Cruz Perez, D. E. (2020). Quality of information about oral cancer in Brazilian Portuguese available on Google, Youtube, and Instagram. *Medicina Oral, Patología Oral y Cirugía Bucal*, *25*(3), e346–e352. http://dx.doi.org/doi:10.4317/medoral.23374. DOI: 10.4317/medoral.23374 PMID: 32040464

Roger, A., Dourgoudian, M., Mergey, V., Laplanche, D., Ecarnot, F., & Sanchez, S. (2023). Effectiveness of Prevention Interventions Using Social Marketing Methods on Behavioural Change in the General Population: A Systematic Review of the Literature. *International Journal of Environmental Research and Public Health, 20*(5), 4576. DOI: 10.3390/ijerph20054576 PMID: 36901585

Sanghavi, B., Sachdev, S. S., Sachdev, J. B., Sonawane, S., Latke, S., Banga, K. S., & Banga, K. (2025). Social media as a tool for oral health promotion: An umbrella review of systematic reviews and content-analysis studies across digital platforms. *Cureus, 17*(7), e87962. DOI: 10.7759/cureus.87962 PMID: 40821201

Sharma, S., Mohanty, V., Balappanavar, A. Y., Chahar, P., Rijhwani, K., & Balappanavar, A. (2022). Role of digital media in promoting oral health: A systematic review. *Cureus, 14*(9), e28893. DOI: 10.7759/cureus.28893 PMID: 36225421

Stark, A. L., Geukes, C., & Dockweiler, C. (2022). Digital health promotion and prevention in settings: Scoping review. *Journal of Medical Internet Research, 24*(1), e21063. DOI: 10.2196/21063 PMID: 35089140

Swenson, E. R., Bastian, N. D., & Nembhard, H. B. (2018). Healthcare market segmentation and data mining: A systematic review. *Health Marketing Quarterly, 35*(3), 186–208. DOI: 10.1080/07359683.2018.1514734 PMID: 30470165

Tiffany, B., Blasi, P., Catz, S. L., & McClure, J. B. (2018). Mobile apps for oral health promotion: Content review and heuristic usability analysis. *JMIR mHealth and uHealth, 6*(9), e11432. DOI: 10.2196/11432 PMID: 30181114

Willis, V. C., Thomas Craig, K. J., Jabbarpour, Y., Scheufele, E. L., Arriaga, Y. E., Ajinkya, M., Rhee, K. B., & Bazemore, A. (2022). Digital health interventions to enhance prevention in primary care: Scoping review. *JMIR Medical Informatics, 10*(1), e33518. DOI: 10.2196/33518 PMID: 35060909

KEY TERMS AND DEFINITIONS

Customers Engagement: The degree to which individuals actively interact with, participate in, or respond to health-related content, services, or communications provided by healthcare organizations through digital or traditional channels.

Digital Health Marketing: The strategic use of digital technologies, online platforms, and electronic communication tools to promote health services, educate individuals, and encourage healthier behaviors and preventive healthcare practices.

Health Communication: The process of creating and sharing health-related information to improve awareness, understanding, decision-making, and behavior among individuals or communities.

Oral Health Promotion: The organized effort to improve oral health awareness, knowledge, and practices through education, preventive initiatives, and supportive interventions aimed at reducing oral diseases.

Preventive Oral Health Behavior: Individual actions and habits undertaken to maintain oral health and prevent dental diseases, including regular tooth brushing, healthy eating, dental checkups, and oral hygiene practices.

Social Media Marketing: The use of social media platforms to communicate, educate, and engage audiences through content intended to promote awareness, services, or behavior change in a specific area, including health.

Trust in Digital Health Information: The extent to which individuals perceive online health information as credible, reliable, accurate, and worthy of being used in making health-related decisions.

Chapter 7
Digital Marketing Tools and Preventive Health Behaviors:
Opportunities and Challenges for Dental Health Promotion

Flaka Hoti
http://orcid.org/0000-0002-4780-5776
University "Fehmi Agani" in Gjakova, Kosovo

Hasime Arif Bacaj Terziqi
http://orcid.org/0009-0001-3411-8272
Faculty of Medicine, University "Fehmi Agani" in Gjakova, Kosovo

Sarab Jawad Mohammed Al-Obaidi
http://orcid.org/0009-0005-2168-7491
Department of Industrial Management, College of Administration and Economics, University of Baghdad, Baghdad, Iraq

Kamel Mouloudj
http://orcid.org/0000-0001-7617-8313
Department of Commercial Sciences, Faculty of Economics, Business, and Management Sciences, University of Medea, Algeria

Ferdi Kamberi
http://orcid.org/0000-0003-1642-736X
Faculty of Social Sciences, University "Fehmi Agani" in Gjakova, Kosovo

Antigona Ukëhaxhaj
http://orcid.org/0000-0003-4128-0769
Faculty of Medicine, University "Fehmi Agani," in Gjakova, Kosovo & National Institute of Public Health Kosovo, Kosovo

ABSTRACT

Digital technologies have transformed healthcare communication and created new opportunities for promoting preventive health behaviors, particularly in public dental health contexts. This chapter examines the role of digital marketing tools in encour-

DOI: 10.4018/979-8-3373-8894-6.ch007

aging preventive health behaviors and improving public dental health promotion. Using a conceptual and literature-based approach, the chapter synthesizes prior research on digital communication technologies, behavioral theories, preventive engagement, and challenges associated with healthcare communication. The findings indicate that digital marketing tools—including mobile health applications, social media platforms, wearable technologies, artificial intelligence, and personalized communication systems—can strengthen preventive behaviors through improved awareness, reminders, self-monitoring, personalization, and patient engagement. However, important challenges remain, including privacy and ethical concerns, digital inequalities, communication barriers, regulatory limitations, and difficulties sustaining long-term behavioral change.

INTRODUCTION

The rapid expansion of digital technologies has transformed how health information is communicated, accessed, and utilized across healthcare systems worldwide (Mouloudj et al., 2023). Digital platforms, mobile technologies, social media, wearable devices, and artificial intelligence (AI) increasingly shape interactions between healthcare providers and the public, creating new opportunities to improve health communication and encourage preventive health behaviors (Franssen et al., 2020; OECD, 2019; Stoumpos et al., 2023). As healthcare systems continue to shift toward prevention-oriented approaches, digital communication tools have gained growing importance in supporting health awareness, patient engagement, self-care, and early intervention (Martínez Asanza et al., 2024). These developments are particularly relevant to public health initiatives that seek to reduce preventable diseases and encourage healthier behavioral practices (Li et al., 2020).

Preventive health behaviors, including healthy lifestyle choices, regular screening, adherence to medical recommendations, and routine self-care practices, play a critical role in improving health outcomes and reducing healthcare burdens (Mouloudj et al., 2026; Parkinson & Naidu, 2024). In the field of oral and dental health, preventive behaviors such as regular tooth brushing, flossing, reduced sugar consumption, smoking avoidance, and periodic dental checkups are essential for preventing oral diseases and maintaining long-term well-being (Martínez Asanza, 2025). Nevertheless, sustaining such behaviors remains challenging because health decisions are influenced not only by individual knowledge but also by social norms, economic conditions, digital literacy, healthcare accessibility, and broader environmental factors (Glanz & Bishop, 2010).

In response to these challenges, digital marketing tools have emerged as increasingly valuable mechanisms for promoting preventive health behaviors. Unlike traditional communication approaches, digital tools facilitate more immediate, personalized, and interactive engagement (Kim & Lee, 2026). Technologies such as mobile health applications (mHealth), social media platforms, wearable devices, online communities, chatbots, and personalized messaging systems allow healthcare organizations to disseminate preventive information, provide reminders, encourage self-monitoring, and strengthen public participation in preventive health practices (Huang et al., 2026; Wells et al., 2022). Research suggests that digital interventions can positively influence behavior change, health engagement, and preventive practices when integrated into individuals' everyday routines and supported by meaningful feedback mechanisms (Lee et al., 2018; Iribarren et al., 2021; Jung & Cho, 2022; Natalucci et al., 2023).

In the context of public dental health promotion, digital marketing tools present important opportunities for improving oral health literacy, increasing awareness of preventive care, encouraging healthier routines, and promoting timely access to dental services (Atherton et al., 2010, Franssen et al., 2020). Social media campaigns, mobile applications, personalized reminders, and digital educational platforms may strengthen engagement with preventive behaviors by making oral health information more accessible and relevant (Mouloudj et al., 2026; Parkinson & Naidu, 2024). However, despite these opportunities, important challenges remain, including privacy concerns, ethical issues related to AI, communication barriers, unequal digital access, misinformation, predatory marketing, and difficulties sustaining long-term behavioral change (Dwivedi et al., 2021; Deniz-Garcia et al., 2023; Huang et al., 2026; Shajari et al., 2023).

Given these opportunities and challenges, there remains a need for a comprehensive understanding of how digital marketing tools contribute to preventive health behaviors and public dental health promotion. Existing discussions are often fragmented across broader healthcare settings, with limited attention to preventive dental contexts.

Accordingly, this chapter aims to examine the role of digital marketing tools in promoting preventive health behaviors, with a particular focus on public dental health promotion. Specifically, the chapter seeks to address the following research questions:

- How do digital marketing tools contribute to promoting preventive health behaviors in healthcare and public dental health contexts?
- What theoretical perspectives explain the influence of digital communication tools on preventive health behaviors?
- How can the effectiveness of digital campaigns for preventive health promotion be evaluated?

- What opportunities and challenges influence the effectiveness of digital marketing tools in promoting preventive dental health behaviors?
- What managerial implications emerge for healthcare organizations and public dental health practitioners seeking to strengthen preventive engagement through digital communication tools?

By addressing these questions, the chapter provides a comprehensive overview of the opportunities and challenges associated with digital marketing tools and their contribution to preventive dental health promotion.

DIGITAL TRANSFORMATION IN THE HEALTHCARE SECTOR

Understanding Digital Transformation in Healthcare

The rapid advancement of digital technologies has transformed how organizations operate, communicate, and deliver services across various sectors, including healthcare (Mouloudj et al., 2023). In contemporary society, digital technologies increasingly influence social interaction, communication patterns, information access, and decision-making processes (Alnaemat & Saleem, 2026). The integration of digital systems, internet-based platforms, cloud computing, AI, automation, and social media into organizational activities are commonly referred to as digitalization (Martínez Asanza, 2025). These technologies facilitate data-driven decision-making, improve communication efficiency, and enhance organizational performance (Almokdad et al., 2026; OECD, 2019).

At a broader level, digital transformation refers to the extensive organizational and structural changes resulting from the strategic integration of digital technologies into operational systems and service delivery models (Martínez Asanza et al., 2024). Across industries, digital transformation has altered how services are designed, delivered, and experienced (Almokdad et al., 2026). While digital technologies offer significant opportunities for improving efficiency, accessibility, and innovation, they also introduce important concerns related to governance, privacy, ethical standards, and digital inequality (Alnaemat & Saleem, 2026; Huang et al., 2026; Li et al., 2020). Consequently, stakeholders must adopt evidence-based and collaborative approaches to ensure an inclusive and sustainable digital future (OECD, n.d.).

In the healthcare sector, digital transformation represents a major shift toward technology-enabled healthcare systems that improve service quality, patient engagement, and healthcare accessibility. Healthcare institutions increasingly utilize digital technologies to address medical challenges, improve healthcare efficiency, and strengthen communication between healthcare providers and patients (Martínez

Asanza, 2025; Parkinson & Naidu, 2024). The digital transformation of healthcare includes internet-based systems, electronic communication platforms, digital patient management tools, and intelligent technologies designed to improve diagnosis, treatment, and preventive care practices (Kim & Lee, 2026; Stoumpos et al., 2023).

More specifically, healthcare systems increasingly rely on technologies such as electronic health records, telemedicine, AI, mobile health applications, wearable devices, and big data analytics (Franssen et al., 2020; Mouloudj et al., 2023). These technologies have significantly improved healthcare delivery by facilitating quicker diagnosis, better patient monitoring, efficient medical information management, and stronger communication between healthcare professionals and patients (Huang et al., 2026). Furthermore, digital technologies enable healthcare services to become more patient-centered by supporting remote consultations, personalized communication, and continuous access to medical information regardless of geographic limitations (Khan et al., 2026; Fernandes Prabhu et al., 2025).

Table 1. Major digital technologies supporting healthcare transformation and preventive health promotion

Digital Technology	Description	Healthcare Benefits	Contribution to Preventive Health Behaviors
Electronic Health Records (EHRs)	Digital systems for storing and managing patient medical data	Improved care coordination and medical information accessibility	Facilitates monitoring of preventive checkups and patient history
Telemedicine	Remote consultation through digital communication technologies	Increased access to healthcare services	Encourages preventive consultations and early intervention
Mobile Health Applications (mHealth)	Smartphone applications supporting health management	Improved patient engagement and health monitoring	Promotes healthy habits and preventive reminders
Artificial Intelligence (AI)	Intelligent systems for diagnosis and predictive analysis	Enhanced healthcare accuracy and efficiency	Supports early disease detection and risk prediction
Big Data Analytics	Analysis of large health-related datasets	Improved decision-making and service planning	Helps identify health risks and behavioral trends
Social Media Platforms	Digital communication channels for information dissemination	Wider health information reach	Supports awareness campaigns and preventive education

Source: Developed by the authors based on OECD (2019), Stoumpos et al. (2023), Khan et al. (2026), Fernandes Prabhu et al. (2025), and UNICEF (n.d.)

Opportunities and Challenges of Digital Transformation for Public Health Promotion

The increasing integration of digital technologies into healthcare systems creates substantial opportunities for enhancing public health outcomes and encouraging preventive health behaviors (Li et al., 2020; Martínez Asanza, 2025). According to UNICEF (n.d.), digital transformation can significantly improve healthcare accessibility, service coordination, workforce efficiency, and patient outcomes. The use of standardized digital systems and data-driven decision-making processes enables healthcare organizations to deliver more efficient, accessible, and personalized healthcare services.

In addition, technologies such as AI, predictive analytics, mobile applications, and digital communication platforms facilitate early disease detection, personalized interventions, and improved health education (Mouloudj et al., 2025). These innovations also provide healthcare organizations with new opportunities to disseminate preventive information and encourage healthier behavioral practices among individuals and communities (Kim & Lee, 2026; Martínez Asanza, 2025). In the context of public health, digital communication channels may strengthen awareness regarding oral hygiene practices, preventive dental visits, healthy dietary habits, and early prevention of oral diseases (Mouloudj et al., 2026; Parkinson & Naidu, 2024).

Despite these opportunities, digital transformation also presents several challenges. Concerns regarding data privacy, cybersecurity, unequal access to digital technologies, digital literacy limitations, and ethical considerations may reduce the effectiveness of technology-enabled healthcare initiatives (Huang et al., 2026; Mouloudj et al., 2023). Moreover, disparities in internet access and technological capabilities may limit participation among vulnerable populations. Therefore, healthcare institutions and policymakers should adopt inclusive and secure digital strategies to maximize the role of digital technologies in promoting preventive health behaviors and improving public dental health outcomes (Kim & Lee, 2026; Martínez Asanza et al., 2024).

DIGITAL MARKETING TOOLS AND STRATEGIES

Digital technologies have transformed the ways healthcare organizations communicate with individuals, disseminate health information, and encourage preventive health behaviors (Kim & Lee, 2026). In the context of public health promotion, digital marketing tools facilitate broader access to health education, personalized communication, behavioral monitoring, and patient engagement (Martínez Asanza, 2025; Mouloudj et al., 2025). Their increasing adoption reflects the expansion of digital ecosystems and growing public interest in technology-enabled healthcare solutions. However, sociological literature suggests that the benefits of these technologies are not equally distributed, as socio-economic status, age, educational level, and digital literacy significantly influence access and usage patterns, potentially reproducing existing health inequalities (Van Dijk, 2020; WHO, 2021). Consequently, healthcare professionals, social workers, and community actors play an important role in supporting vulnerable populations and reducing digital inequalities through technology access and education initiatives (Berkman et al., 2014; Mouloudj et al., 2026).

Among the most widely adopted digital tools are mobile health applications (mHealth), which have experienced considerable growth during the last decade (Mouloudj et al., 2023). Application marketplaces currently provide more than 350,000 health-related mobile applications addressing diverse areas such as chronic disease management, stress reduction, sleep disorders, medication adherence, fitness tracking, mental health, telehealth, and monitoring of vital signs (Wells et al., 2022). Health-based mobile applications are generally defined as software programs downloaded onto smartphones or similar digital devices for medical and health-related purposes, either by patients or healthcare professionals (Wells et al., 2022).

The increasing popularity of mHealth technologies is linked to their ability to provide personalized services, enhance healthcare accessibility, lower healthcare costs, and empower individuals to take greater responsibility for their own health management (Li et al., 2020; Mouloudj et al., 2025). Furthermore, the widespread availability of smartphones and internet connectivity has created favorable conditions for broader adoption of mHealth solutions, particularly among historically underserved populations (van Veen et al., 2019). Research evidence demonstrates that mobile applications can positively influence preventive and self-management behaviors. For example, Lee et al. (2018) found that mHealth interventions contributed to improved health outcomes in chronic disease management through real-time monitoring, personalized information delivery, and automated reminders that strengthened patient engagement and self-management. Similarly, a systematic review and meta-analysis by Iribarren et al. (2021) concluded that mobile app interventions generate moderate improvements in behavioral and clinical outcomes, particularly by increasing engagement and facilitating positive behavioral change.

In the context of preventive health promotion, including public dental health, mobile applications can be particularly useful for encouraging healthy routines, sending reminders for preventive checkups, improving adherence to oral hygiene practices, disseminating educational content, and supporting healthier lifestyle choices (Kim & Lee, 2026; Nejad et al., 2021; Martínez Asanza, 2025). Personalized notifications and real-time monitoring functions may enhance users' awareness and motivate sustained engagement in preventive behaviors (Mouloudj et al., 2026).

Another important technological development is wearable health technology, which includes electronic devices worn on or near the body, or integrated into clothing and accessories, to collect and analyze physiological and behavioral information (Yetisen et al., 2018). Through sensor miniaturization, network connectivity, and predictive analytics, wearable devices continuously collect, transmit, and interpret biometric information (Metcalf et al., 2016). Commonly monitored indicators include body temperature, heart rate, blood pressure, oxygen saturation, posture, physical activity, and movement patterns using technologies such as electrocardiograms (ECGs) and ballistocardiograms (BCGs) (Franseen et al., 2020; Iribarren et al., 2021).

Evidence indicates that wearable technologies can substantially contribute to preventive health behaviors by providing accurate feedback, supporting self-monitoring, and encouraging healthier habits. For example, wearable activity trackers have demonstrated significant potential for increasing physical activity levels, particularly among individuals with chronic conditions (Franseen et al., 2020). Similarly, wearable devices can support behavioral change by offering personalized performance feedback that encourages healthier lifestyles. Regarding mental well-being, wearable technologies enable stress and emotional monitoring through physiological indicators, thereby supporting early identification and management of psychological conditions (Choi et al., 2017; Setz et al., 2010).

Wearable technologies are also increasingly applied in the management of chronic illnesses, including cardiovascular diseases, hypertension, diabetes, Parkinson's disease, stroke rehabilitation, and respiratory disorders through remote monitoring and personalized intervention systems (Burridge et al., 2017; Brown et al., 2017; Lin et al., 2017). In addition, these technologies provide rehabilitation and behavioral support for patients with cancer, autism, and depression (Rossi et al., 2018; Daniels et al., 2018; Valenza et al., 2015). Although these applications extend beyond preventive dental care, they collectively demonstrate the broader capacity of digital tools to support personalized prevention, early intervention, and patient-centered healthcare.

Table 2. Major digital marketing tools supporting preventive health behaviors

Digital Tool	Main Function	Contribution to Preventive Health Behaviors	Potential Relevance to Public Dental Health
Mobile Health Applications (mHealth)	Health monitoring, reminders, education	Encourages self-management and healthy habits	Oral hygiene reminders, appointment tracking, preventive education
Wearable Technologies	Continuous monitoring of physiological indicators	Promotes health awareness and behavior tracking	Monitoring lifestyle factors influencing oral health
Online Health Communities	Peer support and information exchange	Enhances motivation and social support	Sharing oral health experiences and preventive knowledge
Social Media Platforms	Health communication and content dissemination	Expands awareness and preventive education	Promotion of oral health campaigns
AI Chatbots and Virtual Assistants	Automated responses and personalized support	Improves accessibility and health engagement	Appointment scheduling and preventive guidance

Source: Developed by the authors based on cited literature

In addition to mobile and wearable technologies, online health communities and social media platforms have become increasingly important digital communication channels. These online environments create spaces where individuals exchange experiences, seek information, and provide emotional support regarding health-related concerns (Ziebland & Wyke, 2012; Naslund et al., 2016). From a sociological perspective, the theory of social capital developed by Putnam (2000) distinguishes between bonding social capital (stronger internal group connections) and bridging social capital (connections between different groups), both of which influence how health information is shared and trusted within digital communities. In public health contexts, these digital communities can reinforce preventive behaviors by strengthening peer influence, improving health awareness, and facilitating communication between communities and healthcare institutions (Martínez Asanza et al., 2024; Parkinson & Naidu, 2024).

AI is another rapidly growing digital tool that increasingly supports communication and engagement strategies in healthcare. AI-powered chatbots and virtual assistants can provide real-time support by answering patient inquiries, scheduling appointments, disseminating information, and offering personalized recommendations (Huang et al., 2026; Zhao et al., 2026). These tools enhance accessibility by enabling continuous interaction between patients and healthcare providers, thereby improving patient experiences and engagement (Li et al., 2020).

Nevertheless, the growing use of AI raises important ethical and social concerns. Existing evidence suggests that machine learning systems trained on historical healthcare data may unintentionally reproduce or reinforce existing inequalities

(Obermeyer et al., 2019). Therefore, scholars increasingly advocate for human-centered AI approaches that prioritize dignity, transparency, autonomy, and social justice in algorithmic healthcare systems (Shneiderman, 2020). While AI-driven technologies offer significant opportunities for enhancing communication effectiveness and preventive health engagement, their successful implementation requires careful attention to privacy, security, equity, and data quality considerations (Kim & Lee, 2026; Mouloudj et al., 2025).

Overall, digital marketing tools, including mobile applications, wearable technologies, online communities, social media, and AI-driven communication systems, provide substantial opportunities for encouraging preventive health behaviors and strengthening public dental health promotion. However, their effectiveness depends on equitable access, user acceptance, digital literacy, and responsible implementation strategies.

THE ROLE OF DIGITAL MARKETING TOOLS IN PROMOTING PREVENTIVE HEALTH BEHAVIORS FOR PUBLIC DENTAL HEALTH

Preventive health behaviors play an essential role in reducing disease burden and improving long-term public health outcomes (Nejad et al., 2021). The World Health Organization (WHO) continues to emphasize the importance of preventing noncommunicable diseases, obesity, hypertension, physical inactivity, and other health-related risks through effective preventive strategies and public awareness initiatives (WHO, 2023, 2024a, 2024b, 2024c). Within this context, digital communication technologies and marketing tools increasingly support the dissemination of preventive information and encourage healthier behavioral practices (Kim & Lee, 2026).

In healthcare settings, preventive communication becomes more effective when individuals are not only informed about potential health risks but are also guided toward practical actions, available support systems, and timely interventions (Martínez Asanza et al., 2024; Parkinson & Naidu, 2024). Digital platforms facilitate this process by linking health information with reminders, appointment systems, self-care guidance, peer support networks, and personalized feedback mechanisms (Mouloudj et al., 2026). As a result, digital marketing tools have become increasingly relevant for translating preventive knowledge into everyday health practices.

This role is particularly important in public dental health promotion, where preventive behaviors such as regular tooth brushing, flossing, reduced sugar consumption, early dental visits, smoking avoidance, and routine preventive checkups significantly influence oral health outcomes (Atherton et al., 2010; Nejad et al.,

2021). Unlike treatment-oriented approaches, preventive dental health focuses on maintaining healthy behaviors before oral diseases emerge or worsen. In this regard, digital communication tools can strengthen awareness, improve oral health literacy, and support behavior maintenance through continuous engagement.

Digital marketing tools, including mobile applications, wearable devices, social media platforms, online communities, digital reminders, educational websites, and AI-supported communication systems, can make preventive health information more accessible, interactive, and personalized (Huang et al., 2026; Mouloudj et al., 2026). For example, mobile health applications may encourage healthy routines through reminders for tooth brushing, hydration, preventive appointments, and oral care monitoring (Mouloudj et al., 2023). Wearable technologies and smartphone-based health monitoring can also reinforce healthier lifestyles by transforming general recommendations into measurable daily activities, such as physical activity levels, sleep quality, and stress management, all of which indirectly influence oral health and overall well-being.

Research evidence suggests that mobile health interventions and wearable devices can contribute positively to health behavior improvement, including physical activity, nutrition management, self-monitoring, and behavioral adherence, although effectiveness often depends on user engagement, usability, and sustained participation (Jung & Cho, 2022; Natalucci et al., 2023). This distinction is particularly important for preventive health promotion because digital tools do not automatically generate behavioral change; rather, they become effective when individuals integrate them into their daily routines and perceive them as meaningful and easy to use (Kim & Lee, 2026).

Digital technologies may also contribute to healthier dietary practices and improved nutrition literacy. Since dietary behavior strongly influences oral health outcomes, particularly through sugar consumption and nutritional habits, digital interventions that combine education, feedback, motivation, and behavioral monitoring can support healthier decision-making (Chatterjee et al., 2021). Repeated digital reinforcement through reminders, educational content, or personalized messaging can help individuals better understand preventive recommendations and translate them into sustainable habits (Parkinson & Naidu, 2024).

One of the major strengths of digital marketing tools in preventive health promotion is personalization. Digital communication platforms allow messages to be tailored according to demographic characteristics, health conditions, language, literacy levels, cultural background, behavioral history, and interaction patterns (Martínez Asanza et al., 2024). Personalized communication can improve message relevance and reduce the limitations of generic preventive campaigns.

Healthcare market segmentation and data mining techniques can help identify population groups that may benefit from specific preventive interventions or communication strategies (Swenson et al., 2018). Younger populations, for example, may be more responsive to mobile applications and social media campaigns related to oral hygiene, whereas older adults may benefit from simplified interfaces, trust-based communication, and reminder systems for preventive dental visits. Similarly, individuals with chronic diseases may require personalized educational messages connecting oral health maintenance with broader health outcomes (Nejad et al., 2021). In this sense, tailored communication improves the alignment between preventive messages and audience needs.

However, personalization should be implemented responsibly. Preventive communication often involves sensitive personal information, and the use of digital tools should prioritize transparency, privacy protection, scientific credibility, and ethical standards (Martínez Asanza et al., 2024). Data-driven communication strategies should support informed decision-making rather than manipulate behavior or exploit personal data (Huang et al., 2026). Responsible personalization therefore requires balancing technological efficiency with individual autonomy and equity considerations.

Table 3. Contributions of digital marketing tools to preventive dental health behaviors

Digital Marketing Tool	Preventive Function	Contribution to Dental Health Promotion
Mobile Health Applications (mHealth)	Reminders, education, behavioral monitoring	Encourages brushing, flossing, hydration, and preventive dental visits
Social Media Platforms	Health awareness and information dissemination	Promotes oral hygiene campaigns and preventive education
Online Health Communities	Peer interaction and shared experiences	Encourages knowledge exchange and preventive motivation
AI Chatbots and Virtual Assistants	Real-time support and personalized guidance	Provides oral care recommendations and appointment assistance
Wearable Technologies	Lifestyle monitoring and self-tracking	Supports healthy habits indirectly associated with oral health
Personalized Digital Messaging	Tailored communication based on user needs	Improves relevance and engagement with preventive oral health advice

Source: Developed by the authors based on cited literature

Overall, digital marketing tools can contribute substantially to preventive health behaviors when designed as mechanisms for sustained engagement rather than one-way information delivery. Their strength lies in connecting evidence-based information with practical action, personalized communication, self-monitoring, reminders, and social support. In the context of public dental health promotion, these tools can improve oral health awareness, encourage preventive service utilization, support healthier daily routines, and normalize preventive behaviors such as regular oral hygiene and early dental care seeking.

THEORETICAL PERSPECTIVES AND EVALUATION OF DIGITAL CAMPAIGNS FOR PREVENTIVE DENTAL HEALTH PROMOTION

Behavioral Theories Supporting Preventive Health Communication

Understanding why individuals adopt preventive health behaviors is essential for designing effective digital communication strategies. Behavioral theories provide useful frameworks for explaining how digital messages, reminders, social influence, and perceived risks shape customers' willingness to adopt sustainable and healthy practices (Alameri et al., 2026; Mouloudj et al., 2025; Nejad et al., 2021). In the context of public dental health promotion, these theoretical perspectives can help explain behaviors such as regular tooth brushing, flossing, reducing sugar consumption, attending preventive dental checkups, and seeking oral health information (Atherton et al., 2010; Martínez Asanza et al., 2024).

One of the most widely applied behavioral frameworks is the "Health Belief Model" (HBM), originally developed by Rosenstock (1966) and further refined over time. According to HBM, individuals are more likely to adopt preventive behaviors when they perceive themselves as susceptible to a health condition, believe that the condition may have serious consequences, recognize the benefits of taking preventive action, and perceive barriers to action as manageable (Champion & Skinner, 2021). Health-related behaviors are therefore shaped by individuals' beliefs regarding risk, severity, expected outcomes, and practical constraints.

Although the HBM remains influential in health communication research, sociological critiques argue that it tends to emphasize individual perceptions while underestimating structural and social determinants of health behavior. Factors such as socio-economic conditions, cultural norms, social networks, healthcare access, and environmental limitations can strongly influence preventive behaviors regardless of individual motivation. Consequently, scholars increasingly advocate for multi-level interventions that simultaneously address individual beliefs, community support, and structural barriers to behavior change (Glanz & Bishop, 2010; Champion & Skinner, 2021).

Health belief frameworks continue to play an important role in explaining how individuals respond to digital preventive communication. Research suggests that health beliefs significantly shape intentions to adopt preventive behaviors (Mao et al., 2023). In digital contexts, HBM is useful for understanding how people react to online health messages, mobile applications, educational platforms, and social media content. For example, Mao et al. (2023) demonstrated the continuing relevance of HBM in digital environments, showing its usefulness in explaining public responses to health promotion strategies and preventive communication campaigns. Similarly, Yap et al. (2023) found that preventive health behaviors are influenced by perceived benefits, barriers, subjective norms, and perceived health importance, while perceived threat factors such as susceptibility and severity may be less influential. Their findings also suggest that affordability and cultural orientation significantly shape preventive behavior.

Another widely applied framework is the "Theory of Planned Behavior" (TPB), developed by Ajzen (1991). TPB proposes that behavioral intention is the strongest predictor of behavior and is shaped by three key dimensions: attitudes toward the behavior, subjective social norms, and perceived behavioral control. In preventive healthcare settings, TPB helps explain why individuals decide to adopt or reject digital health tools, participate in preventive services, or engage in self-care activities (Mouloudj et al., 2026). Research applying TPB highlights its usefulness for understanding digital engagement in healthcare contexts. For instance, Li et al. (2020) found that perceived behavioral control and illness severity strongly influenced patients' intentions to use online inquiry services provided by internet hospitals. Behavioral intentions were also affected by convenience, emotional preferences, and perceived risks, emphasizing the need for trustworthy and secure digital healthcare systems. Likewise, Gu et al. (2019) reported that attitude, trust, subjective norms, and perceived behavioral control significantly influence continued participation in health-related social media platforms. These findings are particularly relevant for public dental health promotion, where digital campaigns increasingly rely on social media, educational platforms, and mobile technologies to encourage preventive oral health behaviors.

Table 4. Behavioral theories supporting preventive health communication

Theory	Core Components	Contribution to Preventive Health Behaviors	Relevance to Public Dental Health Promotion
Health Belief Model (HBM)	Perceived susceptibility, severity, benefits, and barriers	Explains why individuals adopt preventive actions	Encourages preventive dental visits and oral hygiene behaviors
Theory of Planned Behavior (TPB)	Attitudes, subjective norms, perceived behavioral control	Explains behavioral intentions and decision-making	Helps understand adoption of preventive oral health behaviors and digital tools

Source: Developed by the authors based on Rosenstock (1966), Ajzen (1991)

Evaluating the Effectiveness of Digital Campaigns for Preventive Health Promotion

The effectiveness of digital campaigns depends not only on message visibility but also on their ability to influence meaningful behavioral change. Health communication campaigns are generally based on the assumption that exposure to preventive messages contributes to increased awareness, stronger intentions, and ultimately healthier behaviors (Martínez Asanza et al., 2024; Zhao et al., 2026). According to the Bangkok Charter for Health Promotion in a Globalized World (2005), health promotion involves enabling people to gain greater control over their health and its determinants. This broader perspective emphasizes participation, access, supportive environments, and social empowerment rather than relying solely on information dissemination (Koh et al., 2021).

Evidence increasingly supports the effectiveness of digital communication campaigns in public health promotion. Koh et al. (2021), in their review of 99 public health campaigns across Facebook, Instagram, Twitter, and YouTube, found that campaigns using interactive features and behavior-oriented content achieved stronger audience engagement and visibility. However, the study also highlighted an important limitation: many campaigns focused excessively on engagement indicators such as likes, comments, and shares rather than measuring actual behavioral outcomes.

Similarly, Athey et al. (2022) examined 819 public health interventions implemented through Facebook and Instagram by 174 health organizations, reaching more than two billion users. Their findings indicated that digital campaigns substantially improved public understanding of health topics and vaccines, demonstrating the cost-effectiveness and broad reach of social media communication strategies. Moreover, Siopis et al. (2023), through an analysis of 29 studies, found that digital interventions delivered through smartphone applications, websites, and text messaging systems contributed positively to blood pressure management, further supporting the effectiveness of digital preventive communication strategies.

In the context of public dental health, effective digital campaigns should move beyond awareness creation and focus on measurable preventive outcomes. These may include increased oral hygiene compliance, greater participation in preventive dental visits, improved oral health literacy, healthier dietary behaviors, and stronger long-term engagement with preventive care practices.

Trust, Credibility, and Perceived Usefulness of Digital Health Information

Trust remains one of the most important determinants of whether individuals adopt health information delivered through digital channels. Research consistently demonstrates that people are more likely to use digital information sources when the content is perceived as useful, credible, and relevant to their personal needs. According to Zhang and Kim (2022), perceived usefulness significantly influences both trust and continued use of online health information. Similarly, Boon-itt (2019) found that the quality of health-related websites positively influences perceptions of usefulness, which subsequently strengthens trust and intention to use digital information sources. Information credibility is therefore strongly associated with perceived usefulness and engagement with preventive communication (Mouloudj et al., 2026).

Further evidence is provided by Rowley et al. (2015), who developed the Trust in Online Health Information (TOHI) scale, identifying credibility, usefulness, ease of use, and verification as major determinants of trust in digital health information. Meta-analytic findings also confirm that high-quality and trustworthy information positively influences behavioral intentions to adopt digital information systems (Sun et al., 2022).

For preventive dental health promotion, these findings suggest that digital communication strategies should prioritize evidence-based content, transparency, professional credibility, and practical usefulness (Martínez Asanza et al., 2024). Individuals are more likely to engage with oral health information and preventive guidance when digital messages are perceived as trustworthy, understandable, and directly applicable to everyday health practices.

CHALLENGES OF DIGITAL MARKETING TOOLS IN PROMOTING PREVENTIVE DENTAL HEALTH BEHAVIORS

Privacy, Ethics, and Trust in Digital Health Communication

Privacy and data security represent major challenges in the use of digital marketing tools for preventive health promotion. Many digital communication strategies depend on personal data to segment audiences, personalize messages, predict health interests, and deliver targeted information (Mouloudj et al., 2025). Such data may include demographic characteristics, geographical location, online behavior, application usage, wearable device information, health-related preferences, or indicators associated with disease risks. Although these data can make preventive messages more relevant and personalized, they also create important ethical and legal concerns.

Health-related data are considerably more sensitive than information commonly used in commercial marketing because they may reveal intimate aspects of a person's lifestyle, medical condition, vulnerability, diagnosis, or risk status (Mouloudj et al., 2026). A preventive reminder for dental screening, oral hygiene practices, diabetes monitoring, or nutritional counseling may be beneficial when delivered transparently and appropriately (Martínez Asanza et al., 2024). However, the same communication may feel intrusive if individuals do not understand how their information was collected, why they were targeted, or who has access to their data.

These concerns become increasingly significant with the growth of mobile health applications, wearable devices, AI, and personalized communication systems. Although mHealth applications can improve health education, reminders, monitoring, and feedback, concerns remain regarding their quality, usability, reliability, and ethical use of AI (Deniz-Garcia et al., 2023). Similarly, wearable technologies and AI-supported sensors facilitate real-time monitoring and preventive self-care but simultaneously generate continuous streams of sensitive health-related information (Shajari et al., 2023).

The ethical complexity of digital communication extends beyond privacy concerns. AI-supported systems increasingly enable audience segmentation, behavioral prediction, automated messaging, and personalized targeting (Almokdad et al., 2026). While these capabilities may improve the timing and relevance of preventive communication, they also raise concerns related to transparency, manipulation, discrimination, bias, and the commercialization of sensitive health information. Ethical concerns do not arise from personalization itself, but from situations where personalization becomes opaque, overly persuasive, or exploitative. For example, evidence-based reminders encouraging preventive dental checkups differ fundamentally from emotionally manipulative or commercially driven content lacking scientific credibility.

Research in digital and social media communication emphasizes the importance of algorithmic accountability, platform governance, ethical communication, and responsible use of consumer data in digital environments (Alameri et al., 2026; Dwivedi et al., 2021). These concerns become even more critical in preventive health promotion because they may directly influence health decisions, trust in healthcare services, and long-term preventive behaviors (Huang et al., 2026). Moreover, algorithmic bias remains an important issue. Systems trained on incomplete or unrepresentative data may unintentionally reinforce social inequalities by prioritizing digitally active populations while overlooking communities with greater preventive health needs (Mouloudj et al., 2025). Consequently, digital communication strategies should evaluate not only engagement metrics but also fairness, inclusiveness, and public health impact (Obermeyer et al., 2019).

Trust therefore becomes central to the effectiveness of preventive communication. Responsible digital health promotion requires informed consent, transparent data use, privacy protection, clear boundaries between education and advertising, and strong safeguards against misuse of personal information. Without these protections, personalized communication risks undermining the trust necessary for sustained preventive engagement.

Table 5. Major challenges affecting digital marketing tools in preventive dental health promotion

Challenge	Key Issue	Potential Impact on Preventive Dental Health Behaviors
Privacy and Data Security	Collection and management of sensitive health data	Reduced trust and reluctance to engage with digital preventive tools
Ethical Use of AI	Algorithmic bias, manipulation, opaque personalization	Unequal communication and misinformation risks
Sustaining Long-Term Behavior Change	Difficulty maintaining preventive habits	Reduced long-term adherence to oral hygiene and preventive visits
Communication Barriers	Cultural, linguistic, technological, and literacy limitations	Unequal access to preventive oral health information
Regulatory and Legal Issues	Weak oversight and misleading content	Confusion between evidence-based advice and commercial promotion

Source: Developed by the authors based on cited literature

Long-Term Behavioral Change and Communication Barriers

A persistent challenge in preventive health promotion is that behavioral change is difficult to sustain over time. Digital campaigns may successfully attract attention, increase engagement, or motivate short-term action; however, maintaining preventive behaviors requires more than exposure to information alone (Mouloudj et al., 2026). Preventive behaviors, including oral hygiene practices, routine dental checkups, healthy eating, smoking cessation, medication adherence, and self-care, are shaped by habits, emotions, social norms, economic circumstances, family routines, environmental conditions, and access to healthcare systems (Martínez Asanza et al., 2024).

A common limitation of digital communication strategies is the assumption that increased awareness automatically leads to behavioral change. In reality, individuals may fully understand preventive recommendations yet remain unable or unwilling to implement them due to financial limitations, time constraints, low confidence, lack of social support, or limited access to services. Bailey (2019) emphasizes the importance of goal setting and action planning in supporting behavioral change, while the COM-B model suggests that sustained behavior depends on three interconnected dimensions: capability, opportunity, and motivation (Timlin et al., 2021). This distinction is particularly relevant for public dental health promotion. Messages encouraging preventive dental visits or oral hygiene practices must consider practical realities such as affordability, appointment availability, accessibility of dental services, waiting times, transportation, and trust in healthcare providers (Mouloudj et al., 2025). Without addressing these everyday barriers, even scientifically accurate messages may have limited influence on long-term preventive behavior.

Long-term engagement also requires adaptability. Individuals may ignore repeated notifications, discontinue application use, disable reminders, or disengage if they fail to perceive meaningful benefits. Therefore, digital preventive strategies should integrate realistic goals, feedback systems, self-monitoring, periodic content renewal, and social support mechanisms that reinforce sustained engagement rather than short-term digital activity (Nejad et al., 2021). Communication barriers further complicate preventive health promotion. Health communication is not simply the transmission of information; rather, it is a socially embedded process shaped by beliefs, power relations, culture, and trust (Berkman et al., 2014). The transactional model of communication emphasizes that meaning is co-constructed between participants rather than passively transmitted from sender to receiver. Public health communication research similarly highlights the importance of culturally sensitive messages, participatory design, long-term trust building, and evaluation of broader social outcomes (Zhao et al., 2026).

Barriers to effective communication may be technological, social, cultural, or structural. Marginalized populations and older adults may experience difficulties related to digital access, digital literacy, language barriers, institutional mistrust, stigma, or culturally inappropriate communication approaches (Braveman et al., 2011; Sørensen et al., 2012). Within this context, healthcare professionals, community actors, and social workers frequently function as intermediaries who help bridge communication gaps between healthcare institutions and communities through culturally competent engagement and trust-building practices (Betancourt et al., 2005).

Regulatory and Legal Challenges in Digital Health Communication

Digital communication for preventive health promotion operates within a regulatory environment that often struggles to keep pace with technological developments. Health communication must comply with professional standards, patient confidentiality, data protection regulations, advertising guidelines, consumer protection laws, and public health ethics (Martínez Asanza, 2025; Zhao et al., 2026). However, emerging communication forms, including influencer marketing, AI-generated content, mobile applications, targeted advertising, and platform-based communication, frequently create uncertainty regarding responsibility and accountability (Huang et al., 2026; Martínez Asanza et al., 2024). These challenges become particularly important when preventive health messages originate from actors outside formal healthcare systems, including influencers, commercial brands, wellness companies, private clinics, supplement marketers, or digital platforms (Mouloudj et al., 2025). Individuals may struggle to distinguish evidence-based guidance from sponsored content, personal opinions, or misleading health claims. Such confusion can be especially problematic in preventive areas including oral hygiene, nutrition, weight management, chronic disease prevention, and preventive dental care.

Consequently, preventive communication should maintain clear distinctions between education, promotion, counseling, and clinical advice. Claims should remain evidence-based, conflicts of interest should be transparent, and vulnerable populations should receive protection against misleading or exploitative content. Regulatory responsibility should also be shared among public health institutions, policymakers, professional associations, digital platforms, and advertisers to ensure safe, transparent, and accountable communication practices.

Managerial Implications

The findings of this chapter offer important implications for healthcare managers, dental practitioners, policymakers, and public health organizations seeking to promote preventive dental health behaviors through digital marketing tools. First, managers should adopt a patient-centered digital communication strategy that prioritizes preventive engagement rather than solely promoting treatment services. Digital tools such as mobile applications, social media platforms, reminder systems, chatbots, and personalized messaging can be used to encourage routine oral hygiene practices, preventive dental visits, healthier dietary habits, and early detection behaviors.

Second, healthcare organizations should emphasize personalization and audience segmentation when designing preventive communication strategies. Different population groups vary in their digital literacy, health awareness, age, cultural background, and preventive needs. Therefore, tailored communication approaches may improve message relevance and increase behavioral engagement. However, personalization should remain transparent, ethical, and respectful of patient privacy.

Third, healthcare managers should prioritize trust, credibility, and information quality in digital communication. Preventive dental health campaigns are more likely to succeed when information is evidence-based, easy to understand, culturally sensitive, and delivered through trusted channels.

Finally, managers should recognize that digital communication alone is insufficient to sustain long-term preventive behavior. Effective strategies require integration with accessible healthcare services, continuous patient support, community engagement, and regular evaluation of behavioral outcomes rather than relying solely on digital engagement metrics. Such an approach can strengthen the long-term effectiveness of public dental health promotion initiatives.

LIMITATIONS AND FUTURE RESEARCH

Despite providing important insights into the role of digital marketing tools in promoting preventive health behaviors, this chapter has several limitations that should be acknowledged. First, the discussion is primarily conceptual and literature-based, relying on evidence drawn from prior studies conducted across different healthcare settings and populations. Consequently, the findings may not fully capture contextual differences in digital access, oral health literacy, cultural norms, healthcare infrastructure, and technology adoption across regions or demographic groups. Second, while the chapter emphasizes preventive dental health promotion, some supporting evidence originates from broader healthcare and preventive behavior literature due to the limited availability of studies specifically focused on digital marketing tools in dental health contexts.

Another limitation concerns the rapid evolution of digital technologies. Innovations in AI, wearable technologies, social media algorithms, mobile health applications, and personalized communication systems continue to reshape digital engagement practices. As a result, some technological developments and communication trends may evolve beyond the scope of current evidence.

Future research should prioritize empirical investigations examining the effectiveness of specific digital marketing tools in promoting preventive dental health behaviors across diverse populations. Comparative studies exploring differences based on age, digital literacy, socio-economic background, and cultural context would also be valuable. Furthermore, future research may examine ethical concerns, long-term behavioral sustainability, trust formation, and the effectiveness of AI-driven personalized communication in public dental health promotion.

CONCLUSION

Digital marketing tools have emerged as important mechanisms for promoting preventive health behaviors and supporting public dental health promotion. Through technologies such as mobile health applications, social media platforms, wearable devices, online communities, AI, and personalized communication systems, healthcare organizations can disseminate preventive information, encourage healthier routines, and strengthen engagement with oral health practices. These tools provide opportunities to transform preventive communication from one-way information delivery into more interactive, personalized, and behavior-oriented engagement.

The chapter highlights that preventive dental health behaviors, including oral hygiene maintenance, regular dental checkups, healthy dietary habits, and early preventive care, can be positively influenced when digital communication strategies combine evidence-based information with reminders, self-monitoring, feedback, and social support. Theoretical perspectives such as the Health Belief Model and Theory of Planned Behavior further explain how perceptions, attitudes, social influence, and behavioral intentions shape preventive actions.

However, the effectiveness of digital marketing tools depends on addressing important challenges, including privacy concerns, ethical use of AI, communication barriers, digital inequalities, regulatory limitations, and difficulties in sustaining long-term behavioral change. Therefore, successful public dental health promotion requires responsible, inclusive, and trustworthy digital strategies that prioritize accessibility, credibility, and patient-centered preventive engagement.

REFERENCES

Ajzen, I. (1991). The theory of planned behavior. *Organizational Behavior and Human Decision Processes*, *50*(2), 179–211. DOI: 10.1016/0749-5978(91)90020-T

Alameri, S. A., Mahmoud, B. I., Almado, A. A., Jasim, Z. A., Jahlool, I. H., & Alyousuf, A. N. (2026). Consumer Acceptance of AI-Supported Circular Fashion Services: A Technology Acceptance Perspective. In Mouloudj, K., & Arantes, L. (Eds.), *Ethical Consumption and Responsible Innovation in Fashion through AI* (pp. 35–58). IGI Global., DOI: 10.4018/979-8-3373-7200-6.ch002

Almokdad, E., Mouloudj, K., Kiatkawsin, K., & Lee, C.H. (2026). Designing the right fit: Socially cued versus functional AI interfaces in hospitality self-service technologies. *Journal of Hospitality and Tourism Insights*, Vol. ahead-of-print. https://doi.org/DOI: 10.1108/JHTI-10-2025-1267

Alnaemat, N. D., & Saleem, S. A. (2026). Integrating Digital Technologies Into Fashion Management: Opportunities and Challenges. In Mouloudj, K., & Arantes, L. (Eds.), *Ethical Consumption and Responsible Innovation in Fashion through AI* (pp. 145–168). IGI Global., DOI: 10.4018/979-8-3373-7200-6.ch006

Atherton, H., Huckvale, C., & Car, J. (2010). Communicating health promotion and disease prevention information to patients via email: A review. *Journal of Telemedicine and Telecare*, *16*(4), 172–175. DOI: 10.1258/jtt.2010.004002 PMID: 20511566

Bailey, R. R. (2019). Goal setting and action planning for health behavior change. *American Journal of Lifestyle Medicine*, *13*(6), 615–618. DOI: 10.1177/1559827617729634 PMID: 31662729

Berkman, L. F., Kawachi, I., & Glymour, M. M. (Eds.). (2014). *Social Epidemiology* (2nd ed.). Oxford University Press., DOI: 10.1093/med/9780195377903.001.0001

Betancourt, J. R., Green, A. R., Carrillo, J. E., & Park, E. R. (2005). Cultural competence and health care disparities: Key perspectives and trends. *Health Affairs (Project Hope)*, *24*(2), 499–505. DOI: 10.1377/hlthaff.24.2.499 PMID: 15757936

Boon-itt, S. (2019). Quality of health websites and their influence on perceived usefulness, trust and intention to use: An analysis from Thailand. *Journal of Innovation and Entrepreneurship*, *8*(1), 1–17. DOI: 10.1186/s13731-018-0100-9

Braveman, P. A., Arkin, E., Proctor, D., Kauh, T., & Holm, N. (2011). Systemic and structural racism and health inequities. *Annual Review of Public Health*, *32*, 1–16. DOI: 10.1146/annurev-publhealth-032310-092614

Brown, S. A., Breton, M. D., Anderson, S. M., Kollar, L., Keith-Hynes, P., Levy, C. J., & Kudva, Y. C. (2017). Overnight closed-loop control improves glycemic control in a multicenter study of adults with type 1 diabetes. *The Journal of Clinical Endocrinology and Metabolism*, *102*(10), 3674–3682. DOI: 10.1210/jc.2017-00556 PMID: 28666360

Burridge, J. H., Lee, A. C. W., Turk, R., Stokes, M., Whitall, J., Vaidyanathan, R., & Franco, E. (2017). Telehealth, wearable sensors, and the internet: Will they improve stroke outcomes through increased intensity of therapy, motivation, and adherence to rehabilitation programs? *Journal of Neurologic Physical Therapy : JNPT*, *41*, S32–S38. DOI: 10.1097/NPT.0000000000000183 PMID: 28628594

Champion, V. L., & Skinner, C. S. (2021). Health Belief Model. In Glanz, K., Rimer, B. K., & Viswanath, K. (Eds.), *Health behavior: Theory, Research, and Practice* (pp. 8–38). Jossey-Bass.

Chatterjee, A., Prinz, A., Gerdes, M., & Martinez, S. (2021). Digital interventions on healthy lifestyle management: Systematic review. *Journal of Medical Internet Research*, *23*(11), 1–14. DOI: 10.2196/26931 PMID: 34787575

Choi, Y., Jeon, Y.-M., Wang, L., & Kim, K. (2017). A biological signal-based stress monitoring framework for children using wearable devices. *Sensors (Basel)*, *17*(9), 1936. DOI: 10.3390/s17091936 PMID: 28832507

Daniels, J., Haber, N., Voss, C., Schwartz, J., Tamura, S., Fazel, A., & Winograd, T. (2018). Feasibility testing of a wearable behavioral aid for social learning in children with autism. *Applied Clinical Informatics*, *9*(1), 129–140. DOI: 10.1055/s-0038-1626727 PMID: 29466819

Deniz-Garcia, A., Fabelo, H., Rodriguez-Almeida, A. J., Zamora-Zamorano, G., Castro-Fernandez, M., Alberiche Ruano, M. P., Solvoll, T., Granja, C., Schopf, T. R., Callico, G. M., Soguero-Ruiz, C., & Wägner, A. M. (2023). Quality, usability, and effectiveness of mHealth apps and the role of artificial intelligence: Current scenario and challenges. *Journal of Medical Internet Research*, *25*, 1–17. DOI: 10.2196/44030 PMID: 37140973

Dwivedi, Y. K., Ismagilova, E., Hughes, D. L., Carlson, J., Filieri, R., Jacobson, J., Jain, V., Karjaluoto, H., Kefi, H., Krishen, A. S., Kumar, V., Rahman, M. M., Raman, R., Rauschnabel, P. A., Rowley, J., Salo, J., Tran, G. A., & Wang, Y. (2021). Setting the future of digital and social media marketing research: Perspectives and research propositions. *International Journal of Information Management*, *59*, 1–37. DOI: 10.1016/j.ijinfomgt.2020.102168

Fernandes Prabhu, D., Gurupur, V., Stone, A., & Trader, E. (2025). Integrating artificial intelligence, electronic health records, and wearables for predictive, patient-centered decision support in healthcare. *Health Care, 13*(21), 2753. DOI: 10.3390/healthcare13212753 PMID: 41228120

Franssen, W. M. A., Franssen, G. H. L. M., Spaas, J., Solmi, F., & Eijnde, B. O. (2020). Can consumer wearable activity tracker-based interventions improve physical activity and cardiometabolic health in patients with chronic diseases? A systematic review and meta-analysis of randomised controlled trials. *The International Journal of Behavioral Nutrition and Physical Activity, 17*(1), 57. DOI: 10.1186/s12966-020-00955-2 PMID: 32393357

Glanz, K., & Bishop, D. B. (2010). The role of behavioral science theory in development and implementation of public health interventions. *Annual Review of Public Health, 31*(1), 399–418. DOI: 10.1146/annurev.publhealth.012809.103604 PMID: 20070207

Gu, D., Guo, J., Liang, C., Lu, W., Zhao, S., Liu, B., & Long, T. (2019). Social media-based health management systems and sustained health engagement: TPB perspective. *International Journal of Environmental Research and Public Health, 16*(9), 1495. DOI: 10.3390/ijerph16091495 PMID: 31035585

Huang, Y., Leng, X., & Tian, Z. (2026). Predatory marketing and false health promotion on social media: Risk pathways in diet, fitness, and supplement communication. *Frontiers in Public Health, 14*, 1709812. DOI: 10.3389/fpubh.2026.1709812 PMID: 41810286

Iribarren, S. J., Akande, T. O., Kamp, K. J., Barry, D., Kader, Y. G., & Suelzer, E. (2021). Effectiveness of mobile apps to promote health and manage disease: Systematic review and meta-analysis of randomized controlled trials. *JMIR mHealth and uHealth, 9*(1), e21563. DOI: 10.2196/21563 PMID: 33427672

Jung, J., & Cho, I. (2022). Promoting physical activity and weight loss with mHealth interventions among workers: Systematic review and meta-analysis of randomized controlled trials. *JMIR mHealth and uHealth, 10*(1), e30682. DOI: 10.2196/30682 PMID: 35060913

Khan, P. A., Badole, P. J., & Shaikh, D. (2026). Telemedicine and digital health: The future for pharmaceutical companies and health care. *Indian Journal of Pharmacology, 58*(1), 24–34. DOI: 10.4103/ijp.ijp_452_24 PMID: 41498661

Kim, S., & Lee, S. (2026). Enhancing preventive health risk behaviors: The synergistic effect of anthropomorphism and benefit appeals on social media. *Communication Reports, 39*(1), 1–19. DOI: 10.1080/08934215.2025.2472301

Koh, A., Swanepoel, W., Ling, A., Ho, B. L., Tan, S. Y., & Lim, J. (2021). Digital health promotion: Promise and peril. *Health Promotion International*, *36*(Supplement_1), 70–80. DOI: 10.1093/heapro/daab134 PMID: 34897444

Lee, J. A., Choi, M., Lee, S. A., & Jiang, N. (2018). Effective behavioral intervention strategies using mobile health applications for chronic disease management: A systematic review. *BMC Medical Informatics and Decision Making*, *18*(1), 12. DOI: 10.1186/s12911-018-0591-0 PMID: 29458358

Li, D., Hu, Y., Pfaff, H., Wang, L., Deng, L., Lu, C., Xia, S., Cheng, S., Zhu, X., & Wu, X. (2020). Determinants of patients' intention to use the online inquiry services provided by internet hospitals: Empirical evidence from China. *Journal of Medical Internet Research*, *22*(10), e22716. DOI: 10.2196/22716 PMID: 33006941

Lin, Z., Dai, H., Xiong, Y., Xia, X., & Horng, S. J. (2017, July). Quantification assessment of bradykinesia in Parkinson's disease based on a wearable device. *In 2017 39th annual international conference of the IEEE engineering in medicine and biology society (EMBC)* (pp. 803-806). IEEE. DOI: DOI: 10.1109/EMBC.2017.8036946

Mao, Z., Wang, D., & Zheng, S. (2023). Health belief model and social media engagement: A cross-national study of health promotion strategies against COVID-19 in 2020. *Frontiers in Public Health*, *11*, 1093648. DOI: 10.3389/fpubh.2023.1093648 PMID: 36844861

Martínez Asanza, D. (2025). Emerging Trends and Future Perspectives in Digital Dentistry for Rural Areas: An Update. In Martínez Asanza, D. (Ed.), *Transforming Dental Health in Rural Communities: Digital Dentistry* (pp. 1–36). IGI Global., DOI: 10.4018/979-8-3693-7165-7.ch001

Martínez Asanza, D., Rojas Herrera, I. A., Mouloudj, K., Amable, O. G., & Muzzamil, M. (2024). Impact of Digital Innovations in Preventive Dentistry: A Narrative Review. In Martínez Asanza, D. (Ed.), *Leveraging Digital Technology for Preventive Dentistry* (pp. 55–84). IGI Global., DOI: 10.4018/979-8-3693-3872-8.ch003

Metcalf, D., Milliard, S. T., Gomez, M., & Schwartz, M. (2016). Wearables and the Internet of things for health: Wearable, interconnected devices promise more efficient and comprehensive health care. *IEEE Pulse*, *7*(5), 35–39. DOI: 10.1109/MPUL.2016.2592260 PMID: 28113167

Mouloudj, K., Alameri, S. A. S., Evans, M. A., Almado, A. A. G., Mahmoud, B. I., & Asanza, D. M. (2026). Social marketing for health equity: Promoting preventive health behavior among women in rural communities. *International Journal of Environmental Research and Public Health*, *23*(5), 584. DOI: 10.3390/ijerph23050584 PMID: 42196677

Mouloudj, K., Bouarar, A. C., Martínez Asanza, D., & Dimitrova, M. (2025). Understanding Customers' Intentions to Use Digital Dental Health Services: An Expanded Technology Acceptance Model. In Martínez Asanza, D. (Ed.), *Transforming Dental Health in Rural Communities: Digital Dentistry* (pp. 189–210). IGI Global., DOI: 10.4018/979-8-3693-7165-7.ch007

Mouloudj, K., Bouarar, A. C., Martínez Asanza, D., Saadaoui, L., Mouloudj, S., Njoku, A. U., Evans, M. A., & Bouarar, A. (2023). Factors Influencing the Adoption of Digital Health Apps: An Extended Technology Acceptance Model (TAM). In Bouarar, A., Mouloudj, K., & Martínez Asanza, D. (Eds.), *Integrating Digital Health Strategies for Effective Administration* (pp. 116–132). IGI Global., DOI: 10.4018/978-1-6684-8337-4.ch007

Naslund, J. A., Aschbrenner, K. A., Marsch, L. A., & Bartels, S. J. (2016). The future of mental health care: Peer-to-peer support and social media. *Epidemiology and Psychiatric Sciences*, *25*(2), 113–122. DOI: 10.1017/S2045796015001067 PMID: 26744309

Natalucci, V., Marmondi, F., Biraghi, M., & Bonato, M. (2023). The effectiveness of wearable devices in non-communicable diseases to manage physical activity and nutrition: Where we are? *Nutrients*, *15*(4), 913. DOI: 10.3390/nu15040913 PMID: 36839271

Nejad, M. S., Harooni, J., Charkazi, A., Shams, M., & Latifi, M. (2021). Using social marketing to promote preventive behaviors related to COVID-19. *Journal of Lifestyle Medicine*, *11*(2), 52–56. DOI: 10.15280/jlm.2021.11.2.52 PMID: 34549026

Obermeyer, Z., Powers, B., Vogeli, C., & Mullainathan, S. (2019). Dissecting racial bias in an algorithm used to manage the health of populations. *Science*, *366*(6464), 447–453. DOI: 10.1126/science.aax2342 PMID: 31649194

OECD. (2019). *Vectors of Digital Transformation.* OECD Digital Economy Papers, No. 273. OECD Publishing. Available at: https://doi.org/DOI: 10.1787/20716826

OECD. (n.d.). *Digital transformation (Policy Issue).* OECD. Available at: https://www.oecd.org/en/topics/policy-issues/digital-transformation.html

Parkinson, J., & Naidu, J. (2024). Driving and evaluating social impact in health marketing. *Health Marketing Quarterly*, *41*(2), 113–129. DOI: 10.1080/07359683.2024.2363568 PMID: 39010695

Putnam, R. D. (2000). *Bowling Alone: The Collapse and Revival of American Community*. Simon & Schuster.

Rosenstock, I. M. (1966). Why people use health services. *The Milbank Memorial Fund Quarterly*, *44*(3), 94–127. DOI: 10.2307/3348967 PMID: 5967464

Rossi, A., Frechette, L., Miller, D., Miller, E., Friel, C., Van Arsdale, A., Lin, J., Shankar, V., Kuo, D. Y. S., & Nevadunsky, N. S. (2018). Acceptability and feasibility of a Fitbit physical activity monitor for endometrial cancer survivors. *Gynecologic Oncology*, *149*(3), 470–475. DOI: 10.1016/j.ygyno.2018.04.560 PMID: 29692337

Rowley, J., Johnson, F., & Sbaffi, L. (2015). Students' trust judgements in online health information seeking. *Health Informatics Journal*, *21*(4), 316–327. DOI: 10.1177/1460458214546772 PMID: 25193449

Setz, C., Arnrich, B., Schumm, J., La Marca, R., Tröster, G., & Ehlert, U. (2010). Discriminating stress from cognitive load using a wearable EDA device. *IEEE Transactions on Information Technology in Biomedicine*, *14*(2), 410–417. DOI: 10.1109/TITB.2009.2036164 PMID: 19906598

Shajari, S., Kuruvinashetti, K., Komeili, A., & Sundararaj, U. (2023). The emergence of AI-based wearable sensors for digital health technology: A review. *Sensors (Basel)*, *23*(23), 1–18. DOI: 10.3390/s23239498 PMID: 38067871

Shneiderman, B. (2020). Human-centered artificial intelligence: Reliable, safe & trustworthy. *International Journal of Human-Computer Interaction*, *36*(6), 495–504. DOI: 10.1080/10447318.2020.1741118

Siopis, G., Moschonis, G., Eweka, E., Jung, J., Kwasnicka, D., Asare, B. Y., Kodithuwakku, V., Willems, R., Verhaeghe, N., Annemans, L., Vedanthan, R., Oldenburg, B., Manios, Y., Oldenburg, B., Kwasnicka, D., Gong, E., Jung, J., Asare, B. Y.-A., Kodithuwakku, V., & Bruka, L. (2023). Effectiveness, reach, uptake, and feasibility of digital health interventions for adults with hypertension: A systematic review and meta-analysis of randomised controlled trials. *The Lancet. Digital Health*, *5*(3), 144–159. DOI: 10.1016/S2589-7500(23)00002-X PMID: 36828607

Sørensen, K., Van den Broucke, S., Fullam, J., Doyle, G., Pelikan, J., Slonska, Z., & Brand, H. (2012). Health literacy and public health: A systematic review. *BMC Public Health*, *12*(1), 80. DOI: 10.1186/1471-2458-12-80 PMID: 22276600

Stoumpos, A. I., Kitsios, F., & Talias, M. A. (2023). Digital Transformation in Healthcare: Technology Acceptance and Its Applications. *International Journal of Environmental Research and Public Health*, *20*(4), 3407. DOI: 10.3390/ijerph20043407 PMID: 36834105

Sun, Y. (2022). Consumers' evaluation of web-based health information quality: Ameta-analysis. *Journal of Medical Internet Research, 24*(4), 1–20. https://www.jmir.org/2022/4/e36463/

Swenson, E. R., Bastian, N. D., & Nembhard, H. B. (2018). Healthcare market segmentation and data mining: A systematic review. *Health Marketing Quarterly, 35*(3), 186–208. DOI: 10.1080/07359683.2018.1514734 PMID: 30470165

The Bangkok Charter for Health Promotion in a Globalized World (2005). Bangkok: World Health Organization. Available at: https://www.who.int/healthpromotion/conferences/6gchp/hpr_050829_%20BCHP.pdf?ua=1

Timlin, D., McCormack, J. M., & Simpson, E. E. (2021). Using the COM-B model to identify barriers and facilitators towards adoption of a diet associated with cognitive function. *Public Health Nutrition, 24*(7), 1657–1670. DOI: 10.1017/S1368980020001445 PMID: 32799963

UNICEF. (n.d.). *Digital health.* UNICEF. Available at: https://www.unicef.org/health/digital-health

Valenza, G., Citi, L., Gentili, C., Lanata, A., Scilingo, E. P., & Barbieri, R. (2015). Characterization of depressive states in bipolar patients using wearable textile technology and instantaneous heart rate variability assessment. *IEEE Journal of Biomedical and Health Informatics, 19*(1), 263–274. DOI: 10.1109/JBHI.2014.2307584 PMID: 25561449

Van Dijk, J. (2020). *The Digital Divide*. Polity Press.

van Veen, S., Binz, S., Muminovic, M., Chaudhry, K., Rose, S., Calo, S., Rammal, J., France, J., & Miller, J. B. (2019). Potential of mobile health technology to reduce health disparities in underserved communities. *The Western Journal of Emergency Medicine, 20*(5), 799–802. DOI: 10.5811/westjem.2019.6.41911 PMID: 31539337

Wells, C., & Spry, C. (2022). *An Overview of Smartphone Apps: CADTH Horizon Scan*. Canadian Agency for Drugs and Technologies in Health., Available at https://www.ncbi.nlm.nih.gov/books/NBK595384/ DOI: 10.51731/cjht.2022.269

WHO. (World Health Organization), (2023). *Hypertension: Fact sheet.* Available at: https://www.who.int/news-room/fact-sheets/detail/hypertension

WHO. (World Health Organization), (2024a). *Nearly 1.8 billion adults at risk of disease from not doing enough physical activity*. Available at: https://www.who.int/news/item/26-06-2024-nearly-1-8-billion-adults-at-risk-of-disease-from-not-doing-enough-physical-activity

WHO. (World Health Organization), (2024b). *Noncommunicable diseases: Fact sheet*. Available at: https://www.who.int/news-room/fact-sheets/detail/noncommunicable-diseases

WHO. (World Health Organization), (2024c). *Obesity and overweight: Fact sheet*. Available at: https://www.who.int/news-room/fact-sheets/detail/obesity-and-overweight

World Health Organization. (2021). *Global strategy on digital health 2020–2025*. WHO.

Yap, S. F., Lim, W. M., Gaur, S. S., & Lim, P. Y. (2023). A framework for preventive health marketing. *Journal of Strategic Marketing*, *31*(4), 894–917. DOI: 10.1080/0965254X.2021.2013933

Yetisen, A. K., Martinez-Hurtado, J. L., Ünal, B., Khademhosseini, A., & Butt, H. (2018). Wearables in Medicine. *Advanced Materials*, *30*(33), 1–17. DOI: 10.1002/adma.201706910 PMID: 29893068

Zhang, Y., & Kim, Y. (2022). Consumers' Evaluation of Web-Based Health Information Quality: Meta-analysis. *Journal of Medical Internet Research*, *24*(4), 1–20. DOI: 10.2196/36463 PMID: 35482390

Zhao, F., Huang, X., Huang, L., Gong, Y., Wang, Z., & Liu, H. (2026). Health communication on Chinese social media: A case study of stress urinary incontinence-related videos on TikTok and Bilibili. *Journal of Consumer Health on the Internet*, •••, 1–13. DOI: 10.1080/15398285.2026.2658036

Ziebland, S., & Wyke, S. (2012). Health and illness in a connected world: How might sharing experiences on the internet affect people's health? *The Milbank Quarterly*, *90*(2), 219–249. DOI: 10.1111/j.1468-0009.2012.00662.x PMID: 22709387

KEY TERMS AND DEFINITIONS

Digital Health Communication: The use of digital technologies and online platforms to deliver, exchange, and promote health-related information, education, and preventive messages between healthcare providers, institutions, and the public.

Digital Marketing: The strategic use of digital technologies, online platforms, and communication channels to promote information, services, or behaviors and engage target audiences through interactive and data-driven approaches.

Oral Health Prevention: The set of actions and practices aimed at maintaining oral health and reducing the risk of dental diseases through hygiene, healthy behaviors, and early preventive measures.

Preventive Dental Care: Professional and self-care practices designed to prevent oral diseases, maintain dental health, and reduce the need for restorative or emergency treatments.

Preventive Health Behaviors: Individual actions and lifestyle practices undertaken to prevent illness, reduce health risks, and maintain overall physical and mental well-being.

Chapter 8
Digital Marketing as a Health System Intervention:
Rethinking Promotion, Prevention, and Public Dentistry

L. B. Muralidhar
http://orcid.org/0000-0003-3453-613X
Jain (Deemed to be) University, India

ABSTRACT

Oral health remains persistently marginalised within public health systems, despite its strong associations with nutrition, productivity, and overall well-being. Traditional clinic-centric and episodic health promotion approaches have proven insufficient to address behavioural complexity, structural inequities, and scale constraints. This chapter reconceptualises digital marketing not as a peripheral communication activity but as a systemic lever embedded within oral health systems. Integrating perspectives from public health, marketing, behavioural science, and health systems research. It introduces the concept of the "digital oral health citizen" and advances the Digital Oral Health Intervention Framework (DOHIF), linking behavioural dynamics, technological infrastructures, governance arrangements, and public value creation through feedback-driven learning systems. It concludes by positioning digital marketing as a core public health capability essential for inclusive, preventive, and ethically grounded oral health systems in the digital era.

DOI: 10.4018/979-8-3373-8894-6.ch008

1 INTRODUCTION: FROM COMMUNICATION TOOL TO HEALTH SYSTEM LEVER

The oral health status is peripheral in most of the public health systems, even though it is linked with pain, nutrition, educational status, labour involvement, and overall noncommunicable disease burden, mainly because dental care developed as an independent sector, was treatment-focused, and has gained only partial integration into national policies (Peres et al., 2019; World Health Organisation, 2022). This institutional division has distributive effects on oral disease, as long-term social gradients in oral disease are based on income, education, geography, and health literacy, and these disparities cannot be addressed by service expansion alone (Celeste & Gaida, 2019; Watt & Sheiham, 2012). This global review shows that oral diseases affect nearly half of the world's population and are strongly patterned by social determinants, making them a major but neglected public health and equity challenge (Peres et al., 2019).

Digital marketing should not be viewed as an adjunct to promotion but as a platform-level feature that can influence service visibility, institutional trustworthiness, behavioural expectations, and feasible access. This refocusing is required, as traditional oral health promotion has tended to overemphasise the effectiveness of advice alone. In contrast, the behavioural theory posits that preventive behaviour depends on attitudes, norms, perceived behavioural control, susceptibility, barriers, capability, opportunity, and motivation (Ajzen, 1991; Michie et al., 2011; Rosenstock et al., 1988).

Empirical studies have shown that digital and social media interventions can increase reach, customise communication, maintain engagement, and enhance hygiene practices, preventive awareness, appointment-seeking, and perceptions of care, particularly through interactive formats. Nevertheless, their importance extends beyond that as the search is better optimised, analytics is better targeting, and platform design influences norms, reminders, and referral pathways (Abroms et al., 2012; Azzopardi-Muscat & Sørensen, 2019; Sharma et al., 2022; Kepper et al., 2024).

The gains are not absolute, as being digital by age, disability, language, education, and connection can only increase inequity rather than decrease it, compounded by algorithmic bias. This threat is enhanced by the global inequality in need and access: approximately 3.5 billion people are affected by oral diseases, and 2.6 billion people were offline in 2024, and the lowest connectivity is located in the environment with the greatest disease burden (International Telecommunication Union, 2024; Khoury et al., 2024; Mittelstadt et al., 2016; World Health Organization, 2022).

The key contribution of the chapter is hence the conceptualisation of digital marketing in public dentistry as a system capability that connects prevention, service navigation, governance, and adaptive learning, the value of which is based on fair design, staffing adjustment, and policy support and not on the technical deployment of the same, which is why the practical relevance of the chapter consists in the question of which population is prioritised, which digital bottleneck is addressed, which service endpoint is linked, and which indicator demonstrates altered behaviour or service use (Null et al., 2021; Peters, 2019; Rothschild, 1999). The authors propose a digital public health framework in which digital technologies are treated as system-level capabilities that must be designed and governed for equity, integration, and measurable health impact, rather than as isolated communication tools (Azzopardi-Muscat & Sørensen, 2019).

1.1 Chapter roadmap and synthesis

To ensure the argument's flow is clear from the very beginning, the chapter may be understood as the gradual development of ideas, from conceptual foundations, through implementation and system integration. The roadmap minimises redundancy, as each major section adds a layer to the same argument rather than reopening it in parallel (Peters, 2019; Azzopardi-Muscat & Sørensen, 2019; Null et al., 2021). Sections 2, 3 and 4 define the conceptual centre as the connection between systems thinking, digital citizenship and preventive infrastructure. In sections 5 to 7, the campaign strategy is followed by advanced technologies and governance, so that the operational choices are read sequentially rather than in isolation. Sections 8 and 9 synthesise ethical tensions and trends at the empirical level and in comparative lessons, explaining what the evidence substantiates and where the boundaries lie. The discussion is then incorporated into sections 10-12 with DOHIF, followed by translation into implications, implementation priorities, and final claims.

2. CONCEPTUAL REFRAMING: DIGITAL MARKETING WITHIN HEALTH SYSTEMS

The complexity of oral health is a public health system rather than a limited clinical field, since the distribution of diseases, service utilisation, and preventive behaviour are shaped by interactive social, behavioural, institutional, and informational circumstances rather than solitary clinical events (Peters, 2019). Therefore, systems thinking is required, as it shifts the focus from episodic treatment to the interaction among upstream determinants, risk environments, service organisation, and patterned behavioural responses. Of particular significance is this view in oral health, where not only biological vulnerability but also food systems, commercial exposure, socioeconomic inequality, health literacy, and long-term policy neglect also play a role in disease burden (Peres et al., 2019; World Health Organisation, 2022).

The social determinants framework reinforces this discussion by demonstrating that income, education, housing, insecure employment, and the inability to access preventive and restorative care are influenced by the social determinants (Celeste & Gaida, 2019; Watt & Sheiham, 2012). The same can be found in behavioural epidemiology: individual choice alone does not determine sugar consumption, oral hygiene, or attendance at the dentist; opportunity structures, social organisation, and cumulative disadvantage are the driving forces behind these practices. These inequalities have been exacerbated by the globalisation of ultra-processed foods and high-sugar diets, which have disproportionately affected low-income populations exposed to unhealthy food environments and with poor preventive systems (Peres et al., 2019; World Health Organisation, 2022).

These conditions demonstrate how far the linear preventive models can go. Where the behaviour is shaped by lack, disjointed services, and commercial persuasion, the information is insufficient. Oral health communication should thus be conducted within a broader intervention ecology. In this regard, digital marketing must be redefined in terms of health-system capability rather than as a promotional method. According to recent studies, repeated communication, segmentation, feedback, and workflow alignment are the elements that can be supported by digital platforms in preventing, navigating, empowering, and integrating services (Bales et al., 2024; Jivraj et al., 2022; Azzopardi-Muscat & Sørensen, 2019).

These functions can be used in the context of oral health, where they may mitigate informational asymmetry through enhancing discoverability of clinics, normalisation of preventive visits, prevention of reminders, and translation of clinical knowledge into accessible formats. Nevertheless, there is no structural inequality that is dissolved through digital systems. The lack of literacy, language, connectivity, and platform visibility, along with algorithmic bias and poor governance, can replicate exclusion and push prevention towards surveillance (Lupton, 2017; OECD, 2022). A complex approach to oral-health interventions by integrating behavioural theory, digital public health, service-dominant logic, and learning health systems, thus, will continue to be needed to design equitable, accountable, and measurable interventions (Ajzen, 1991; Michie et al., 2011; Null et al., 2021; Rothschild, 1999).

With this conceptual reframing in place, the following section shifts the system logic's focus to the character who has to manoeuvre through it: the digital oral health citizen. That transition continues to guide the chapter towards the abstract architecture of lived experience, enhancing the flow of theory and access to it.

3. RESEARCH METHODOLOGY

This book chapter adopts a narrative review methodology supported by conceptual synthesis. Peer-reviewed literature, policy reports, systematic reviews, and recent empirical studies on digital marketing, public dentistry, oral-health promotion, digital health equity, teledentistry, and governance are examined. The review prioritises studies published from 2019 onward while also including foundational behavioural and social marketing theories. Evidence is analysed thematically across prevention, access, technology, ethics, policy, and implementation. Comparative examples from high-income and low- and middle-income contexts are used to identify practical lessons. The synthesis informs the proposed Digital Oral Health Intervention Framework for public dentistry. The keywords namely, "digital marketing", "public dentistry", "oral health promotion", "digital public health", "digital health equity", "oral health inequalities", "teledentistry", "health communication", "social marketing", "digital health literacy", "behaviour change", "preventive dentistry", "AI in oral healthcare", "search engine optimisation AND health access", "oral health governance", "public health digital interventions", "health systems thinking", "digital oral health", "equity in digital health" "community oral health" and "digital behaviour change interventions" were used for searching the references. The databases, namely "PubMed / MEDLINE', "Scopus", "Web of Science", "Google Scholar", "ScienceDirect ", "SpringerLink", "Wiley Online Library", "Taylor & Francis Online", "PLOS ONE Database", "JMIR (Journal of Medical Internet Research)", "Cochrane Library (for systematic reviews)", "WHO Institutional Repository", "OECD iLibrary" and "CDC Digital Health Resources" were primarily searched.

4. THE DIGITAL ORAL HEALTH CITIZEN: BEHAVIOUR, INEQUALITY, AND ACCESS

The idea of the digital oral health citizen suggests that the decision-making process regarding symptoms, provider quality, credibility, risk, and affordability is shifting toward a situational, pre-clinical, and more digital information-based setting rather than being made through formal care channels (Lupton, 2017). This transition is, however, not a distribution of the informational power equally. Though digital technologies have the potential to decrease the distance between the population and the services, they also pose new inequalities in cases where there is a variety in access to the correct information, skills in navigation, and visibility of the platform among the social groups (Kepper et al., 2024).

Thus, the digital oral health citizen cannot be viewed as an empowered patient in general. This topic is largely about the interplay among behavioural ability, digital literacy, market forces, platform architecture, and structural inequality. Digital health literacy is not limited to understanding preventive advice in oral health. It also involves the capacity to find credible information, differentiate evidence-based advice from marketing, decode risk communication, and transform online contact into corresponding help-seeking behaviour (Loncar-Turukalo et al., 2019).

Since the oral health information spaces are filled with publicly institutionalised clinics, influencers, advertisers, and AI-mediated systems, equity of access is not the case. Consumers with lower evaluative ability are at greater risk from straightforward stories, commercial propaganda, and visual cues that appear knowledgeable while hiding the facts (Lupton, 2017; Sharma et al., 2022). The behavioural theory explains the reason why this is important. Perceived susceptibility, severity, barriers, benefits, attitudes, norms, and perceived control are variables that are influenced by perceived control as much as by prior knowledge or clinical advice (Ajzen, 1991; Rosenstock et al., 1988).

Neutral sequence is thus not present in platform-mediated patient journeys, which are usually organised using search engines, maps, reviews, booking systems, and teleconsultation portals and which create visibility, credibility, and urgency (Null et al., 2021). However, digitisation does not eliminate established social differences but superimposes them. The access to available services, availability of shared devices, and access to culturally oriented content remain to be the prerogative of income, education, geography, language, and institutional trust, with rural, low-income, and minority populations being characterized by poor connection, reliance on shared devices, and content inadequately aligned with their culture (Celeste & Gaida, 2019; Peres et al., 2019; World Health Organisation, 2021, 2022).

Further, algorithm-based systems can amplify marginalisation by favouring users with digital visibility and commercial appeal and by redirecting public communicative efforts to groups with a high disease burden and limited digital footprint (Mittelstadt et al., 2016). When it comes to oral health, digital citizenship is never universal but, instead, stratified and, as a result, there are equity-focused digital capability, culturally responsive communication, and responsible platform governance as the key policy imperatives (Khoury et al., 2024 ; OECD, 2022).

As soon as the inequality has been demonstrated at the level of the digital citizen, the next question to ask is how public communication can intervene upstream. The next segment thus does not merely consider digital marketing as a form of messaging, but rather as a proactive infrastructure that should be found in daily life and at access points.

5. DIGITAL MARKETING AS PREVENTIVE INFRASTRUCTURE

The analytical importance of digital marketing to the oral health of populations lies in the fact that it is not merely additional communication but rather the preventive infrastructure embedded in daily settings, where health meanings, dietary behaviours, symptom perception, and care-seeking beliefs are established. The traditional prevention methods, such as school programmes, clinical counselling, pamphlets, and occasional public campaigns, remain significant. However, they are usually intermittent, not deeply embedded in everyday life, and do not fit well in the digital environment where behavioural evaluations are formed nowadays.

In comparison, digital marketing is constant, permeates media spaces, and can serve as a reminder, behavioural trigger, narrative framing, and direction at the point of oral health practice, making it preventive rather than persuasive on a one-off basis (Azzopardi-Muscat & Sørensen, 2019). This continuity is particularly relevant in dentistry, since oral disease is cumulative and its prevention requires repeated behaviours rather than single actions (Peres et al., 2019; World Health Organisation, 2022). This mechanism is illustrated using content-driven prevention. Advice can be converted into practice when behaviourally sequenced and placed in the audience's context through educational posts, short-form videos, podcasts, and email reminders. Their influence does not lie solely in the transfer of information. Based on the Theory of Planned Behaviour and the Health Belief Model, such content can reinforce the perception of susceptibility, help clarify benefits, redefine norms, and enhance the perception of behavioural control by making oral hygiene seem possible and socially acceptable (Ajzen, 1991; Rosenstock et al., 1988).

This meaning is supported by the Behaviour Change Wheel, which demonstrates that digital content can influence capability through knowledge, motivation through emotional and normative framing, and opportunity through reminders that facilitate the organisation of action in context (Michie et al., 2011). There is general evidence supporting these assertions, and research shows that blogs, visual materials, social media posts, and online campaigns can enhance awareness of hygiene practices and attitudes towards preventive actions, especially among younger and digitally literate demographics (Sharma et al., 2022).

However, the evidence base is rather limited, as most of the evidence is based on the measures of engagement, awareness, and self-reported intentions instead of the results regarding the behavioural changes in the long run or clinical outcomes, which creates an enormous inferential gap between communication performance and population-level prevention (Sharma et al., 2022). Digital spaces are also a type of social ecosystem that can facilitate peer learning, community mobilisation, and the formation of trust, but can also promote aestheticised, diluted, or misleading messages in the absence of strong governance (Lupton, 2017). Thus, public spending on discoverability, credible digital content, culturally responsive content, referral linkage, and equity-oriented analytics serves as a preventive measure for system-building rather than as optional promotion (OECD, 2022; Kepper et al., 2024).

Since prevention has been identified as the chapter's infrastructural concern, the discussion reduces to the campaign's strategy. This shift connects the expansive preventive argument to the specific decisions that determine how the focus, streams, and standards of evaluation are distributed within public dentistry.

6. STRATEGIC DIGITAL CAMPAIGNS FOR PUBLIC DENTISTRY

The nature of strategic digital campaigns in public dentistry differs in that they are not aimed at market growth but at population health, and the logic of segmentation, targeting, and assessment is altered. Efficiency, profitability and conversion potential are usually the reasons why segmentation is used in a commercial environment. In community dentistry, by contrast, it ought to be explained by epidemiological necessity, avoidable threats, and disparities in access to care.

The key strategic issue thus shifts from placing greater emphasis on who can be accessed most readily to how communicative attention can be allocated to prioritise prevention, early care-seeking, and service uptake among groups that are unevenly positioned within oral health systems. This frames digital strategy as a societal value rather than promotional optimisation. The campaign can achieve significant participation but provide minimal benefit to the population's oral health when it fails to produce positive changes in awareness, behaviour, or service use among the groups with the highest oral disease burden (Celeste & Gaida, 2019; World Health Organisation, 2022).

6.1 Segmentation and targeting as public-value choices

In this reasoning, the segmentation of the audience is necessary because oral health risks, behavioural obstacles, and access limitations are socially stratified among children, adolescents, pregnant women, older adults, migrants, rural population, and low-income families. The generic campaigns can have extensive nominal coverage but are behaviourally inactive to the neediest. Online solutions enable more narrowly segmented targeting based on demographic, geographic, behavioural, and interest-based indicators, and can be used to design messages tailored to specific life stages, risk situations, and decision-making circumstances (Abroms et al., 2012).

This is in line with the Health Belief Model and the Theory of Planned Behaviour, as customised communication can address group-specific beliefs about susceptibility, benefits, barriers, norms, and perceived behavioural control (Ajzen,

1991; Rosenstock et al., 1988). Nevertheless, it is not possible to reduce the public-dentistry segmentation to platform-behaviour technical clustering. It entails structural analysis of audiences that is based on social determinants, cumulative disadvantage, and unequal ability to translate information into action (Kepper et al., 2024; Watt & Sheiham, 2012). Social marketing is useful because it shifts the focus of targeting from engagement-related metrics to living conditions, motivations, and service conditions (Rothschild, 1999).

Simultaneously, narrow targeting can stigmatise populations, create blind spots in the changing vulnerability, and be reproduced by exclusion since digital systems are based on faulty data, proxy variables, and algorithm assumptions, which in most cases tend to make poor, old, rural, and other disadvantaged groups less visible (Khoury et al., 2024; Mittelstadt et al., 2016). The most appropriate response is a proportional digital universalism: provide basic information to everyone, and increase targeting where the need and underutilization are highest, applying surveillance, service intelligence, and knowledge of the community instead of the obscure platform information (OECD, 2022; Kepper et al., 2024).

6.2 Evaluation and operational logic

Assessment should also not be limited to clicks, impressions, watch time, and engagement rates. They are also handy process metrics, yet they are poor proxies for impact when used as outcomes, given the possibility of high platform performance without oral-hygiene behaviour, booking completion, preventive attendance, or equitable service uptake. A better model distinguishes among five interconnected levels: reach, comprehension, behavioural intention, service uptake, and health outcome. To this end, online indicators are supposed to go hand in hand with off-platform outcomes like appointment requests, visits completed, follow-up continuity, fewer missed appointments, uptake by underserved populations, and, in case possible, clinical measures like plaque scores, gingival bleeding, or untreated decay (Michie et al., 2011; Null et al., 2024). The resulting operational pathway is straightforward: define the issue, identify the priority audience, align the channel with the barrier, connect communication to a booking or referral destination, and measure process and outcome indicators. The campaign strategy must, however, be evaluated not by its ability to maximise visibility or attention, but rather by its ability to enhance equitable prevention and service utilisation (Buck et al., 2024; Farrokhi et al., 2023; Scheerman et al., 2024).

These strategic decisions raise the question of which technologies can help them implement them. The following section shifts the focus from the campaign logic to system enablers, demonstrating how AI, messaging, and teledentistry can either expand or limit the pathway described above.

7. ADVANCED TECHNOLOGIES AS SYSTEM ENABLERS

Advanced digital technologies are useful as system enablers for oral health in the public sector, as they can enhance how needs are defined, the tailoring of communication, and the connection of patients to service pathways. However, the value of these technologies depends on governance, since the same systems can also enhance surveillance, reproduce bias, and widen inequity if safeguards are weak (Khoury et al., 2024; Lupton, 2017; OECD, 2022).

It is not a technical novelty, however, but the reorganisation of relationships among communication, epidemiology, and access in public dentistry that is the key issue for analysis. The significance of artificial intelligence is particularly high since it can customize messages based on demographic, behavioural, geographic, and service-use trends related to poor oral health or low attendance of preventive care, which will facilitate language-adapted, life-stage-adapted, inferred barriers-adapted, and need-probable customization and Such tailoring can enhance perceived vulnerability, decrease barriers, be socially appropriate, and enhance perceived behavioural control as proposed by the Health Belief Model and the Theory of Planned Behaviour in oral health where fear, literacy, cost, cultural belief and practical constraint interact (Ajzen, 1991; Rosenstock et al., 1988).

Nevertheless, communicative justice does not align with accessibility, as automated systems can fail to translate culturally sensitive meanings, lose contextual nuance, and reproduce training-data bias (Mittelstadt et al., 2016; World Health Organisation, 2021). Predictive analytics also provides a strategic value by integrating clinical, service, demographic, and engagement data to identify the emergent risk and underserved populations; however, individuals with the least service contact can be least readable by analytics systems to ensure resource allocation is based on the administrative visibility instead of the actual need (Celeste & Gaida, 2019; Azzopardi-Muscat & Sørensen, 2019).

7.1 Emerging conversational platforms: AI chatbots and messaging systems

Scalable, low-complexity tasks, such as responding to routine questions, referring clients to facilities, clarifying their eligibility, and sending reminders in vernacular mobile channels, can be handled using conversational platforms, including AI chatbots and messaging apps (Choonhawarakorn et al., 2025; Farrokhi et al., 2023). They deliver optimal visibility when they operate under escalation principles, human control, integration of services into a data repository, and accuracy and differentiated application across groups of people (Benzian et al., 2025; OECD, 2022). Teledentistry can best be applied in the same logic of hybrid: it can minimise the difference between awareness and care but only in the case of regulation, reimbursement, infrastructure, and clinical appropriateness, since many oral conditions need direct examination and treatment (Null et al., 2021).

Provided they are enablers of technologies rather than standalone tools, the value they bring to society depends on the institutional circumstances in which they operate. The following paragraphs then switch from technological capability to governance capacity, and thus the chapter's flow aligns with the shift from the tool to the system.

8. GOVERNANCE, POLICY, AND INSTITUTIONAL ECOSYSTEMS

Governance can be used to either make or replicate the exclusion caused by digital marketing in the field of public oral health. As soon as communication, predictive analytics, platform infrastructures, and teledentistry start to influence discoverability, trust, and access, they become policy concerns and not some second-tier technical decisions, where oral health has traditionally been characterised by ineffective prevention and poor organisational integration (OECD, 2022; Azzopardi-Muscat & Sørensen, 2019).

The global normativity is founded on effective normativity. The World Health Organisation associates digital technologies in oral health with universal health coverage, equity and health promotion. In addition, it highlights that overall social trends in oral diseases in the population do not change (World Health Organisation, 2021, 2022). The same position is expressed by the Organisation for Economic Co-Operation and Development (OECD), which identifies stewardship, interoperability, transparency, and institutional controls as the main factors of building credible digital health governance (OECD, 2022). Taken together, these frameworks suggest that not only should the digital transformation be effective, but it should also support values such as equity, trust, and system resilience. However, the principles are not applied equally to digital marketing, which is still often presumed to be a neutral communication or a commercial activity that does not fall under health control. This distinction can no longer be analytically feasible.

8.1 Institutional implementation framework for policymakers

This chapter is enhanced by an explicit implementation framework that transforms high policy ambition into a working sequence of five interconnected steps: situational assessment, infrastructure and workforce preparedness, pilot deployment, outcome evaluation, and scale-up with governance review. The situational assessment aims to determine the disease burden, target populations, digital access, service bottlenecks, language needs, and the baseline discoverability of public services. The next step should be to define staffing, procurement, referral design, data governance, and core monitoring dashboards in line with the preparedness plan.

The deployment of pilots to specific channels, facilities, or geographies should be restricted until operational viability is established, especially in resource-constrained systems. Process, service, equity, and cost indicators should be incorporated into the evaluation process, whereas scale-up should be undertaken once feasibility, affordability, and measurable benefit are established. This simulated reasoning is analytically significant because implementation failures are also frequently a sign of the system's limitations rather than poor communication design. This is evident in rural South India, where, despite the presence of dentists and basic infrastructure in community health centres, there is a shortage of dental assistants and hygienists, resulting in service delivery issues. Only 13.9% of respondents had used the centres in the past year to access oral healthcare, with awareness and perceived accessibility closely linked to utilisation (Panditi et al., 2025).

In this regard, operational fit and reach, such as staff capacity, referral functionality, waiting times, and completion rates of digitally confident and underserved users, should be used to judge pilots (Adeniyi et al., 2024; Panditi et al., 2025). This means that targeting justification, language and accessibility standards, referral capacity, consent, data-use policies, escalation responsibility, and subgroup performance review, have become a minimum governance checklist to policymakers because digital marketing has become the key determinant of the discoverability, promptness, and access paths, and regulatory guidance is not yet developed to regulate segmentation, algorithmic visibility, and platform dependence in oral-health systems (OECD, 2022; World Health Organisation, 2021; Null et al., 2021;Khoury et al., 2024).

As soon as governance is foregrounded, the ethical questions can be posed in sharper form than they are currently spread out throughout the chapter. Consequently, the following section separates ethics and trust as the tests for assessing whether digitally mediated influence remains valid in oral public health.

9. ETHICS, TRUST, AND CONTESTED TERRAINS

The ethical environment of online marketing in oral healthcare remains significant, and the most critical concerns can be summarised briefly. As soon as the digital communication goes beyond delivering information and providing personalised prompting, predictive profiling, and service navigation, the key ethical question is what kinds of influence are acceptable in prevention and what protection they have. It is particularly pertinent to oral health since the most at risk of preventive care tend to be the least digitally literate, with low bargaining power, and in the institutional view (Celeste & Gaida, 2019; Peres et al., 2019).

The initial ethical code is that of persuasion and manipulation. Communicating about health to the masses can be as simple as brushing their teeth, reducing sugar intake, or visiting the dentist. Justification is more difficult, however, when the targeting is opaque, emotionally excessive, or aimed at exploiting vulnerability rather than at informed action. Among the factors that predetermine behaviour in oral health, proportionality and transparency are thus more justifiable than optimisation (Ajzen, 1991; Rosenstock et al., 1988; Rothschild, 1999).

The second border is the usage of data and dependence on the platform. Behavioural data, search history, patterns of service use and traces of engagement could enhance timing and relevance. Nevertheless, they also transform communication into a potential surveillance site in cases of weak consent, opaque profiling, or commercial infrastructures, which can be observed and acted upon by public institutions. That is why digital oral-health programmes must be based on data reduction, transparent justification, auditing, and the identification of additional ways to support human services in the event of inadequate automated pathways (Lupton, 2017; OECD, 2022).

The third barrier is that of trust. Communication with the public is most acceptable when users can distinguish between service support and commercial persuasion, understand why they are being sent a message, and are confident that data use, targeting, and referral decisions are made in the public interest. Ethics must also serve as a facilitating governance condition to be implemented, rather than as a separate theme repeated throughout (Mittelstadt et al., 2016; Verdejo & Gutiérrez-Santiuste, 2019).

10. EVIDENCE, TRENDS, AND COMPARATIVE LESSONS

This section strengthens the chapter by identifying ethics, evidence, and application within a cumulative analysis sequence, clarifying that the empirical literature on digital public oral health is growing. However, it is methodologically uneven and continues to rely on short-term, intermediate, and self-reported outcomes rather than sustained clinical effects, continuity of care, and strong equity indicators (Farrokhi et al., 2023). The systematic reviews, randomised and quasi-experimental studies, case analyses of service visibility, and teledentistry reviews form the evidence base. However, the variety of outcome indicators limits the power of causal inferences, and a careful interpretation of the existing results as indicative of causality is necessary. Synthesising multiple reviews, this umbrella review finds that social media can be a powerful but uneven tool for oral-health promotion, with promising effects on awareness alongside concerns about misinformation and uneven reach.

Currently, better discoverability, customised communication, and enhanced service linkage are the aspects that have the most support, while arguments regarding sustained population-level benefit are more tentative (Kitsaras et al., 2023; Scheerman et al., 2024). To have a more stringent interpretation, implementation science and longitudinal evaluation would have to be used more closely. RE-AIM frameworks are very helpful since they bridge the outcomes of reach, adoption, implementation, maintenance and service. Meanwhile, new digital oral health research indicates that a set of engagement metrics cannot determine the effectiveness of any intervention unless it is accompanied by longer follow-up and behaviourally or clinically significant endpoints (Holtrop et al., 2021; Borrelli et al., 2025).

The literary references set towards two things simultaneously, making it read like a trend chapter. Oral disease has been an issue that is widespread all over the world, with close to half of the global population being afflicted by it, and digital access is unevenly distributed across geographical areas and income brackets. The primary current is not the growth of digital-only, but an augmented reliance on digital channels, the value of which to the population depends on whether the systems can realise the reach to deliverable, equitable, and quantifiable results (International Telecommunication Union, 2024; World Health Organisation, 2022).

This involves examining the relationship among digital uptake, oral health inequality, institutional capacity, and service design in high-income and low- and middle-income settings. Data from high-income settings offer the best example of system integration rather than communication alone. Informational friction can be minimised, continuity of care can be enhanced by search visibility, multilingual public-facing content, and teledentistry, but only in the case when the institutions of the public invest in the correct information about the services and usable navigation paths and coordinated referral systems (Null et al., 2021).

In comparison, the low- and middle-income setting evidence is more ambivalent, yet tends to be more disclosing, since it demonstrates that digital communication can compensate for the weak outreach, workforce shortage, and poor awareness among the population, despite the inequality in access to devices, navigation abilities, language literacy, and trust being able to recreate the exclusion. Cross-context comparison is thus crucial and the most justifiable conclusion is conditional, in that digital marketing can make a significant contribution to the oral health of the population only under the conditions of its attachment to the trusted institutions, relevance to service pathways, multilingual and low-literacy design, and equity-sensitive outcomes, rather than scale or engagement itself(Adeniyi et al., 2024; Abroms et al., 2012; Khoury et al., 2024; Kepper et al., 2024).

On the whole, the literature allows us to come to the conditional conclusion that digital marketing can play a significant role in the promotion of oral health of the population only in the case when it is institutionally trusted, contextual, linked to service pathways, and measured with the help of measures beyond the engagement level.

10.1 Applied case examples and LMIC lessons

The chapter can be made more practical through several concrete examples. Tailored video-based oral hygiene advice in a randomised controlled trial, as opposed to conventional advice, showed better improvements in the health of the gums in three months, which proves that digital delivery can influence a quantifiable clinical outcome as long as the content is behaviourally specific and personalised (Buck et al., 2024). The Happy Teeth gamified app significantly improved children's oral health knowledge, behaviours and clinical outcomes compared with traditional education alone, demonstrating the value of theory-informed gamification. A mobile-app education programme for parents of children with congenital heart disease enhanced parental KAP scores and improved children's oral-hygiene indices, suggesting targeted mHealth can reduce infection risk in high-risk groups

The view of the developing countries should also be discussed further. The digital oral-health strategy should be perceived in India in conjunction with the disproportionate lack of readiness in the population-system: public programmes are aimed at increasing the oral-health services, but their usage is low in those areas where there is a lack of awareness, personnel, and operational assistance meaning that communication is not enough to offset the lack of a sufficient delivery capacity (Panditi et al., 2025). Elsewhere in Sub-Saharan Africa, a different lesson emerges from community-based integration models. A suggested oral-health integration in the Chamas programme in Kenya informs on how trusted community spaces, common sites, and cost-effective prevention can develop a feasible base on which digital or hybrid engagement can be established, yet only in the case of sustainability, workforce support, and implementation assessment being established at the beginning (Adeniyi et al., 2024).

These cases combined make the chapter more practical in its argument. They demonstrate that the digital strategy is most plausible when aligned with readiness to deliver and community trust and a realistic service pathway: where staffing is sparse, communication should make navigation easy and preserve the limited capacity; where already trusted community platforms can be used, the digital outreach can be employed to enhance attendance, follow-up and prevention at a relatively low cost. The inclusion of this comparative interpretation would help make the chapter's treatment of trends more empirically grounded and more beneficial to managers operating in resource-constrained environments (Adeniyi et al., 2024; Panditi et al., 2025).

The examples of cases also help justify the implementation choices considered previously in the chapter. The Buck et al. (2024) trial demonstrates that behaviourally specific and personalised content can affect a clinical outcome during a specific follow-up period. In contrast, the Choonhawarakorn et al. study demonstrates that low-cost messaging can reinforce routine preventive behaviour when timing and reinforcement are incorporated into delivery. Taken together, these studies reinforce the thesis that the implementation strategy should be evaluated by the achievement of the pathways and the quantifiable benefit, but not by the digital activity itself (Choonhawarakorn et al., 2025).

Table 1. Comparative synthesis of recent evidence on digital oral-health interventions

Study	Design	Digital approach	Main finding	Relevance/gap
Farrokhi et al. (2023).	Systematic review of 10 intervention studies	Social-media oral-health promotion	Positive effects on knowledge, attitudes, and some preventive behaviours across platforms such as Instagram, WhatsApp, Telegram, YouTube, and Snapchat.	Strong on intervention mapping; limited by heterogeneity and short follow-up.
Li et al. (2023).	Case-based health service access study	Search engine optimisation and digital discoverability	Clinic discoverability affects whether users can locate timely, lower-cost services, making visibility part of access rather than mere branding.	Useful for access theory, but not designed to measure long-term clinical outcomes.
Buck et al. (2024).	Randomised controlled trial	Tailored video-based oral-hygiene advice	Personalised video advice improved gingival health over three months compared with conventional oral-hygiene advice.	Supports tailored digital content; evidence remains short-term and clinically narrow.
Benzian et al. (2025).	Overview of 30 systematic reviews	Teledentistry for access and quality	Teledentistry improved access, efficiency, and patient-centred care, but equity, privacy, and safety were less frequently studied, and the quality of reviews was often low.	Shows implementation promise while underscoring the need for stronger methods and governance analysis.

The evidence and discussions in the case lay the groundwork for the chapter's integrative move. The following part brings these strands together into DOHIF, so that the case concludes within a framework rather than a series of isolated observations. Synthesising multiple reviews, this umbrella review finds that social media can be a powerful but uneven tool for oral-health promotion, with promising effects on awareness alongside concerns about misinformation and uneven reach

10.2 Comparative synthesis of recent empirical evidence

To make the literature review more than a narrative summary, Table 1 summarises recent empirical and review-based findings on digital marketing, service access, and oral-health behaviour. The table presents the methodological profiles of both studies, as well as the key findings and limitations for theory construction in this chapter.

These studies lead to a similar trend. Digital interventions are most effective when customised, recurring, and directly connected to service pathways; they are least persuasive when success is assumed based solely on platform activity. The main gap in the research is, then, not the possibility that digital tools can impact awareness, but the possibility that they can create lasting and equitable impacts on attendance, prevention, and continuity of care across various health-system settings. It is also based on this comparative synthesis that the Digital Oral Health Intervention Framework can be justified, as the behavioural, infrastructural, and governance aspects must be viewed and discussed as a unified unit rather than as independent variables.

11. TOWARD AN INTEGRATIVE FRAMEWORK: DIGITAL MARKETING–ENABLED ORAL HEALTH SYSTEMS

Figure 1. Digital oral health intervention framework

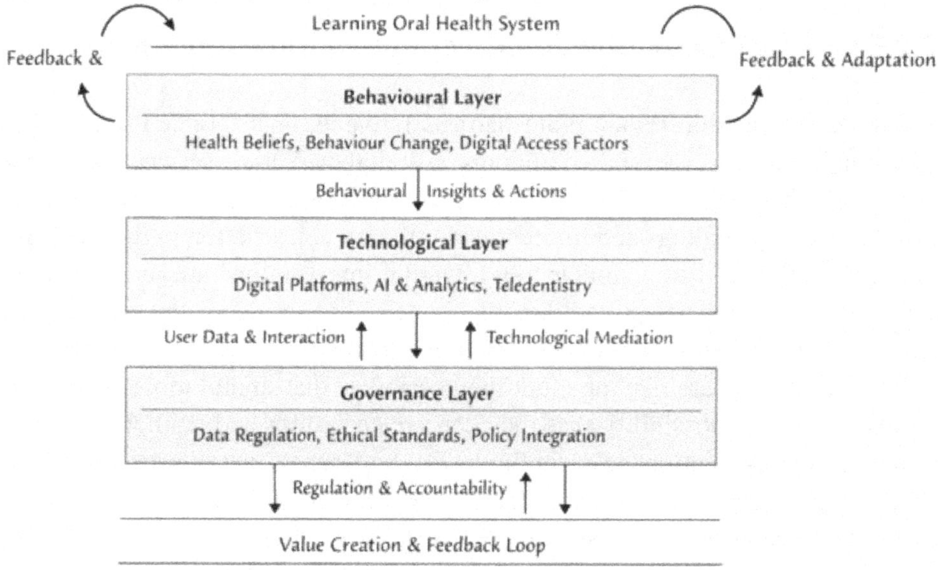

The prevention, behaviour, access, governance, and ethics literature conclusively demonstrates that digital marketing has become part of the oral-health system, influencing service visibility, trust formation, behaviour and navigation, and the institutional feedback loop, rather than simply relaying information. Nevertheless, the chapter also reveals that the corresponding theoretical traditions are not successfully incorporated. The intention and action, the infrastructure, and the governance structures elucidate behavioural, digital-health, and governance models, but rarely work together to explain the role of communicative power in the performance of the oral-health system.

The Digital Oral Health Intervention Framework (DOHIF) proposed herein fills this gap by theorising digital oral health systems as stratified socio-technical systems in which behavioural processes, technological infrastructures, and governance regimes can and do co-exist and interact to influence prevention and service outcomes. The analytical usefulness of it is the systematic manner in which it considers digital marketing as a system-enabling mechanism whereby the needs are identified, understood, taken action on, and managed within the institution with feedback loops of intervention, service utilisation, data creation, and policy revision (Peters, 2019).

The behavioural layer is based on the Health Belief Model, the Theory of Planned Behaviour, and the Behaviour Change Wheel as it stipulates the mediation of the susceptibility, benefits, barriers, norms, control, capability, opportunity, and motivation by reminders, booking systems, multilingual communication, search discoverability, and perceived responsiveness (Ajzen, 1991; Michie et al., 2 The infrastructures that may alleviate or exacerbate friction and inequity are search systems, social media, messaging, artificial intelligence, predictive analytics, and teledentistry included in the technological layer, and the data stewardship, consent, transparency, accountability, and regulatory coordination included in the governance layer as endogenous determinants of system quality (Khoury et al., 2024; Mittelstadt et al., 2016; Null et al., 2021; OECD, 2022; World Health Organization, 2021; Kepper et al., 2024).

DOHIF, in turn, conceptualises the notions of public value as behavioural, service, and systemic, including self-care, attendance, earlier diagnosis, missed appointments, resource allocation, and institutional legitimacy (Azzopardi-Muscat & Sørensen, 2019; Verdejo & Gutiérrez-Santiuste, 2019; World Health Organisation, 2022).

11.1 Reading DOHIF as a problem-trend-outcome model

A further account of DOHIF will allow us to demonstrate how the chapter depicts the issues, problems, and tendencies rather than enumerating them individually. The framework could be interpreted as a chain of interconnected background conditions that lead to digital mechanisms and, eventually, system outcomes, read left to right. Low perceived risk, fear, confusion, and weak preventive routines are among the issues captured at the behavioural level. On the technological front, it includes trends such as search-mediated care paths, platform dependence, conversational messaging, AI-aided customisation, and teledentistry. At the governance level, it is data that reflects issues of data stewardship, privacy, targeting legitimacy, accountability, and institutional capacity. DOHIF can thus be utilised as both a conceptual diagram and an operational reading tool: it can assist in explaining which problem is under consideration, which digital mechanism is being applied, under what governance conditions, and what measurable outcome is attained.

Table 2. Operational explanation of the Digital Oral Health Intervention Framework (DOHIF)

DOHIF layer	Issue or trend illustrated	Mechanism in practice	Indicative measures
Behavioural	Low perceived risk, weak routines, dental anxiety, social-norm effects	Targeted reminders, tailored education, peer cues, low-friction booking prompts	Knowledge gain, intention, self-care routines, attendance conversion
Technological	Search-driven discovery, platform visibility, messaging ecosystems, and AI-enabled targeting	SEO, service directories, chatbots, messaging services, teleconsultation, analytics	Discoverability, response time, booking completion, drop-off rates, and service navigation success
Governance	Privacy concerns, algorithmic bias, unequal data visibility, and weak accountability	Consent design, audit trails, procurement rules, equity review, referral and escalation protocols	Equity of reach, complaints, audit findings, safe escalation, trust and legitimacy indicators
System outcomes	Fragmented communication and limited proof of value	Linking outreach to triage, follow-up, and service delivery	Missed appointments, preventive uptake, continuity of care, plaque/gingival measures where feasible

Such working reading facilitates analysis. Rather than positioning digital marketing as a generic layer of communications, it demonstrates the interaction of particular trends, including platform-mediated search, AI-assisted messaging or data-driven targeting, to particular risks, including inequality, bias, weak trust, and unequal institutional preparedness. It also explains why a more powerful evaluation is required: the framework becomes comprehensive when the chapters and future studies can relate digital action to behavioural, service, equity, and clinical outcomes rather than to exposure metrics.

DOHIF can be operationalised into six steps to practitioners and policymakers that include: (1) define the oral-health problem and priority population; (2) identify the digital barrier or opportunity in the care pathway; (3) select the channel or tool most relevant to that bottleneck; (4) specify the service linkage, including booking, triage, referral, or follow-up; (5) assign behavioural, service, It was read in this manner, the framework can be viewed as a managerial planning and evaluation tool, not only a concept map, which directly addresses the fact that operations need to be further operationalised in a public-dentistry environment (Null et al., 2021; Azzopardi-Muscat & Sørensen, 2019; Scheerman et al., 2024).

The primary contribution that DOHIF makes is thus the connection between marketing systems and the values of the health system. It does not adhere to conventional barriers of communication and service provision and proves that digital marketing impacts access, responsiveness, prevention, efficiency, and equity. Simultaneously, it remains critical and non-acclaimant by staying sensitive to foregrounding contextual dependency, quality of governance, and the threat of the exclusion to offer an analytical expression of how digital oral health systems can be successful, unsuccessful, and which of the numerous layers must be remodelled so that communicative power can be used to serve a fair system performance instead of digital visibility (Kepper et al., 2024).

With the framework in place, the last thing to do is explain its implications for scholarship, public management, and future research. The following part is an implication rather than a synthesis, continuing the chapter's flow, since it concerns explanation and use.

12. IMPLICATIONS AND FUTURE RESEARCH DIRECTIONS

Oral-health communication is not the only focus of the analysis; it also demonstrates that digital marketing has now become an upstream element of health-system design. Not a downstream promotional tool, since visibility, trust, searchability, personalised prompting, and platform interaction actively influence prevention, access, and use of services in digitally mediated oral-health systems (Kepper et al., 2024). Social marketing and the scholarship of public-health is another area where this argument reorients by focusing on complex adaptive systems in which communicative infrastructures are important in influencing responsiveness, legitimacy, and public value and reveal the shortcomings of commercial measures, like optimisation, conversion, and audience efficiency, to measure success (Peters, 2019).

The future theory should therefore address the contradictions among persuasion and autonomy, precision and inclusion, and platform capability and institutional control. The service-dominant logic comes in handy in the present case, since it views access and trust as co-created during interactions among citizens, providers, institutions, and digital systems rather than being passed on through one-way communication (Verdejo & Gutiérrez-Santiuste, 2019). In practice, it can be assumed that educational materials, search methods, social media use, reminder services, and teledentistry platforms should be considered interconnected elements that can guide users from awareness to action and from initial contact to care continuity (Abroms et al., 2012; Null et al., 2021).

A defensible implementation argument does not purport to claim that digital communication is necessarily cheap. Instead, it implies that online public-health dentistry campaigns can be cost-saving or cost-effective by reducing missed appointments, enhancing the triage process, focusing workforce time on users with higher needs, and prolonging preventive communication without necessarily having to work with them face-to-face at each point. Nevertheless, syntheses of evidence on teledentistry also indicate that formal economic assessment remains limited and that most claims of returns on investment are based more on perceived efficiencies than on robust comparative designs (Benzian et al., 2025; Scheerman et al., 2024).

That is why policymakers and population managers should allocate funds to digital campaigns, as service-improvement interventions should be budgeted with clear business cases. These would include an approximation of start-up costs, recurrent staffing needs, technology purchases, content adaptation, training, compliance with governance requirements, and the opportunity cost of unmanaged demand. They ought also to establish a minimum set of measures, such as no-show reduction, time first to contact, booking completion, uptake among underserved groups, administrative workload, and, where possible, preventive clinical markers, as campaigns only measured by visibility indicators would not tell whether they reinforce oral-health systems in the face of the reality of limited financial resources (Panditi et al., 2025; Scheerman et al., 2024).

The need and barriers should dominate segmentation; therefore, rather than just engagement potential, populations with high disease burden, low service uptake, and high barriers to care should be prioritised by public actors. Multilingual content, low-literacy forms, culturally adapted narratives, and mobile-friendly interfaces should be considered minimum design standards for communicative accessibility (Celeste & Gaida, 2019; Loncar-Turukalo et al., 2019). Assessment must also shift to evaluating attendance, uptake of preventive check-ups, triage completion, follow-up continuity, and distributional effects in underserved groups (Azzopardi-Muscat & Sørensen, 2019).

One method of operationalising this logic is a return-on-investment dashboard, which connects areas of spending on one side and service impacts on the other, such as an investment in start-ups and recurrent costs versus reduction of no-show, completed preventive visits, triage efficiency, administrative time saved, and uptake by high-need groups (Benzian et al., 2025; Scheerman et al., 2024).

Meanwhile, digital strategy should also be governance-sensitive and globally inclusive, rather than universalising models based on digitally mature systems. Adopting digital marketing not only improves oral health; when used as a publicly responsible system of prevention, navigation, and justice, it delivers measurable behavioural, service, and clinical results. For NGOs, hybrid implementation and service-readiness research seem to have the greatest potential, whereas analysis of practice alone is less significant (Adeniyi et al., 2024; Bales et al., 2024; Panditi et al., 2025).

There is a direct policy implication of these findings. Supposing that access, trust, and prevention are conditioned by digital oral-health communication, it will be necessary to regulate it as a health-system architecture rather than as an unregulated supplement. Proportionality, transparency, privacy protection, inclusion, and accountability should be applied throughout the ethical-by-design implementation. Clear justification for the use of data, minimally intrusive data collection, intelligible consent, and regular auditing of exclusionary effects should be employed (OECD, 2022; World Health Organisation, 2021; Mittelstadt et al., 2016).

The public authorities are also to invest in public-interest digital infrastructure, interoperable data systems, and procurement standards that maintain the public sector's autonomy. The research agenda is also urgent requiring since the existing evidence continues to be heavily dependent upon engagement indicators, short-term knowledge change, and self-reported behavioural intention with little strong evidence on sustained self-care, preventive attendance, follow-up continuity, distributional equity, and algorithmic accountability remains limited; future longitudinal, comparative, mixed-methods, and participatory research must therefore test whether digital interventions alter clinical pathways, access patterns, trust, and exclusion over time and across settings (Farrokhi et al., 2023; Sharma et al., 2022; Khoury et al., 2024).

13. CONCLUSION

Collectively, the facts discussed in this chapter justify a radical conceptual change: digital marketing needs to be reframed as a central communications process rather than an adjunctive support for oral health services in the modern health system. Its importance lies in how it balances behavioural knowledge, technological infrastructure, service navigation, and adaptive feedback to create prevention, access, and trust. Simultaneously, the chapter demonstrates that digital strategies can only create value for people when aligned with social determinants, connected to service capacity, and regulated to minimise rather than reproduce exclusion.

In line with that, the chapter is now more focused on its mixed audience: it does not lose the theoretical importance to scholars and policy analysts but explains the implementation questions that are of interest to the administrators and programme managers, such as service readiness, referral linkage, measurement, and equity monitoring (Null et al., 2021; Azzopardi-Muscat & Sørensen, 2019).

The main issue, consequently, is how to match the prevention, equity, and innovation, rather than letting innovation run its course. Digital communication has the potential to enhance discoverability, personalise preventive care, and bridge the gap between outreach and care. However, these advantages are contingent on literacy, accessibility, good governance and independence of the public sector. The chapter, hence, recommends transdisciplinary cooperation among researchers in public health, dental researchers, marketers, behavioural scientists, technology scholars, and policymakers, as well as enhanced assessment of behavioural, service, equity, and clinical outcomes.

Digital marketing offers a revolutionary way to implement health system reforms by enabling more focused and effective promotion and preventive and public dental activities. Digital channels such as social media, search engines, and email campaigns are being used by health organisations to target different audiences with tailored messages that promote healthy behaviours, increase oral health knowledge, and encourage preventive care. Digital marketing uses data analytics and audience segmentation to identify at-risk populations and send instructional content or reminders for dental check-ups, immunisations, and early disease diagnosis. This adjustment not only increases public engagement and health literacy but also advances the overarching objectives of preventive dentistry and population health management, resulting in better health outcomes and more effective allocation of healthcare resources.

REFERENCES

Abroms, L. C., & Millan Lounsbury, N. (2012). Digital and social media campaigns: Expanding the reach of public health interventions. *Oral Health Promotion and Education*, *4*(2), 1–15.

Adeniyi, A., Akama, G., Lukandu, O., Ikemeri, J. E., Jumah, A., Chelagat, S., Kasuya, A., Ruhl, L., Songok, J., & Christoffersen-Deb, A. (2024). Reducing maternal and child oral health disparities in Sub-Saharan Africa through a community-based strategy. *Frontiers in Oral Health*, *5*, 1429332. DOI: 10.3389/froh.2024.1429332 PMID: 39005710

Ajzen, I. (1991). The theory of planned behaviour. *Organizational Behavior and Human Decision Processes*, *50*(2), 179–211. DOI: 10.1016/0749-5978(91)90020-T

Azzopardi-Muscat, N., & Sørensen, K. (2019). Towards an equitable digital public health era: Promoting equity through a health literacy perspective. *European Journal of Public Health*, *29*(Supplement_3), 13–17. DOI: 10.1093/eurpub/ckz166 PMID: 31738443

Bales, G. C., Curtan, S., Agarwal, N., Ronis, S. D., & Nelson, S. (2024). Adoption of New Oral Health Interventions in Primary Care: Qualitative Findings. *AJPM Focus*, *3*(3), 100214. DOI: 10.1016/j.focus.2024.100214 PMID: 38586824

Benzian, H., Guo, H., & Alqahtani, N.. (2025). Teledentistry for improving access to, and quality of oral health care: Overview of systematic reviews and meta-analyses. *Journal of Medical Internet Research*, *27*, e65211. DOI: 10.2196/65211 PMID: 40737673

Borrelli, B., Endrighi, R., Heeren, T., Adams, W. G., Gansky, S. A., Werntz, S., Rueras, N., Stephens, D., Ameli, N., & Henshaw, M. M. (2025). Parent-targeted oral health text messaging for underserved children attending pediatric clinics: A randomised clinical trial. *JAMA Network Open*, *8*(1), e2452780. DOI: 10.1001/jamanetworkopen.2024.52780 PMID: 39745701

Buck, D., Seong, J., Daud, A., Davies, M., Newcombe, R., & West, N. X. (2024). A randomised controlled trial to evaluate the effectiveness of personalised oral hygiene advice delivered via video technology. *Journal of Dentistry*, *149*, 105243. DOI: 10.1016/j.jdent.2024.105243 PMID: 39019247

Celeste, R. K., & Gaida, J. E. (2019). Social determinants of oral health inequalities. *Journal of Dental Research*, *98*(11), 1234–1241. DOI: 10.1177/0022034519876518 PMID: 31379234

Choonhawarakorn, K., Kasemkhun, P., & Leelataweewud, P. (2025). Effectiveness of a message service on child oral health practice via a social media application: A randomized controlled trial. *International Journal of Paediatric Dentistry*, *35*(2), 446–455. DOI: 10.1111/ipd.13256 PMID: 39104027

Farrokhi, F., Ghorbani, Z., Farrokhi, F., Namdari, M., & Salavatian, S. (2023). Social media as a tool for oral health promotion: A systematic review. *PLoS One*, *18*(12), e0296102. DOI: 10.1371/journal.pone.0296102 PMID: 38113216

Holtrop, J. S., Estabrooks, P. A., Gaglio, B., Harden, S. M., Kessler, R. S., King, D. K., Kwan, B. M., Ory, M. G., Rabin, B. A., Shelton, R. C., & Glasgow, R. E. (2021). Understanding and applying the RE-AIM framework: Clarifications and resources. *Journal of Clinical and Translational Science*, *5*(1), e126. DOI: 10.1017/cts.2021.789 PMID: 34367671

International Telecommunication Union. (2024). Facts and Figures 2024: Internet use. ITU. https://www.itu.int/itu-d/reports/statistics/facts-figures-2024/

Jivraj, A., Barrow, J., & Listl, S. (2022). Value-based oral health care: Implementation lessons from four case studies. *The Journal of Evidence-Based Dental Practice*, *22*(1, Suppl), 101662. DOI: 10.1016/j.jebdp.2021.101662 PMID: 35063180

Kepper, M. M., Fowler, L. A., Kusters, I. S., Davis, J. W., Baqer, M., Sagui-Henson, S., Xiao, Y., Tarfa, A., Yi, J. C., Gibson, B., Heron, K. E., Alberts, N. M., Burgermaster, M., Njie-Carr, V. P. S., & Klesges, L. M. (2024). Expanding a behavioral view on digital health access: Drivers and strategies to promote equity. *Journal of Medical Internet Research*, *26*, e51355. DOI: 10.2196/51355 PMID: 39088246

Khoury, Z. H., Ferguson, A., Price, J. B., Sultan, A. S., & Wang, R. (2024). Responsible artificial intelligence for addressing equity in oral healthcare. *Frontiers in Oral Health*, *5*, 1408867. DOI: 10.3389/froh.2024.1408867 PMID: 39092200

Kitsaras, G., Gomez, J., Hogan, R., & Ryan, M. (2023). Evaluation of a digital oral health intervention (Know Your OQ™) to enhance knowledge, attitudes and practices related to oral health. *BDJ Open*, *9*(1), 40. DOI: 10.1038/s41405-023-00166-4 PMID: 37633985

Loncar-Turukalo, T., Zdravevski, E., Da Silva, J. M., Chouvarda, I., & Trajkovik, V. (2019). Literature on wearable technology for connected health: Scoping review of research trends, advances, and barriers. *Journal of Medical Internet Research*, *21*(9), e14017. DOI: 10.2196/14017 PMID: 31489843

Lupton, D. (2017). *Digital health: Critical and cross disciplinary perspectives*. Routledge., DOI: 10.4324/9781315648835

Michie, S., van Stralen, M. M., & West, R. (2011). The behaviour change wheel: A new method for characterising and designing behaviour change interventions. *Implementation Science : IS*, *6*(1), 42. DOI: 10.1186/1748-5908-6-42 PMID: 21513547

Mittelstadt, B. D., Allo, P., Taddeo, M., Wachter, S., & Floridi, L. (2016). The ethics of algorithms: Mapping the debate. *Big Data & Society*, *3*(2), 2053951716679679. DOI: 10.1177/2053951716679679

Null, J. H.. (2021). Teledentistry and telehealth: Policy, practice, and evidence. *Journal of Dental Education*, *85*(10), 1321–1334.

OECD. (2022). *Health Data Governance for the Digital Age: Implementing the OECD Recommendation on Health Data Governance*. OECD Publishing., DOI: 10.1787/68b60796-

Panditi, M., Anusha, K., & Palle, E.. (2025). Availability and utilisation of oral healthcare services at rural community health centres in South India: A mixed methods study. *BMC Oral Health*, *25*(1), 977. DOI: 10.1186/s12903-025-06327-1 PMID: 40598131

Peres, M. A., Macpherson, L. M., Weyant, R. J., Daly, B., Venturelli, R., Mathur, M. R., Listl, S., Celeste, R. K., Guarnizo-Herreño, C. C., Kearns, C., Benzian, H., Allison, P., & Watt, R. G. (2019). Oral diseases: A global public health challenge. *Lancet*, *394*(10194), 249–260. DOI: 10.1016/S0140-6736(19)31146-8 PMID: 31327369

Peters, D. H. (2019). The application of systems thinking in health: Why use systems thinking? *Health Research Policy and Systems*, *12*(1), 51. DOI: 10.1186/1478-4505-12-51 PMID: 25160707

Rosenstock, I. M., Strecher, V. J., & Becker, M. H. (1988). Social learning theory and the Health Belief Model. *Health Education Quarterly*, *15*(2), 175–183. DOI: 10.1177/109019818801500203 PMID: 3378902

Rothschild, M. L. (1999). Carrots, sticks, and promises: A conceptual framework for the management of public health and social issue behaviors. *Journal of Marketing*, *63*(4), 24–37. DOI: 10.1177/002224299906300404

Scheerman, J. F. M., Qari, A. H., Varenne, B., Bijwaard, H., Swinckels, L., Giraudeau, N., van Meijel, B., & Mariño, R. (2024). A systematic umbrella review of the effects of teledentistry on costs and oral-health outcomes. *International Journal of Environmental Research and Public Health*, *21*(4), 407. DOI: 10.3390/ijerph21040407 PMID: 38673320

Sharma, S., Mohanty, V., Balappanavar, A. Y., Chahar, P., & Rijhwani, K. (2022). Role of Digital Media in Promoting Oral Health: A Systematic Review. *Cureus*, *14*(9), e28893. DOI: 10.7759/cureus.28893 PMID: 36225421

Verdejo, A. V., & Gutiérrez-Santiuste, E. (2019). Service-dominant logic in public services: Value co-creation in e-government. *Public Management Review*, *21*(7), 1011–1031. DOI: 10.1080/14719037.2018.1529878

Watt, R. G., & Sheiham, A. (2012). Integrating the common risk factor approach into a social determinants framework. *Community Dentistry and Oral Epidemiology*, *40*(6), 473–481. DOI: 10.1111/j.1600-0528.2012.00680.x PMID: 22429083

World Health Organisation. (2021). *Improving oral health through the use of digital technology*. https://www.who.int/publications/i/item/9789240035225.https://www.who.int/publications/i/item/9789240061484

World Health Organization. (2022). *Global oral health status report: Towards universal health coverage for oral health by 2030*. World Health Organization. https://www.who.int/publications/i/item/9789240061484

KEY TERMS AND DEFINITIONS

Behaviour Change Wheel (BCW): The Behaviour Change Wheel is a behavioural framework developed by Michie et al. (2011) that explains behaviour through the interaction of capability, opportunity, and motivation, and guides the design of interventions to influence health-related practices.

Digital Health Literacy: Digital health literacy is the ability to locate, understand, evaluate, and apply online health information and digital services effectively for informed oral-health decision-making and appropriate help-seeking behaviour

Digital Marketing in Public Oral Health: Digital marketing in public oral health refers to the strategic use of digital platforms, online communication tools, social media, search systems, messaging services, and data-driven technologies to promote oral-health awareness, preventive behaviours, service navigation, and equitable access to dental care within population health systems.

Digital Oral Health Citizen: The digital oral health citizen is an individual who engages with oral health information, risk assessment, provider selection, and care-seeking decisions through digital environments such as search engines, social media, telehealth platforms, and online communication systems.

Digital Oral Health Intervention Framework (DOHIF): The Digital Oral Health Intervention Framework (DOHIF) is a conceptual model proposed in the chapter that integrates behavioural processes, digital technologies, governance systems, and service pathways to explain how digital marketing influences prevention, access, equity, and oral-health outcomes.

Preventive Infrastructure: Preventive infrastructure refers to the integrated communication, technological, and institutional systems that support continuous oral-health promotion, early intervention, behavioural reinforcement, and access to preventive services within everyday social settings.

Teledentistry: Teledentistry is the use of digital communication technologies, remote consultations, virtual monitoring, and electronic information exchange to improve access, continuity, and coordination of oral health services and professional support.

Chapter 9

Digital Marketing for Dental Public Health Using TikTok

Supaprawat Siripipatthanakul
http://orcid.org/0000-0001-6671-2682
Bangkok Thonburi University, Thailand

Astri Dwi Andriani
http://orcid.org/0000-0003-3951-4829
Putra Indonesia University, Indonesia

ABSTRACT

Short-form video content has shed light on health communication, and public dental health is at a crossroads. This chapter introduces TikTok and GenAI as a two-engine system to enhance oral health worldwide. This study proposes a three-part strategy to address dental misinformation and DIY dental care: (1) AI-Based Content Engineering, where AI-powered LLMs and synthetic avatars deliver effective and non-intimidating education; (2) Algorithm Implementation, where Gen Z and Alpha demographics are targeted with local clinical access through Gen Z and Alpha-friendly edutainment; and (3) Targeted Dental Public Health. GenAI lowers production obstacles, enabling practitioners to maintain a high-rate evidence-based engagement cycle. This synergy increases the public's Knowledge, Attitudes, and Practices (KAP) and introduces Digital Care Ethics, which promotes clinically responsible, technologically enhanced oral health services.

DOI: 10.4018/979-8-3373-8894-6.ch009

1. INTRODUCTION

The innovative era of global health communication has ushered in a tectonic shift from stagnant, text-heavy information repositories to a dynamic, hyper-visual social ecosystem. With no tolerance for medical knowledge being consumed and transmitted by any means, the rise of short-form video content has reshaped the context in which knowledge is delivered and received in public health efforts, as these efforts aim to remain relevant and competitive in a more digital world. Digital ecosystems amalgamate interrelated tools, platforms, and stakeholders to facilitate healthcare delivery. There has been less focus on their contribution to improving communication and collaboration, especially in resource-constrained environments. The digital ecosystems support these functions, highlighting essential components, applications, obstacles, and facilitators (Devkota, 2024; Mwogosi & Mambile, 2025). It is not just a media shift but a paradigm shift in the attention economy, in which once-dominant long-form media like YouTube are now being challenged by TikTok's fast-paced format. For democratic access to oral hygiene education, this development represents an unprecedented opportunity to democratize dental health by creating easily digestible content for the public.

The global trend of audiences shifting to short-form video is supported by compelling statistics. By 2024, TikTok had surpassed 1.5 billion monthly active users, and its engagement rates were significantly higher than those of legacy platforms (Digital Global Overview, 2024). In many countries with some of the highest TikTok penetration rates worldwide, the platform has emerged as a focal point for edutainment. This shift is driven by the fact that short clips offer users cognitive comfort by transforming complex dental procedures into less intimidating stories. Therefore, public dental health strategies must address this format to avoid losing the attention of younger demographics to non-professional influencers.

However, as a consequence of this democratization, a serious problem has emerged: the proliferation of misinformation about dental care and DIY dental treatments, leading to a frightening trend. Controversial topics such as the dangerous trend of teeth filing or caustic chemical whitening methods have been viewed by millions of people, ultimately displacing evidence-based clinical guidance. Quantitative research shows that the most popular dental videos on TikTok are created by amateurs, and many include medically inaccurate recommendations (Gušić et al., 2024). This public health crisis of misinformation is an epidemic that requires a strong, professional counter-narrative to the narratives that drive these trends.

Case studies worldwide also demonstrate the pervasiveness of this digital health threat. In the US, the American Association of Orthodontists (AAO, 2022) issued an official statement warning against DIY gap-closing tutorials using non-medical rubber bands, which could lead to long-term tooth loss. The British Dental Association

(BDA, 2023) faced increasing pressure from patients requesting corrective treatment after following the trend of using "at-home veneers." These examples demonstrate that digital failures have created a credibility gap between viral entertainment and clinical safety. Reclaiming the role of health information custodians is timely for professionals, and the urgency of this research is to offer a framework to facilitate this reclaim (Thorat et al., 2024).

The key to achieving a much-needed balance between medical expertise and digital marketing creativity is integrating GenAI (Generative AI). Historically, practitioners' digital presence has been hampered by the time-consuming process of content creation (Khan et al., 2021).

Rapidly creating appropriate, engaging, and culturally specific content is possible using GenAI tools, such as Large Language Models for scripting or AI-based video synthesis (Andriani, 2025). With AI, the number of vulnerable DIY trends will multiply exponentially as effective, professionally verified, AI-driven educational videos proliferate.

In Southeast Asia, particularly Thailand and Indonesia, the combination of a mobile-first population and the application of AI has created a laboratory for innovation. Quantitative surveys show that patients are increasingly receptive to AI-generated health guidance when it is endorsed by a trusted institution. For example, AI avatars have been tested in Thailand and used in a Bangkok public health campaign to model post-operative care, where adherence was higher than with conventional pamphlets (Thonburi Health Report, 2024). This study examines how these local achievements can be translated into a global plan, using TikTok as a complex behavior change tool.

Furthermore, this research is urgent given the evolving nature of health literacy. In the modern era, literacy is characterized by the ability to navigate a digital ecosystem and distinguish fact from fiction (Nutbeam & Lloyd, 2021). By not creating dental professionals on TikTok, professionals are allowing unqualified creators to overqualify the field. The presence on TikTok is a moral issue. Analyzing the intersection of AI-assisted content and public health will enable this research to offer practitioners a roadmap for proactively teaching myth-busting and addressing myths before they become established behaviors (Willis et al., 2022).

For policy considerations, this study is generalized to formulate ethical principles for promoting AI-based health. With the rapid development of GenAI, the distinction between human and machine medical advice is blurring (Veseli & Bencharit, 2026). It highlights the need for a Digital Care Ethics framework to ensure that AI tools do not replace the patient-provider relationship but instead complement it. This chapter contributes to the literature by proposing a framework that balances AI efficiency with rigorous medical ethics, making global dental health strategies both innovative and technologically responsible (International Dental Federation [FDI], 2023).

Scalability is significant for the potential for global impact. With TikTok, AI can be used to optimize campaigns that can reach millions of people simultaneously in rural areas, unlike the limited geographic reach of traditional interventions (Global Oral Health Initiative, 2023). To illustrate this point, a single viral video on fluoride use, converted into multiple languages by AI, can be more effective than a decade of local workshops. It is crucial for quantifying this effect and for providing evidence-based recommendations to organizations such as the WHO on incorporating short-form videos into global oral health action plans.

This chapter explains that the future of community dental care is digital, visual, and automated. By merging the viral aspect of TikTok with the accuracy of Generative AI, we can usher in a time where a fair amount of oral health education is a basic human right. Experts and practitioners widely recognize this chapter as a crucial resource. There is now a call to embrace a New Era of Health Communication to counter the spread of misinformation and build a more informed and healthier world. There are still many traditional dentists who are reluctant to embrace TikTok, believing it is more for fun than for work. Part of the hesitation stems from a lack of clarity about how to incorporate clinical expertise into a short-form video story and from fear of not being taken seriously. Such resistance is a missed opportunity to engage with patients authentically. When dental companies humanize themselves on TikTok, I'm even more impressed. It's a great way to bridge the gap between clinical professionalism and accessible, personable care.

2. LITERATURE REVIEW

Digital marketing for public dental health promotion on TikTok is a successful strategy for educating and engaging the public, especially youth. Dentists can leverage AI-generated content techniques to produce engaging short-form TikTok videos on oral hygiene and practice marketing.

2.2 The Way AI is Going to Improve TikTok Dental Marketing.

The introduction of Artificial Intelligence (AI) in social media marketing has completely transformed the healthcare communication workflow, particularly content production and ideation. According to recent research, the main challenges for dental professionals entering the digital environment include content fatigue and the laborious task of scriptwriting.

Large Language Models (LLMs) are generative AI models that automatically generate evidence-based video scripts and identify hashtags at high speed to address current dental trends. Such automation not only saves up to 70 percent of time during the brainstorming phase but also keeps educational content organized, engaging (Wintz et al., 2024), and optimized for the TikTok algorithm. By automating the creative process, AI allows public health professionals to focus more on clinical accuracy and maintain a consistent digital presence, both of which are crucial for retaining an audience.

Beyond textual insights, AI has revolutionized the aesthetic and functional nature of dental education on TikTok. High-fidelity 3D dental models and AI avatars can be created using emerging text-to-video and synthetic media technologies, allowing complex procedures in oral surgery or orthodontics to be frozen without the ethical and privacy concerns associated with capturing real patient images. These AI-powered visual tools can help introduce transparency into procedures, making seemingly daunting dental procedures less intimidating for laypeople. Andriani (2025) stated that consuming visual content created or enhanced with AI tools significantly boosts user engagement because these tools can produce smooth, professional animations that were previously available only to large companies with substantial marketing budgets.

TikTok's competitive advantage lies in its recommendation engine, which is increasingly powered by targeted messaging and AI-assisted trend analysis. AI programs have the potential to sift through vast amounts of social listening data and identify new public health concerns, including the growing popularity of dangerous DIY dental tricks (Gušić et al., 2024). With AI to address these trending topics in real time, dental practitioners can implement reactive education, creating materials that directly target and debunk misinformation before it goes viral. This fact-based strategy will ensure that government messages about the importance of dental health aren't presented in a vacuum but instead address the concerns and anxieties in online communities (Thorat et al., 2024). Safe DIY dental tricks include improving everyday hygiene, such as warm saltwater rinses to relieve gum inflammation, oil pulling with coconut oil to reduce plaque, and eating crunchy, fibrous foods like apples to naturally clean teeth.

The efficiency of content creation on TikTok is also enhanced by AI's ability to tailor health messages to different demographics. One size doesn't fit all in global public health; today, AI tools can transform the same educational idea into a variety of formats, languages, and cultural contexts (Federation of International Dentistry [FDI], 2023). For example, an AI system can reframe a basic script about the importance of fluoride into a comic sketch for younger audiences or a more serious lecture for older audiences, while maintaining its underlying medical quality. Veseli and Bencharit (2026) stated that this hyper-personalization is crucial to overcome cultural barriers in dental health, especially in geographically and linguistically diverse regions such as Southeast Asia.

Additionally, AI can be used in TikTok marketing through predictive analytics to help practitioners identify the best time and format for maximum reach. Based on interaction data, machine learning models can determine which types of dental content are most effective, such as before-and-after videos, myth-busting sessions, or clinic tours (Digital Global Overview, 2024). It enables a more scientific marketing approach by directing resources toward content types that positively affect patient attitudes and behaviors. The predictive features make TikTok not just a simple social app but a highly sophisticated public health intervention tool that can positively impact dental literacy levels in the community.

Finally, the literature suggests that the development of AI and TikTok has triggered a vicious cycle of interaction and feedback. Sentiment analysis tools, powered by AI, allow dentists to aggregate large volumes of candid comments and reviews to identify which misconceptions or questions are prevalent and need clarification (Willis et al., 2022). This real-time feedback enables a dynamic, far more responsive public health communication process than traditional media. As technology matures, the combination of AI-driven visuals, computer-aided ideation, and personalized messaging will likely serve as the template for a global approach to improving oral health outcomes amid digital transformation (de Ahumada Servant et al., 2025).

2.2 The major TikTok strategies in Public Dental Health.

The key to an effective public presence in dental health on TikTok is strategically placing educational content and actively busting myths. Unlike conventional health brochures, TikTok's short-form format allows practitioners to present brushing and flossing methods in a highly visual, easily repeatable way, which has been shown to improve patient retention and motor skill acquisition (Wintz et al., 2024). TikTok acts as a frontline against the harmful DIY dental care trend in the so-called infodemic. By implementing image conversion or merging features, dental practitioners can directly counter harmful information, such as at-home tooth filing or charcoal whitening, with evidence-based clinical correction. Professional myth-busting videos are more engaging than traditional tutorials because they tap into the audience's curiosity while restoring clinical authority.

One key psychological approach to online dental marketing is humanizing the practice and its medical team. Dental anxiety is a major barrier to service utilization in any country worldwide, but TikTok offers a unique way to alleviate this anxiety by showcasing the behind-the-scenes life of a dental office. By engaging with the dental team and participating in non-clinical moments, practitioners can create a sense of parasocial interaction: viewers form a personal connection with the provider even before they enter the office (Andriani, 2025). Research has shown that clinics that humanize their staff by posting humorous or touching stories have higher patient trust and reduced pre-appointment anxiety measured among new patients (Sivrikaya et al., 2021).

Professionals need to navigate TikTok's cultural ecosystem by using trending sounds and challenges to maximize organic reach. This isn't just a popularity game, but a strategic move to keep up with trends, where the platform's algorithm ranks content based on high-volume audio and hashtags. Making dental health information appear trending, such as through a catchy dance or a viral audio video, helps overcome the resistance typically associated with boring health advertising. However, the literature also emphasizes the need to maintain professional credibility; effective techniques include adapting to trends, as they can convey serious health messages without making specialist practices seem clichéd (Gušić et al., 2024).

The effectiveness of digital interactions in generating specific health outcomes depends on the effectiveness of the so-called Call to Action (CTA). While awareness is crucial, successful public health marketing must encourage users to change their behavior, such as scheduling a checkup appointment or visiting an educational website. Research on digital health communication shows that videos with a single, clearly structured call to action (CTA), either in the video caption or linked in the bio, achieve significantly higher click-through rates than videos without direct instruction (Thorat et al., 2024). As part of a digital push within a public health framework, this CTA helps transform informed consumers into active participants in their personal oral health care.

Furthermore, this combination of steps forms a patient funnel that resembles the modern patient journey. The phases of educational content are Awareness, Humanization, and Trend Promotion/CTA (Digital Health Overview, 2024). In social dental health projects, especially in developing countries such as Southeast Asia, this is crucial for addressing systemic barriers to access. By providing free, high-quality education and a direct path to professional consultation, TikTok's strategy democratizes dental knowledge and makes oral health care accessible to groups traditionally underserved by conventional medical marketing systems.

Finally, TikTok marketing can be sustainable for public health, depending on the consistency of content and community engagement. The TikTok algorithm rewards active users who consistently create content and engage with their audience through the comments section. This interactive component will also enable the creation of a two-way health communication model, in which practitioners can answer specific patient questions in real time, thereby eliminating doubts that can prevent patients from seeking professional help (Willis et al., 2022). With the evolution of platforms, myth-busting learning, humanized branding, and algorithm-aware trend engagement will become the new standard for digital health promotion worldwide (International Dental Federation [FDI], 2023).

2.3 The Impact of Social Media and TikTok on Dental Public Health

The move from text-based health promotion to video-based communication has significantly improved user engagement, an important indicator of success in promoting public well-being. Unlike traditional websites or paper brochures, TikTok's algorithmic structure prioritizes so-called "high-engagement" content, in other words, videos that receive likes, shares, and comments, and distributes them to a wider audience rather than to followers. Research shows that the active format of short videos leads to higher engagement than conventional social media platforms. Features such as auto-playing videos and the For You Page (FYP) remove barriers between users and health messages. This is not merely a superficial reaction, but a cognitive interaction between the population and information about dental health, creating a context in which oral health care becomes a common topic of social conversation, rather than a neglected health condition.

Social media has changed oral health education and healthcare communication. This review discusses how social media can quickly reach large audiences, enhance patient engagement, and support health professionals in improving oral health. Facebook, Instagram, YouTube, and TikTok are used to disseminate evidence-based information on dental care and to modify behavior through interactive, multimedia content. Social media campaigns promote oral health, preventive dentistry, and community support. Still, disinformation, unsubstantiated health advice, and ethical issues continue. Social media helps patients and healthcare providers communicate, learn, and enhance health literacy. Despite concerns, social media can improve oral health education if professionals collaborate with influencers to provide accurate, reliable information. AI and AR could personalize and improve dental health promotion in the digital age (Arora et al., 2025).

TikTok's broader and unparalleled reach provides a competitive advantage in addressing global health challenges across its diverse population. With over one billion active users, the platform is not limited by geographic or socioeconomic boundaries, allowing public dental health campaigns to reach underserved populations who lack access to regular dental visits. Research has shown that TikTok can specifically target Generation Z and Millennials, reaching audiences that are inaccessible to traditional health advertising methods but are highly engaged in digital health circles. Through TikTok's global platform, evidence-based campaigns by dental institutions can reach millions of users across multiple continents simultaneously, thereby making preventive oral health education a global right. Social media has changed the way health information is obtained, how people engage in health-promoting actions, and how people form attitudes about wellness. Fundraising (Paul & Headley-Johnson, 2025; Alhersh, 2026). Growing empirical evidence supports the view that TikTok is an effective tool for dental health pedagogy. Recent intervention studies have demonstrated a direct association between increased dental health literacy (KAP) and the consumption of educational entertainment about dental health. For example, quantitative results showed that users who surveyed professional dental health content creators had better knowledge of periodontal disease prevention and proper toothbrushing techniques than the control group. Narratives that are more visual on the platform are better suited to the literacy needs than traditional methods. This is especially true when complex medical data needs to be represented visually.

"TikTok's effects go beyond changing behavior to acquiring knowledge, influencing real-life health decisions. Social proof plays a key role in normalizing dental checkups and preventing dental phobia, as people emulate the healthy habits of trusted influencers or professionals. When professional dental content goes viral, it creates momentum that encourages audiences to make oral health a part of their overall lifestyle. These changes can significantly impact public health policymakers' decisions, as they demonstrate that digital interventions can produce long-term reductions in disease rates and the global burden of preventable oral conditions. Scalability initiatives for health based on TikTok also provide cost-effective solutions for resource-constrained government health departments. Producing and distributing AI-powered TikTok videos costs significantly less than traditional TV/print advertising, while also delivering a higher Return on Engagement (ROE). Digital campaigns in Southeast Asia used localized TikTok content to bring traffic to community centers, showing how online awareness can translate into real-world clinical behavior. That's why TikTok is a must-use tool in health strategies worldwide, where the goal is to achieve the best results on a limited budget.

TikTok's long-term impact on public health is enhanced by its use of Continuous Learning, which exposes users to repetitive information. The nature of TikTok content means users will see the same health messages multiple times, further strengthening the habit-forming effects of oral hygiene training. This gradual delivery of information, as Willis et al. (2022) noted, is more efficient for long-term retention than intensive one-on-one educational sessions. A consistent, active presence on these platforms will allow dental practitioners to ensure that messages about the importance of maintaining public health are consistently conveyed, ultimately resulting in a more informed and health-literate global.

2.4 Best Practices

Consistency is a key factor in TikTok's algorithmic success, as it requires regular content sharing to remain visible online and earn audience trust. Compared with traditional, cyclical, and seasonal media campaigns, TikTok's "For You Page" (FYP) algorithm favors accounts that post high-quality, frequent content, as this signals to the platform that a creator is an active and relevant participant in the ecosystem (Wintz et al., 2024). According to digital health communication, posting content three to five times a week is considered sufficient to keep the target audience in the cognitive loop. Frequent posting in public dental health can help to establish preventive information as a routine behavior (e.g., proper flossing practices or the effectiveness of fluoride), which is a fundamental psychological motivator for long-term behavior change. By utilizing TikTok's advanced geographic targeting capabilities, public health programs that have historically aimed to increase global consciousness can now be directed toward local and clinical needs. The viral reach has a positive impact on general education, but the ability to tag specific sites and use region-specific hashtags means people can see the content at a variety of easily accessible local dental clinics. Such hyper-local targeting is especially important in geographically diverse regions such as Southeast Asia, where digital reach must be aligned with existing physical infrastructure. Partnering with other healthcare professionals and digital creators can be a powerful force multiplier for reaching and increasing the credibility of public health messages about dental health.

The number of Likes, Comments, and Reposts for the top 100 most popular micro-videos varied significantly. Citizens were most likely to view cartoon or documentary-style videos. In a similar vein, content that taught about illnesses or promoted professional health was regularly seen. The most popular content included original music, formal Mandarin, subtitles, and was less than 60 seconds. The fact that the majority of PHCs find it difficult to use TikTok is regarded as a missed opportunity, particularly given its growing popularity and the daily increase in account creation (Zhu et al., 2020). Dental professionals can leverage existing communities and share health information through duets, collaborations, or livestreams with doctors, nutritionists, or other established health influencers. This multidisciplinary approach increases not only demographic coverage but also understanding of oral health within the health system. Collaborative credibility is more effective than individual professional content in changing skeptical views, because social consensus about healthy oral habits is reinforced by recommendations from multiple credible individuals.

Ethical consistency and professional integrity are also key components of best practices in collaborative and trend-driven marketing. As collaborations expand, dental professionals should ensure that their partners have produced evidence-based content that is not commercially biased (Federation of International Dentistry [FDI], 2023). According to the literature, the optimal approach to best-practice structures involves a compromise between the creative freedom of digital artists and the clinical rigor of dental practitioners. This combination ensures that the final product is entertaining enough to be selected by the TikTok algorithm, yet factual enough to meet high medical ethical standards (Veseli & Bencharit, 2026).

Furthermore, active, real-time community engagement, including responding to user feedback and answering frequently asked questions, is a behavioral pattern that helps distinguish a successful health advocate from a passive advertiser. This two-way communication model allows professionals to be recognized more as community workers, rather than as powerful protectors. Research also shows that active participation in the comments section can be a powerful way to reduce so-called dental anxiety by offering direct, personal reassurance to fearful patients (Sivrikaya et al., 2021). By focusing on engagement, dental clinics can create a loyal digital community that becomes a source of patient referrals and health advocates, given its self-directed nature (Willis et al., 2022).

Finally, implementing data-driven improvements is a best practice that ensures the viability of a digital dental strategy. By regularly auditing TikTok's "Creator Analytics," practitioners can identify which formats, timings, and types of collaborations generate the highest engagement and retention of health knowledge (Thorat et al., 2024). This iterative process allows public health initiatives to remain agile, adapting to rapidly changing digital trends while maintaining a focus on core health outcomes. As the digital landscape continues to evolve, a commitment to these best practices in consistency, targeting, and collaboration will remain the definitive blueprint for successful digital transformation in the public dental sector (de Ahumada Servant et al., 2025).

3. METHODOLOGY

3.1 Data Collection

This chapter employed a narrative review and thematic content analysis. A narrative review is a type of academic literature review that summarizes, synthesizes, and critiques published research on a specific topic. Unlike systematic reviews, they rely on the author's expertise to tell a compelling, thematic story rather than following rigid protocols. This methodology facilitates the integration of multiple qualitative studies to produce a thorough, evidence-based synthesis. Narrative analysis was used in this review, and content analysis was conducted on scholarly papers indexed in Google Scholar, Web of Science, and Scopus from 2020 to 2025.

3.2 Data Analysis

The methodology is adapted to search for previous studies for inclusion criteria based on related topics and keywords, such as Digital Marketing, Generative AI, TikTok, Public Dental Health, Health Literacy, Edutainment, Oral Care, and Global

Health Strategy. The scholarly papers, mainly published between 2015 and 2025, were selected through purposive sampling. The exclusion criteria include papers not published in English or outside the publication period, as well as duplicate papers. The thematic content analysis was conducted by two academic editors, the authors of this chapter.

4. RESULTS AND DISCUSSIONS

Figure 1. The theoretical framework

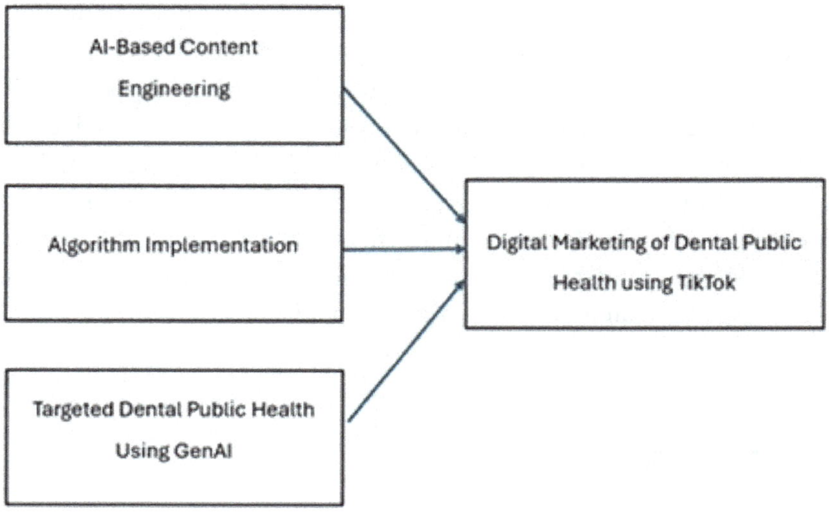

Figure 1 shows digital marketing for dental public health on TikTok across three dimensions: (1) AI-based content engineering, (2) algorithm implementation, and (3) targeted dental public health using GenAI.

The three key dimensions to revolutionize digital marketing for dental public health on TikTok are:

(1) AI-based content engineering that leverages artificial intelligence to automatically generate, personalize, and optimize short-form video content that appeals to diverse audiences and promotes oral health messages.
(2) algorithm implementation where marketers strategically analyze and adapt to TikTok's recommendation system to maximize content visibility and engagement among target demographics using real-time data.

(3) targeted dental public health using GenAI that leverages generative AI to craft hyper-personalized public health campaigns, ensuring that educational materials address specific community needs, cultural preferences, and emerging dental health trends for maximum impact and behavioral change.

4.1 Generative AI: The Engine of Modern Dental Content Creation

The introduction of Generative Artificial Intelligence (GenAI) into public dental health will shift the paradigm by replacing manual content creation with automated and scalable communication models. With increasingly competitive digital dental marketing, the need for high-quality, scientific, and engaging content has outpaced the logistical capabilities of traditional dental practices. GenAI is a force multiplier, enabling practitioners to balance their professional competencies with the demands of innovative social media platforms like TikTok. With the help of advanced machine learning frameworks, the dental profession can now produce a vast amount of educational content that was previously available only to large media outlets, ensuring that evidence-based oral health information continues to dominate the digital attention economy.

The first pillar of this AI transformation is automated ideation, which encompasses the broad application of LLMs such as ChatGPT and Gemini. These tools have transformed the early stages of content strategy by enabling sophisticated keyword research and the identification of misinformation in public health discourse. For example, an LLM can handle queries from thousands of users and accurately pinpoint the most prevalent dental myths in a given geographic area, such as claims about the efficacy of charcoal whitening or DIY teeth-straightening devices. This allows public health educators to move away from disseminating broad information and instead develop highly targeted myth-busting campaigns that address the most urgent and important understandings held by the population with laser-like accuracy.

The balance between clinical rigor and ease of viewing short videos can only be maintained through the LLM's role in scripting. The linguistic architecture of TikTok writing must capture the viewer's attention within the first 3 seconds and deliver a compelling medical message in under a minute. This is a creative translation, and AI tools are particularly well-suited to it, taking dense clinical instructions on periodontal disease or fluoride varnish and converting them into a highly readable script. This would maintain the professional integrity of dental advice but optimize it for the platform's unique consumption patterns, ultimately resulting in higher health literacy among lay audiences (Wintz et al., 2024).

The autonomous creation of AI-generated avatars and synthetic media is the second pillar of GenAI in dentistry, addressing one of the limitations of medical education:

the visual intimidation factor. Most oral surgical interventions that appear normal to a practitioner may appear frightening or even frightening to a phobic patient when shown in a real-life clinical video. The solution is to use AI-generated avatars and synthetic 3D models to create artificial prints of dental implant placement or root canal treatments, offering a sterile, anatomically correct printing process. These avatars can explain the process in a non-threatening, non-stigmatizing manner, putting patients at ease before surgery and reducing their anxiety before entering the clinic (Veseli & Bencharit, 2026).

Synthetic media is also being used to address key ethical and privacy concerns associated with conventional medical video recording. Recording high-quality video of live patients requires complex consent models and often violates patient privacy, even when the footage is de-identified. These barriers can be removed through AI avatars, allowing dental educators to present a limitless range of clinical situations, from pediatric practices to geriatric prosthetics, without direct contact. Such capabilities enable a more diverse representation of patient groups in health campaigns, allowing members of all ethnicities and age groups to feel represented in the dental health stories they read on social media (Gušić et al., 2024).

The third pillar, AI-based analytics, offers the navigational insights necessary for success in the volatile TikTok ecosystem. Trending Topic Analysis is an AI-based trend-tracking technology that goes beyond simple hashtag tracking, using sentiment analysis and predictive modeling to understand the velocity of dental trends. A practitioner might have time to identify a trend and show that it has reached its peak by the time it takes to do so manually. AI analytics tools can detect early signs of emerging trends, such as specific "voice challenges" or "visual challenges" used in the healthcare niche. Dental professionals can capitalize on these trends by using professional content at the right time and increasing organic impressions (Digital Global Overview, 2024).

More granular audience segmentation is also possible using AI-based analytics tools. AI doesn't need to target large audiences with a single message; engagement statistics can identify which content formats appeal to specific subpopulations. For example, data might indicate that teenage boys are more interested in technology-oriented dental content (e.g., how AI scanning works), while young parents are more interested in preventive pediatric content. This level of granularity enables more effective allocation of digital resources within public health departments, ensuring the right messages reach the right audience at the right time (Thorat et al., 2024).

Bring these three pillars of AI together in Ideation, Synthetic Media, and Analytics, and you get a closed-loop system for continuous improvement. The AI analytics not only feed back into the LLM, but also make subsequent rounds of scripting more sophisticated and synthetic media production more refined, based on user data interactions. It represents a public health response that is nimble and adaptable to address new challenges or waves of misinformation in dentistry in real time. This AI-powered workflow is crucial to ensuring that oral health education is available at all times, especially in regions like Southeast Asia, where the professional-to-patient ratio in the medical field is very low but mobile access is high.

However, the use of these tools must be governed by a robust ethical framework, particularly regarding the transparency of AI-generated content. With the integration of synthetic media and reality, it has been argued that a dental professional should share the current reality when using AI-generated avatars or scripts, a practice known as Digital Care Ethics. This transparency is crucial to the credibility-trust axis, which is a paradigm for the medical profession. The goal of implementing Generative AI is not to replace the dentist's voice but to augment it, so that key services are handled effectively by machine intelligence (Federation of International Dentistry [FDI], 2023).

Generative AI tools represent the most significant technological leap in health communication since the advent of the internet itself. By automating ideas, humanizing procedures through synthetic media, and navigating trends through advanced analytics, the dental profession can finally compete on equal footing with commercial interests and widespread misinformation. This study argues that mastery of GenAI is no longer optional for modern dental practitioners but rather a core competency for cultivating a globally aware, health-literate, and caries-free society in the 21st century (Andriani, 2025).

TikTok's technical drivers of organic reach are the power of sound and participation trends. It's an audio-based platform; responding to “trending sounds” signals to the algorithm to boost content to the For You Page (FYP). However, this presents a paradox that strains credibility for dental professionals. Practitioners should incorporate professional adaptations, such as using popular songs or challenges as background music for serious medical advice, to maintain professional integrity (Gušić et al., 2024). For example, the syncopated rhythm used to time a “proper toothbrushing challenge” can make a mundane activity go viral. This ensures the message reaches millions of users who might not otherwise seek dental advice, thus effectively disguising public health education as entertainment.

A key aspect of this implementation strategy is the conversion mechanism. No viral video should simply aim to raise awareness: it should drive users toward specific dental outcomes. This is achieved through “Micro-Calls to Action” (Micro-CTAs). Rather than simply telling users to schedule an appointment, TikTok CTAs can be more effective by suggesting they save the video for their next brushing session or by asking them to comment with the word “dental,” which reminds them they've already tried. This seamless interaction conditions the algorithm to identify the material as useful and gradually nudges users toward greater health-seeking actions. The overall impact of individual micro-interventions will be a measurable increase in community dental literacy and a decrease in behavioral intentions. Quantitative analysis of successful dental accounts shows that the Human-Education Trends (EHT) ratio is crucial for long-term intention.

The importance of the Comments Section as a secondary educational space cannot be overstated. One implementation strategy is Community Management, where dentists or their AI-assisted bots respond to specific questions in real time. This transforms a one-way broadcast into a two-way consultation. When a practitioner answers a common question like, "Why do my gums bleed when I floss?", the answer is shared with thousands of other users in the comments section. This passive consultation model significantly reduces the barrier to entry for people hesitant to visit a clinic, providing the first step toward professional care (Willis et al., 2022).

The shared "visual identity" of dental practices on TikTok also helps build trust. This involves using uniform colors, professional attire, and a designated section of the clinic as a filming studio. This uniformity signals to viewers that the product is created by a legitimate, organized group of professionals. A familiar visual identity (a type of TikTok content) is a marker of trust amid the chaotic flow of information (Digital Global Overview, 2024). In public health initiatives, branding will help people build a Digital Dental Home and be confident that they can always access accurate information.

Table 1. Strategic framework for TikTok dental public health promotion implementation

Strategy Pillars	Content Techniques	Objectives	Algorithmic/ Psychological Drivers
Education (Myth-Busting)	Stitching harmful trends; "Green screen" evidence analysis.	Correcting misinformation & establishing authority.	**Cognitive Conflict:** Triggers high retention by challenging false beliefs.
Tutorials (60s Health Hacks)	Rapid-fire brushing/ flossing tips; "3 steps to..." videos.	Skill acquisition & habit formation.	**Snackable Learning:** Reduces cognitive load for better recall.
Humanizing (BTS)	Day-in-the-life; Meet the team; Clinic tour.	Reducing dental phobia & building trust.	**Parasocial Interaction:** The viewer feels a personal bond with the provider.
Trend Participation	Using viral audio, participating in "safe" medical challenges.	Increasing organic reach/ discoverability.	**Audio Recognition:** Triggers FYP (For You Page) distribution.
Call to Action (CTA)	Link-in-bio; "Comment for part 2"; Interactive polls.	Conversion from viewer to patient.	**Nudge Theory:** Small digital actions lead to real-world behavioral change.

Source: Authors' elaboration based on the studies of Fraticelli et al. (2021), and RE et al. (2022).

Table 1 presents the Strategic Framework for TikTok Dental Public Health Promotion, emphasizing the main pillars of education, tutorials, humanization, trend engagement, and calls to action. It describes content tactics such as re-purposing toxic trends and quick-fire brushing demos, and mentions aims such as skill learning and habit formation. The chart also highlights key psychological variables underlying the effectiveness of TikTok-based oral health promotion, including cognitive conflict, snackable learning, parasocial interaction, auditory recognition, and the use of nudge theory.

4.2 TikTok as the Dental Public Health Marketing Tool

TikTok's potential impact on public health in dentistry lies in its potential to expand the reach of interventions previously limited by geographic constraints and traditional media. As a platform, TikTok is not just another communication channel; it is a key part of the health ecosystem, redefining how reach is measured in the 21st century. By transforming passive observers into active participants, public health campaigns can leverage TikTok's proprietary infrastructure to facilitate connections between dentists and communities that are traditionally unreachable through conventional health promotion strategies.

Serving younger audiences, namely Generation Z and Generation Alpha, is perhaps the most pressing use of TikTok to promote dental health among the public. This generation is notoriously difficult to reach through conventional media channels, including television, print, and even email, because their information-seeking behavior is driven by short-form, peer-approved, and visual content formats (de Ahumada Servant et al, 2025). TikTok's For You Page (FYP) algorithm subtly becomes a health educator for this population, delivering dental health information in a format they readily rely on. By engaging this group during their most vulnerable period through edutainment, health professionals working to prevent dental disease can foster preventive oral hygiene habits that help reduce the lifetime prevalence of dental disease and address the problem at its most advanced stage (Wintz et al., 2024).

One example of TikTok's gradual yet significant impact is the increase in users' dental health literacy. Users' repeated exposure to accurate clinical information in a non-stressful environment using the TikTok app helps normalize dental health as part of overall wellness. Studies show that when users regularly consume professional content, they experience increased self-efficacy (confidence in their ability to perform oral health activities appropriately) (Guši et al., 2024). This increased literacy is fundamental to disease prevention, as a more educated population is less susceptible to harmful DIY trends and consults professionals sooner when they show signs of disease, ultimately reducing overall healthcare expenditures.

Local healthcare access and clinic utilization represent a significant step toward strategically leveraging geographic targeting on TikTok. While viral content gains recognition worldwide, the combination of location-based tagging and a local feed algorithm allows people within a specific radius to access public clinics. This hyper-local strategy can help ensure that a teenager in Bangkok or a young parent in Yogyakarta is shown content produced by a local community health center, thereby minimizing the psychological distance between the teenager or parent and the care professional. For public health policymakers, this implies that digital campaigns can be directly connected to local health infrastructure to make the abstract video a reality, such as a visit to a local practitioner for a checkup or fluoride treatment.

To measure success in this new era, it's necessary to stop using vanity metrics (likes and views) and start using impact metrics (engagement, behavior change, and literacy). Engagement statistics, such as saves or shares, can better reflect the value of educational videos than views, as they indicate that users want to repeat or share the information with their networks. Furthermore, changes in behavioral intent can be monitored through click-through rates (CTRs) on link-in-bio tools that generate appointment-booking portals or tele-dentistry appointments. Using these data-driven methods allows public health departments to determine the Return on Health Investment (ROHI) of each digital campaign they launch.

Table 2. Metrics and the framework for digital dental public health interventions

Dimensions	Core Strategy	Primary Metrics	Dental Public Health Outcomes
Demographics	Gen Z/Alpha tailored content (Short-form, visual).	Completion Rate & Repatch Rate.	Increased early-life preventative habits.
Geographics	Geo-tagging & Regional Hashtags.	Localized FYP Impressions & Store/ Clinic Visits.	Enhanced access to local public health services.
Literacy Impacts	Myth-busting & Explainer Videos.	Video "Saves" & Comment Sentiment Analysis.	Reduction in DIY-related oral injuries & misinformation.
Behavioral Impacts	Micro-CTAs & Link-in-Bio.	Click-Through Rate (CTR) to Booking Systems.	Improved clinic attendance & patient compliance.

Source: Authors' elaboration based on the studies of Tımarcıoğlu et al. (2026) and Wood (2024).

Table 2 illustrates the dimensions (demographics, geographics, literacy impacts, and behavioral impacts), the core strategy, the primary metrics, and the dental public health outcomes.

By tailoring concise, visually appealing materials for Gen Z and Alpha demographics, dental public health initiatives can increase completion and engagement rates, promoting early preventive dental practices. Utilizing geo-tagging and regional hashtags ensures that content targets local audiences, as evidenced by increased localized "For You Page" (FYP) impressions and increased visits to stores or clinics, thereby enhancing access to local dental services. Producing myth-busting and explanatory videos encourages viewers to retain reliable information and participate constructively in discussions, thereby reducing DIY-related mouth injuries and misinformation. Utilizing micro-calls to action (CTAs) and conspicuous link-in-bio features increases click-through rates to booking systems, hence improving clinic attendance and augmenting patient compliance.

4.3 Related Studies

Surve et al. (2025) conducted a study based on research from 2019 to 2024, aggregating content analyses from TikTok, YouTube, Instagram, Facebook, and Twitter to evaluate the reach, quality, and impact of dental and nondental social media influencers. Dental influencers often disseminate trustworthy and preventive health information. Conversely, nondental influencers often disseminate disinformation, promote unproven products, and exacerbate self-esteem concerns. Children's behavior and attitudes were positively shaped by gamified brushing routines and adversely by hazardous do-it-yourself (DIY) trends and excessive commercialization. Discrepancies in readability and engagement were seen in professional content. Social media influencers significantly affect children's dental practices. Collaboration among dental experts and prominent influencers, together with enhanced regulation and digital literacy, can facilitate the dissemination of safe and effective oral health messaging. The strategic use of SMIs enables pediatric dentistry practitioners to improve oral health awareness, counter misconceptions, and promote healthier behaviors in children.

Mulawarman & Yahya (2025) concluded the rapid advancement of digital technology compels educational institutions to innovate their advertising strategies, especially by leveraging social media. Social media provides extensive, adaptable, and readily available platforms for engaging prospective students and enhancing university reputation. The digital marketing plans on social media use both primary data (observations and student surveys) and secondary sources. The effective use of digital media, such as Instagram and TikTok, significantly increases public awareness of and engagement with educational institutions.

BinHamdan et al. (2025) show that social media platforms are vital yet paradoxical tools for transmitting oral health information in Saudi Arabia. Individuals who engaged with dental-specific accounts exhibited markedly fewer misunderstandings, but reliance on social media as an information source was associated with a higher prevalence of misconceptions. These findings underscore the need to disseminate credible information from trusted sources to counter misconceptions. Strategic partnerships with dental professionals are essential for improving the dissemination of accurate oral health information, raising public awareness, and reducing misunderstandings about oral health.

Fraticelli et al. (2021) concluded that neglecting oral hygiene in adolescents adversely impacts dental caries, periodontal disorders, and their social and emotional well-being. Consequently, the TikTok platform (ByteDance, Beijing, China) serves as a potent medium for disseminating health-related information and educational content. This study aims to evaluate the quality of TikTok videos tagged #oralhealtheducation. Sixty-nine videos were recognized. Three oral health doctors, three health education professionals, and ten members of TikTok's target demographic saw and assessed the films using a qualitative questionnaire. The OHP identified erroneous or inaccurate information in 11.6% (8 out of 69) of the videos. In both instances, at least two HEPs indicated they were unable to determine whether this content was present or whether the film adhered to dental ethics guidelines. Disagreement was evident among the pros. The assessment revealed that TikTok's target demographic rated the observed items highly, with an average score of 2.5, compared with professionals, whose average score was below 2.5 on a 0-5 scale. Users are encouraged to approach TikTok videos about oral health with skepticism. The involvement of health professionals in creating and approving the videos could enhance their effectiveness in addressing teenagers' needs.

Digital marketing for dental public health on TikTok uses concise, captivating video content to educate the public, counter misconceptions, and advocate for preventive oral care for a diverse audience. By employing a genuine, accessible tone, dental professionals can leverage trends, instructional tutorials, and myth-busting content, such as demonstrating proper brushing techniques or explaining the risks of viral DIY hacks, to make vital health information go viral and be easily shared. This technique enhances public health literacy, alleviates dental anxiety, establishes practitioners as credible authorities, and engages younger populations who frequently use the platform to acquire information.

5. CONCLUSIONS

The arrival of TikTok and Generative AI in collective dental health heralds a new chapter in medical communication: the democratization of clinical knowledge and the personalization of healthcare therapies. This chapter illustrates that the TikTok Revolution is not only a social media fad but a paradigm change in the global health ecosystem. Generative AI's creative power and the platform's appealing short-form video format allow dental professionals to close the longstanding gap between medical knowledge and public health literacy. Moving from archaic, passive strategies to nimble, AI-powered, edutainment-oriented strategies provides a scalable fix for the rising tide of dental misinformation and encourages a culture of proactive oral hygiene among a digitally savvy populace. The strategic synergies outlined in this chapter, from automated ideation and synthetic avatars to spatially focused behavioral nudges, provide a potent model for enhancing global health equity. By combining AI algorithms with clinical expertise, clinical authorities are creating a powerful public health tool that can reach underserved groups and break down the mental barrier posed by dental anxiety. Yet the successful application of this digital strategy still relies on a fine ethical balance.

As AI becomes a prominent player in content development, the dental profession must not lose sight of values such as transparency, clinical accuracy, and patient safety, so that the digital transformation leads to an improvement, not a commercialization, of care. Public dental health's TikTok digital marketing leverages short, entertaining videos to educate diverse audiences, especially Gen Z and Millennials, about oral hygiene and preventive care, and to counter widespread myths about dental health. By using trending audio, hashtags, and creative formats, dentists and public health professionals can turn boring topics into entertaining, shareable content that builds trust, reduces dental anxiety, and raises awareness of oral health issues. Good ideas include films on how to brush, office tours to demystify the practice and show the behind-the-scenes, and smile transformations. Additionally, this type of content invites people to engage directly and connects them with professional dental advice.

The shift to TikTok and Generative AI will bring about a paradigm shift in medical communication, positioning this study at the forefront of the competition in the "Health 5.0" era. Public Dental Health: Integration of Generative AI in Oral Health Education and Training, a framework that aims to codify the application of a combination of viral social mechanisms and machine intelligence to close the growing gap between clinical knowledge and general public health knowledge. By emphasizing these new tools, practitioners can reestablish their position as powerful gatekeepers in a digital environment where people are increasingly influenced by unverified influencers and anecdotal health claims.

Rewriting established public health theories, including the Health Belief Model (HBM), in the context of AI-enhanced healthcare marketing is a crucial part of this framework. The concept of Edutainment in this new era can be considered a pedagogical bridge between rigorous educational knowledge acquired in dentistry and entertainment, ensuring high retention rates in an era of intermittent attention. This chapter examines how TikTok videos can be used to educate younger audiences about the susceptibility and severity of oral diseases by extending the so-called Infoware model to older generations, incorporating Generative AI as a key driver of content creation. Developing the meaning of these developments is necessary to understand the possibilities of algorithmic information delivery beyond mere interaction and ultimately generating tangible changes in knowledge, attitudes, and preventive practices (KAP) levels internationally.

To change viewing from passive scrolling to active behavior change for oral hygiene, a public dental health strategy on TikTok needs a nuanced approach. This process, called 'From Algorithm to Brushing,' requires a multifaceted approach to match clinical accuracy with the culturally specific grammar of short videos. The lateral communication model employed by TikTok is different from the top-down communication model used in conventional health interventions. Professionals have to use the lateral communication model in a high-skill, high-engagement environment. Below, three key pillars of this implementation are discussed: pedagogical strategies, psychological branding, and optimization algorithms.

The solution to TikTok's attention-deficit problem is educational information in high-impact tactics like myth-busting and 60-second lessons. The most successful ways of busting myths use what's called the Curiosity Gap and Cognitive Conflict – the psychological arousal that happens in a professional when exposing a dangerous but popular trend, like harmful DIY teeth filing or damaging lemon-juice whitening. This trend can have lasting effects, and practitioners can demonstrate this with AI-enhanced graphics or macro photography to produce genuine shock and help stop the spread of disinformation. The medical needs need to be re-branded as life hacks. 60-second brushing and flossing tutorials need to be promoted to a predominantly young audience, with an emphasis on immediate benefits (you will look better and have fresher breath).

Humanizing the dental profession is a crucial psychological intervention that will help break the white coat barrier and reduce the prevalence of odontophobia (fear of dental care) worldwide. Showcasing BTS content: Demystifying the clinical environment can be done through anything from preparing tools and equipment to sterilization processes to the dental team's morning meeting. Such transparency builds parasocial trust, in which patients feel they have already established a relationship with the provider before the first physical interaction. They can tell their health story, leverage personal stories or humor, capitalize on trending vignettes, and be perceived as an approachable health partner rather than a distant clinical force.

The use of so-called Visual Anchors contributes to procedural transparency. A 3D model of caries development with AI support can be more convincing than a ten-minute lecture. This visual anchor provides patients with a mental map of how the process connects to the "why." For instance, a synthetic avatar that experiences a painless and relaxed root canal can directly combat the stereotype of torture that is often associated with dentistry in the media. The dental profession can change public perception of the importance of oral health by restoring the narrative with high-quality images that TikTok could use for its dental digital marketing.

6. RECOMMENDATION FOR FURTHER RESEARCH

Future studies should focus on longitudinal measurements to determine whether high TikTok use is associated with long-term changes in oral health behaviors and a significant reduction in the global DMFT (Decayed, Missing, and Filled Teeth) index.

1. AI Ethics and Policy Frameworks are crucial because Generative AI (Gen AI) urgently requires a policy framework, and as the technology advances, more international policy frameworks must be developed to regulate AI-based medical guidance and ensure that synthetic media and automated scripts meet international clinical standards.
2. Cross-Cultural Comparative Analysis is a comparative study of the impact of cultural specificities in Indonesia and Thailand, as well as other countries, on the acceptance of AI-based dental marketing, which could be completed and lead to a more culturally specific approach to global health.
3. Algorithmic Bias and Health Equity is important for scholars to explore the possibility of algorithmic bias on social media sites to ensure equitable distribution of social health messages to various socioeconomic and linguistic groups.

By adopting 21st-century tools, the public dental health sector can become a less reactive, more proactive, and more digital-first clinical service. This chapter serves as a timeless call to action for researchers and policymakers to practice how to combine technology and empathy so that healthy smiles in the age of artificial intelligence can become a universal right.

It is recommended that, for further study, the chapter provide a solid contemporary context for the "tectonic shift" in health communication toward short-form video. The literature review highlights the "credibility gap" associated with viral DIY dentistry trends. However, the literature review repeatedly praises GenAI. To provide balance, further studies should include more critical analyses of the limits of AI-generated medical advice. Socioeconomic hurdles that may impede TikTok engagement in "resource-constrained environments" are not explored in this chapter. It is advisable to add a "digital divide" section to discuss how data costs and hardware limitations in rural Southeast Asia may further hinder this model's scalability. The demonstration of the dental "infodemic" of teeth filing and caustic whitening deception. Proposing a "Digital Care Ethics" framework to recover professional power is beneficial. Practitioners could benefit from an "Action Plan" table to implement these ethics. AAO and BDA case studies support the focus on DIY trends as a concern. The "Humanizing" section should be strengthened with more examples of how to maintain professional boundaries while remaining "accessible" in further.

REFERENCES

Alhersh, B. A. (2026). The Influence of Social Media Exposure on Dietary Behaviors and Dental Caries Prevalence Among Pediatric Patients. https://www.preprints.org/manuscript/202602.1878

American Association of Orthodontists (AAO). (2022). Consumer alert: The dangers of DIY orthodontic treatments. https://www2.aaoinfo.org/danger-of-diy/

Andriani, A. D. (2025). The Future of Digital Content: AI-Generated Texts, Images, Videos, and Real-Time Production. In *Impacts of AI-Generated Content on Brand Reputation* (pp. 149–176). IGI Global Scientific Publishing., https://www.igi-global.com/chapter/the-future-of-digital-content/383241 DOI: 10.4018/979-8-3373-4327-3.ch006

Arora, M., Sachdeva, P., Gupta, N., Gambhir, N., Singh, D., & Tuli, A. (2025). Scrolling toward smiles: The role of social media in dental health promotion. *Santosh University Journal of Health Sciences, 11*(2), 275–279. https://journals.lww.com/sujh/fulltext/2025/07000/scrolling_toward_smiles__the_role_of_social_media.15.aspx?context=latestarticles

BinHamdan. R. H., Alsadhan, S. A., Gazzaz, A. Z., & AlJameel, A. H. (2025). Social media use and oral health–related misconceptions in Saudi Arabia: cross-sectional study. *JMIR Formative Research, 9*, e70071. https://formative.jmir.org/2025/1/e70071

British Dental Association (BDA). (2023). Social media trends and oral health risks. *BDA Press Release*. https://www.bda.org/

de Ahumada Servant, P., Martín-Martín, D., & Romero, I. (2025). Digital transformation of oral health care: Measuring the digitalization of dental clinics. *Social Indicators Research, 178*(3), 1145–1167. DOI: 10.1007/s11205-024-03366-z

Devkota, H. P. (2024). Healthcare communication in the age of social media and digital health technologies. *Japanese Journal of Pharmaceutical Education, 8*. Advance online publication. DOI: 10.24489/jjphe.2024-055

Digital Global Overview. (2024). The state of social media: Algorithmic trends and engagement. *We Are Social & Meltwater*. https://datareportal.com/reports/digital-2024-global-overview-report

Florida Dental Association. (2023). AI-driven content strategies for the modern practice. *FDI World Dental Press*. https://www.fdiworlddental.org/fdi-annual-report-2023

Fraticelli, L., Smentek, C., Tardivo, D., Masson, J., Clément, C., Roy, S., Dussart, C., Bourgeois, D., & Carrouel, F. (2021). Characterizing the content related to oral health education on TikTok. *International Journal of Environmental Research and Public Health, 18*(24), 13260. DOI: 10.3390/ijerph182413260 PMID: 34948869

Gušić, I., Stojilković, M., Alija, S., Prodanović, D., Mirnić, J., & Veljović, T. (2024). The impact of social media on the selection of dentists based on their social media presence among residents of Vojvodina, Serbia: A cross-sectional study. *BMC Public Health, 24*(1), 3348. DOI: 10.1186/s12889-024-20884-0 PMID: 39616357

International Dental Federation (FDI). (2023). Digital promotion of oral health: Best practices for social media. *FDI World Dental Press.* https://www.fdiworlddental.org/fdi-annual-report-2023

Khan, M. I., Saleh, M. A., & Quazi, A. (2021, January). Social media adoption by health professionals: A TAM-based study. In *Informatics* (Vol. 8, No. 1, p. 6). MDPI. https://www.mdpi.com/2227-9709/8/1/6

Mulawarman, W. G., & Yahya, M. (2025). Digital promotion strategies utilizing social media to improve the image of educational institutions. *Journal of Educational Management Research, 4*(3), 1010–1022. DOI: 10.61987/jemr.v4i3.1055

Mwogosi, A., & Mambile, C. (2025). Digital ecosystems for healthcare communication and collaboration: A scoping review. *Digital Health, 11*, 20552076251377933. DOI: 10.1177/20552076251377933 PMID: 40949671

Nutbeam, D., & Lloyd, J. E. (2021). Understanding and Responding to Health Literacy as a Social Determinant of Health. *Annual Review of Public Health, 42*(1), 159–173. DOI: 10.1146/annurev-publhealth-090419-102529 PMID: 33035427

Paul, B., & Headley-Johnson, S. A. (2025, October). The impact of social media on health behaviors, a systematic review. In *Healthcare* (Vol. 13, No. 21, p. 2763). https://pmc.ncbi.nlm.nih.gov/articles/PMC12608964/

Re, P. R., Harliani, N. D., & Purnama, T.RE. (2022). TikTok Media as an Effort to Increase Dental Health Knowledge for High School Students. *Journal of Drug Delivery and Therapeutics, 12*(5), 146–148. Advance online publication. DOI: 10.22270/jddt.v12i5.5669

Sivrikaya, E. C., Yilmaz, O., & Sivrikaya, P. (2021). Dentist-patient communication on dental anxiety using the social media: A randomized controlled trial. *Scandinavian Journal of Psychology, 62*(6), 780–786. DOI: 10.1111/sjop.12769 PMID: 34333783

Surve, K. S., Padawe, D., & Takate, V. (2025). Digital Dilemma: The Intersection of Social Media Influencers and Pediatric Dental Health. *Journal of Clinical Insights and Research in Dentistry, 1*(2), 82–88. DOI: 10.5005/jcird-11034-0015

Thonburi Health Report. (2024). AI and patient compliance in urban Thailand. *Bangkok Metropolitan Administration.* https://ir.thg.co.id

Thorat, V., Rao, P., Joshi, N., Talreja, P., & Shetty, A. R. (2024, May 07). Role of Artificial Intelligence (AI) in Patient Education and Communication in Dentistry. *Cureus, 16*(5), e59799. DOI: 10.7759/cureus.59799 PMID: 38846249

Tımarcıoğlu, G., Kargu, E. C., Çerçi Akçay, H., & Tımarcıoğlu, B. (2026). Evaluating the reliability and educational quality of YouTube™ and TikTok™ videos on custom subperiosteal implants: a cross-sectional methodological analysis. *BMC Oral Health.* https://link.springer.com/article/10.1186/s12903-026-08290-x

Veseli, E., & Bencharit, S. (2026). FDI guidelines for AI in dental education: FDI guidelines for AI in dental education. *British Dental Journal, 240*(5), 317–317. DOI: 10.1038/s41415-026-9690-y PMID: 41826442

Willis, V. C., Thomas Craig, K. J., Jabbarpour, Y., Scheufele, E. L., Arriaga, Y. E., Ajinkya, M., Rhee, K. B., & Bazemore, A. (2022). Digital Health Interventions to Enhance Prevention in Primary Care: Scoping Review. *JMIR Medical Informatics, 10*(1), e33518. DOI: 10.2196/33518 PMID: 35060909

Wintz, D., Wright, K., & Schaffer, K. B. (2024). Medical influence: What does success look like? *Palliative Care and Social Practice, 18*, 26323524241297695. Advance online publication. DOI: 10.1177/26323524241297695 PMID: 39539771

Wood, N. H. (2024). From Trends to Trust: Harnessing Social Media for the Future of Dentistry. *South African Dental Journal, 79*(10), 521–524. https://www.scielo.org.za/scielo.php?pid=S0011-85162024001000001&script=sci_arttext

Zhu, C., Xu, X., Zhang, W., Chen, J., & Evans, R. (2020). How health communication via TikTok makes a difference: A content analysis of TikTok accounts run by Chinese provincial health committees. *International Journal of Environmental Research and Public Health, 17*(1), 192. https://www.mdpi.com/1660-4601/17/1/192. DOI: 10.3390/ijerph17010192 PMID: 31892122

KEY TERMS AND DEFINITIONS

Digital Marketing: Digital marketing involves promoting products or services through online channels, such as search engines, social media, email, and websites, to engage consumers. It uses digital technologies to run targeted, measurable campaigns that enhance brand exposure, engagement, and sales, often yielding a superior ROI compared to conventional tactics.

Dental Public Health: Dental public health is a specialist discipline dedicated to the prevention, control, and promotion of oral health through coordinated community initiatives, rather than solely individual patient treatment. It aims to improve population-level outcomes through measures such as water fluoridation, education, and expanded access to care for marginalized groups. Principal activities include school-centered preventive measures, public health monitoring, and policy formulation to address disparities in oral diseases.

DIY Dental Tricks: Do-it-yourself dental procedures, often driven by exorbitant costs or limited access to care, pose significant, long-term risks to public health. Prevalent and hazardous procedures include the use of abrasive substances (such as charcoal and baking soda), home teeth whitening with high-concentration peroxides, do-it-yourself tooth alignment, and attempts to remove plaque or extract teeth with home-made implements.

Digital marketing for dental public health on TikTok: It can be transformed through three principal dimensions: (1) AI-driven content creation, which utilizes artificial intelligence to autonomously generate, customize, and enhance short-form video content that appeals to varied audiences and disseminates oral health messages; (2) algorithmic strategy, wherein marketers systematically analyze and adapt to TikTok's recommendation framework, employing real-time data to optimize content visibility and engagement among targeted demographics; and (3) targeted dental public health initiatives utilizing generative AI, which formulates hyper-personalized public health campaigns, ensuring that educational resources cater to specific community needs, cultural inclinations, and emerging dental health trends for maximal impact and behavioral modification.

Chapter 10
Global Strategies in Digital Marketing for Public Dental Health Promotion

Mohammad Rakibul Islam Bhuiyan
http://orcid.org/0000-0003-4284-6461
Begum Rokeya University, Rangpur, Bangladesh

ABSTRACT

This chapter explores the transformative impact of digital marketing and social media promotion on public dental health, emphasizing global strategies to enhance patient engagement, awareness, and care. It examines the adoption of digital tools, such as social media platforms, e-commerce, influencer marketing, and digital payments, to improve the accessibility and effectiveness of dental health campaigns. A systematic review of 1,218 Scopus-indexed publications (2020–2025) using PRISMA protocols identifies key trends and challenges in the sector. Findings highlight that digital marketing can bridge gaps in patient education, especially among younger, digitally savvy populations. The chapter introduces a conceptual framework linking digital technologies with improved business outcomes while promoting sustainability in dental health practices. It emphasizes the need to better understand the influence of digital strategies on patient behaviors and the integration of teledentistry services to support digital literacy and foster inclusive digital infrastructure in developing economies.

DOI: 10.4018/979-8-3373-8894-6.ch010

1.0 INTRODUCTION

Digital marketing has rapidly transformed the landscape of public dental health promotion, offering new avenues to reach diverse populations and influence oral health behaviors (Srivastava et al., 2023). Multiple studies highlight that digital strategies—including social media campaigns, mobile applications, and teledentistry—significantly increase patient engagement, improve oral health literacy, and can lead to measurable improvements in oral hygiene practices across age groups. Social media platforms such as Facebook, Instagram, WhatsApp, and YouTube are widely used for disseminating oral health information and engaging both patients and professionals (Jayasinghe et al., 2024).

Oral diseases remain among the most prevalent noncommunicable diseases globally. The World Health Organization reports that oral diseases affect nearly 3.7 billion people worldwide—approximately 45% of the global population—over the life course from early childhood to old age. Untreated dental caries in permanent teeth is the single most common health condition according to the Global Burden of Disease 2021, affecting approximately 2.5 billion people, while severe periodontal disease affects more than 1 billion people, complete tooth loss (edentulism) affects approximately 350 million people, and oral cancers account for approximately 389,000 new cases and 188,000 deaths annually. Three out of four people affected by oral diseases live in middle-income countries, and oral diseases disproportionately affect the most vulnerable and socially disadvantaged populations, with people of low socioeconomic status carrying a significantly higher burden throughout the life course. The economic burden is substantial: global direct health expenditures on the main oral diseases exceeded US$380 billion in 2019, representing approximately 4.8% of global direct health expenditures.

Despite being largely preventable, prevention and treatment for oral health conditions are expensive and usually not included in national universal health coverage (UHC) benefit packages, and most low- and middle-income countries do not have sufficient services available (Bhuiyan et al., 2025a). These epidemiological realities have motivated WHO's strategic calls for population-level prevention, multisectoral action, and scalable delivery models to reach underserved groups (Petersen & Kwan, 2009). Empirical and programmatic analyses reinforce the potential for coordinated, large-scale interventions: Pine and Dugdill's (2011) analysis of a global public–private partnership illustrates how pooled resources, shared governance, and cross-sector collaboration can extend oral-health promotion at scale, while reviews of mass-media and social media campaigns (Goldberg et al., 2022; Potts & Radford, 2019) show that media approaches can achieve broad reach and engagement but also exhibit variable effectiveness depending on design, evaluation metrics, and contextual adaptation.

Most industries such as healthcare have been revolutionized by the use of digital marketing and social media promotion. Digital platforms are becoming complementary or substituting traditional marketing in the dentistry sector, as they provide dentists and other dental health professionals with new ways of accessing and interacting with patients.

1.1 Rationale for the Chapter

Instagram, Facebook, TikTok, and YouTube are digital platforms that have emerged as formidable instruments of educating more people about health. The social media allows direct interaction with the audiences in real-time where dental professionals can interact with their existing and potential customers. Also, influencer utilization within the healthcare industry has proven to be very promising in fostering trust, as well as, promoting positive dental-related habits (Nagpal & Sharma, 2019). The chapter extended an in-depth overview of the relationship between social media campaigns and influencer marketing and how they can be applied to disseminate oral health messages and empower consumers to make informed choices on the topic of their dental health.

Moreover, dental marketing on the digital platform has the potential to close the divide between the dental practitioners and the digital-native generations (Gen Z and Millennials) that, more frequently, refer online in search of health information. In this chapter, the ways the digital tools and the role of oral health promotion intersect explored, and how the former can be used effectively to address the barriers in dental care access and raise awareness about such topics as preventive dental hygiene, orthodontics, and cosmetic dentistry.

1.2 Significance of the Work

Despite rising interest in digital health and the widespread adoption of social media platforms, a clear research gap exists in systematically evaluating how modern digital marketing techniques—targeted social advertising, influencer partnerships, platform analytics, embedded e-commerce, and integrated tele-dentistry pathways—perform specifically for public dental health promotion across diverse socio-economic, geographic, and settings. While individual campaign evaluations demonstrate reach (Potts & Radford, 2019) and scoping reviews summarize mass-media evidence (Goldberg et al., 2022), there is limited empirical synthesis linking contemporary digital marketing modalities to measurable public dental health outcomes, equity considerations, and implementation scalability. This gap is particularly urgent given the post-COVID acceleration of digital health transformation: multiple recent reviews and policy analyses document rapid adoption of digital health technologies and service innovations after 2020, reshaping patient engagement, care delivery, and health communication ecosystems (Milne & Costa, 2020; Mosnaim et al., 2020; Mfouth Kemajou et al., 2024). Emerging studies forecasting digital-health innovation strategies and practitioner attitudes further justify focusing on how digital marketing can be purposefully integrated into oral health promotion with attention to effectiveness, equity, and governance (Garg et al., 2025; Askedal et al., 2025; Anshasi et al., 2025).

The use of social media has transformed the method of transmitting dental health websites have millions of users that are active, which gives dental health campaigns a rare chance to inform people about such important issues as regular check-ups, how to brush their teeth, and what is flossing (Bhuiyan et al., 2025a). Digital marketing campaigns can be used to reach the specific demographics such as the younger generation that are more digitally oriented and therefore are an effective tool in promoting oral health education (Salman, 2024). Considering the fact that the majority of the population is unaware of the fundamental practices of oral health, the distribution of such information via social media can enhance the dental health literacy of the overall population on a massive scale (Farrokhi et al., 2023).

In addition, the social media has high potential of consumer interaction, which promotes immediate communication between dental professionals and their patients. Digital platforms, unlike traditional marketing, in which one-way communication is usually involved. Social media has become a vital resource of the promotion of oral health and support in the context of the post-COVID world where most people are now more accustomed to obtaining information about their health online (Farrokhi et al., 2023).

This chapter offers an all-encompassing approach to digital transformation within dental health enable conventional players to compete in a challenging global environment. Digital marketing strategies hold significant potential to bridge gaps in public dental health access, particularly among underserved and low-income populations (Northridge et al., 2020). By leveraging digital platforms, oral health campaigns can reach communities that traditionally lack access to preventive dental care, thereby reducing the burden of untreated dental diseases at the population level.

1.3 Research Gap

Despite the growing body of literature on digital marketing in healthcare, a critical gap remains in understanding how global digital marketing strategies can be systematically applied to public dental health promotion. Most existing studies focus on general healthcare marketing or commercial dental practices in developed economies, with limited attention to cross-cultural, globally applicable frameworks (Holden, 2019; Bhuiyan et al., 2025a). Furthermore, the integration of tools such as social media campaigns, influencer marketing, tele-dentistry, and digital payment systems specifically for public oral health awareness — particularly in developing economies — remains underexplored. The role of digital literacy barriers and infrastructure gaps in shaping the effectiveness of these strategies across diverse global contexts has also received insufficient scholarly attention (Krishnan, 2025). This chapter addresses these gaps by proposing a conceptual framework that connects global digital marketing innovations with improved public dental health outcomes, patient engagement, and sustainability (Mackey & Nayyar, 2016).

1.4 Objectives

The primary objective of this chapter is to examine how global digital marketing strategies and social media promotion can enhance public dental health awareness, patient engagement, and access to dental care services through digital transformation. The following sub-objectives are consistent with the primary objectives.

1. To explore the role of digital marketing in dental health promotion.
2. To examine the impact of social media platforms on oral health awareness campaigns.
3. To identify barriers to digital transformation in dental healthcare services.
4. To assess the influence of influencer marketing on patient behavior and preventive dental care.
5. To evaluate the role of digital platforms in building patient trust and engagement.
6. To analyze the application of PRISMA methodology in reviewing digital dental health marketing literature.

2.0 LITERATURE REVIEW

2.1 Digital marketing and digital transformation in healthcare and dentistry

Digital marketing and digital transformation have fundamentally reshaped healthcare and dentistry by enabling interactive, patient-centered, and technology-driven communication systems. According to digital marketing literature, digital marketing integrates websites, social media platforms, mobile applications, analytics, and automation tools to improve patient engagement and service delivery (Dwivedi et al., 2021). Dwivedi et al. (2021) emphasized that digital and social media marketing allows healthcare providers to establish real-time communication, personalized interactions, and stronger online visibility compared to traditional one-way promotional methods. In dentistry, digital transformation extends beyond promotion and includes online appointment systems, tele-dentistry, digital payment systems, and data-driven patient relationship management, all of which improve operational efficiency and patient satisfaction. Moreover, Zare and Persaud (2024) argued that digital transformation involves a broader organizational change where healthcare institutions redesign value creation and patient interaction through digital technologies. These technological advancements have become increasingly important in post-COVID healthcare environments, where patients rely heavily on online information and virtual healthcare accessibility.

The literature further demonstrates that social media and electronic word-of-mouth (e-WOM) significantly influence dental healthcare communication and patient decision-making. Platforms such as Facebook, Instagram, TikTok, and YouTube are widely used to disseminate oral health information, promote preventive dental care, and build trust between dental professionals and patients. Farrokhi et al. (2023) found that social media campaigns enhance oral health literacy and increase public awareness regarding dental hygiene practices. Influencer marketing has also emerged as an important strategy in dental health promotion, particularly among younger populations such as Gen Z and Millennials. Research by Lou and Yuan (2019) suggested that trusted influencers can positively affect patient attitudes, treatment adherence, and preventive dental behaviors by providing relatable and credible health-related content. These findings indicate that digital transformation and social media marketing are becoming essential strategic tools for sustainable and patient-centered dental healthcare services.

2.2 Dental Health Marketing through Social Media Promotion and Electronic Word-of-Mouth (e-WOM).

Social media promotion is one of the most basic elements of digital marketing, as it implies using social networking platforms such as Facebook, Instagram, TikTok, and YouTube to address patients, influence their behavior patterns, and establish long-term relationships (Dwivedi et al., 2021). The recent healthcare environment after the COVID-19 reveals that patients are more dependent on peer-generated information when determining the authenticity, safety, and quality of health care services before making their decisions. Social media is, thus, an effective instrument of developing trust and reducing the information asymmetry between the dental providers and their potential patients (Dwivedi et al., 2021). Digital/social media marketing in healthcare literature demonstrates that such variables as the format-message fit (e.g., video tutorials on how to maintain oral health), the number of posts, and influencer partnerships may all contribute to engagement, brand image, and patient acquisition to a considerable extent (Dwivedi et al., 2021). Influencer marketing is simply the next logical evolution of e-WOM, where influencers and opinion leaders might have a substantial influence on awareness, the attitude of the patients, and treatment decisions (Lou & Yuan, 2019)

2.3 Dental Health Marketing for Sustainable Healthcare Promotion

Dental health marketing has evolved beyond traditional promotional activities and is now increasingly recognized as an experiential, educational, and sustainable approach to healthcare communication. Contemporary dental marketing emphasizes patient-centered experiences, preventive oral health education, and long-term relationship building between dental professionals and patients. According to Koththagoda and Thushara (2016), healthcare marketing strategies are most effective when they integrate educational communication with personalized patient engagement. In dentistry, this involves promoting oral hygiene awareness, preventive care behaviors, and treatment transparency through digital platforms and interactive communication channels. Furthermore, experiential healthcare marketing focuses on creating memorable and trustworthy patient experiences that improve satisfaction, engagement, and loyalty. The Experience Economy perspective suggests that consumers increasingly value emotionally engaging and personalized healthcare experiences rather than purely transactional services (Brodie et al., 2011). Digital technologies such as virtual consultations, educational videos, social media storytelling, and patient testimonials allow dental practitioners to provide interactive and informative healthcare experiences that strengthen patient trust and improve treatment adherence.

Sustainability has also become an important dimension of modern dental health marketing, particularly as patients become more socially and environmentally conscious in selecting healthcare providers. Wallace and MacEntee (2012) emphasized that accessible oral health education and community-based healthcare communication can reduce inequalities in dental care access and improve public oral health outcomes. In this context, digital marketing serves not only as a commercial tool but also as a mechanism for promoting sustainable healthcare behaviors and inclusive oral health awareness.

The focus of dental marketing is based on the genuineness, patient education, and meaningful communication between the medical care provider and patients (Uddin et al., 2024). According to researchers, one of the digital health marketing can expand access to preventive oral health education, empowering communities to make informed decisions about their dental care and reducing systemic inequalities in oral health outcomes (Wallace & MacEntee, 2012). These qualities are consistent with the Experience Economy model, which highlights that memorable experience, e.g., personalized patient care is currently a significant point of value in the contemporary healthcare.

2.4 Social Media Dental health marketing

The growing significance of electronic word-of-mouth (e-WOM) further strengthens the effectiveness of social media dental marketing. Online reviews, patient comments, ratings, and shared treatment experiences strongly influence public perceptions of credibility, trustworthiness, and healthcare quality. Filieri et al. (2015) explained that consumer-generated content significantly affects trust formation and behavioral intentions in digital environments. Similarly, Farrokhi et al. (2023) found that social media-based oral health campaigns improve public awareness, oral health literacy, and preventive dental practices across different age groups. Social media also enables dental practices to employ visual storytelling strategies, including before-and-after treatment images, educational videos, live consultations, and patient success stories, which enhance emotional engagement and strengthen patient confidence in dental services. Platforms such as TikTok and Instagram are particularly effective due to their visual and short-form content formats, which align with the communication preferences of Gen Z and Millennial audiences.

Influencer marketing has additionally become an essential component of social media dental health promotion. Health influencers, dental professionals, and online opinion leaders can significantly shape patient attitudes toward preventive care, oral hygiene routines, and treatment acceptance. Research by Lou and Yuan (2019) demonstrated that influencer credibility, authenticity, and relatability positively affect consumer trust and behavioral intentions. The visual storytelling-oriented social media and their emphasis on the engagement with patients can be especially effective in marketing the dental health services. The use of social media advertisements facilitates the transformation of the Internet interest into the face-to-face appointment by encouraging effortless ability to the booking platforms and inviting patients to use dental services (Dwivedi et al., 2021).

2.5 Theoretical Grounding: Health Behavior Models in Digital Dental Marketing

The effectiveness of digital marketing strategies in public dental health promotion can be better understood through established health behavior theories. The Health Belief Model (HBM) suggests that individuals are more likely to seek dental care when they perceive themselves as susceptible to oral diseases and recognize the severity of untreated conditions. Digital marketing tools, particularly social media campaigns and influencer-generated content, directly address these perceptions by delivering visually compelling educational content that raises awareness of dental caries, gum disease, and the long-term consequences of neglecting oral hygiene. For instance, TikTok and Instagram campaigns featuring real patient experiences can heighten perceived susceptibility, while testimonial-based content reduces perceived barriers to seeking care, such as cost, fear, or lack of awareness of available services.

Similarly, the Theory of Planned Behavior (TPB) offers a complementary lens, suggesting that an individual's intention to adopt preventive dental behaviors is shaped by their personal attitudes toward oral health, the influence of social norms, and their perceived ability to act (Rajeh, 2022). Influencer marketing, in this context, plays a powerful role in shaping subjective norms — when trusted online figures normalize regular dental check-ups or promote oral hygiene routines, their followers are more likely to adopt similar behaviors. Furthermore, tele-dentistry services and online booking platforms enhance perceived behavioral control by removing logistical barriers to accessing dental care, particularly among populations in low-resource settings. Anchoring digital dental marketing strategies within these theoretical frameworks transforms promotional efforts from mere commercial outreach into evidence-based public health interventions.

3.0 METHODOLOGY

3.1 Methods

The approach that was used in this paper is systematic review as per PRISMA (Preferred Reporting Items to Systematic Reviews and Meta-Analyses). This procedure ensure a clear, reproducible, and all-inclusive literature review to identify and combine relative researches on the digital revolution of dental marketing and social media advertising (Page et al., 2021; Kumar & Mirchandani, 2013). The systematic review is a proper way of presenting an exhaustive report of the current trends, technology, and marketing innovations in the dental health industry.

3.2 Research Design

This study employs a systematic review methodology following the PRISMA guidelines. This synthesis of literature is known to be systematic and reproducible and this is the main focus of this review. A systematic review is a method of evaluating literature on comprehensive documentation of the study selection, and publication of findings using the best-evidence synthesis (Page et al., 2021). This chapter uses this design to explore the existing digital transformation in dental health marketing, that is, the adoption of social media and digital marketing strategies to market dental services, products, and care strategies with the reference to studies published since 2020.

3.3 Database and Search Strategy

The database used is an important factor to the rigor and credibility of a systematic review. The use of Scopus, a multidisciplinary peer-reviewed journal database, has been applied in this study. The search word such as "Digital Transformation, Digital Marketing, Social Media Promotion, and Dental Health Marketing", has been developed to identify the studies that have a direct connection to the current research. English papers were included in this literature review and only documents published in the last five years, 2020-2025, were taken into account. The analyzed materials are journal articles, reviews, book chapters, and conference papers all of which are part of the scientific communication of the healthcare industry. Using a combination of keywords and filters, in accordance with the principles of systematic reviews (Higgins et al., 2021) the relevance and quality of the hits in the search were ensured, which effectively reduced irrelevant hits. This study adopted the PRISMA framework to conduct a systematic literature review on digital marketing and dental healthcare promotion. The literature search was primarily conducted using the Scopus database because of its comprehensive coverage of high-quality peer-reviewed journals in healthcare, business, and digital technology research (Higgins et al., 2021. The search process focused on identifying studies related to digital marketing, social media marketing, digital transformation, and dental healthcare communication.

Figure 1. PRISMA-based methodology (Scopus Database, 2025)

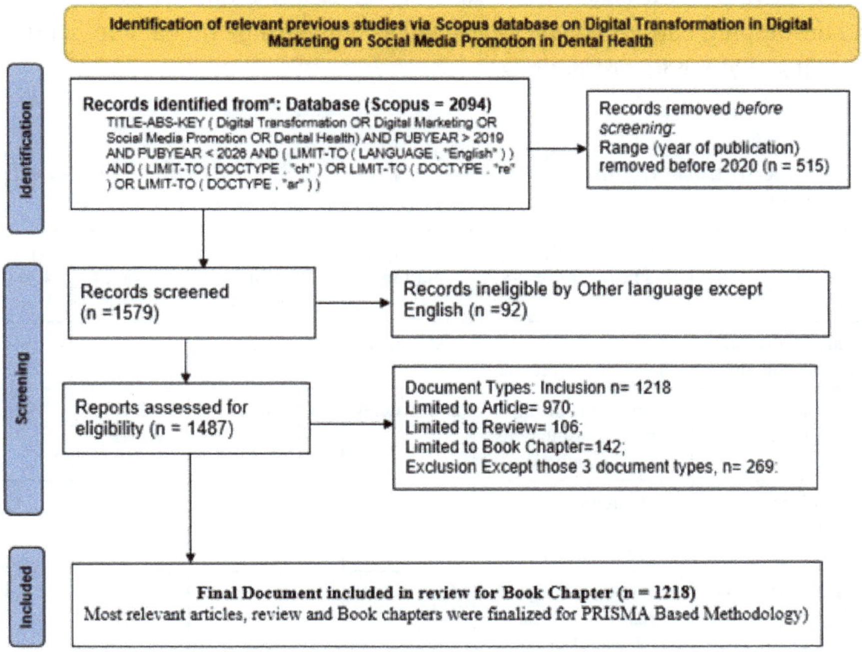

The following search string was applied in the Scopus database:

("digital marketing" OR "social media marketing" OR "digital transformation") AND ("dental health" OR dentistry OR "oral healthcare" OR "dental marketing")

Several filters were applied to refine the search results and ensure the inclusion of recent and relevant studies. The inclusion criteria were:

- Publication years: **2020–2025**
- Language: **English**
- Document type: **Journal articles and review papers**
- Subject areas: **Healthcare, dentistry, business, management, and information technology**

Studies that were non-English, conference abstracts, editorials, book chapters, duplicated records, or unrelated to dental healthcare marketing were excluded from the final review process. The selected articles were further screened based on title relevance, abstract evaluation, and full-text assessment to ensure alignment with the objectives of this study. This systematic filtering process improved the reliability, transparency, and academic rigor of the literature review methodology.

As synthesized in Table 1, the screened corpus of 1,218 articles was categorized into distinct thematic clusters, establishing a clear differentiation between developed and developing nations (LMICs), as well as comparing clinical tele-dentistry with general social media promotions.

Table 1. Granular thematic and geographical breakdown of the screened corpus (N = 1,218)

Thematic Clusters	Primary Digital Platform Focus	Developed Nations	LMICs / Developing Nations	Total Articles Count	Percentage of Corpus (%)
Social Media Oral Health Promotion	Instagram, TikTok, YouTube, Facebook	322 Articles	215 Articles	537 Articles	44.1%
Clinical Tele-Dentistry & Triage	Mobile Health Apps, Virtual Consultations, AI Chatbots	210 Articles	114 Articles	324 Articles	26.6%
Patient Behavior & Engagement	Search Engines (SEO), E-commerce Dental Booking	115 Articles	72 Articles	187 Articles	15.3%
Ethical Concerns & Misinformation	Cross-border digital trends, Unverified Dental Hacks	98 Articles	72 Articles	170 Articles	14.0%
Total Reviewed Dataset	Omni-channel Digital Scope	745 Articles (61.2%)	473 Articles (38.8%)	1,218 Articles	100%

Source: Author Contribution.

3.4 Selection Technique

Selection was guided by PRISMA flowchart protocol, which guarantees that the screening and selection of the eligible studies are systematic. The Scopus database search provided 2,094 records on the first search. The initial screening step was the deletion of duplicates and the exclusion of the records that failed to fit the inclusion criteria, including papers in non-English or those that were not published after 2020. Following this preliminary screening, 1,579 records were evaluated on their suitability to the themes of dental health promotion and social media and digital marketing. The inclusion criteria were narrowed down to the quality and relevance of the studies with reference to their suitability to dental marketing strategies and innovations. Having used these refined criteria, the resulting number of documents was 1,218 documents and they included journal articles, review articles and book chapters (Page et al., 2021).

3.5 Analysis Technique

Since the literature on the digital transformation technologies and marketing strategies is heterogeneous, especially relating to the dentistry industry, this study employs a systematic review methodology following the PRISMA guidelines. Analysis provides the knowledge of how these tools are applied in practice, what challenges are related to them and how they affect the marketing of dental health as a whole. The systematic synthesis of the studies gives an implicit conclusion on the effectiveness of digital transformation in the dental health sector and gives important trends and gaps. The approach aids in combining concepts, emphasizing new trends, and providing a viable knowledge base in subsequent research and practices in the industry (Thomas & Harden, 2008; Vashishth et al., 2024).

4.0 RESULTS

The systematic review identified significant trends in the application of digital marketing and digital transformation strategies in public dental health promotion. As presented in Table 1, a total of 1,218 Scopus-indexed publications published between 2020 and 2025 were systematically analyzed using the PRISMA methodology. The findings reveal that social media oral health promotion constituted the largest thematic cluster, accounting for 537 articles (44.1% of the reviewed corpus), highlighting the growing importance of platforms such as Facebook, Instagram, TikTok, and YouTube in promoting oral health awareness and patient engagement. Clinical tele-dentistry and virtual consultation studies represented 324 articles (26.6%), indicating the rapid expansion of remote dental healthcare services in the post-COVID digital healthcare environment. In addition, 187 articles (15.3%) focused on patient behavior and engagement through SEO, e-commerce, and digital communication tools, while 170 articles (14.0%) examined ethical concerns, misinformation, and patient data privacy associated with digital dental marketing practices.

The geographical distribution of the reviewed studies also demonstrates a clear imbalance between developed and developing regions. As summarized in Table 1, 745 articles (61.2%) originated from developed nations, whereas 473 articles (38.8%) focused on low- and middle-income countries (LMICs), suggesting that digital dental healthcare research remains more concentrated in technologically advanced economies. Furthermore, the review identified seven core digital marketing strategies that shape contemporary public dental health promotion, as detailed in Table 2. These strategies include social media marketing, influencer marketing, search engine optimization (SEO), e-commerce integration, digital payment systems, tele-dentistry services, and data-driven personalized campaigns. Together, these findings demonstrate that digital transformation in dental healthcare extends beyond promotional communication and increasingly integrates patient engagement, healthcare accessibility, trust-building, and operational efficiency. The relationships among these identified strategies and their outcomes are synthesized within the proposed conceptual framework illustrated in Figure 2.

4.1 Domains of Conceptual Framework

The conceptual framework comprises four interconnected domains: Digital Technologies, Marketing Innovations, Business Outcomes, and Cultural Sustainability. These domains collectively illustrate how digital transformation enables innovative marketing practices and influences patient engagement, competitiveness, healthcare accessibility, and long-term sustainability in public dental health promotion. The framework emphasizes that digital technologies such as social media platforms, tele-dentistry systems, online payment services, and data-driven marketing tools facilitate stronger relationships between dental professionals and patients while improving healthcare communication and service delivery. As illustrated in Figure 2, the interaction between these domains creates a cyclical process in which technological innovation supports marketing effectiveness, patient trust, and sustainable healthcare outcomes.

The simple model highlights the importance of digital technologies in conventional dental health marketing. Practices are adopting new technologies to produce social media content to promote their services, engage with influencers to share oral health campaigns, and design unique packaging for dental care services (Anshasi et al., 2025). These developments are useful in improving competitiveness in the market, patient engagement, brand loyalty, and sustainability in communicating oral health education. The cyclical relationship between technology, innovation, and intricate business outcomes is improving and changing the dental industry for the better (Carausu et al., 2018).

4.2 Conceptual Framework

Dental health marketing is evolving through digital technologies, including online payment systems, e-commerce platforms for dental products, and social media engagement. These technologies help practices operate more efficiently and expand their reach. The digital payment systems and e-commerce transactions provide valuable consumer insights, allowing for data-driven decisions that enhance operational efficiency and customer experience. Social media enables dental practices to have direct communication with patients and build a community of users. Social media marketing is used by dental marketers to conduct targeted advertising, collect customer feedback, and create engaging multimedia content (Kumar & Mirchandani, 2013; Chaffey & Smith, 2017).

Figure 2. Conceptual framework

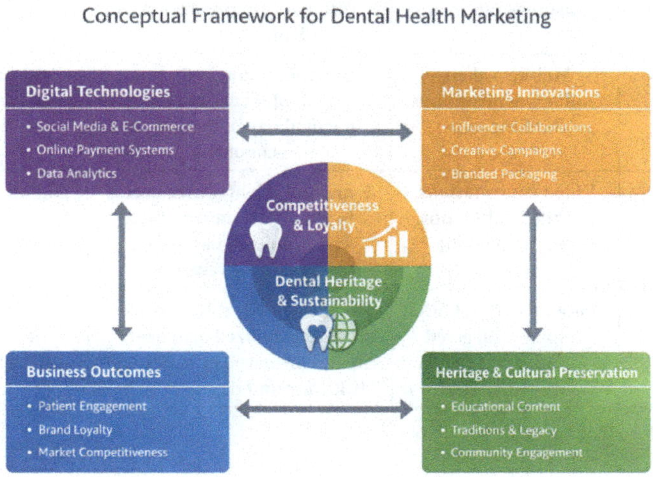

As illustrated in Figure 2 and further detailed in Table 2, seven core digital marketing strategies have been identified.

Table 2. Classification and operational framework of global digital marketing strategies in public dental health

Digital Marketing Strategy	Key Tools/Platforms	Application in Public Dental Health Promotion	Framework Domain
Social Media Marketing	Facebook, Instagram, TikTok, YouTube	Disseminating oral health education, patient testimonials, and preventive care campaigns to mass audiences	Digital Technologies & Marketing Innovations
Influencer Marketing	Health influencers, Opinion leaders, Brand ambassadors	Building patient trust, normalizing dental care-seeking behaviors among Gen Z and Millennials	Marketing Innovations
Search Engine Optimization (SEO) & Content Marketing	Google, Dental blogs, Patient testimonials, Educational videos	Improving online visibility of dental practices and driving patient traffic through credible health content	Digital Technologies

continued on following page

Table 2. Continued

Digital Marketing Strategy	Key Tools/Platforms	Application in Public Dental Health Promotion	Framework Domain
E-Commerce Integration	Online dental product stores, Direct-to-consumer platforms	Expanding access to dental care services, generating additional revenue streams for dental practices	Business Outcomes (Competitiveness)
Digital Payment Systems	Mobile wallets, Online payment apps, Banking apps	Reducing financial barriers to dental care access, particularly in developing economies	Business Outcomes (Engagement & Loyalty)
Tele-Dentistry Services	Video consultations, Mobile health apps, Online booking systems	Expanding dental care access to rural and underserved communities, improving patient convenience	Digital Technologies
Data-Driven Personalized Campaigns	Data analytics, CRM systems, Targeted advertising	Designing culturally sensitive and personalized oral health campaigns based on consumer behavior and demographics	Marketing Innovations & Business Outcomes

Source: Author Contribution.

4.3 Regional Infrastructure Barriers and Patient Data Privacy in Developing Economies

While digital marketing holds transformative potential for public dental health promotion, significant operational barriers persist in developing economies (Khandelwal et al., 2022). Erratic internet connectivity, frequent power outages, and limited smartphone penetration severely restrict the reach of social media campaigns and tele-dentistry services in rural and underserved communities. Furthermore, the absence of national electronic health record (EHR) systems in many low-income countries creates fragmented patient data management, undermining the continuity and quality of digital dental care delivery.

Beyond infrastructure, critical ethical and legal concerns surround patient data privacy in digital dental consultations. Many developing nations lack comprehensive data protection legislation governing the collection, storage, and sharing of sensitive health information (Conduah et al., 2025). Tele-dentistry platforms must therefore adopt internationally recognized privacy frameworks, such as GDPR-aligned protocols, to ensure patient confidentiality and informed consent. Policymakers must urgently establish clear legal parameters for digital dental consultations, safeguarding patient rights while enabling equitable access to technology-driven oral health services across diverse global contexts (Wang & Xie, 2026).

4.4 Marketing Innovations

Marketing innovation refers to the application of new brand management techniques, packaging designs, and social media strategies. The distinguishing features of dental services are often reflected in their packaging (e.g., eco-friendly toothpaste tubes) and the narrative behind their services (e.g., emphasis on patient care and sustainability). Innovations in social media have a strong impact on the visibility of dental practices, enhancing brand awareness and engagement (Riaj et al., 2025). These innovations assist in repositioning dental practices in competitive markets where traditional approaches may no longer suffice. Based on previous marketing efforts, dental practices must prioritize digital strategies over traditional methods, using data analytics to optimize campaigns and achieve better results (Mangold & Faulds, 2009).

4.5 Business Outcomes: Competitiveness, Participation, and Loyalty

Successful digital transformation in dental practices leads to increased competitiveness, better patient engagement, and stronger brand loyalty. Effective digital marketing strategies improve patient engagement by making oral health education more accessible, fostering long-term preventive care compliance and strengthening the trust between communities and dental health providers (Dwivedi et al., 2021). Engagement is further boosted when there is direct interaction through online campaigns and co-creation of content. Emotional loyalty to the dental practice is also enhanced when patients connect on a personal level with the brand (Brodie et al., 2011). Lim (2020) suggests that patient loyalty can be fostered through personalized experiences and reward systems, thus ensuring long-term engagement.

5.0 DISCUSSION

The digital transformation of the dental industry has reached a great milestone as indicated by the systematic review that has identified that it was a turning point in an industry that was mostly based on time-proven practices and traditional approaches. The findings explain how dental practices need to adopt digital marketing and promotion through social media to stay competitive in the present global healthcare market (Dwivedi et al., 2021).

The digital transformation of dental health services presents a critical opportunity to advance health equity by making preventive oral health education accessible to diverse populations, particularly in developing economies where traditional dental care infrastructure remains limited (Theriault & Bridge, 2023).

The conceptual framework developed in the present paper connects digital technologies and marketing innovations with the following significant business performance, including competitiveness, patient engagement, and loyalty, at the same time providing the continuity of quality care (Kumar & Mirchandani, 2013; Chaffey & Smith 2017). Digital-first approach, unique patient care packages, and personalized storytelling are new marketing innovations that have become critical in helping to reposition dental practices in an ever-competitive market (Mangold & Faulds, 2009). These initiatives create a more interactive marketplace, enhance patient relations, and develop long-term loyalty due to their ability to change people in an emotional manner and provide tailored interactions (Brodie et al., 2011).

The existing literature is mostly too generalized and lacks the focus on features of developing economies, including the issue of digital illiteracy and excessive costs of applying digital solutions (Salah & Ayyash, 2024; James, 2021; Nazaruddin et al., 2024). This chapter seeks to fill these gaps by presenting a recent and comprehensive model and realistic recommendations to dental professionals, marketers, and policymakers.

This chapter identifies **six key global strategies** in digital marketing for public dental health promotion, as follows:

1. **Social Media Marketing and Patient Engagement** — Utilizing platforms such as Facebook, Instagram, TikTok, and YouTube to disseminate oral health education, promote preventive care, and foster real-time interaction between dental professionals and patients across diverse global populations (Acosta et al., 2025).
2. **Influencer Marketing for Health Behavior Change** — Collaborating with credible health influencers and opinion leaders to build trust, normalize dental care-seeking behaviors, and reach digitally-native demographics such as Gen Z and Millennials.
3. **Search Engine Optimization (SEO) and Content Marketing** — Developing SEO-driven educational content, patient testimonials, and oral health blogs to improve the online visibility of dental health campaigns and services globally (Ghalavand et al., 2025).
4. **E-Commerce and Digital Payment Integration** — Leveraging e-commerce platforms and mobile payment systems to improve accessibility to dental products and services, particularly in developing economies where financial barriers limit care access.

5. **Tele-Dentistry and Virtual Consultation Promotion** — Using digital platforms to promote and deliver remote dental consultations, thereby expanding access to care in underserved and geographically isolated communities worldwide.
6. **Data-Driven and Personalized Marketing Campaigns** — Applying data analytics and consumer insights to design targeted, and personalized oral health campaigns that are adaptable to diverse global contexts.

These six strategies are discussed throughout the chapter and are synthesized within the proposed conceptual framework linking digital technologies, marketing innovations, and improved public dental health outcomes.

5.1 Recommendations

This analysis yields actionable recommendations for dental service providers, businesses, policymakers, and industry stakeholders. Digital-first online marketing should prioritize patient communication, brand building, preventive oral health education, and improving community access to care (Dwivedi et al., 2021). Collaborating with credible influencers enables practices to reach younger audiences and build trust through reliable information (Lou & Yuan, 2019). Eco-friendly packaging aligns with environmentally conscious consumers, supporting long-term patient retention and loyalty (Trivium Packaging, 2024). Data analytics should drive personalized marketing messages and product recommendations tailored to individual patient needs (Chaffey & Smith, 2017; Kumar & Mirchandani, 2013). Virtual consultations and digital dental education experiences advertised on online platforms enhance patient engagement and meaningful interactions (Nazaruddin et al., 2024). Dental practitioners would benefit from training workshops on e-commerce, digital marketing, and tele-dentistry adoption. Finally, increased investment in research on cultural contexts in emerging economies will strengthen evidence for improving dental health outcomes through digital technologies (James, 2021; Salah & Ayyash, 2024).

5.2 Implications

5.2.1 Practical Applications of Dental Health Services and Marketing Activities

The evidence synthesis provides practical guidelines through which dental health services can operate effectively in the digital era to continue providing quality care while remaining competitive. Both large and small dental practices increasingly need to adopt a digital-first operational model. Patient interaction and the simplification of payment processes are critical for improving operational efficiency;

therefore, the adoption of digital payment technologies such as mobile wallets, online payment systems, and online appointment scheduling platforms has become essential. Effective implementation of these technologies can enhance operational performance, reduce overhead costs, and expand access to previously underserved patient populations. Previous studies have shown that digital transformation in dental healthcare contributes to improved patient engagement, better service delivery, and greater accessibility to preventive oral healthcare services, particularly in underserved communities (Farrokhi et al., 2023; Tarazona-Montoya et al., 2024).

One of the most significant practical implications of adopting digital technologies in dental health marketing is revenue diversification and patient outreach expansion. Omnichannel strategies allow traditional dental practices to combine physical appointments with online consultations, e-commerce dental product sales, and direct digital communication with patients. Through these integrated approaches, dental healthcare providers can reach broader audiences, especially younger populations such as Gen Z and Millennials who increasingly rely on online healthcare services and social media platforms for health-related information. Convenience, preventive healthcare education, and social responsibility are among the key factors influencing this demographic's healthcare decisions. Dental practices that integrate these values into their marketing strategies are more likely to strengthen patient loyalty and increase market competitiveness (Dwivedi et al., 2021).

Digital technologies also play a critical role in improving patient care and treatment efficiency. Real-time data collection and digital monitoring systems can improve the management of patient treatment and enhance both healthcare quality and patient satisfaction. Tele-dentistry platforms, virtual consultations, and digital patient management systems help dental practices deliver timely and efficient healthcare services while improving accessibility for patients in remote or underserved areas. In addition, personalized communication strategies supported by digital technologies can contribute to stronger patient retention and building trust through transparent and traceable healthcare interactions (Lou and Yuan, 2019; Khatun et al., 2025).

5.2.2 Theory and Framework Development Implications

This systematic review contributes to the theoretical understanding of the relationship between digital transformation, patient engagement, and organizational performance in dental healthcare services. The findings demonstrate that digital technologies are reshaping traditional dental marketing by shifting healthcare communication from transactional service delivery toward interactive and experience-oriented patient engagement (Dwivedi et al., 2021). This transformation aligns with the Experience Economy perspective, which emphasizes personalized and emotionally engaging healthcare experiences as key drivers of patient satisfaction and loyalty (Brodie et al., 2011).

The review also highlights the importance of organizational resilience and institutional adaptation in the post-COVID digital healthcare environment. Dental practices that adopted tele-dentistry, online appointment systems, and digital communication platforms demonstrated greater continuity and operational flexibility during healthcare disruptions (Khatun et al., 2025). These findings support institutional theory by suggesting that patients increasingly expect seamless digital healthcare experiences, and dental organizations that fail to adapt to these expectations may lose competitiveness and patient trust.

5.2.3 Policy Implication and Institutional Support Requirement

The implications of the findings for policymakers and government institutions are substantial, particularly in developing economies where access to quality dental healthcare remains limited. Governments should prioritize digital literacy initiatives for dental practitioners by offering subsidized training programs focused on online appointment systems, tele-dentistry services, and digital healthcare marketing. These initiatives can equip dental professionals with the technological capabilities required to integrate digital solutions into their practices and serve patients more effectively (Nazaruddin et al., 2024).

In addition, policymakers should support the development of digital infrastructure in rural and underserved regions. The successful digital transformation of dental healthcare services depends heavily on reliable broadband internet access, mobile payment systems, and telecommunication networks that enable remote consultations and digital patient engagement. Improving this infrastructure can significantly enhance healthcare accessibility and reduce disparities in oral healthcare delivery (James, 2021; Salah and Ayyash, 2024).

5.2.4 Social and Economic Implications of Patients and Communities

The social and economic effects of digital transformation on dental healthcare services are deeply rooted in patients and communities. The use of digital technologies in dental health services can improve patient access to treatment, decrease barriers to care, and foster healthier communities (Tarazona-Montoya et al., 2024). Through digital platforms, dental services can extend healthcare accessibility to patients living in rural and underserved regions where conventional face-to-face dental services may be difficult to obtain (Kok Wah, 2026). This transformation has the potential to improve oral health outcomes and reduce health inequities among underserved populations.

Digital transformation can also empower marginalized groups, including women involved in dental healthcare practices. Many women participate in both administrative and clinical components of dental care, and digital technologies provide opportunities to improve workflow efficiency and promote services directly to patients. Online marketing platforms enable women entrepreneurs in the dental sector to strengthen brand visibility, establish professional credibility, and expand patient outreach. Additionally, digital payment systems and e-commerce platforms facilitate direct-to-patient sales of dental products, thereby increasing economic participation and self-sufficiency (de Oliveira Collet et al., 2024).

A notable example is the World Health Organization digital oral health campaign conducted on TikTok and Instagram through the BrushChallenge initiative, which promoted community oral hygiene awareness (Al-Khalifa et al., 2025). By collaborating with verified dental influencers and key opinion leaders (KOLs), the campaign disseminated short and engaging educational videos demonstrating correct brushing techniques. This strategy generated billions of views globally and significantly improved oral health literacy among younger audiences. Socially, the campaign democratized dental education across diverse populations (Hyde et al., 2017). Economically, the preventive approach may reduce long-term public healthcare expenditures by minimizing severe dental decay and reducing the need for costly clinical interventions.

5.3 Limitations and Future Directions

The reviewed body of work on digital marketing tends to focus on the general retail or unrelated market, which makes it important to focus more on the specifics of the dental health industry (Salah & Ayyash, 2024). The digital means of cultural preservation have not been developed in any comprehensive theoretical framework when applied to dental health promotion (James, 2021). The contextual elements in emerging economies, including the low level of digital skills and high prices of adopting digital marketing, receive less attention in the research about dental marketing (Nazaruddin et al., 2024). The current analysis focuses on marketing and promotional factors the most, not on other spheres, including the involvement of the digital technologies in dental health management and patients care.

Table 3. A list of study of limitations and future directions

Study Limitations	Implications for Current Findings	Future Research Directions
Limited Dental-Specific Research	The lack of dental-specific studies reduces the ability to tailor digital marketing strategies to the dental sector's particular needs and patient behaviors.	Future studies should focus on the adoption and impact of digital marketing strategies specifically in the dental health sector, considering unique factors such as patient trust, engagement, and treatment adherence.
Influencer Marketing Impact	While influencers have been widely used in other industries, the direct influence of influencers on dental health behaviors like seeking preventive care or adhering to dental treatments remains unclear.	Research should explore how influencer marketing can be more effectively leveraged in dentistry, including its impact on changing patient behaviors towards preventive care and treatment adherence.
Lack of Long-Term Studies on Patient Retention	Short-term research provides insights into immediate effectiveness but lacks understanding of long-term patient retention and health outcomes resulting from digital marketing efforts.	Longitudinal studies are needed to assess the sustained impact of digital marketing strategies on patient retention, health outcomes, and long-term behavior changes in oral health care.
Limited Data on Tele-Dentistry Integration	While tele-dentistry is an emerging tool for increasing access to dental care, there is limited research on how digital marketing can promote tele-dentistry services effectively.	Future studies should explore how digital marketing can enhance tele-dentistry adoption, focusing on patient perceptions, engagement, and the role of tele-dentistry in improving access to care.
Environmental and Sustainability Implications	As consumers become more environmentally conscious, incorporating sustainability into dental marketing could enhance brand loyalty and consumer engagement.	Future research should investigate how sustainable practices in digital marketing (e.g., eco-friendly packaging, promoting green initiatives) can influence consumer decisions and brand perception in the dental industry.

Source: Author Contribution.

CONCLUSION

This systematic review with 1,218 Scopus-indexed articles (2020-2025) examines the digital marketing and social media promotion has a significant potential to revolutionize the traditional field of dental health. The framework proposed connects the concept of digital innovation to the enhancement of patient engagement and oral health outcomes and how the intentional implementation of digital strategies can result in competitiveness, patient trust, and treatment adherence. One of the tools that can be considered useful in promoting preventive care in dental clinics and enhancing accessibility to dental services is digital channels. It is mandated that by successfully going through this digital transition, there must be a long-term mindset to digital literacy, development of infrastructures and innovative strategies that can reach the modern consumers and simultaneously guarantee quality and accessibility of dental health services. The chapter has various contributions. It gives a narrow study of the dental health sector that covers recent studies (2020-2025), where there is a gap in the earlier general study. It brings together the promotion of dental health and the ambition of improving patient care to fill the gap in the theoretical models that associate digital marketing strategies with increased health outcomes and business performance. Especially the focus on developing economies introduces the following factors, i.e., the lack of digital literacy, the lack of access to technology, and the prohibitively high prices of the digital adoption. The systematic review procedure, which is carried out using PRISMA, offers a strong and dependable foundation on the conclusions and recommendations.

REFERENCES

Acosta, J. M., Detsomboonrat, P., Pisarnturakit, P. P., & Urwannachotima, N. (2025). The use of social media on enhancing dental care and practice among dental professionals: Cross-sectional survey study. *JMIR Formative Research, 9*(1), e66121. DOI: 10.2196/66121 PMID: 39757575

Al-Khalifa, K. S., AlSheikh, R., Alakloby, B. O., Alharbi, H. M., Alghamdi, R. F., Ali, S., & Al Dehailan, L. (2025). Instagram's impact on dental consumers: Analyzing toothpaste hashtags. *Frontiers in Oral Health, 5*, 1420500. DOI: 10.3389/froh.2024.1420500 PMID: 39839664

Anshasi, R. J., Alsubahi, N., Alhusein, A. A., Khassawneh, A. A. L., Alrawad, M., & Alsyouf, A. (2025). Evolving perspectives in dental marketing: A study of Jordanian dentists' attitudes towards advertising and practice promotion. *Heliyon, 11*(1), e41143. Advance online publication. DOI: 10.1016/j.heliyon.2024.e41143 PMID: 39844992

Askedal, K., Hausvik, G. I., & Vesterfjell, A. (2025). Accelerating Digital Service Innovation in a Post-COVID Era: Key Recommendations for Healthcare Managers. *Information Systems Journal, 35*(6), 1565–1581. DOI: 10.1111/isj.12596

Bhuiyan, M. R. I., Akter, M. S., Amin, A., & Hossain, R. (2025a). The mediating effect of innovation capabilities, information quality and supply chain resilience in the relationship between big data analytics capability (BDAC) and healthcare performance. *SAGE Open, 15*(3), 21582440251362262. DOI: 10.1177/21582440251362262

Brodie, R. J., Hollebeek, L. D., Jurić, B., & Ilić, A. (2011). Customer engagement: Conceptual domain, fundamental propositions, and implications for research. *Journal of Service Research, 14*(3), 252–271. DOI: 10.1177/1094670511411703

Carausu, E. M., Dascalu, C. G., Lupu, I. C., Burlea, L. S., Feier, R. D., & Zegan, G. (2018). Marketing in Dentistry: Opinion Survey on Promotion of the Dental Office. *Revista de Cercetare si Interventie Sociala, 63*. https://www.ceeol.com/search/article-detail?id=733472

Chaffey, D., & Smith, P. R. (2017). *Digital marketing excellence: Planning, optimizing, and integrating online marketing* (6th ed.). Routledge., DOI: 10.4324/9781315640341

Conduah, A. K., Ofoe, S., & Siaw-Marfo, D. (2025). Data privacy in healthcare: Global challenges and solutions. *Digital Health, 11*, 20552076251343959. DOI: 10.1177/20552076251343959 PMID: 40475296 de Oliveira Collet, G., de Morais Ferreira, F., Ceron, D. F., de Lourdes Calvo Fracasso, M., & Santin, G. C. (2024). Influence of digital health literacy on online health-related behaviors influenced by internet advertising. *BMC Public Health*, *24*(1), 1949. DOI: 10.1186/s12889-024-19506-6 PMID: 39033160

Dwivedi, Y. K., Ismagilova, E., Hughes, D. L., Carlson, J., Filieri, R., Jacobson, J., Jain, V., Karjaluoto, H., Kefi, H., Krishen, A. S., Mäntymäki, M., Methuku, S., Mix, D. B., Ngobo, P. V., Papamichail, K. N., Pikoos, A., Porra, J., Raman, R., Rana, N. P., & Rauch, D. A. (2021). Setting the future of digital and social media marketing research: Perspectives and research propositions. *International Journal of Information Management*, *59*, 102168. DOI: 10.1016/j.ijinfomgt.2020.102168

Farrokhi, F., Ghorbani, Z., Farrokhi, F., Namdari, M., & Salavatian, S. (2023). Social media as a tool for oral health promotion: A systematic review. *PLoS One*, *18*(12), e0296102. DOI: 10.1371/journal.pone.0296102 PMID: 38113216

Garg, V., Kumar, H., Bansal, R., & Bhardwaj, A. (2025). Envisioning Digital Health Technology Innovations for 2025: Enhancing Digital Interventions in the Post-COVID-19 Era. In *Innovations in Healthcare Technologies in India: An Initiative of ICMR-CIBioD (Centre for Innovation and Bio-Design)* (pp. 1-17). Singapore: Springer Nature Singapore. https://doi.org/DOI: 10.1007/978-981-97-0244-2_1

Ghalavand, H., Panahi, S., & Nouri, M. (2025). Opportunities and challenges of social media for oral health literacy improvement: A qualitative investigation based on Iranian dentists' perspectives. *BMC Health Services Research*, *25*(1), 673. DOI: 10.1186/s12913-025-12845-z PMID: 40346510

Goldberg, E., Eberhard, J., Bauman, A., & Smith, B. J. (2022). Mass media campaigns for the promotion of oral health: A scoping review. *BMC Oral Health*, *22*(1), 182. DOI: 10.1186/s12903-022-02212-3 PMID: 35568896

Higgins, J. P., Thomas, J., Chandler, J., Cumpston, M., Li, T., Page, M. J., & Welch, V. A. (Eds.). (2021). *Cochrane Handbook for Systematic Reviews of Interventions* (2nd ed.). John Wiley & Sons.

Holden, A. C. (2019). Dentistry and oral health in online media sources: A discourse analysis. *Community Dental Health*, *36*(3), 221–228. DOI: 10.1922/CDH_4623Holden08 PMID: 31468748

Hyde, S., Dupuis, V., Mariri, B. P., & Dartevelle, S. (2017). Prevention of tooth loss and dental pain for reducing the global burden of oral diseases. *International Dental Journal*, *67*, 19–25. DOI: 10.1111/idj.12328 PMID: 29023745

James, J. (2021). Confronting the scarcity of digital skills among the poor in developing countries. *Development Policy Review*, *39*(2), 324–339. DOI: 10.1111/dpr.12479

Jayasinghe, Y. A., Kanmodi, K. K., Jayasinghe, R. M., & Jayasinghe, R. D. (2024). Assessment of patterns and related factors in using social media platforms to access health and oral health information among Sri Lankan adults, with special emphasis on promoting oral health awareness. *BMC Public Health*, *24*(1), 1472. DOI: 10.1186/s12889-024-19008-5 PMID: 38824505

Khandelwal, R., Kolte, A., & Rossi, M. (2022). A study on entrepreneurial opportunities in digital health-care post-Covid-19 from the perspective of developing countries. *foresight, 24*(3-4), 527-544. DOI: 10.1108/FS-02-2021-0043

Khatun, M., Hossain, R., Bhuiyan, M. R., Tabassum, M. N., & Riaj, M. A. (2025). Green Entrepreneurship and Digital Transformation for Sustainable Development: A Systematic Review. In Mouloudj, K., & Bouarar, A. (Eds.), *Digitizing Green Entrepreneurship* (pp. 153–180). IGI Global Scientific Publishing., DOI: 10.4018/979-8-3693-7442-9.ch006

Kok Wah, J. N. (2026). Empowering healthier decisions: The impact of consumer innovativeness on linking perceived benefits with protective health behaviors through digital marketing in the health-care sector. *International Journal of Pharmaceutical and Healthcare Marketing*, *20*(1), 18–44. DOI: 10.1108/IJPHM-07-2024-0073

Krishnan, V. (2025). Digital Opinion Leaders: The new age influencers! *Journal of the World Federation of Orthodontists*, *14*(3), 123–124. DOI: 10.1016/j.ejwf.2025.05.003 PMID: 40456597

Kumar, V., & Mirchandani, R. (2013). Increasing the ROI of social media marketing. *IEEE Engineering Management Review*, *41*(3), 17–23. DOI: 10.1109/EMR.2013.6596535

Lou, C., & Yuan, S. (2019). Influencer marketing: How message value and source credibility affect consumer trust of branded content on social media. *Journal of Interactive Advertising*, *19*(1), 58–73. DOI: 10.1080/15252019.2018.1533501

Mackey, T. K., & Nayyar, G. (2016). Digital danger: A review of the global public health, patient safety and cybersecurity threats posed by illicit online pharmacies. *British Medical Bulletin*, *118*(1), 110–126. DOI: 10.1093/bmb/ldw016 PMID: 27151957

Mangold, W. G., & Faulds, D. J. (2009). Social media: The new hybrid element of the promotion mix. *Business Horizons*, *52*(4), 357–365. DOI: 10.1016/j.bushor.2009.03.002

Mfouth Kemajou, P., Mbanya, A., & Coppieters, Y. (2024). Digital approaches in post-COVID healthcare: A systematic review of technological innovations in disease management. *Biology Methods and Protocols*, *9*(1), bpae070. Advance online publication. DOI: 10.1093/biomethods/bpae070 PMID: 39440031

Milne, R., & Costa, A. (2020). Disruption and dislocation in post-COVID futures for digital health. *Big Data & Society*, *7*(2), 2053951720949567. DOI: 10.1177/2053951720949567 PMID: 36789368

Mosnaim, G. S., Stempel, H., Van Sickle, D., & Stempel, D. A. (2020). The adoption and implementation of digital health care in the post–COVID-19 era. *The Journal of Allergy and Clinical Immunology. In Practice*, *8*(8), 2484–2486. DOI: 10.1016/j.jaip.2020.06.006 PMID: 32585407

Nagpal, A., & Sharma, G. (2019). Daunting for developing countries. *British Dental Journal*, *227*(3), 175–175. DOI: 10.1038/s41415-019-0612-0 PMID: 31399649

Nazaruddin, I., Utami, E. R., & Rahmawati, E. (2024). Digitalization challenges for SMEs: A systematic literature review perspective and future research. *JBTI: Jurnal Bisnis: Teori dan Implementasi, 15*(1), 15-43. https://doi.org/DOI: 10.18196/jbti.v15i1.20410

Northridge, M. E., Kumar, A., & Kaur, R. (2020). Disparities in access to oral health care. *Annual Review of Public Health, 41*(1), 513–535. DOI: 10.1146/annurev-publhealth-040119-094318 PMID: 31900100

Page, M. J., McKenzie, J. E., Bossuyt, P. M., Boutron, I., Hoffmann, T. C., Mulrow, C. D., Shamseer, L., Tetzlaff, J. M., Akl, E. A., Brennan, S. E., Chou, R., Glanville, J., Grimshaw, J. M., Hróbjartsson, A., Lalu, M. M., Li, T., Loder, E. W., Mayo-Wilson, E., McDonald, S., & Moher, D. (2021). The PRISMA 2020 statement: An updated guideline for reporting systematic reviews. *BMJ (Clinical Research Ed.)*, *372*(71), n71. Advance online publication. DOI: 10.1136/bmj.n71 PMID: 33782057

Petersen, P. E., & Kwan, S. (2009). World Health Organization global oral health strategies for oral health promotion and disease prevention in the twenty-first century. *Prävention und Gesundheitsförderung*, *4*(2), 100–104. DOI: 10.1007/s11553-009-0169-x

Pine, C. M., & Dugdill, L. (2011). Analysis of a unique global public-private partnership to promote oral health. *International Dental Journal*, *61*, 11–21. DOI: 10.1111/j.1875-595X.2011.00036.x PMID: 21770936

Potts, G., & Radford, D. R. (2019). # Teeth&Tweets: The reach and reaction of an online social media oral health promotion campaign. *British Dental Journal, 227*(3), 217–222. DOI: 10.1038/s41415-019-0593-z PMID: 31399680

Rajeh, M. T. (2022). Modeling the theory of planned behavior to predict adults' intentions to improve oral health behaviors. *BMC Public Health, 22*(1), 1391. DOI: 10.1186/s12889-022-13796-4 PMID: 35858885

Riaj, M. A., Tabassum, M. N., Hossain, R., Bhuiyan, M. R., & Khatun, M. (2025). Digitalization Transformation in Entrepreneurship and Enterprise Green Innovation. In Mouloudj, K., & Bouarar, A. (Eds.), *Digitizing Green Entrepreneurship* (pp. 181–204). IGI Global Scientific Publishing., DOI: 10.4018/979-8-3693-7442-9.ch007

Salah, O. H., & Ayyash, M. M. (2024). E-commerce adoption by SMEs and its effect on marketing performance: An extended of TOE framework with ai integration, innovation culture, and customer tech-savviness. *Journal of Open Innovation, 10*(1), 100183. DOI: 10.1016/j.joitmc.2023.100183

Salman, F. D. (2024). Marketing Strategies in Dentistry: Navigating Social Media, Influencers, and Traditional Channels for Oral Health Promotion. In *Leveraging Digital Technology for Preventive Dentistry* (pp. 279-304). DOI: DOI: 10.4018/979-8-3693-3872-8.ch010

Srivastava, R., Tangade, P., & Priyadarshi, S. (2023). Transforming public health dentistry: Exploring the digital foothold for improved oral healthcare. *International Dental Journal of Student's Research, 11*(2), 61–67. Advance online publication. DOI: 10.18231/j.idjsr.2023.013

Tarazona-Montoya, R., Devece, C., Llopis-Albert, C., & García-Agreda, S. (2024). Effectiveness of digital marketing and its value in new ventures. *The International Entrepreneurship and Management Journal, 20*(4), 2839–2862. DOI: 10.1007/s11365-024-00959-5

Theriault, H., & Bridge, G. (2023). Oral health equity for rural communities: Where are we now and where can we go from here? *British Dental Journal, 235*(2), 99–102. DOI: 10.1038/s41415-023-6058-4 PMID: 37500855

Thomas, J., & Harden, A. (2008). Methods for the thematic synthesis of qualitative research in systematic reviews. *BMC Medical Research Methodology, 8*(1), 45. DOI: 10.1186/1471-2288-8-45 PMID: 18616818

Trivium Packaging. (2024). 2024 Global buying green report. https://buyinggreen.triviumpackaging.com/

Uddin, K. S., Bhuiyan, M. R. I., & Hamid, M. (2024). Perception towards the acceptance of digital health services among the people of Bangladesh. *WSEAS Transactions on Business and Economics, 21*, 1557–1570. DOI: 10.37394/23207.2024.21.127

Vashishth, T. K., Sharma, V., Sharma, K. K., Kumar, B., Chaudhary, S., & Panwar, R. (2024). Industry 4.0 Trends and Strategies: A Modern Approach with Focus on Knowledge Management. *Knowledge Management and Industry Revolution, 4*(0), 111–158. DOI: 10.1002/9781394242641.ch5

Wallace, B. B., & MacEntee, M. I. (2012). Access to dental care for low-income adults: Perceptions of affordability, availability and acceptability. *Journal of Community Health, 37*(1), 32–39. DOI: 10.1007/s10900-011-9412-4 PMID: 21590434

Wang, X., & Xie, F. (2026). Global artificial intelligence governance research in the digital and intelligent era: Advances, trends and countermeasures. *Journal of Knowledge Management, 30*(1), 30–68. DOI: 10.1108/JKM-01-2025-0006

Zare, J., & Persaud, A. (2024). Digital transformation and business model innovation: A bibliometric analysis of existing research and future perspectives. *Management Review Quarterly, 75*(3), 1999–2032. DOI: 10.1007/s11301-024-00426-z

KEY TERMS AND DEFINITIONS

Cross-Border Misinformation: The rapid dissemination of unverified, false, or scientifically inaccurate health claims across international digital platforms, which poses a significant threat to global public health safety.

Digital Health Literacy: The ability of individuals to seek, find, understand, evaluate, and apply health-related information from digital sources to make informed decisions about their dental and general health care.

Digital Health Marketing: The strategic use of internet-based channels, search engines, and social media networks by dental professionals and public health bodies to communicate, educate, and engage target audiences about oral healthcare solutions.

Influencer Marketing in Healthcare: A digital communication strategy involving collaborations between public health institutions and digital key opinion leaders (KOLs) or dental professionals to disseminate validated medical information and combat online misinformation.

PRISMA Protocol (Preferred Reporting Items for Systematic Reviews and Meta-Analyses): An evidence-based minimum set of items and steps designed to help authors transparently report why a systematic review was done, what the authors did, and what they found.

Public Dental Health Promotion: A science-based branch of public health focused on improving oral health, preventing dental diseases, and enhancing community awareness regarding oral hygiene through organized institutional and digital efforts.

Tele-Dentistry: A subfield of telehealth that utilizes digital information, imaging, and communication technologies to provide remote dental consultations, triage, guidance, and oral health education.

Compilation of References

Abdolkhani, R., Gray, K., Borda, A., & DeSouza, R. (2019). Patient-generated health data management and quality challenges in remote patient monitoring. *JAMIA Open*, *2*(4), 471–478. DOI: 10.1093/jamiaopen/ooz036 PMID: 32025644

Abroms, L. C., & Millan Lounsbury, N. (2012). Digital and social media campaigns: Expanding the reach of public health interventions. *Oral Health Promotion and Education*, *4*(2), 1–15.

Acosta, J. M., Detsomboonrat, P., Pisarnturakit, P. P., & Urwannachotima, N. (2025). The use of social media on enhancing dental care and practice among dental professionals: Cross-sectional survey study. *JMIR Formative Research*, *9*(1), e66121. DOI: 10.2196/66121 PMID: 39757575

Adams, K., Snyder, J., Crooks, V. A., & Berry, N. S. (2018). A critical examination of empowerment discourse in medical tourism: The case of the dental tourism industry in Los Algodones, Mexico. *Globalization and Health*, *14*(1), 70. DOI: 10.1186/s12992-018-0392-3

Adane, K., Gizachew, M., & Kendie, S. (2019). The role of medical data in efficient patient care delivery: A review. *Risk Management and Healthcare Policy*, *12*, 67–73. DOI: 10.2147/RMHP.S179259 PMID: 31114410

Adeniyi, A., Akama, G., Lukandu, O., Ikemeri, J. E., Jumah, A., Chelagat, S., Kasuya, A., Ruhl, L., Songok, J., & Christoffersen-Deb, A. (2024). Reducing maternal and child oral health disparities in Sub-Saharan Africa through a community-based strategy. *Frontiers in Oral Health*, *5*, 1429332. DOI: 10.3389/froh.2024.1429332 PMID: 39005710

Afeche, P., Araghi, M., & Baron, O. (2017). Customer acquisition, retention, and service access quality: Optimal advertising, capacity level, and capacity allocation. *Manufacturing & Service Operations Management*, *19*(4), 674–691. DOI: 10.1287/msom.2017.0635

Ahmad, N. S., Musa, R., & Harun, M. H. M. (2016). The impact of social media content marketing (SMCM) towards brand health. *Procedia Economics and Finance*, *37*, 331–336. DOI: 10.1016/S2212-5671(16)30133-2

Ajzen, I. (1991). The theory of planned behavior. *Organizational Behavior and Human Decision Processes*, *50*(2), 179–211. DOI: 10.1016/0749-5978(91)90020-T

Alameri, S. A., Mahmoud, B. I., Almado, A. A., Jasim, Z. A., Jahlool, I. H., & Alyousuf, A. N. (2026). Consumer Acceptance of AI-Supported Circular Fashion Services: A Technology Acceptance Perspective. In Mouloudj, K., & Arantes, L. (Eds.), *Ethical Consumption and Responsible Innovation in Fashion through AI* (pp. 35–58). IGI Global., DOI: 10.4018/979-8-3373-7200-6.ch002

Alauddin, M. S., Baharuddin, A. S., & Mohd Ghazali, M. I. (2021). The Modern and Digital Transformation of Oral Health Care: A Mini Review. *Health Care*, *9*(2), 118. DOI: 10.3390/healthcare9020118 PMID: 33503807

Al-Gasawneh, J. A., Alghizzawi, M., & Al Attyia, N. F. Y. (2025). The Influence Factor of Digital Marketing on Customer Satisfaction. In Alzoubi, H. M., Al-Gasaymeh, A. S., & Vasudevan, S. (Eds.), *Bridging Digital Innovation and Technology for Business Transformation—ICTIM* (pp. 125–130). Springer., DOI: 10.1007/978-3-031-90558-2_16

Alhersh, B. A. (2026). The Influence of Social Media Exposure on Dietary Behaviors and Dental Caries Prevalence Among Pediatric Patients. https://www.preprints.org/manuscript/202602.1878

Alhumainy, N., Alnajrani, T. M., Thobaiti, A. A. A., Alharthi, A. A. A., Alkhalide, H. M., Alghamdi, J. D. S., Alharthi, N. S., Alotaibi, A. A. G., Aldajani, H. M. H., & Al-Tarad, R. D. S. (2024). Enhancing primary care delivery: A comprehensive review of collaboration among multidisciplinary teams. *Journal of Posthumanism*, *4*(3), 2209–2223. DOI: 10.63332/joph.v4i3.3786

Ali, S. K., Khan, H., Shah, J., & Nadeem Ahmed, K. (2023). An electronic health record system implementation in a resource limited country-lessons learned. *Digital Health*, *9*, 20552076231203660. DOI: 10.1177/20552076231203660 PMID: 37744747

ALKasassbeh. H., Alghizzawi, M., Abu-AlSondos, I.A., Yaseen, S.G., Almuhaisen, O., Al-Daoud, K.I. (2025). Digital Marketing and Consumer Satisfaction. In S.G. Yaseen (Eds.), *Applied Artificial Intelligence in Business* (pp. 349–360), Springer. DOI: 10.1007/978-3-031-90271-0_25

Al-Khalifa, K. S., AlSheikh, R., Alakloby, B. O., Alharbi, H. M., Alghamdi, R. F., Ali, S., & Al Dehailan, L. (2025). Instagram's impact on dental consumers: Analyzing toothpaste hashtags. *Frontiers in Oral Health*, *5*, 1420500. DOI: 10.3389/froh.2024.1420500 PMID: 39839664

Almarshadi, R., Hamdi, S., Hadi, F., Alshehri, A., Alsahafi, R., Aljohani, N., Alyamani, R., Alhbchi, M., Alqahtani, N., Almutiri, R., Alqadi, T., Alhabardi, A., Abu Aziz, K., & Alshammeri, T. (2025). Redefining Digital Dentistry: Multidisciplinary Applications of 3D Printing for Personalized Dental Care. *Cureus*, *17*(6), e86791. DOI: 10.7759/cureus.86791 PMID: 40718273

Almodawer, Y., Alam, S. S., Sinniah, S., & Ali, M. H. (2025a). Health tourism in Malaysia: Understanding the drivers of satisfaction and revisit intention. *Tourism Recreation Research*, *50*(5), 1088–1109. DOI: 10.1080/02508281.2024.2379686

Almokdad, E., Mouloudj, K., Kiatkawsin, K., & Lee, C.H. (2026). Designing the right fit: Socially cued versus functional AI interfaces in hospitality self-service technologies. *Journal of Hospitality and Tourism Insights*, Vol. ahead-of-print. https://doi.org/DOI: 10.1108/JHTI-10-2025-1267

Almokdad, E., Mouloudj, K., & Lee, C. H. (2025). Rehumanizing AI-Driven Service: How Employee Presence Shapes Consumer Perceptions in Digital Hospitality Settings. *Journal of Theoretical and Applied Electronic Commerce Research*, *20*(3), 209. DOI: 10.3390/jtaer20030209

Almokdad, E., Mouloudj, K., Njoku, A., Bouarar, A. C., Evans, M. A., Asanza, D. M., & Mouloudj, S. (2026). Exploring healthcare workers' intentions to volunteer in digital healthcare services for underserved communities: An extended TAM-based study. *Electronic Journal of General Medicine*, *23*(1), em714. DOI: 10.29333/ejgm/17915

Alotaibi, H. N. (2025). Patient Satisfaction with CAD/CAM 3D-Printed Complete Dentures: A Systematic *Analysis of the Clinical Studies. Health Care*, *13*(4), 388. DOI: 10.3390/healthcare13040388 PMID: 39997262

Alqabbani, Y. N., Alfhaed, N. K., Almasaad, K. F., Mahanshi, R. Y., Farooqi, F., Al-Khalifa, K. S., & Gaffar, B. O. (2025). The impact of dental photography in social media platforms on patients' selection of dentists and type of treatment. *BMC Oral Health*, *25*(1), 111. DOI: 10.1186/s12903-025-05483-8 PMID: 39838400

Álvarez, H. (2025). *Salutogenic Marketing*. Aim and Scope. Salud Uninorte., DOI: 10.14482/sun.41.01.001.245

Alyahya, M., Agag, G., & Abdelwahab, M. (2026). AI-enabled complaint handling and customer recommendation: A quasi-experimental difference-in-differences (DiD) perspective. *Journal of Retailing and Consumer Services*, *92*, 104803. DOI: 10.1016/j.jretconser.2026.104803

Alyami, M. H. (2024). The Applications of 3D-Printing Technology in Prosthodontics: A Review of the Current Literature. *Cureus*, *16*(9), e68501. DOI: 10.7759/cureus.68501 PMID: 39364461

Alyousuf, A. N., Sabeeh, A. O., Alnaemat, N. D., Mouloudj, K., & Hussein, S. A. (2026). Understanding Gen Z's Adoption of AI Technologies in Green Product Purchases: An Extension of the Technology Acceptance Model. In Mouloudj, K., & Bouarar, A. (Eds.), *Insights on Consumer Psychology in the Digital Landscape* (pp. 369–392). IGI Global., DOI: 10.4018/979-8-3373-2424-1.ch013

American Association of Orthodontists (AAO). (2022). Consumer alert: The dangers of DIY orthodontic treatments. https://www2.aaoinfo.org/danger-of-diy/

Anagun, Y., Bolel, N. S., Isik, S., & Ozkan, S. E. (2022). Deep Learning-based customer complaint management. *Journal of Organizational Computing and Electronic Commerce*, *32*(3–4), 217–231. DOI: 10.1080/10919392.2023.2210049

Andriani, A. D. (2025). The Future of Digital Content: AI-Generated Texts, Images, Videos, and Real-Time Production. In *Impacts of AI-Generated Content on Brand Reputation* (pp. 149–176). IGI Global Scientific Publishing., https://www.igi-global.com/chapter/the-future-of-digital-content/383241 DOI: 10.4018/979-8-3373-4327-3.ch006

Anshasi, R. J., Alsubahi, N., Alhusein, A. A., Khassawneh, A. A. L., Alrawad, M., & Alsyouf, A. (2025). Evolving perspectives in dental marketing: A study of Jordanian dentists' attitudes towards advertising and practice promotion. *Heliyon*, *11*(1), e41143. Advance online publication. DOI: 10.1016/j.heliyon.2024.e41143 PMID: 39844992

Antonopoulou, V., Meyer, C., Chadwick, P., Gibson, B., Sniehotta, F. F., Vlaev, I., Vassova, A., Goffe, L., Lorencatto, F., McKinlay, A., & Chater, A. M. (2024). Understanding healthcare professionals' responses to patient complaints in secondary and tertiary care in the UK: A systematic review and behavioural analysis using the Theoretical Domains Framework. *Health Research Policy and Systems*, *22*(1), 137. DOI: 10.1186/s12961-024-01209-4 PMID: 39354470

Anyikwa, C. L., & Ogwo, C. E. (2025). Enhancing oral health outcomes through public health policy reform. *Frontiers in Oral Health*, *6*, 1604465. DOI: 10.3389/froh.2025.1604465 PMID: 40551851

Apel, Z., Fagundes, N., Sharmin, N., Nassar, U., Gow, G., Apel, D., & Perez, A. (2024). Social Media in Oral Health Education: A Scoping Review. *European Journal of Dental Education : Official Journal of the Association for Dental Education in Europe, 29*(1), 50–63. DOI: 10.1111/eje.13053 PMID: 39462438

Arora, M., Sachdeva, P., Gupta, N., Gambhir, N., Singh, D., & Tuli, A. (2025). Scrolling toward smiles: The role of social media in dental health promotion. *Santosh University Journal of Health Sciences, 11*(2), 275–279. https://journals.lww.com/sujh/fulltext/2025/07000/scrolling_toward_smiles__the_role_of_social_media.15.aspx?context=latestarticles

Ashley, C., & Tuten, T. (2015). Creative strategies in social media marketing: An exploratory study of branded social content and consumer engagement. *Psychology and Marketing, 32*(1), 15–27. DOI: 10.1002/mar.20761

Asiri, F. Y. I., Tennant, M., & Kruger, E. (2024). Oral health behaviour, care utilisation, and barriers among students with disabilities: A parental perspective. *Health Care, 12*(19), 1955. DOI: 10.3390/healthcare12191955 PMID: 39408135

Askedal, K., Hausvik, G. I., & Vesterfjell, A. (2025). Accelerating Digital Service Innovation in a Post-COVID Era: Key Recommendations for Healthcare Managers. *Information Systems Journal, 35*(6), 1565–1581. DOI: 10.1111/isj.12596

Atanda, A. J., Livinski, A. A., London, S. D., Boroumand, S., Weatherspoon, D., Iafolla, T. J., & Dye, B. A. (2022). Tooth retention, health, and quality of life in older adults: A scoping review. *BMC Oral Health, 22*(1), 185. DOI: 10.1186/s12903-022-02210-5 PMID: 35585618

Atherton, H., Huckvale, C., & Car, J. (2010). Communicating health promotion and disease prevention information to patients via email: A review. *Journal of Telemedicine and Telecare, 16*(4), 172–175. DOI: 10.1258/jtt.2010.004002 PMID: 20511566

Attia, A. (2023). Effect of sustainable supply chain management and customer relationship management on organizational performance in the context of the Egyptian textile industry. *Sustainability (Basel), 15*(5), 4072. DOI: 10.3390/su15054072

Ayalon, L. (2025). Toward an intragroup approach to alleviate ageism in the second half of life. *The Gerontologist, 65*(10), gnaf169. Advance online publication. DOI: 10.1093/geront/gnaf169 PMID: 40720236

Azzopardi-Muscat, N., & Sørensen, K. (2019). Towards an equitable digital public health era: Promoting equity through a health literacy perspective. *European Journal of Public Health, 29*(Supplement_3), 13–17. DOI: 10.1093/eurpub/ckz166 PMID: 31738443

Badewy, R., Singh, H., Quiñonez, C., & Singhal, S. (2021). Impact of Poor Oral Health on Community-Dwelling Seniors: A Scoping Review. *Health Services Insights*, *14*, 1178632921989734. DOI: 10.1177/1178632921989734 PMID: 33597810

Bahadori, S., Buckle, P., Ascensao, T. S., Ghafur, S., & Kierkegaard, P. (2025). Evolving digital health technologies: Aligning with and enhancing the national institute for health and care excellence evidence standards framework. *JMIR mHealth and uHealth*, *13*, e67435. DOI: 10.2196/67435 PMID: 40845677

Bailey, R. R. (2019). Goal setting and action planning for health behavior change. *American Journal of Lifestyle Medicine*, *13*(6), 615–618. DOI: 10.1177/1559827617729634 PMID: 31662729

Bales, G. C., Curtan, S., Agarwal, N., Ronis, S. D., & Nelson, S. (2024). Adoption of New Oral Health Interventions in Primary Care: Qualitative Findings. *AJPM Focus*, *3*(3), 100214. DOI: 10.1016/j.focus.2024.100214 PMID: 38586824

Bambauer-Sachse, S., & Stuhldreier, S. M. (2026). Effective complaint management on social networks: The impact of response strategy, type and account on consumer reactions. *Journal of Services Marketing*, *40*(10), 1–21. DOI: 10.1108/JSM-03-2025-0215

Barranca-Enríquez, A., & Romo-González, T. (2022). Your health is in your mouth: A comprehensive view to promote general wellness. *Frontiers in Oral Health*, *3*, 971223. DOI: 10.3389/froh.2022.971223 PMID: 36186536

Barreda-Gutiérrez, M., Cantarero-Prieto, D., & Pascual Sáez, M. (2024). Age, Technology, and the Digital Divide: Are They Directly Related to Mental Health Problems? *Health Care*, *12*(23), 2454. DOI: 10.3390/healthcare12232454 PMID: 39685075

Bashirian, S., Khoshravesh, S., Ayubi, E., Karimi-Shahanjarini, A., Shirahmadi, S., & Solaymani, P. (2023). The impact of health education interventions on oral health promotion among older people: A systematic review. *BMC Geriatrics*, *23*(1), 548. Advance online publication. DOI: 10.1186/s12877-023-04259-5 PMID: 37697260

Beaven, A., & Marshman, Z. (2024). Barriers and facilitators to accessing oral healthcare for older people in the UK: A scoping review. *British Dental Journal*. Advance online publication. DOI: 10.1038/s41415-024-7740-x PMID: 39152268

Beck Guimarães, M., Vaz Machry, R., Fernandes de Carvalho, J. C., Machado Mota, M., Favero Bulgarelli, A., De Rezende Pinto, L., & Marchini, L. (2025). Ageism on geriatric dentistry Instagram posts. *PAJAR - Pan-American. Journal of Aging Research*, *13*(1), e48238. DOI: 10.15448/2357-9641.2025.1.48238

Beltrán, V., Muñoz-Sepúlveda, F., Acevedo, C., Navarro, P., Venegas, B., Salgado, C., Uribe, P., & Engelke, W. (2024). A rural teledentistry care experience: A geriatric approach to assessing oral health status and treatment needs in older adults from Mapuche community in Chile. *Frontiers in Public Health, 12*, 1356622. DOI: 10.3389/fpubh.2024.1356622 PMID: 38903581

Bełżek, A., Żerebiec, M., Saj, N., Rupeć, Z., Kamiński, P., Kaczmarski, M., & Turżańska, K. (2025). Advances in 3D printed orthotics for rehabilitation. *Wiadomosci lekarskie (Warsaw, Poland)*: 1960), 78(3), 539–543. DOI: 10.36740/WLek/202602

Ben-Omran, M., Livinski, A., Kopycka-Kedzierawski, D., Boroumand, S., Williams, D., Weatherspoon, D., Iafolla, T., Fontelo, P., & Dye, B. (2021). The use of teledentistry in facilitating oral health for older adults: A scoping review. *The Journal of the American Dental Association, 152*(12), 998–1011.e17. Advance online publication. DOI: 10.1016/j.adaj.2021.06.005 PMID: 34521539

Berkman, L. F., Kawachi, I., & Glymour, M. M. (Eds.). (2014). *Social Epidemiology* (2nd ed.). Oxford University Press., DOI: 10.1093/med/9780195377903.001.0001

Betancourt, J. R., Green, A. R., Carrillo, J. E., & Park, E. R. (2005). Cultural competence and health care disparities: Key perspectives and trends. *Health Affairs (Project Hope), 24*(2), 499–505. DOI: 10.1377/hlthaff.24.2.499 PMID: 15757936

Bhamra, I. B., Gallagher, J. E., & Patel, R. (2024). Telehealth technologies in care homes: A gap for dentistry? *Journal of Public Health (Oxford, England), 46*(1), e106–e135. DOI: 10.1093/pubmed/fdad258 PMID: 38102945

Bhuiyan, M. R. I., Akter, M. S., Amin, A., & Hossain, R. (2025a). The mediating effect of innovation capabilities, information quality and supply chain resilience in the relationship between big data analytics capability (BDAC) and healthcare performance. *SAGE Open, 15*(3), 21582440251362262. DOI: 10.1177/21582440251362262

BinHamdan. R. H., Alsadhan, S. A., Gazzaz, A. Z., & AlJameel, A. H. (2025). Social media use and oral health–related misconceptions in Saudi Arabia: cross-sectional study. *JMIR Formative Research, 9*, e70071. https://formative.jmir.org/2025/1/e70071

Bolukbasi, G., & Dundar, N. (2024). Oral health in older adults: Current insights and tips. *Journal of Gerontology and Geriatrics, 72*(2), 96–107. DOI: 10.36150/2499-6564-N700

Boon-itt, S. (2019). Quality of health websites and their influence on perceived usefulness, trust and intention to use: An analysis from Thailand. *Journal of Innovation and Entrepreneurship, 8*(1), 1–17. DOI: 10.1186/s13731-018-0100-9

Borrelli, B., Endrighi, R., Heeren, T., Adams, W. G., Gansky, S. A., Werntz, S., Rueras, N., Stephens, D., Ameli, N., & Henshaw, M. M. (2025). Parent-targeted oral health text messaging for underserved children attending pediatric clinics: A randomised clinical trial. *JAMA Network Open*, *8*(1), e2452780. DOI: 10.1001/jamanetworkopen.2024.52780 PMID: 39745701

Borthakur, P. P. (2024). The Role and Future Directions of 3D Printing in Custom Prosthetic Design. *Engineering Proceedings*, *81*(1), 10. DOI: 10.3390/engproc2024081010

Bouarar, A. C., Mouloudj, K., Čaušević, A., & Mouloudj, S. (2025). Investigating intentions to visit Sarajevo city: Expanding the theory of planned behavior. *Tourism and Hospitality Management*, *31*(3), 371–383. DOI: 10.20867/thm.31.3.4

Bovsh, A. L., Mouloudj, K., Rasulova, A. M., & Tkachuk, T. M. (2024). Viral Content in Event Management of Hospitality and Socio-Cultural Activities. In S. Kulshreshtha & C. Webster (Eds.), *New Technologies in Virtual and Hybrid Events* (pp. 229-258). IGI Global. DOI: 10.4018/979-8-3693-2272-7.ch012

Braveman, P. A., Arkin, E., Proctor, D., Kauh, T., & Holm, N. (2011). Systemic and structural racism and health inequities. *Annual Review of Public Health*, *32*, 1–16. DOI: 10.1146/annurev-publhealth-032310-092614

Breitsohl, J., Khammash, M., & Griffiths, G. (2010). E-business complaint management: Perceptions and perspectives of online credibility. *Journal of Enterprise Information Management*, *23*(5), 653–660. DOI: 10.1108/17410391011083083

Brinkhof, L. P., de Wit, S., Murre, J. M. J., & Ridderinkhof, K. R. (2023). Mitigating the Harmful Impact of Ageism among Older Individuals: The Buffering Role of Resilience Factors. *Geriatrics (Basel, Switzerland)*, *9*(1), 1. DOI: 10.3390/geriatrics9010001 PMID: 38392100

British Dental Association (BDA). (2023). Social media trends and oral health risks. *BDA Press Release*. https://www.bda.org/

Brodie, R. J., Hollebeek, L. D., Jurić, B., & Ilić, A. (2011). Customer engagement: Conceptual domain, fundamental propositions, and implications for research. *Journal of Service Research*, *14*(3), 252–271. DOI: 10.1177/1094670511411703

Brown, S. A., Breton, M. D., Anderson, S. M., Kollar, L., Keith-Hynes, P., Levy, C. J., & Kudva, Y. C. (2017). Overnight closed-loop control improves glycemic control in a multicenter study of adults with type 1 diabetes. *The Journal of Clinical Endocrinology and Metabolism*, *102*(10), 3674–3682. DOI: 10.1210/jc.2017-00556 PMID: 28666360

Buck, D., Seong, J., Daud, A., Davies, M., Newcombe, R., & West, N. X. (2024). A randomised controlled trial to evaluate the effectiveness of personalised oral hygiene advice delivered via video technology. *Journal of Dentistry*, *149*, 105243. DOI: 10.1016/j.jdent.2024.105243 PMID: 39019247

Bui, T. T., Tran, Q. T., Alang, T., & Le, T. D. (2023). Examining the relationship between digital content marketing perceived value and brand loyalty: Insights from Vietnam. *Cogent Social Sciences*, *9*(1), 2225835. DOI: 10.1080/23311886.2023.2225835

Burridge, J. H., Lee, A. C. W., Turk, R., Stokes, M., Whitall, J., Vaidyanathan, R., & Franco, E. (2017). Telehealth, wearable sensors, and the internet: Will they improve stroke outcomes through increased intensity of therapy, motivation, and adherence to rehabilitation programs? *Journal of Neurologic Physical Therapy : JNPT*, *41*, S32–S38. DOI: 10.1097/NPT.0000000000000183 PMID: 28628594

Butt, I., Iqbal, T., & Zohaib, S. (2019). Healthcare marketing: A review of the literature based on citation analysis. *Health Marketing Quarterly*, *36*(4), 271–290. DOI: 10.1080/07359683.2019.1680120 PMID: 31646959

Calderon, S. J., Comnick, C. L., Villhauer, A., Marshall, T., Dahl, J.-U., Banas, J. A., & Drake, D. R. (2023). A social media intervention for promoting oral health behaviors in adolescents: A non-randomized pilot clinical trial. *Oral*, *3*(2), 203–214. DOI: 10.3390/oral3020018 PMID: 38162993

Callaway, J., Strozza, C., Christensen, K., Doblhammer, G., Rau, R., & Sogaard, J. (2025). Ageing populations: new challenges in longevity. *BMC public health challenges*, 25(1), 4395. DOI: 10.1186/s12889-025-25531

Carausu, E. M., Dascalu, C. G., Lupu, I. C., Burlea, L. S., Feier, R. D., & Zegan, G. (2018). Marketing in Dentistry: Opinion Survey on Promotion of the Dental Office. *Revista de Cercetare si Interventie Sociala, 63*. https://www.ceeol.com/search/article-detail?id=733472

Celeste, R. K., & Gaida, J. E. (2019). Social determinants of oral health inequalities. *Journal of Dental Research*, *98*(11), 1234–1241. DOI: 10.1177/0022034519876518 PMID: 31379234

Chaffey, D., & Smith, P. R. (2017). *Digital marketing excellence: Planning, optimizing, and integrating online marketing* (6th ed.). Routledge., DOI: 10.4324/9781315640341

Champion, V. L., & Skinner, C. S. (2021). Health Belief Model. In Glanz, K., Rimer, B. K., & Viswanath, K. (Eds.), *Health behavior: Theory, Research, and Practice* (pp. 8–38). Jossey-Bass.

Cham, T. H., Lim, Y. M., Sia, B. C., Cheah, J. H., & Ting, H. (2021). Medical tourism destination image and its relationship with the intention to revisit: A study of Chinese Medical tourists in Malaysia. *Journal of China Tourism Research, 17*(2), 163–191. DOI: 10.1080/19388160.2020.1734514

Chan, A. K. Y., Lin, C. P., Ijarogbe, O., Kateeb, E., Ogawa, H., Shah, S. M., Fernandez, F., Chen, T. C., Renn, T. Y., Chu, C. H., & Chang, W. J. (2025). Promoting Oral Health for Older Adults in the Asia-Pacific Region. *International dental journal*, 75 Suppl 2(Suppl 2), 100886. DOI: 10.1016/j.identj.2025.100886

Chan, A. K. Y., Tamrakar, M., Jiang, C. M., Lo, E. C. M., Leung, K. C. M., & Chu, C. H. (2021). Common Medical and Dental Problems of Older Adults: A Narrative Review. *Geriatrics (Basel, Switzerland)*, *6*(3), 76. DOI: 10.3390/geriatrics6030076 PMID: 34449647

Chang, H. H., Wong, K. H., & Fang, P. W. (2014). The effects of customer relationship management relational information processes on customer-based performance. *Decision Support Systems*, *66*, 146–159. DOI: 10.1016/j.dss.2014.06.010

Chatterjee, S., & Chaudhuri, R. (2023). Customer relationship management in the digital era of artificial intelligence. In S.S. Kamble, R.S. Mor, A. Belhadi (Eds.), *Digital Transformation and Industry 4.0 for Sustainable Supply Chain Performance* (pp. 175–190). *EAI/Springer Innovations in Communication and Computing*, Springer. https://doi.org/DOI: 10.1007/978-3-031-19711-6_8

Chatterjee, A., Prinz, A., Gerdes, M., & Martinez, S. (2021). Digital interventions on healthy lifestyle management: Systematic review. *Journal of Medical Internet Research*, *23*(11), 1–14. DOI: 10.2196/26931 PMID: 34787575

Chatterjee, S., & Chaudhuri, R. (2022). Adoption of Artificial Intelligence Integrated Customer Relationship Management in Organizations for Sustainability. In Vrontis, D., Thrassou, A., Weber, Y., Shams, S. M. R., Tsoukatos, E., & Efthymiou, L. (Eds.), *Business under Crisis* (Vol. III, pp. 137–156). Palgrave Studies in Cross-disciplinary Business Research. Palgrave Macmillan., DOI: 10.1007/978-3-030-76583-5_6

Chávez, E. M., Kossioni, A., & Fukai, K. (2022). Policies supporting oral health in ageing populations are needed worldwide. *International Dental Journal*, *72*(4, 4S), S27–S38. DOI: 10.1016/j.identj.2022.06.014 PMID: 36031323

Chen, Q., Gong, Y., Lu, Y., & Luo, X. (2025). The golden zone of AI's emotional expression in frontline chatbot service failures. *Internet Research*, *35*(3), 1065–1103. DOI: 10.1108/INTR-07-2023-0551

Choi, H.-K., Kim, S.-S., & Kim, B.-S. (2023). Perceived justice and customer loyalty in the situation of beauty service failure. *SAGE Open*, *13*(4), 1–14. DOI: 10.1177/21582440231217729

Choi, Y., Jeon, Y.-M., Wang, L., & Kim, K. (2017). A biological signal-based stress monitoring framework for children using wearable devices. *Sensors (Basel)*, *17*(9), 1936. DOI: 10.3390/s17091936 PMID: 28832507

Chong, J. L., Lim, K. K., & Matchar, D. B. (2019). Population segmentation based on healthcare needs: A systematic review. *Systematic Reviews*, *8*(1), 202. DOI: 10.1186/s13643-019-1105-6 PMID: 31409423

Chong, J. L., Low, L. L., Matchar, D. B., Malhotra, R., Lee, K. H., Thumboo, J., & Chan, A. W. M. (2020). Do healthcare needs-based population segments predict outcomes among the elderly? Findings from a prospective cohort study in an urbanized low-income community. *BMC Geriatrics*, *20*(1), 78. DOI: 10.1186/s12877-020-1480-9 PMID: 32103728

Choonhawarakorn, K., Kasemkhun, P., & Leelataweewud, P. (2025). Effectiveness of a message service on child oral health practice via a social media application: A randomized controlled trial. *International Journal of Paediatric Dentistry*, *35*(2), 446–455. DOI: 10.1111/ipd.13256 PMID: 39104027

Coltman, T., Devinney, T. M., & Midgley, D. F. (2011). Customer relationship management and firm performance. *Journal of Information Technology*, *26*(3), 205–219. DOI: 10.1057/jit.2010.39

Conduah, A. K., Ofoe, S., & Siaw-Marfo, D. (2025). Data privacy in healthcare: Global challenges and solutions. *Digital Health*, *11*, 20552076251343959. DOI: 10.1177/20552076251343959 PMID: 40475296

D'Aiuto, F., Suvan, J., Siripaiboonpong, N., Gatzoulis, M. A., & D'Aiuto, F. (2025). The root of the matter: Linking oral health to chronic diseases prevention. *International Journal of Cardiology. Congenital Heart Disease*, *19*(100574), 100574. DOI: 10.1016/j.ijcchd.2025.100574 PMID: 40066344

da Mata, C., & Allen, P. F. (2023). Providing Oral Healthcare to Older Patients—Do We Have What It Takes? *International Journal of Environmental Research and Public Health*, *20*(13), 6234. DOI: 10.3390/ijerph20136234 PMID: 37444082

Da Silva Mulder, J., Pinto, M., Aníbal, I., Dornellas, A., Garrido, D., Huanca, C., Haddad, A., & Abdala, C. (2024). Teledentistry Applied to Health and Education Outcomes: Evidence Gap Map. *Journal of Medical Internet Research*, *26*, e60590. Advance online publication. DOI: 10.2196/60590 PMID: 39602783

Damen, D. J., Schoonman, G. G., Maat, B., Habibović, M., Krahmer, E., & Pauws, S. (2022). Patients managing their medical data in personal electronic health records: Scoping review. *Journal of Medical Internet Research, 24*(12), e37783. DOI: 10.2196/37783 PMID: 36574275

Daniels, J., Haber, N., Voss, C., Schwartz, J., Tamura, S., Fazel, A., & Winograd, T. (2018). Feasibility testing of a wearable behavioral aid for social learning in children with autism. *Applied Clinical Informatics, 9*(1), 129–140. DOI: 10.1055/s-0038-1626727 PMID: 29466819

Dar, H., & Kashyap, K. (2025). Structural equation modeling (SEM) approach for envisaging the connotation among medical tourists' satisfaction, attitude and loyalty: A case of Delhi-NCR, India. *International Journal of Spa and Wellness, 8*(2), 246–264. DOI: 10.1080/24721735.2025.2455867

Das, S., & Hassan, H. K. (2022). Impact of sustainable supply chain management and customer relationship management on organizational performance. *International Journal of Productivity and Performance Management, 71*(6), 2140–2160. DOI: 10.1108/IJPPM-08-2020-0441

Davari, L. D., Morris, M., & Allison, P. J. (2025). Policy options to complement the new Canadian dental program enabling high quality care for people with disabilities and older adults. *Gerodontology, 42*(3), 307–320. DOI: 10.1111/ger.12813 PMID: 40163434

de Ahumada Servant, P., Martín-Martín, D., & Romero, I. (2025). Digital transformation of oral health care: Measuring the digitalization of dental clinics. *Social Indicators Research, 178*(3), 1145–1167. DOI: 10.1007/s11205-024-03366-z

de la Hoz-Correa, A., & Muñoz-Leiva, F. (2019). The role of information sources and image on the intention to visit a medical tourism destination: A cross-cultural analysis. *Journal of Travel & Tourism Marketing, 36*(2), 204–219. DOI: 10.1080/10548408.2018.1507865

de Oliveira Collet, G., de Morais Ferreira, F., Ceron, D. F., de Lourdes Calvo Fracasso, M., & Santin, G. C. (2024). Influence of digital health literacy on online health-related behaviors influenced by internet advertising. *BMC Public Health, 24*(1), 1949. DOI: 10.1186/s12889-024-19506-6 PMID: 39033160

de Oliveira Júnior, A. J., Oliveira, J. M., Bretz, Y. P., & Mialhe, F. L. (2023). Online social networks for prevention and promotion of oral health: A systematic review. *Canadian Journal of Dental Hygiene : CJDH = Journal Canadien de l'Hygiène Dentaire : JCHD, 57*(2), 83. PMID: 37464997

Değirmencioğlu, E., & Kılıçoğlu, H. (2024). Evaluating the impact of social media marketing from the perspective of orthodontists. *BMC Oral Health, 24*(1), 779. DOI: 10.1186/s12903-024-04558-2 PMID: 38992712

Deniz-Garcia, A., Fabelo, H., Rodriguez-Almeida, A. J., Zamora-Zamorano, G., Castro-Fernandez, M., Alberiche Ruano, M. P., Solvoll, T., Granja, C., Schopf, T. R., Callico, G. M., Soguero-Ruiz, C., & Wägner, A. M. (2023). Quality, usability, and effectiveness of mHealth apps and the role of artificial intelligence: Current scenario and challenges. *Journal of Medical Internet Research, 25*, 1–17. DOI: 10.2196/44030 PMID: 37140973

Dettori, M., & Castiglia, P. (2022). COVID-19 and Digital Health: Evolution, Perspectives and Opportunities. *International Journal of Environmental Research and Public Health, 19*(14), 8519. DOI: 10.3390/ijerph19148519 PMID: 35886366

Deutsch, A., & Jay, E. (2021). Optimising oral health in frail older people. *Australian Prescriber, 44*(5), 153–160. DOI: 10.18773/austprescr.2021.037 PMID: 34728880

Devkota, H. P. (2024). Healthcare communication in the age of social media and digital health technologies. *Japanese Journal of Pharmaceutical Education, 8*. Advance online publication. DOI: 10.24489/jjphe.2024-055

Dickie de Castillos, E., & Rodriguez-Junior, S. A. (2023). Scientific production on Gerodontology as a dental specialty-Bibliometric literature review. *FisiSenectus, 11*(1), 11–22. DOI: 10.22298/rfs.2023.v11.n1.7593

Dickinson, R., Vahia, I., Singh, A., Gupta, S., Alkhatib, F., Handa, I., & Sekhon, H. (2024). Exploring digital ageism: A systematic literature review on social media and aging. *The American Journal of Geriatric Psychiatry : Official Journal of the American Association for Geriatric Psychiatry, 32*(4), S130–S131. DOI: 10.1016/j.jagp.2024.01.220

Digital Global Overview. (2024). The state of social media: Algorithmic trends and engagement. *We Are Social & Meltwater*. https://datareportal.com/reports/digital-2024-global-overview-report

Ding, H., Zhang, M., Lo, B., Chan, K. K. F., Lo, E. C. M., & Tsoi, J. K. H. (2023). A Personalised 3D-Printed Dental Plaque Removal Mouthguard for Older Adults. *International Dental Journal, 73*(6), 828–833. DOI: 10.1016/j.identj.2023.04.005 PMID: 37202299

Douma, M. C., Rejeb, M. B., Zardoub, N., Braham, A., Chouchene, H., Boualleg-ue, O., & Latiri, H. S. (2024). Impact of implementing electronic nursing records on quality and safety indicators in care. *The Libyan Journal of Medicine*, *19*(1), 2421625. DOI: 10.1080/19932820.2024.2421625 PMID: 39570988

Drafta, S., Macris, A., & Petre, A. (2025). Innovations on the horizon: Teledentistry, artificial intelligence, and hybrid models to improve oral health for vulnerable communities. *Frontiers in Oral Health*, *6*, 1649715. Advance online publication. DOI: 10.3389/froh.2025.1649715 PMID: 40860795

Drossos, D., Coursaris, C., & Kagiouli, E. (2024). Social media marketing content strategy: A comprehensive framework and empirically supported guidelines for brand posts on Facebook pages. *Journal of Consumer Behaviour*, *23*(3), 1175–1192. DOI: 10.1002/cb.2269

Dubovitskaya, A., Baig, F., Xu, Z., Shukla, R., Zambani, P. S., Swaminathan, A., Jahangir, M. M., Chowdhry, K., Lachhani, R., Idnani, N., Schumacher, M., Aberer, K., Stoller, S. D., Ryu, S., & Wang, F. (2020). ACTION-EHR: Patient-centric blockchain-based electronic health record data management for cancer care. *Journal of Medical Internet Research*, *22*(8), e13598. DOI: 10.2196/13598 PMID: 32821064

Dwivedi, Y. K., Ismagilova, E., Hughes, D. L., Carlson, J., Filieri, R., Jacobson, J., Jain, V., Karjaluoto, H., Kefi, H., Krishen, A. S., Kumar, V., Rahman, M. M., Raman, R., Rauschnabel, P. A., Rowley, J., Salo, J., Tran, G. A., & Wang, Y. (2021). Setting the future of digital and social media marketing research: Perspectives and research propositions. *International Journal of Information Management*, *59*, 1–37. DOI: 10.1016/j.ijinfomgt.2020.102168

Elmessiry, A., Cooper, W. O., Catron, T. F., Karrass, J., Zhang, Z., & Singh, M. P. (2017). Triaging patient complaints: Monte Carlo cross-validation of six machine learning classifiers. *JMIR Medical Informatics*, *5*(3), e19. DOI: 10.2196/medinform.7140 PMID: 28760726

Emami, E., Harnagea, H., Shrivastava, R., Ahmadi, M., & Giraudeau, N. (2022). Patient satisfaction with e-oral health care in rural and remote settings: A systematic review. *Systematic Reviews*, *11*(1), 234. Advance online publication. DOI: 10.1186/s13643-022-02103-2 PMID: 36309732

Emmanuel, A. K., Obasi, D. E., Gbadebo, A. J., Omolara, A. B., Emuobor, R. O., Oboite, D. U., Omoijate, A., & Karanji, C. (2024b). Impact of ageism on the social wellbeing of older adults: Evidence from a geriatric home in Lagos, Nigeria. *International Journal of Engineering and Management Research*, *14*(6), 46–54. DOI: 10.31033/ijemr.14.6.46-54

Emmesjö, L., Hallgren, J., & Gillsjö, C. (2025). Older adults' digital technology experiences: A qualitative study. *BMC Digital Health, 3*(1), 24. Advance online publication. DOI: 10.1186/s44247-025-00163-7

Ernst, H., Hoyer, W. D., Krafft, M., & Krieger, K. (2011). Customer relationship management and company performance—The mediating role of new product performance. *Journal of the Academy of Marketing Science, 39*(2), 290–306. DOI: 10.1007/s11747-010-0194-5

Esperança, M., Freitas, D., Paixão, P. V., Marcos, T. A., Martins, R. A., & Ferreira, J. C. (2025). Proactive complaint management in public sector informatics using AI: A semantic pattern recognition framework. *Applied Sciences (Basel, Switzerland), 15*(12), 6673. DOI: 10.3390/app15126673

Etemad-Sajadi, R., & Bohrer, L. (2019). The impact of service recovery output/process on customer satisfaction and loyalty: The case of the airline industry. *Tourism and Hospitality Research, 19*(2), 259–266. DOI: 10.1177/1467358417743080

Fan, Y., Wu, L. Z., Lyu, Y., & Kwan, H. K. (2025). Don't expect robots to be creative: Why and when organizational dehumanization is a creativity killer. *International Journal of Hospitality Management, 130*, 104229. DOI: 10.1016/j.ijhm.2025.104229

Farrokhi, F., Ghorbani, Z., Farrokhi, F., Namdari, M., & Salavatian, S. (2023). Social media as a tool for oral health promotion: A systematic review. *PLoS One, 18*(12), e0296102. DOI: 10.1371/journal.pone.0296102 PMID: 38113216

Farrukh, M., Shahzad, I. A., Sajid, M., Sheikh, M. F., & Alam, I. (2022). Revisiting the intention to travel framework in the perspective of medical tourism: The role of eWord-of-mouth and destination image. *International Journal of Healthcare Management, 15*(1), 28–35. DOI: 10.1080/20479700.2020.1836733

Farzad, M., Allahi, M. N., Hashemi, N., Mohammadi, M., & Zadeh, N. A. (2026). Influence of social media on the oral health-related quality of life and cognitive function in elderly individuals: A cross-sectional study. *Journal of Education and Health Promotion, 15*(1), 34. DOI: 10.4103/jehp.jehp_1336_24 PMID: 41788952

Fengmin, Z., Baijun, W., Jiangtao, B., Li, L., & Patwary, A. K. (2022). Investigating revisit intention of medical tourists in China through nutritional knowledge, perceived medical quality, and trust in the physiologist: A recommendation on health tourism policy measures. *Frontiers in Public Health, 10*, 893497. DOI: 10.3389/fpubh.2022.893497

Fernandes Prabhu, D., Gurupur, V., Stone, A., & Trader, E. (2025). Integrating artificial intelligence, electronic health records, and wearables for predictive, patient-centered decision support in healthcare. *Health Care, 13*(21), 2753. DOI: 10.3390/healthcare13212753 PMID: 41228120

Fernández, C., Maturana, C., Coloma, S. A. C., & Giacaman, R. (2021). Teledentistry and mHealth for Promotion and Prevention of Oral Health: A Systematic Review and Meta-analysis. *Journal of Dental Research, 100*(9), 914–927. DOI: 10.1177/00220345211003828 PMID: 33769123

Fierro, J. C., Polo, I. M., & Oliván, F. J. S. (2014). From Dissatisfied Customers to Evangelists of the Firm: A Study of the Spanish Mobile Service Sector. *Business Research Quarterly, 17*(3), 191–204. DOI: 10.1016/j.cede.2013.10.001

Flor, A., Ferreira, M. R., Oliveira, Ó., & Pereira, O. (2025). Cultivating continuing learning and active aging through digital literacy: A digital and social approach. Tec empresarial, 19(3), 98–119. DOI: 10.18845/te.v19i3.8137

Florida Dental Association. (2023). AI-driven content strategies for the modern practice. *FDI World Dental Press*. https://www.fdiworlddental.org/fdi-annual-report-2023

Folorunsho, S., Ajayi, V., Sanmori, M., Suleiman, M., Abdullateef, R., & Abdulganiyu, A. (2025). Access to and utilization of dental care services by older adults in Nigeria: Barriers and facilitators. *Special Care in Dentistry : Official Publication of the American Association of Hospital Dentists, the Academy of Dentistry for the Handicapped, and the American Society for Geriatric Dentistry, 45*(3), e70040. DOI: 10.1111/scd.70040 PMID: 40326488

Franssen, W. M. A., Franssen, G. H. L. M., Spaas, J., Solmi, F., & Eijnde, B. O. (2020). Can consumer wearable activity tracker-based interventions improve physical activity and cardiometabolic health in patients with chronic diseases? A systematic review and meta-analysis of randomised controlled trials. *The International Journal of Behavioral Nutrition and Physical Activity, 17*(1), 57. DOI: 10.1186/s12966-020-00955-2 PMID: 32393357

Fraticelli, L., Smentek, C., Tardivo, D., Masson, J., Clément, C., Roy, S., Dussart, C., Bourgeois, D., & Carrouel, F. (2021). Characterizing the content related to oral health education on TikTok. *International Journal of Environmental Research and Public Health, 18*(24), 13260. DOI: 10.3390/ijerph182413260 PMID: 34948869

Freire, Y., Sánchez, M. G., Suárez, A., Joves, G., Nowak, M., & Díaz-Flores García, V. (2023). Influence of the use of social media on patients changing dental practice: A web-based questionnaire study. *BMC Oral Health, 23*(1), 365. DOI: 10.1186/s12903-023-03078-9 PMID: 37277765

Fung, C. K. C., Ha, D. H., Walsh, L. J., & Lopez Silva, C. P. (2024). A Pilot Study to Assess the Feasibility of Real-Time Teledentistry in Residential Aged Care Facilities. *Health Care, 12*(22), 2216. DOI: 10.3390/healthcare12222216 PMID: 39595415

Furman, E., Diamant, A., & Kristal, M. (2021). Customer acquisition and retention: A fluid approach for staffing. *Production and Operations Management, 30*(11), 4236–4257. DOI: 10.1111/poms.13520

Gaffar, B., Farooqi, F. A., Nazir, M. A., Bakhurji, E., Al-Khalifa, K. S., Alhareky, M., & Virtanen, J. I. (2022). Oral health-related interdisciplinary practices among healthcare professionals in Saudi Arabia: Does integrated care exist? *BMC Oral Health, 22*(1), 75. DOI: 10.1186/s12903-022-02113-5 PMID: 35300658

Gan, T., Zheng, J., Li, W., Li, J., & Shen, J. (2023). Health and wellness tourists' motivation and behavior intention: The role of perceived value. *International Journal of Environmental Research and Public Health, 20*(5), 4339. DOI: 10.3390/ijerph20054339

Garg, V., Kumar, H., Bansal, R., & Bhardwaj, A. (2025). Envisioning Digital Health Technology Innovations for 2025: Enhancing Digital Interventions in the Post-COVID-19 Era. In *Innovations in Healthcare Technologies in India: An Initiative of ICMR-CIBioD (Centre for Innovation and Bio-Design)* (pp. 1-17). Singapore: Springer Nature Singapore. https://doi.org/DOI: 10.1007/978-981-97-0244-2_1

Gelibolu, M., & Mouloudj, K. (2025). Motivators and demotivators of consumers' smart voice assistant usage for online shopping. *Journal of Theoretical and Applied Electronic Commerce Research, 20*(3), 152. DOI: 10.3390/jtaer20030152

Ghalavand, H., Panahi, S., & Nouri, M. (2025). Opportunities and challenges of social media for oral health literacy improvement: A qualitative investigation based on Iranian dentists' perspectives. *BMC Health Services Research, 25*(1), 673. DOI: 10.1186/s12913-025-12845-z PMID: 40346510

Ghezzi, E. M., Niessen, L. C., & Jones, J. A. (2023). Innovations in Geriatric Oral Health Care. *Clinics in Geriatric Medicine, 39*(2), 343–357. DOI: 10.1016/j.cger.2023.01.005 PMID: 37045537

Ghorbanian- Zolbin, M., Kujala, S., Widén, G., Eriksson-Backa, K., & Huvila, I. (2025). Digital inclusion among older adults: Identifying potential solutions. Human Technology An Interdisciplinary. *Journal On Humans In ICT Environments*, 21(1), 51–72. DOI: 10.14254/1795-6889.2025.21-1.3

Gianfredi, V., Nucci, D., Pennisi, F., Veronesse, N., & Soysal, P. (2025). Aging, longevity, and healthy aging: The public health approach. *Aging Clinical and Experimental Research, 37*(1), 125. DOI: 10.1007/s40520-025-03021-8 PMID: 40244306

Gibbons, J. B., Hermosilla, M., & Trujillo, A. (2025). On the motivation for pharmaceutical manufacturer coupons: Brand loyalty or customer acquisition? *Health Services Research, 60*(2), e14379. DOI: 10.1111/1475-6773.14379 PMID: 39219365

Gip, H., Guchait, P., Paşamehmetoğlu, A., & Khoa, D. T. (2023). How organizational dehumanization impacts hospitality employees service recovery performance and sabotage behaviors: The role of psychological well-being and tenure. *International Journal of Contemporary Hospitality Management, 35*(1), 64–91. DOI: 10.1108/IJCHM-02-2022-0155

Glanz, K., & Bishop, D. B. (2010). The role of behavioral science theory in development and implementation of public health interventions. *Annual Review of Public Health, 31*(1), 399–418. DOI: 10.1146/annurev.publhealth.012809.103604 PMID: 20070207

Glick, M., Williams, D. M., Kleinman, D. V., Vujicic, M., Watt, R. G., & Weyant, R. J. (2017). A new definition for oral health developed by the FDI World Dental Federation opens the door to a universal definition of oral health. *American Journal of Orthodontics and Dentofacial Orthopedics, 151*(2), 229–231. DOI: 10.1016/j.ajodo.2016.11.010 PMID: 28153139

Goldberg, E., Eberhard, J., Bauman, A., & Smith, B. J. (2022). Mass media campaigns for the promotion of oral health: A scoping review. *BMC Oral Health, 22*(1), 182. DOI: 10.1186/s12903-022-02212-3 PMID: 35568896

Golossenko, A., Palumbo, H., Mathai, M., & Tran, H. A. (2023). Am I being dehumanized? Development and validation of the experience of dehumanization measurement. *The British Journal of Social Psychology, 62*(3), 1285–1329. DOI: 10.1111/bjso.12633 PMID: 36861855

Gryglewska, B., Perera, I., Klimek, E., Fedyk-Łukasik, M., Piotrowicz, K., Mocanu, I., Muntianu, L., & Gąsowski, J. (2022). Teledentistry and oral health in older adults - aspects for implementation of the "Patient centric solution for smart and sustainable healthcare *(ACESO)" project. Folia Medica Cracoviensia, 62*(2), 5–16. DOI: 10.24425/fmc.2022.141697 PMID: 36256891

Gu, D., Guo, J., Liang, C., Lu, W., Zhao, S., Liu, B., & Long, T. (2019). Social media-based health management systems and sustained health engagement: TPB perspective. *International Journal of Environmental Research and Public Health, 16*(9), 1495. DOI: 10.3390/ijerph16091495 PMID: 31035585

Gušić, I., Stojilković, M., Alija, S., Prodanović, D., Mirnić, J., & Veljović, T. (2024). The impact of social media on the selection of dentists based on their social media presence among residents of Vojvodina, Serbia: A cross-sectional study. *BMC Public Health*, *24*(1), 3348. DOI: 10.1186/s12889-024-20884-0 PMID: 39616357

Győrffy, Z., Boros, J., Döbrössy, B., & Girasek, E. (2023). Older adults in the digital health era: Insights on the digital health related knowledge, habits and attitudes of the 65 year and older population. *BMC Geriatrics*, *23*(1), 779. DOI: 10.1186/s12877-023-04437-5 PMID: 38012565

Habibi, A., & Rasoolimanesh, S. M. (2021). Experience and service quality on perceived value and behavioral intention: Moderating effect of perceived risk and fee. *Journal of Quality Assurance in Hospitality & Tourism*, *22*(6), 711–737. DOI: 10.1080/1528008X.2020.1837050

Haislip, J. Z., & Richardson, V. J. (2017). The effect of customer relationship management systems on firm performance. *International Journal of Accounting Information Systems*, *27*, 16–29. DOI: 10.1016/j.accinf.2017.09.003

Han, H., & Hwang, J. (2018). Growing competition in the healthcare tourism market and customer retention in medical clinics: New and experienced travellers. *Current Issues in Tourism*, *21*(6), 680–702. DOI: 10.1080/13683500.2015.1104292

Han, H., & Hyun, S. S. (2015). Customer retention in the medical tourism industry: Impact of quality, satisfaction, trust, and price reasonableness. *Tourism Management*, *46*, 20–29. DOI: 10.1016/j.tourman.2014.06.003

Hapsari, A., & Asaari, A. (2025). *The Role of Personalized Marketing and Service Quality in Enhancing Patient Engagement in Health Care. JKBM*. JURNAL KONSEP BISNIS DAN MANAJEMEN., DOI: 10.31289/jkbm.v11i2.14678

Hartshorn, J. E., & Nair, R. U. (2023). Dental innovations which will influence the oral health care of baby boomers. *Special Care in Dentistry : Official Publication of the American Association of Hospital Dentists, the Academy of Dentistry for the Handicapped, and the American Society for Geriatric Dentistry*, *43*(3), 359–369. DOI: 10.1111/scd.12835 PMID: 36782274

Hat, N. D., Tan, K. L., Ngoc Vi, N. L., Phu, N. A., & Ting, H. (2025). The influence of customer relationship management in enhancing hospitality business performance: The conditional mediation of digital marketing capabilities. *International Journal of Hospitality & Tourism Administration*, *26*(3), 520–546. DOI: 10.1080/15256480.2024.2346142

Heikal, M. M. A., Nabi, N. A., & Elkerdawy, M. W. (2022). A study comparing patient satisfaction and retention of CAD/CAM milled complete dentures and 3D printed CAD/CAM complete dentures versus conventional complete dentures: A randomized clinical trial. *Brazilian Dental Science*, *25*(1), e2785. DOI: 10.4322/bds.2022.e2785

Heileman, M. D., Kodzi, E. T.Jr, & Pett, T. L. (2026). The choice of customer relationship management approach in the supply chain: Examining small business performance. *Vision: The Journal of Business Perspective*, *30*(2), 213–228. DOI: 10.1177/09722629221092091

Hennig-Thurau, T., Gwinner, K. P., Walsh, G., & Gremler, D. D. (2004). Electronic word of-mouth via consumer-opinion platforms: What motivates consumers to articulate themselves on the Internet? *Journal of Interactive Marketing*, *18*(1), 38–52. DOI: 10.1002/dir.10073

Higgins, J. P., Thomas, J., Chandler, J., Cumpston, M., Li, T., Page, M. J., & Welch, V. A. (Eds.). (2021). *Cochrane Handbook for Systematic Reviews of Interventions* (2nd ed.). John Wiley & Sons.

Hirmas-Adauy, M., Castillo-Laborde, C., Awad, C., Jasmen, A., Mattoli, M., Molina, X., Olea, A., Matute, I., Soto, F., Rubilar, P., Urrejola, O., Alfaro, T., Abusleme Lama, M. T., & Esnouf, S. (2024). Navigating Through Innovation in Elderly's Health: A Scoping Review of Digital Health Interventions. *Public Health Review*, *45*, 1607756. DOI: 10.3389/phrs.2024.1607756 PMID: 39749218

Holden, A. C. (2019). Dentistry and oral health in online media sources: A discourse analysis. *Community Dental Health*, *36*(3), 221–228. DOI: 10.1922/CDH_4623Holden08 PMID: 31468748

Hollebeek, L. D., & Macky, K. (2019). Digital content marketing's role in fostering consumer engagement, trust, and value: Framework, fundamental propositions, and implications. *Journal of Interactive Marketing*, *45*(1), 27–41. DOI: 10.1016/j.intmar.2018.07.003

Holtrop, J. S., Estabrooks, P. A., Gaglio, B., Harden, S. M., Kessler, R. S., King, D. K., Kwan, B. M., Ory, M. G., Rabin, B. A., Shelton, R. C., & Glasgow, R. E. (2021). Understanding and applying the RE-AIM framework: Clarifications and resources. *Journal of Clinical and Translational Science*, *5*(1), e126. DOI: 10.1017/cts.2021.789 PMID: 34367671

Homburg, C., Fürst, A., & Koschate, N. (2010). On the importance of complaint handling design: A multi-level analysis of the impact in specific complaint situations. *Journal of the Academy of Marketing Science*, *38*(3), 265–287. DOI: 10.1007/s11747-009-0172-y

Horsfall, D., Lunt, N., King, H., Hanefeld, J., & Smith, R. D. (2013). The Impact of the Internet on Medical Tourism. In Botterill, D., Pennings, G., & Mainil, T. (Eds.), *Medical Tourism and Transnational Health Care* (pp. 223–239). Palgrave Macmillan., DOI: 10.1057/9781137338495_14

Huang, Y., Leng, X., & Tian, Z. (2026). Predatory marketing and false health promotion on social media: Risk pathways in diet, fitness, and supplement communication. *Frontiers in Public Health*, *14*, 1709812. DOI: 10.3389/fpubh.2026.1709812 PMID: 41810286

Huenchuan, S. (Ed.). (2018). Envejecimiento, personas mayores y Agenda 2030 para el Desarrollo Sostenible: perspectiva regional y de derechos humanos, Libros de la CEPAL, No 154 (LC/PUB.2018/24-P), Santiago: Comisión Económica para América Latina y el Caribe (CEPAL); 2018. https://repositorio.cepal.org/handle/11362/44369 (accessed on 16 March 2026).[REMOVED HYPERLINK FIELD]

Hui, J. C. Y., Hu, L. L., Chan, A. K. Y., & Chu, C. H. (2026). Interdisciplinary Strategies for Improving Oral Health in Older Adults: A Comprehensive Review. *Geriatrics (Basel, Switzerland)*, *11*(1), 22. DOI: 10.3390/geriatrics11010022 PMID: 41744900

Hur, W. M., Chung, J., & Park, H. (2025). Beyond Hallyu celebrity appeal: Understanding celebrity attractiveness and content creativity as strategic marketing resources in Taiwan. *Asia Pacific Business Review*, •••, 1–26. DOI: 10.1080/13602381.2025.2512815

Hyde, S., Dupuis, V., Mariri, B. P., & Dartevelle, S. (2017). Prevention of tooth loss and dental pain for reducing the global burden of oral diseases. *International Dental Journal*, *67*, 19–25. DOI: 10.1111/idj.12328 PMID: 29023745

Ingle, N. A., Al-Hashimi, H., Alhammad, A. T., Aldajani, H. A., Alabsi, N. F., & Albuolayan, N. A. (2025). Impact of 3D printing and CAD/CAM technology on orthodontic treatment outcomes: A systematic review and meta-analysis. *Journal of Pharmacy & Bioallied Sciences*, *17*(Suppl 1), S226–S228. DOI: 10.4103/jpbs.jpbs_639_25 PMID: 40510977

International Dental Federation (FDI). (2023). Digital promotion of oral health: Best practices for social media. *FDI World Dental Press*. https://www.fdiworlddental.org/fdi-annual-report-2023

International Telecommunication Union. (2024). Facts and Figures 2024: Internet use. ITU. https://www.itu.int/itu-d/reports/statistics/facts-figures-2024/

Iribarren, S. J., Akande, T. O., Kamp, K. J., Barry, D., Kader, Y. G., & Suelzer, E. (2021). Effectiveness of mobile apps to promote health and manage disease: Systematic review and meta-analysis of randomized controlled trials. *JMIR mHealth and uHealth*, *9*(1), e21563. DOI: 10.2196/21563 PMID: 33427672

Istanbulluoglu, D., & Sakman, E. (2024). Successful complaint handling on social media predicts increased repurchase intention: The roles of trust in company and propensity to trust. *European Management Journal*, *42*(1), 11–22. DOI: 10.1016/j.emj.2022.06.004

Jalilvand, M. R., & Heidari, A. (2017). Comparing face-to-face and electronic word-of-mouth in destination image formation: The case of Iran. *Information Technology & People*, *30*(4), 710–735. DOI: 10.1108/ITP-09-2016-0204

James, J. (2021). Confronting the scarcity of digital skills among the poor in developing countries. *Development Policy Review*, *39*(2), 324–339. DOI: 10.1111/dpr.12479

Janto, M., Iurcov, R., Daina, C. M., Neculoiu, D. C., Venter, A. C., Badau, D., Cotovanu, A., Negrau, M., Suteu, C. L., Sabau, M., & Daina, L. G. (2022). Oral Health among Elderly, Impact on Life Quality, Access of Elderly Patients to Oral Health Services and Methods to Improve Oral Health: A Narrative Review. *Journal of Personalized Medicine*, *12*(3), 372. DOI: 10.3390/jpm12030372 PMID: 35330372

Jasim, Z. A., Alameri, S. A., Almado, A. A., Abdulrahman, F. Y., & Alyousuf, A. N. (2026). Investigating the Impact of Ethical Organizational Culture on Employee Retention. In Rodrigues, R., Mohanty, V., & Figueiredo, P. (Eds.), *Organizational Culture and Employee Experience in the AI-Driven Organization* (pp. 85–110). IGI Global., DOI: 10.4018/979-8-2600-0610-8.ch004

Javadi, S. K. H. S., Jamieson, L., Nouri, A., Sohn, W., & Rudman, A. (2025, December 10). (2025). Exploring Digital Health Technologies for Enhancing Oral Health: A Scoping Review of Interventions for Older Adults. *Gerodontology*, ger.70033. Advance online publication. DOI: 10.1111/ger.70033 PMID: 41368693

Jayachandran, S., Sharma, S., Kaufman, P., & Raman, P. (2005). The role of relational information processes and technology use in customer relationship management. *Journal of Marketing*, *69*(4), 177–192. DOI: 10.1509/jmkg.2005.69.4.177

Jayapal, J. (2025). Unveiling the impact of AI-driven personalization on customer loyalty in online shopping: The moderating effects of privacy concerns. *Journal of Promotion Management*, *31*(5), 865–894. DOI: 10.1080/10496491.2025.2525099

Jayasinghe, Y. A., Kanmodi, K. K., Jayasinghe, R. M., & Jayasinghe, R. D. (2024). Assessment of patterns and related factors in using social media platforms to access health and oral health information among Sri Lankan adults, with special emphasis on promoting oral health awareness. *BMC Public Health*, *24*(1), 1472. DOI: 10.1186/s12889-024-19008-5 PMID: 38824505

Jiang, C. M., Chu, C. H., Duangthip, D., Ettinger, R. L., Hugo, F. N., Kettratad-Pruksapong, M., Liu, J., Marchini, L., McKenna, G., Ono, T., Rong, W., Schimmel, M., Shah, N., Slack-Smith, L., Yang, S. X., & Lo, E. C. M. (2021). Global Perspectives of Oral Health Policies and Oral Healthcare Schemes for Older Adult Populations. *Frontiers in Oral Health*, *2*, 703526. DOI: 10.3389/froh.2021.703526 PMID: 35048040

Jiménez-Herrero, F. (1998). Gerodontología antaño, una disciplina descuidada: Revisión bibliográfica. *Revista Española de Geriatría y Gerontología*, *33*(91), 9148–9154.

Jiménez-Herrero, F. (2003). 25 años de la especialidad de Geriatría y Gerontología. *Revista Española de Geriatría y Gerontología*, *38*(6), 338–354. DOI: 10.1016/S0211-139X(03)74911-7

Jivraj, A., Barrow, J., & Listl, S. (2022). Value-based oral health care: Implementation lessons from four case studies. *The Journal of Evidence-Based Dental Practice*, *22*(1, Suppl), 101662. DOI: 10.1016/j.jebdp.2021.101662 PMID: 35063180

Jo, S.-R., Shin, B.-R., & Jang, J.-H. (2025). Multidisciplinary Professionals' Perceptions of Home-Visit Oral Care for Older Adults in Integrated Community Care: A Focus Group Interview Study. *Health Care*, *13*(18), 2365. DOI: 10.3390/healthcare13182365 PMID: 41008493

Jung, J., & Cho, I. (2022). Promoting physical activity and weight loss with mHealth interventions among workers: Systematic review and meta-analysis of randomized controlled trials. *JMIR mHealth and uHealth*, *10*(1), e30682. DOI: 10.2196/30682 PMID: 35060913

Jutai, J. W., Hatoum, F., Bhardwaj, D., & Hosseini, M. (2024). Implementation of digital health technologies for older adults: A scoping review. *Frontiers in Aging*, *5*, 1349520. DOI: 10.3389/fragi.2024.1349520 PMID: 38784681

Kallás, M. S., Guardeiro, B., Henrique, E. A., Silva, D. G., Takashi, D. A., & Marchini, L. (2024). Telehealth in geriatric dentistry: A comparative analysis of concordance between virtual and in-person examinations for hospitalized older patients. *Special Care in Dentistry : Official Publication of the American Association of Hospital Dentists, the Academy of Dentistry for the Handicapped, and the American Society for Geriatric Dentistry, 44*(6), 1680–1687. DOI: 10.1111/scd.13036 PMID: 38984414

Kamran, S., & Attiq, M. (2011). Value recovery with customer dissatisfaction: A study of restaurant services in Pakistan. *Tourism and Hospitality Research, 11*(3), 169–180. DOI: 10.1177/1467358411415088

Kamyabi, M., Özgit, H., & Ahmed, J. N. (2025). Sustaining digital marketing strategies to enhance customer engagement and brand promotion: Position as a moderator. *Sustainability (Basel), 17*(7), 3270. DOI: 10.3390/su17073270

Katusiime, J., Tumuhimbise, W., Rwambuka Mugyenyi, G., Kobutungi, P., Mugaba, A., Zender, R., Pinkwart, N., & Musiimenta, A. (2022). The role of mobile health technologies in promoting COVID-19 prevention: A narrative review of intervention effectiveness and adoption. *Digital Health, 8*, 1–12. DOI: 10.1177/20552076221131146 PMID: 36276182

Kaur, A., & Bala, R. (2024). Role of Big Data in Customer Acquisition and Retention. In Malik, R., Sharma, A., & Chaudhary, P. (Eds.), *Augmenting Customer Retention Through Big Data Analytics* (pp. 263–276). Apple Academic Press., DOI: 10.1201/9781003538486-16

Keeling, A., Downey, J., Halkes, M., & Wei, Y. (2025). The impact of patient-generated health data from mobile health technologies on health care management and clinical decision-making: Narrative scoping review. *Journal of Medical Internet Research, 27*, e77359. DOI: 10.2196/77359 PMID: 41417964

Kengne-Talla, P., Allison, P., Bussières, A., Rodrigues, A., Bergeron, F., Giraudeau, N., & Emami, E. (2025). Teledentistry for Improving Access To, and Quality of Oral Health Care: Overview of Systematic Reviews and Meta-Analyses. *Journal of Medical Internet Research, 27*, e65211. https://www.jmir.org/2025/1/e65211. DOI: 10.2196/65211 PMID: 40737673

Kepper, M. M., Fowler, L. A., Kusters, I. S., Davis, J. W., Baqer, M., Sagui-Henson, S., Xiao, Y., Tarfa, A., Yi, J. C., Gibson, B., Heron, K. E., Alberts, N. M., Burgermaster, M., Njie-Carr, V. P. S., & Klesges, L. M. (2024). Expanding a behavioral view on digital health access: Drivers and strategies to promote equity. *Journal of Medical Internet Research, 26*, e51355. DOI: 10.2196/51355 PMID: 39088246

Khan, M. I., Saleh, M. A., & Quazi, A. (2021, January). Social media adoption by health professionals: A TAM-based study. In *Informatics* (Vol. 8, No. 1, p. 6). MDPI. https://www.mdpi.com/2227-9709/8/1/6

Khandelwal, R., Kolte, A., & Rossi, M. (2022). A study on entrepreneurial opportunities in digital health-care post-Covid-19 from the perspective of developing countries. *foresight, 24*(3-4), 527-544. DOI: 10.1108/FS-02-2021-0043

Khan, P. A., Badole, P. J., & Shaikh, D. (2026). Telemedicine and digital health: The future for pharmaceutical companies and health care. *Indian Journal of Pharmacology*, *58*(1), 24–34. DOI: 10.4103/ijp.ijp_452_24 PMID: 41498661

Khan, R. U., Salamzadeh, Y., Iqbal, Q., & Yang, S. (2022). The Impact of customer relationship management and company reputation on customer loyalty: The mediating role of customer satisfaction. *Journal of Relationship Marketing*, *21*(1), 1–26. DOI: 10.1080/15332667.2020.1840904

Khattak, O., Hashem, A. S., Alqarni, M. S., Almufarrij, R. A. S., Siddiqui, A. Y., Anis, R., Ahmad, S., Fareed, M. A., Alothmani, O. S., Alkhershawy, L. H. S., Alabidin, W. W. Z., Issrani, R., & Agarwal, A. (2025). Deep Learning Applications in Dental Image-Based Diagnostics: A Systematic Review. *Health Care*, *13*(12), 1466. DOI: 10.3390/healthcare13121466 PMID: 40565492

Khatun, M., Hossain, R., Bhuiyan, M. R., Tabassum, M. N., & Riaj, M. A. (2025). Green Entrepreneurship and Digital Transformation for Sustainable Development: A Systematic Review. In Mouloudj, K., & Bouarar, A. (Eds.), *Digitizing Green Entrepreneurship* (pp. 153–180). IGI Global Scientific Publishing., DOI: 10.4018/979-8-3693-7442-9.ch006

Khoury, Z. H., Ferguson, A., Price, J. B., Sultan, A. S., & Wang, R. (2024). Responsible artificial intelligence for addressing equity in oral healthcare. *Frontiers in Oral Health*, *5*, 1408867. DOI: 10.3389/froh.2024.1408867 PMID: 39092200

Kim, H. Y., & McGill, A. L. (2025). AI-induced dehumanization. *Journal of Consumer Psychology*, *35*(3), 363–381. DOI: 10.1002/jcpy.1441

Kim, J. (2025). Healthcare Professionals' Perceptions and Experiences of Ageism: A Qualitative Study. *International Journal of Environmental Research and Public Health*, *22*(3), 350. DOI: 10.3390/ijerph22030350 PMID: 40238402

Kim, S., & Lee, S. (2026). Enhancing preventive health risk behaviors: The synergistic effect of anthropomorphism and benefit appeals on social media. *Communication Reports*, *39*(1), 1–19. DOI: 10.1080/08934215.2025.2472301

King, G. J., Chao, X., & Duenyas, I. (2016). Dynamic customer acquisition and retention management. *Production and Operations Management*, *25*(8), 1332–1343. DOI: 10.1111/poms.12559

Kitsaras, G., Gomez, J., Hogan, R., & Ryan, M. (2023). Evaluation of a digital oral health intervention (Know Your OQ™) to enhance knowledge, attitudes and practices related to oral health. *BDJ Open*, *9*(1), 40. DOI: 10.1038/s41405-023-00166-4 PMID: 37633985

Koh, A., Swanepoel, W., Ling, A., Ho, B. L., Tan, S. Y., & Lim, J. (2021). Digital health promotion: Promise and peril. *Health Promotion International*, *36*(Supplement_1), 70–80. DOI: 10.1093/heapro/daab134 PMID: 34897444

Koh, S. W. C., Wong, E. R. N., Tan, J. C. M., van der Lubbe, S. C., Goh, J. C., Ching, E. S. Y., Chia, I. W. Y., Low, S. H., Ang, P. Y., Quek, Q., Motani, M., & Valderas, J. M. (2025). Classifying patient complaints using artificial intelligence–powered large language models: Cross-sectional study. *Journal of Medical Internet Research*, *27*, e74231. DOI: 10.2196/74231 PMID: 40768757

Kok Wah, J. N. (2026). Empowering healthier decisions: The impact of consumer innovativeness on linking perceived benefits with protective health behaviors through digital marketing in the health-care sector. *International Journal of Pharmaceutical and Healthcare Marketing*, *20*(1), 18–44. DOI: 10.1108/IJPHM-07-2024-0073

Kopmaz, B., Kitapci, N. S., Kitapci, O. C., Bulu, S. B., Aksu, P. K., Koksal, L., & Mumcu, G. (2019). Dental websites as new media tools for patients in dental health tourism. *Acta Informatica Medica*, *27*(2), 128–132. DOI: 10.5455/aim.2019.27.128-132

Krishnan, V. (2025). Digital Opinion Leaders: The new age influencers! *Journal of the World Federation of Orthodontists*, *14*(3), 123–124. DOI: 10.1016/j.ejwf.2025.05.003 PMID: 40456597

Krishnaraju, V., Mathew, S. K., & Sugumaran, V. (2016). Web personalization for user acceptance of technology: An empirical investigation of E-government services. *Information Systems Frontiers*, *18*(3), 579–595. DOI: 10.1007/s10796-015-9550-9

Kulhánek, A., Lukavská, K., Gabrhelík, R., Burda, V., Holter, M., & Brendryen, H. (2022). Comparing Reminders Sent via SMS Text Messaging and Email for Improving Adherence to an Electronic Health Program: Randomized Controlled Trial. *JMIR mHealth and uHealth*, *10*(3), e31040. Advance online publication. DOI: 10.2196/31040 PMID: 35302945

Kumar, V., & Mirchandani, R. (2013). Increasing the ROI of social media marketing. *IEEE Engineering Management Review, 41*(3), 17–23. DOI: 10.1109/EMR.2013.6596535

Lal, M., & Kashyap, H. (2024). Consumer complaint satisfaction and customer retention: A study of complaint satisfaction in electronic industry. *Jindal Journal of Business Research, 13*(1), 82–99. DOI: 10.1177/22786821231183745

Lam, L., Ng, F., Fung, C., Poon, W., & Smith, G. D. (2026). Digital Health and Technology Adoption. In: Fong, B.Y.F. (Eds.), *The Handbook of Public Health in the Asia-Pacific* (pp. 1–13), *Handbooks in Asian Studies*, Springer. DOI: 10.1007/978-981-97-1788-0_6-1

Lau, M. H. M. (2023). Beyond Ageism: A Qualitative Study of Intersecting Forms of Prejudice towards Retired Older People. *Societies (Basel, Switzerland), 13*(1), 13. DOI: 10.3390/soc13010013

Lee, J. A., Choi, M., Lee, S. A., & Jiang, N. (2018). Effective behavioral intervention strategies using mobile health applications for chronic disease management: A systematic review. *BMC Medical Informatics and Decision Making, 18*(1), 12. DOI: 10.1186/s12911-018-0591-0 PMID: 29458358

Leelavathi, R., Philip, B., Madhusudhanan, R., Sony, N., & Mukthar, K. P. J. (2024). AI-Driven Customer Relationship Management (CRM): A Review of Implementation Strategies. In El Khoury, R. (Eds.), *Anticipating Future Business Trends: Navigating Artificial Intelligence Innovations* (pp. 283–295). Studies in Systems, Decision and Control, Vol. 536. Springer. https://doi.org/DOI: 10.1007/978-3-031-63402-4_22

León, S., Giacaman, R. A., Araya-Bustos, F., Venegas, S., Saavedra, N., Hugo, F. N., De Marchi, R. J., Muñoz, M.-F., Salazar, C., Castrejón-Pérez, R. C., Bustillos, L., Fortanete, A., de López, A. C., Aredes, J. E., Marín-Zuluaga, D., & Elias-Boneta, A. (2024). Current status of geriatric dentistry education in selected dental schools in Latin America and the Caribbean. *Gerodontology, 41*(3), 385–392. DOI: 10.1111/ger.12714 PMID: 37792411

Leung, K. C.-M., & Chu, C.-H. (2023). Dental Care for Older Adults. *International Journal of Environmental Research and Public Health, 20*(1), 214. DOI: 10.3390/ijerph20010214 PMID: 36612536

Lhoest-Snoeck, S., van Nierop, E., & Verhoef, P. C. (2014). For new customers only: A study on the effect of acquisition campaigns on a service company's existing customers' CLV. *Journal of Interactive Marketing, 28*(3), 210–224. DOI: 10.1016/j.intmar.2014.02.004

Li, D., Hu, Y., Pfaff, H., Wang, L., Deng, L., Lu, C., Xia, S., Cheng, S., Zhu, X., & Wu, X. (2020). Determinants of patients' intention to use the online inquiry services provided by internet hospitals: Empirical evidence from China. *Journal of Medical Internet Research, 22*(10), e22716. DOI: 10.2196/22716 PMID: 33006941

Lin, Z., Dai, H., Xiong, Y., Xia, X., & Horng, S. J. (2017, July). Quantification assessment of bradykinesia in Parkinson's disease based on a wearable device. *In 2017 39th annual international conference of the IEEE engineering in medicine and biology society (EMBC)* (pp. 803-806). IEEE. DOI: DOI: 10.1109/EMBC.2017.8036946

Lin, J., Bates, S. M., Allen, L. N., Wright, M., Mao, L., & Kidd, M. (2025). Integrating mobile health app data into electronic medical or health record systems and its impact on health care delivery and patient health outcomes: Scoping review. *JMIR mHealth and uHealth, 13*(1), e66650. DOI: 10.2196/66650 PMID: 40549960

Lipsky, M. S., Singh, T., Zakeri, G., & Hung, M. (2024). Oral Health and Older Adults: A Narrative Review. *Dentistry Journal, 12*(2), 30. DOI: 10.3390/dj12020030 PMID: 38392234

Liu, J., Zhou, L., Yang, L., & Liu, D. (2024). The dehumanization of service robots influences hospitality consumption emotion. *International Journal of Hospitality Management, 119*, 103707. DOI: 10.1016/j.ijhm.2024.103707

Liu, Y., Liu, X., Wang, M., & Wen, D. (2021). How to catch customers' attention? A study on the effectiveness of brand social media strategies in digital customer engagement. *Frontiers in Psychology, 12*, 800766. DOI: 10.3389/fpsyg.2021.800766 PMID: 34975700

Li, X., Shu, Q., Kong, C., Wang, J., Li, G., Fang, X., Lou, X., & Yu, G. (2025). An intelligent system for classifying patient complaints using machine learning and natural language processing: Development and validation study. *Journal of Medical Internet Research, 27*, e55721. DOI: 10.2196/55721 PMID: 39778195

Loncar-Turukalo, T., Zdravevski, E., Da Silva, J. M., Chouvarda, I., & Trajkovik, V. (2019). Literature on wearable technology for connected health: Scoping review of research trends, advances, and barriers. *Journal of Medical Internet Research, 21*(9), e14017. DOI: 10.2196/14017 PMID: 31489843

López García, J. J., Lizcano, D., Ramos, C. M., & Matos, N. (2019). Digital marketing actions that achieve a better attraction and loyalty of users: An analytical study. *Future Internet, 11*(6), 130. DOI: 10.3390/fi11060130

Lou, C., & Yuan, S. (2019). Influencer marketing: How message value and credibility affect consumer trust of branded content on social media. *Journal of Interactive Advertising, 19*(1), 58–73. DOI: 10.1080/15252019.2018.1533501

Lu, L., Gursoy, D., Chi, C. G.-Q., & Xiao, G. (2018). Developing a consumer complaining and recovery effort scale. *Journal of Hospitality & Tourism Research (Washington, D.C.), 42*(5), 686–715. DOI: 10.1177/1096348015597033

Luo, C., Hasan, N. A. M., Zamri bin Ahmad, A. M., & Lei, G. (2025). Influence of short video content on consumers purchase intentions on social media platforms with trust as a mediator. *Scientific Reports, 15*(1), 16605. DOI: 10.1038/s41598-025-94994-z PMID: 40360752

Lupton, D. (2017). *Digital health: Critical and cross disciplinary perspectives*. Routledge., DOI: 10.4324/9781315648835

Mackey, T. K., & Nayyar, G. (2016). Digital danger: A review of the global public health, patient safety and cybersecurity threats posed by illicit online pharmacies. *British Medical Bulletin, 118*(1), 110–126. DOI: 10.1093/bmb/ldw016 PMID: 27151957

Madsen, J. Ø., Guldbæk, R. S., Hæsum, L. K. E., & Thorup, C. B. (2025). Health care professionals´ knowledge of and ability to identify citizens' digital health literacy from a shared perspective of education, practice, policy and politics. *Health and Technology, 15*(4), 769–776. DOI: 10.1007/s12553-025-00994-4

Mahmoud, M. A., Hinson, R. E., & Adika, M. K. (2018). The effect of trust, commitment, and conflict handling on customer retention: The mediating role of customer satisfaction. *Journal of Relationship Marketing, 17*(4), 257–276. DOI: 10.1080/15332667.2018.1440146

Maksimova, M., Solvak, M., & Krimmer, R. (2021). Data-Driven Personalized E-Government Services: Literature Review and Case Study. In Edelmann, N. (Eds.), *Electronic Participation* (Vol. 12849, pp. 151–165). Springer., DOI: 10.1007/978-3-030-82824-0_12

Maleki, A., Ahadinezhad, B., Alizadeh, A., & Khosravizadeh, O. (2025). Using a social marketing approach to increase the pap-smear test uptake: Randomized controlled trial among women residing in urban region. *BMC Women's Health, 25*(1), 114. DOI: 10.1186/s12905-025-03642-1 PMID: 40082980

Mangold, W. G., & Faulds, D. J. (2009). Social media: The new hybrid element of the promotion mix. *Business Horizons, 52*(4), 357–365. DOI: 10.1016/j.bushor.2009.03.002

Mao, Z., Wang, D., & Zheng, S. (2023). Health belief model and social media engagement: A cross-national study of health promotion strategies against COVID-19 in 2020. *Frontiers in Public Health, 11*, 1093648. DOI: 10.3389/fpubh.2023.1093648 PMID: 36844861

Mara, M. (2023). Interdisciplinary education and health care in geriatric dental medicine. *Clinics in Geriatric Medicine, 39*(2), 327–341. DOI: 10.1016/j.cger.2023.01.006 PMID: 37045536

Marković, S., Lončarić, D., & Lončarić, D. (2014). Service quality and customer satisfaction in the health care industry-towards health tourism market. *Tourism and Hospitality Management, 20*(2), 155–170. DOI: 10.20867/thm.20.2.1

Martínez Asanza, D., Rojas Herrera, I. A., Mouloudj, K., Amable, O. G., & Muzzamil, M. (2024). Impact of Digital Innovations in Preventive Dentistry: A Narrative Review. In Asanza, D. (Ed.), *Leveraging Digital Technology for Preventive Dentistry* (pp. 55–84). IGI Global., DOI: 10.4018/979-8-3693-3872-8.ch003

Martínez-Asanza, D. Rojas- Herrera, I.A., Njoku, A., Reyes- Puig, A.C., Mouloudj, F., Gómez- Capote, I., et al. (2024). Study Plans and Programs Supporting Geriatric Dentistry Teaching in Cuba: An Update. In: Martínez- Asanza D, Editor. *Geriatric Dentistry in the Age of Digital Technology*. (pp. 174–191). IGI Global. DOI: 10.4018/979-8-3693-0260-6.ch007

Martínez-Asanza, D., Gbenou-Morgan, Y., & Rosales-Reyes, S. Á. (2020b). Gerodontología: Introducción de un nuevo término en la asignatura Atención integral a la familia II. *Medicentro Electrónica, 24*(1), 149–158. http://scielo.sld.cu/scielo.php?script=sci_arttext&pid=S1029-30432020000100149&lng=es

Martínez-Asanza, D. (2025). Emerging Trends and Future Perspectives in Digital Dentistry for Rural Areas: An Update. In Martínez-Asanza, D. (Ed.), *Transforming Dental Health in Rural Communities: Digital Dentistry* (pp. 1–20). IGI Global., DOI: 10.4018/979-8-3693-7165-7.ch001

Martínez-Asanza, D. (Ed.). (2024). *Geriatric Dentistry in the Age of Digital Technology*. IGI Global., DOI: 10.4018/979-8-3693-0260-6

Martínez-Asanza, D., Álvarez Pérez, A., Guanche Martínez, A. S., & Gómez Capote, I. (2026). Gerodontology in Cuba as a strategic discipline for healthy aging. *Revista Cubana de Medicina Militar, 55*(1), e026076903. https://revmedmilitar.sld.cu/index.php/mil/article/view/76903

Martínez-Asanza, D., Álvarez Pérez, A., & Rojas Herrera, I. A. (2025c). Dental education in gerontogeriatrics as a public health imperative for the Americas. *Revista Cubana de Medicina Militar*, *54*(3), e025076624. https://revmedmilitar.sld.cu/index.php/mil/article/view/76624

Martínez-Asanza, D., Guanche-Martínez, A. S., & Reyes-Puig, A. C. (2020a). La odontogeriatría en la formación y superación de especialistas en Cuba. *Revista Cubana de Medicina Militar*, *49*(3), e502.

Martínez-Asanza, D., Njoku, A., Baviskar, S., Evans, M. A., & Mouloudj, K. (2025a). Oral Hygiene Care of Older Adults and Caregiver Education: A Systematic Review. *Hygiene*, *5*(4), 50. DOI: 10.3390/hygiene5040050

Martínez-Asanza, D., Rojas Herrera, I. A., & Rodríguez Washington, N. (2025b). Distinguishing between Gerodontology and Geriatric Dentistry: Key perspectives on oral health in older adults. *Gerodontology*, *42*(3), 434–435. DOI: 10.1111/ger.12820 PMID: 40470572

Meira, T. M., Prestes, J., Gasparello, G. G., Antelo, O. M., Pithon, M. M., & Tanaka, O. M. (2021). The effects of images posted to social media by orthodontists on public perception of professional credibility and willingness to become a client. *Progress in Orthodontics*, *22*(1), 7. DOI: 10.1186/s40510-021-00353-9 PMID: 33682012

Metcalf, D., Milliard, S. T., Gomez, M., & Schwartz, M. (2016). Wearables and the Internet of things for health: Wearable, interconnected devices promise more efficient and comprehensive health care. *IEEE Pulse*, *7*(5), 35–39. DOI: 10.1109/MPUL.2016.2592260 PMID: 28113167

Mfouth Kemajou, P., Mbanya, A., & Coppieters, Y. (2024). Digital approaches in post-COVID healthcare: A systematic review of technological innovations in disease management. *Biology Methods and Protocols*, *9*(1), bpae070. Advance online publication. DOI: 10.1093/biomethods/bpae070 PMID: 39440031

Michea, M. A., Barahona, P., Dreyer, E., Rojas, M., & Celis, A. (2023). Elderly, ageing and oral fragility. *Journal of Dental Health, Oral Disorders & Therapy*, *14*(2), 28–30. DOI: 10.15406/jdhodt.2023.14.00590

Michie, S., van Stralen, M. M., & West, R. (2011). The behaviour change wheel: A new method for characterising and designing behaviour change interventions. *Implementation Science : IS*, *6*(1), 42. DOI: 10.1186/1748-5908-6-42 PMID: 21513547

Milne, R., & Costa, A. (2020). Disruption and dislocation in post-COVID futures for digital health. *Big Data & Society*, *7*(2), 2053951720949567. DOI: 10.1177/2053951720949567 PMID: 36789368

Min, S., Zhang, X., Kim, N., & Srivastava, R. K. (2016). Customer Acquisition and Retention Spending: An Analytical Model and Empirical Investigation in Wireless Telecommunications Markets. *JMR, Journal of Marketing Research, 53*(5), 728–744. DOI: 10.1509/jmr.14.0170

Miranda-Rosero, O., Sabando-Arteaga, J., & Castro-Freire, D. (2025). *Impacto de estrategias de marketing digital en odontología en la captación y fidelización de pacientes*. Revista Metropolitana de Ciencias Aplicadas., DOI: 10.62452/cf9cjr37

Miranzadeh, F., Sefidkar, R., & Rezaeipandari, H. (2025). Effectiveness of an educational intervention in modifying ageism among nurses in caring for older adults: A randomized controlled trial. *BMC Nursing, 24*(1), 1132. DOI: 10.1186/s12912-025-03798-z PMID: 40890733

Mirzoev, T., & Kane, S. (2018). Key strategies to improve systems for managing patient complaints within health facilities – what can we learn from the existing literature? *Global Health Action, 11*(1), 1458938. DOI: 10.1080/16549716.2018.1458938 PMID: 29658393

Mittelstadt, B. D., Allo, P., Taddeo, M., Wachter, S., & Floridi, L. (2016). The ethics of algorithms: Mapping the debate. *Big Data & Society, 3*(2), 2053951716679679. DOI: 10.1177/2053951716679679

Modha, B. (2023). Exploring customer journeys in the context of dentistry: A case study. *Dentistry Journal, 11*(3), 75. DOI: 10.3390/dj11030075

Moeini, A., & Torabi, S. (2025). The Role of Artificial Intelligence in Dental Diagnosis and Treatment Planning. *Journal of Oral and Dental Health Nexus, 2*(1), 14–26. DOI: 10.61838/kman.jodhn.2.1.2

Mosnaim, G. S., Stempel, H., Van Sickle, D., & Stempel, D. A. (2020). The adoption and implementation of digital health care in the post–COVID-19 era. *The Journal of Allergy and Clinical Immunology. In Practice, 8*(8), 2484–2486. DOI: 10.1016/j.jaip.2020.06.006 PMID: 32585407

Mouloudj, K., Alameri, S. A. S., Evans, M. A., Almado, A. A. G., Mahmoud, B. I., & Asanza, D. M. (2026). Social marketing for health equity: Promoting preventive health behavior among women in rural communities. *International Journal of Environmental Research and Public Health, 23*(5), 584. DOI: 10.3390/ijerph23050584 PMID: 42196677

Mouloudj, K., Bouarar, A. C., Martínez Asanza, D., Saadaoui, L., Mouloudj, S., Njoku, A. U., Evans, M. A., & Bouarar, A. (2023). Factors Influencing the Adoption of Digital Health Apps: An Extended Technology Acceptance Model (TAM). In Bouarar, A., Mouloudj, K., & Martínez Asanza, D. (Eds.), *Integrating Digital Health Strategies for Effective Administration* (pp. 116–132). IGI Global., DOI: 10.4018/978-1-6684-8337-4.ch007

Mubarak, F., & Suomi, R. (2022). Elderly Forgotten? Digital Exclusion in the Information Age and the Rising Grey Digital Divide. *Inquiry : a Journal of Medical Care Organization, Provision and Financing*, *59*, 469580221096272. DOI: 10.1177/00469580221096272 PMID: 35471138

Mulawarman, W. G., & Yahya, M. (2025). Digital promotion strategies utilizing social media to improve the image of educational institutions. *Journal of Educational Management Research*, *4*(3), 1010–1022. DOI: 10.61987/jemr.v4i3.1055

Mwogosi, A., & Mambile, C. (2025). Digital ecosystems for healthcare communication and collaboration: A scoping review. *Digital Health*, *11*, 20552076251377933. DOI: 10.1177/20552076251377933 PMID: 40949671

Nagpal, A., & Sharma, G. (2019). Daunting for developing countries. *British Dental Journal*, *227*(3), 175–175. DOI: 10.1038/s41415-019-0612-0 PMID: 31399649

Narteh, B., Agbemabiese, G. C., Kodua, P., & Braimah, M. (2013). Relationship marketing and customer loyalty: Evidence from the Ghanaian luxury hotel industry. *Journal of Hospitality Marketing & Management*, *22*(4), 407–436. DOI: 10.1080/19368623.2012.660564

Naslund, J. A., Aschbrenner, K. A., Marsch, L. A., & Bartels, S. J. (2016). The future of mental health care: Peer-to-peer support and social media. *Epidemiology and Psychiatric Sciences*, *25*(2), 113–122. DOI: 10.1017/S2045796015001067 PMID: 26744309

Natalucci, V., Marmondi, F., Biraghi, M., & Bonato, M. (2023). The effectiveness of wearable devices in non-communicable diseases to manage physical activity and nutrition: Where we are? *Nutrients*, *15*(4), 913. DOI: 10.3390/nu15040913 PMID: 36839271

Nazari, A., Hajihashemi, M., Safavi, S. R., Ataei, R., & Hosseinnia, M. (2025). Health promotion theory-based educational interventions for improving oral health in children and adolescents: A systematic review and meta-analysis. *BMC Oral Health*, *25*(1), 1153. DOI: 10.1186/s12903-025-06549-3 PMID: 40653471

Nazaruddin, I., Utami, E. R., & Rahmawati, E. (2024). Digitalization challenges for SMEs: A systematic literature review perspective and future research. *JBTI: Jurnal Bisnis: Teori dan Implementasi, 15*(1), 15-43. https://doi.org/DOI: 10.18196/jbti.v15i1.20410

Nazeli, B., Sugiarto, Y., & Wahyudi, A. (2023). Digital Marketing Analysis in Dental Healthcare: The Role of Digital Marketing in Promoting Dental Health in the Community. *East Asian Journal of Multidisciplinary Research, 2*(11), 4337–4360. DOI: 10.55927/eajmr.v2i11.6643

Nejad, M. S., Harooni, J., Charkazi, A., Shams, M., & Latifi, M. (2021). Using social marketing to promote preventive behaviors related to COVID-19. *Journal of Lifestyle Medicine, 11*(2), 52–56. DOI: 10.15280/jlm.2021.11.2.52 PMID: 34549026

Ng, N. Y., & Ruger, J. P. (2014). Ethics and Social Value Judgments in Public Health. *Encyclopedia of Health Economics*, 287-291. DOI: 10.1016/B978-0-12-375678-7.00415-6

Nguyen Huu, T., Nguyen Ngoc, H., Nguyen Dai, L., Nguyen Thi Thu, D., Truc, L. N., & Nguyen Trong, L. (2024). Effect of tourist satisfaction on revisit intention in Can Tho City, Vietnam. *Cogent Business & Management, 11*(1), 2322779. DOI: 10.1080/23311975.2024.2322779

Nguyen, N. X., Tran, K., & Nguyen, T. A. (2021). Impact of service quality on in-patients' satisfaction, perceived value, and customer loyalty: A mixed-methods study from a developing country. *Patient Preference and Adherence, 15*, 2523–2538. DOI: 10.2147/PPA.S333586

Niederdeppe, J., Boyd, A. D., King, A. J., & Rimal, R. N. (2025). Strategies for Effective Public Health Communication in a Complex Information Environment. *Annual Review of Public Health, 46*(1), 411–431. DOI: 10.1146/annurev-publhealth-071723-120721 PMID: 39656948

Nilsson, A., Young, L., Glass, B., Lee, A., Nimmo, A., & Brumpton, K. (2021). Gerodontology in the dental School curriculum: A scoping. *Gerodontology, 00*(4), 1–13. DOI: 10.1111/ger.12555 PMID: 33977554

Nisizaki & Derregibus. (2014). Protocolos de tratamiento y prevención en Gerodontología. *Odontoestomatología, 16*(23), 44–53. http://www.scielo.edu.uy/scielo.php?pid=S1688-93392014000100006&script=sci_arttext&tlng=pt

Nitschke, S., Hahnel, S., Sobota, B. A. J., & Jockusch, J. (2022). Undergraduate Dental Education in Gerodontology in German between 2004 and 2019- A case for compulsory teaching? *European Journal of Dental Education : Official Journal of the Association for Dental Education in Europe*, *26*(523), 523–538. DOI: 10.1111/eje.12729 PMID: 34826171

Northridge, M. E., Kumar, A., & Kaur, R. (2020). Disparities in access to oral health care. *Annual Review of Public Health*, *41*(1), 513–535. DOI: 10.1146/annurev-publhealth-040119-094318 PMID: 31900100

Nuansi, P., & Ngamcharoenmongkol, P. (2021). Proactive complaint management: Effects of customer voice initiation on perceived justices, satisfaction, and negative word-of-mouth. *SAGE Open*, *11*(3), 1–17. DOI: 10.1177/21582440211040788

Null, J. H.. (2021). Teledentistry and telehealth: Policy, practice, and evidence. *Journal of Dental Education*, *85*(10), 1321–1334.

Nuseir, M. T., El Refae, G. A., Aljumah, A., Alshurideh, M., Urabi, S., & Kurdi, B. A. (2023). Digital Marketing Strategies and the Impact on Customer Experience: A Systematic Review. In Alshurideh, M., Al Kurdi, B. H., Masa'deh, R., Alzoubi, H. M., & Salloum, S. (Eds.), *The Effect of Information Technology on Business and Marketing Intelligence Systems* (pp. 21–44). Springer., DOI: 10.1007/978-3-031-12382-5_2

Nutbeam, D., & Lloyd, J. E. (2021). Understanding and Responding to Health Literacy as a Social Determinant of Health. *Annual Review of Public Health*, *42*(1), 159–173. DOI: 10.1146/annurev-publhealth-090419-102529 PMID: 33035427

Obermeyer, Z., Powers, B., Vogeli, C., & Mullainathan, S. (2019). Dissecting racial bias in an algorithm used to manage the health of populations. *Science*, *366*(6464), 447–453. DOI: 10.1126/science.aax2342 PMID: 31649194

Odoom, R., & Agyeman, D. O. (2019). Technology and Social Media in Healthcare Delivery. In Hinson, R., Osei-Frimpong, K., Adeola, O., & Aziato, L. (Eds.), *Health Service Marketing Management in Africa* (pp. 267–279). Productivity Press., DOI: 10.4324/9780429400858-21

OECD. (2019). *Vectors of Digital Transformation.* OECD Digital Economy Papers, No. 273. OECD Publishing. Available at: https://doi.org/DOI: 10.1787/20716826

OECD. (2022). *Health Data Governance for the Digital Age: Implementing the OECD Recommendation on Health Data Governance*. OECD Publishing., DOI: 10.1787/68b60796-

OECD. (n.d.). *Digital transformation (Policy Issue)*. OECD. Available at: https://www.oecd.org/en/topics/policy-issues/digital-transformation.html

Ofori, D., & Appiah-Nimo, C. (2022). Relationship management, competitive advantage and performance of hotels: A resource-based view. *Journal of African Business, 23*(3), 712–730. DOI: 10.1080/15228916.2021.1924573

Ogbeide, G.-C. A., Böser, S., Harrinton, R. J., & Ottenbacher, M. C. (2017). Complaint management in hospitality organizations: The role of empowerment and other service recovery attributes impacting loyalty and satisfaction. *Tourism and Hospitality Research, 17*(2), 204–216. DOI: 10.1177/1467358415613409

Olubodun, T., Balogun, M. R., Odeyemi, K. A., Osibogun, A., Odukoya, O. O., Banjo, A. A., Sonusi, S. E., Olubodun, A. B., Ogundele, O. O. P., & Dolapo, D. C. (2022). Effect of social marketing on the knowledge, attitude, and uptake of pap smear among women residing in an urban slum in Lagos, Nigeria. *BMC Women's Health, 22*(1), 42. DOI: 10.1186/s12905-022-01620-5 PMID: 35164717

Owhoeke, N., Oparaku, O., & Ordu, B. (2023). Digital Infrastructure and Sustainable Development of Marketing Education Curriculum in Tertiary Institutions in Nigeria. *International Journal of Research and Scientific Innovation*. .DOI: 10.51244/IJRSI.2023.101006

Ozay, D., Jahanbakht, M., Shoomal, A., & Wang, S. (2024). Artificial Intelligence (AI)-based Customer Relationship Management (CRM): A comprehensive bibliometric and systematic literature review with outlook on future research. *Enterprise Information Systems, 18*(7), 2351869. DOI: 10.1080/17517575.2024.2351869

Page, M. J., McKenzie, J. E., Bossuyt, P. M., Boutron, I., Hoffmann, T. C., Mulrow, C. D., Shamseer, L., Tetzlaff, J. M., Akl, E. A., Brennan, S. E., Chou, R., Glanville, J., Grimshaw, J. M., Hróbjartsson, A., Lalu, M. M., Li, T., Loder, E. W., Mayo-Wilson, E., McDonald, S., & Moher, D. (2021). The PRISMA 2020 statement: An updated guideline for reporting systematic reviews. *BMJ (Clinical Research Ed.), 372*(71), n71. Advance online publication. DOI: 10.1136/bmj.n71 PMID: 33782057

Palsgaard, P., Maino Vieytes, C. A., Peterson, N., Francis, S. L., Monroe-Lord, L., Sahyoun, N. R., Ventura-Marra, M., Weidauer, L., Xu, F., & Arthur, A. E. (2022). Healthcare Professionals' Views and Perspectives towards Aging. *International Journal of Environmental Research and Public Health, 19*(23), 15870. DOI: 10.3390/ijerph192315870 PMID: 36497945

Panditi, M., Anusha, K., & Palle, E.. (2025). Availability and utilisation of oral healthcare services at rural community health centres in South India: A mixed methods study. *BMC Oral Health*, *25*(1), 977. DOI: 10.1186/s12903-025-06327-1 PMID: 40598131

Paoli, A., Iaccarino, G., Lucidi, F., Pagnini, F., Boccuzzo, G., & Illario, M. (2025). Multidimensional determinants of active and healthy aging trajectories: A position paper from the Age-It Research Program. *The Journals of Gerontology. Series B, Psychological Sciences and Social Sciences*, *80*(Supplement_2), S145–S157. DOI: 10.1093/geronb/gbaf196 PMID: 41442760

Parkinson, J., & Davey, J. (2023). The importance of health marketing and a research agenda. *Health Marketing Quarterly*, *40*(4), 347–351. DOI: 10.1080/07359683.2024.2271780 PMID: 37897233

Parkinson, J., & Naidu, J. (2024). Driving and evaluating social impact in health marketing. *Health Marketing Quarterly*, *41*(2), 113–129. DOI: 10.1080/07359683.2024.2363568 PMID: 39010695

Pasaribu, S. B., Novitasari, D., Goestjahjanti, F. S., & Hendratono, T. (2022). The impact and challenges of digital marketing in the health care industry during the digital era and the COVID-19 pandemic. *Frontiers in Public Health*, *10*, 969523. DOI: 10.3389/fpubh.2022.969523 PMID: 35968423

Passos, K. K. M., da Silva Leonel, A. C. L., Bonan, P. R. F., de Castro, J. F. L., dos Anjos Pontual, M. L., de Moraes Ramos-Perez, F. M., & da Cruz Perez, D. E. (2020). Quality of information about oral cancer in Brazilian Portuguese available on Google, Youtube, and Instagram. *Medicina Oral, Patología Oral y Cirugía Bucal*, *25*(3), e346–e352. http://dx.doi.org/doi:10.4317/medoral.23374. DOI: 10.4317/medoral.23374 PMID: 32040464

Patel, R., & Gallagher, J. E. (2024). Healthy ageing and oral health: Priority, policy and public health. *BDJ Open*, *10*(1), 79. DOI: 10.1038/s41405-024-00262-z PMID: 39379352

Patil, S., Albogami, S., Hosmani, J., Mujoo, S., Kamil, M. A., Mansour, M. A., Abdul, H. N., Bhandi, S., & Ahmed, S. S. S. J. (2022). Artificial Intelligence in the Diagnosis of Oral Diseases: Applications and Pitfalls. *Diagnostics (Basel)*, *12*(5), 1029. DOI: 10.3390/diagnostics12051029 PMID: 35626185

Paul, B., & Headley-Johnson, S. A. (2025, October). The impact of social media on health behaviors, a systematic review. In *Healthcare* (Vol. 13, No. 21, p. 2763). https://pmc.ncbi.nlm.nih.gov/articles/PMC12608964/

Peres, M. A., Macpherson, L. M., Weyant, R. J., Daly, B., Venturelli, R., Mathur, M. R., Listl, S., Celeste, R. K., Guarnizo-Herreño, C. C., Kearns, C., Benzian, H., Allison, P., & Watt, R. G. (2019). Oral diseases: A global public health challenge. *Lancet, 394*(10194), 249–260. DOI: 10.1016/S0140-6736(19)31146-8 PMID: 31327369

Perez Guzman, S., & Ajami, D. S. (2026). Evolution of Digital Technologies in Healthcare. In Scholz, S., Wüchner-Fuchs, M., & Höller, K. (Eds.), *Advancements in Digital Health and Care* (pp. 3–10). Springer., DOI: 10.1007/978-3-032-16837-5_1

Peters, D. H. (2019). The application of systems thinking in health: Why use systems thinking? *Health Research Policy and Systems, 12*(1), 51. DOI: 10.1186/1478-4505-12-51 PMID: 25160707

Petersen, P. E., & Kwan, S. (2009). World Health Organization global oral health strategies for oral health promotion and disease prevention in the twenty-first century. *Prävention und Gesundheitsförderung, 4*(2), 100–104. DOI: 10.1007/s11553-009-0169-x

Piedra-Andrade, M. N., Astudillo, P. A., Bravo, M. E., Cordero Coronel, M. I., & Bravo Calderón, M. E. (2024). Marketing and patient acquisition strategies in dental clinics: Development and implementation of digital marketing campaigns to attract new patients and effectiveness of social networks as a marketing tool for dental clinics. *Research. Social Development, 13*(10), e101131047175. DOI: 10.33448/rsd-v13i10.47175

Pine, C. M., & Dugdill, L. (2011). Analysis of a unique global public-private partnership to promote oral health. *International Dental Journal, 61*, 11–21. DOI: 10.1111/j.1875-595X.2011.00036.x PMID: 21770936

Pioch, C., Henschke, C., Lantzsch, H., Busse, R., & Vogt, V. (2023). Applying a data-driven population segmentation approach in German claims data. *BMC Health Services Research, 23*(1), 591. DOI: 10.1186/s12913-023-09620-3 PMID: 37286993

Ponathil, A., Khasawneh, A., Byrne, K., & Chalil Madathil, K. (2021). Factors affecting the choice of a dental care provider by older adults based on online consumer reviews. *IISE Transactions on Healthcare Systems Engineering, 11*(1), 51–69. DOI: 10.1080/24725579.2020.1854394

Potts, G., & Radford, D. R. (2019). # Teeth&Tweets: The reach and reaction of an online social media oral health promotion campaign. *British Dental Journal, 227*(3), 217–222. DOI: 10.1038/s41415-019-0593-z PMID: 31399680

Poudel, P., Paudel, G., Acharya, R., George, A., Borgnakke, W. S., & Rawal, L. B. (2024). Oral health and healthy ageing: A scoping review. *BMC Geriatrics*, *24*(1), 33. DOI: 10.1186/s12877-023-04613-7 PMID: 38191307

Prosser, G. M., Louca, C., & Radford, D. R. (2022). Potential educational and workforce strategies to meet the oral health challenges of an increasingly older population: A qualitative study. *BDJ Open*, *8*(1), 6. DOI: 10.1038/s41405-022-00098-5 PMID: 35273157

Putnam, R. D. (2000). *Bowling Alone: The Collapse and Revival of American Community*. Simon & Schuster.

Qalati, S. A., Vela, E. G., Li, W., Dakhan, S. A., Hong Thuy, T. T., & Merani, S. H. (2021). Effects of perceived service quality, website quality, and reputation on purchase intention: The mediating and moderating roles of trust and perceived risk in online shopping. *Cogent Business & Management*, *8*(1), 1869363. DOI: 10.1080/23311975.2020.1869363

Raj, E. F. I. (2024). Applications of Data Science and Artificial Intelligence Methodologies in Customer Relationship Management. In Kautish, S., Chatterjee, P., Pamucar, D., Pradeep, N., & Singh, D. (Eds.), *Computational Intelligence for Modern Business Systems. Disruptive Technologies and Digital Transformations for Society 5.0* (pp. 227–242). Springer., DOI: 10.1007/978-981-99-5354-7_12

Rajeh, M. T. (2022). Modeling the theory of planned behavior to predict adults' intentions to improve oral health behaviors. *BMC Public Health*, *22*(1), 1391. DOI: 10.1186/s12889-022-13796-4 PMID: 35858885

Ramos, K., & Cuamea, O. (2023). Dental tourism: Factors influencing travelers' revisit intention to the Mexican border. *International Journal of Tourism Cities*, *9*(3), 806–831. DOI: 10.1108/IJTC-03-2023-0046

Rani, H., Azizan, A. A., Walad, N. I. A., Hassan, S. A. A., Dom, T. N. M., Yeoh, D. S. H., Tay, J. W. C., Rosli, M. S. A., Aun, N. S. M., Aziz, A. F. A., Thwin, K. M., & Tew, I. M. (2025). Challenges and Recommendations for Oral Healthcare of Older Adults in a Long-Term Care Facility. *Health Care*, *13*(20), 2642. DOI: 10.3390/healthcare13202642 PMID: 41154320

Reinartz, W., Krafft, M., & Hoyer, W. D. (2004). The customer relationship management process: Its measurement and impact on performance. *JMR, Journal of Marketing Research*, *41*(3), 293–305. DOI: 10.1509/jmkr.41.3.293.35991

Re, P. R., Harliani, N. D., & Purnama, T.RE. (2022). TikTok Media as an Effort to Increase Dental Health Knowledge for High School Students. *Journal of Drug Delivery and Therapeutics*, *12*(5), 146–148. Advance online publication. DOI: 10.22270/jddt.v12i5.5669

Roba, G. B., & Maric, P. (2023). AI in Customer Relationship Management. In Kryvinska, N., Greguš, M., Fedushko, S. (Eds.), *Developments in Information and Knowledge Management Systems for Business Applications* (pp. 469–487). Studies in Systems, Decision and Control, Vol. 462. Springer. https://doi.org/DOI: 10.1007/978-3-031-25695-0_21

Roger, A., Dourgoudian, M., Mergey, V., Laplanche, D., Ecarnot, F., & Sanchez, S. (2023). Effectiveness of Prevention Interventions Using Social Marketing Methods on Behavioural Change in the General Population: A Systematic Review of the Literature. *International Journal of Environmental Research and Public Health*, *20*(5), 4576. DOI: 10.3390/ijerph20054576 PMID: 36901585

Rokhshad, R., Mohammad-Rahimi, H., Price, J. B., Shoorgashti, R., Abbasiparashkouh, Z., Esmaeili, M., Sarfaraz, B., Rokhshad, A., Motamedian, S. R., Soltani, P., & Schwendicke, F. (2024). Artificial intelligence for classification and detection of oral mucosa lesions on photographs: A systematic review and meta-analysis. *Clinical Oral Investigations*, *28*(1), 88. DOI: 10.1007/s00784-023-05475-4 PMID: 38217733

Rosales, A., & Fernández-Ardèvol, M. (2020). Ageism in the era of digital platforms. *Convergence (London)*, *26*(5–6), 1074–1087. DOI: 10.1177/1354856520930905 PMID: 33239961

Rosenstock, I. M. (1966). Why people use health services. *The Milbank Memorial Fund Quarterly*, *44*(3), 94–127. DOI: 10.2307/3348967 PMID: 5967464

Rosenstock, I. M., Strecher, V. J., & Becker, M. H. (1988). Social learning theory and the Health Belief Model. *Health Education Quarterly*, *15*(2), 175–183. DOI: 10.1177/109019818801500203 PMID: 3378902

Rossi, A., Frechette, L., Miller, D., Miller, E., Friel, C., Van Arsdale, A., Lin, J., Shankar, V., Kuo, D. Y. S., & Nevadunsky, N. S. (2018). Acceptability and feasibility of a Fitbit physical activity monitor for endometrial cancer survivors. *Gynecologic Oncology*, *149*(3), 470–475. DOI: 10.1016/j.ygyno.2018.04.560 PMID: 29692337

Rothschild, M. L. (1999). Carrots, sticks, and promises: A conceptual framework for the management of public health and social issue behaviors. *Journal of Marketing*, *63*(4), 24–37. DOI: 10.1177/002224299906300404

Rowley, J., Johnson, F., & Sbaffi, L. (2015). Students' trust judgements in online health information seeking. *Health Informatics Journal, 21*(4), 316–327. DOI: 10.1177/1460458214546772 PMID: 25193449

Sahab, L., Newton, J. T., & Sabbah, W. (2025). Oral Health and Healthy Aging: A Systematic Review of Longitudinal Studies. *Dentistry Journal, 13*(7), 303. DOI: 10.3390/dj13070303 PMID: 40710148

Salah, O. H., & Ayyash, M. M. (2024). E-commerce adoption by SMEs and its effect on marketing performance: An extended of TOE framework with ai integration, innovation culture, and customer tech-savviness. *Journal of Open Innovation, 10*(1), 100183. DOI: 10.1016/j.joitmc.2023.100183

Salman, F. D. (2024). Marketing Strategies in Dentistry: Navigating Social Media, Influencers, and Traditional Channels for Oral Health Promotion. In *Leveraging Digital Technology for Preventive Dentistry* (pp. 279-304). DOI: DOI: 10.4018/979-8-3693-3872-8.ch010

Sanghavi, B., Sachdev, S. S., Sachdev, J. B., Sonawane, S., Latke, S., Banga, K. S., & Banga, K. (2025). Social media as a tool for oral health promotion: An umbrella review of systematic reviews and content-analysis studies across digital platforms. *Cureus, 17*(7), e87962. DOI: 10.7759/cureus.87962 PMID: 40821201

Scheerman, J. F. M., Qari, A. H., Varenne, B., Bijwaard, H., Swinckels, L., Giraudeau, N., van Meijel, B., & Mariño, R. (2024). A systematic umbrella review of the effects of teledentistry on costs and oral-health outcomes. *International Journal of Environmental Research and Public Health, 21*(4), 407. DOI: 10.3390/ijerph21040407 PMID: 38673320

Schwendicke, F., Uribe, S. E., Walji, M., Lam, W., & Tichy, A. (2025). Electronic Health Records in Dentistry: Relevance, Challenges and Policy Directions. *International Dental Journal, 75*(6), 103964. DOI: 10.1016/j.identj.2025.103964 PMID: 41106216

Setz, C., Arnrich, B., Schumm, J., La Marca, R., Tröster, G., & Ehlert, U. (2010). Discriminating stress from cognitive load using a wearable EDA device. *IEEE Transactions on Information Technology in Biomedicine, 14*(2), 410–417. DOI: 10.1109/TITB.2009.2036164 PMID: 19906598

Shah, A., Arman, M., & Khan, S. (2025). Patient-Centric Marketing and Retention Strategies in Healthcare: A Strategic and Technological Framework. *Journal of Business and Management Studies*. .DOI: 10.32996/jbms.2025.7.2.17

Shajari, S., Kuruvinashetti, K., Komeili, A., & Sundararaj, U. (2023). The emergence of AI-based wearable sensors for digital health technology: A review. *Sensors (Basel), 23*(23), 1–18. DOI: 10.3390/s23239498 PMID: 38067871

Sharma, S., Mohanty, V., Balappanavar, A. Y., Chahar, P., Rijhwani, K., & Balappanavar, A. (2022). Role of digital media in promoting oral health: A systematic review. *Cureus, 14*(9), e28893. DOI: 10.7759/cureus.28893 PMID: 36225421

Sharma, V. K., Sharma, V., & Kumar, D. (2025). Customer relationship management in healthcare: Strategies for adoption in a public health system. *Journal of Marketing Theory and Practice, 33*(4), 560–585. DOI: 10.1080/10696679.2024.2394485

Shen, X., & Wang, J. (2024). How short video marketing influences purchase intention in social commerce: The role of users' persona perception, shared values, and individual-level factors. *Humanities & Social Sciences Communications, 11*(1), 290. DOI: 10.1057/s41599-024-02808-w

Shigli, K., Nayak, S., Lagali-Jirge, V., Nerali, J. T., Vadavi, D., Oginni, F. O., & Kusurkar, R. A. (2025). Dental teachers' perceptions about the status of geriatric dentistry in the dental curriculum: A qualitative exploration in the Indian context. *Gerodontology, 42*(2), 256–268. DOI: 10.1111/ger.12793 PMID: 39428127

Shivakumar, A. T., Srinivas, S., Kalgeri, S. H., Kishor, M., & Avarebeel, S. (2026). A transformative interprofessional model for geriatric oral health care - A proposed working model. *Frontiers in Dental Medicine, 7*, 1757007. DOI: 10.3389/fdmed.2026.1757007 PMID: 41867639

Shmarina, E., Ericson, D., Åkerman, S., & Axtelius, B. (2021). Salutogenic factors for oral health among older people: An integrative review connecting the theoretical frameworks of Antonovsky and Lalonde. *Acta Odontologica Scandinavica, 79*(3), 218–231. DOI: 10.1080/00016357.2020.1849790 PMID: 33596156

Shneiderman, B. (2020). Human-centered artificial intelligence: Reliable, safe & trustworthy. *International Journal of Human-Computer Interaction, 36*(6), 495–504. DOI: 10.1080/10447318.2020.1741118

Sidharthan, S., Ramanarayanan, V., Karuveettil, V., & Ravindran, G. C. (2024). Utilization of dental health services and its associated factors among adult population in Ernakulam district, Kerala, India: A mixed-method analysis. *Journal of Oral Biology and Craniofacial Research, 14*(2), 133–142. DOI: 10.1016/j.jobcr.2024.01.010 PMID: 38352196

Singh, V., Jain, A., & Choraria, S. (2016). Exploring the role of complaint handling among complaining consumers. *Vision: The Journal of Business Perspective*, *20*(4), 331–344. DOI: 10.1177/0972262916668739

Siopis, G., Moschonis, G., Eweka, E., Jung, J., Kwasnicka, D., Asare, B. Y., Kodithuwakku, V., Willems, R., Verhaeghe, N., Annemans, L., Vedanthan, R., Oldenburg, B., Manios, Y., Oldenburg, B., Kwasnicka, D., Gong, E., Jung, J., Asare, B. Y.-A., Kodithuwakku, V., & Bruka, L. (2023). Effectiveness, reach, uptake, and feasibility of digital health interventions for adults with hypertension: A systematic review and meta-analysis of randomised controlled trials. *The Lancet. Digital Health*, *5*(3), 144–159. DOI: 10.1016/S2589-7500(23)00002-X PMID: 36828607

Sivrikaya, E. C., Yilmaz, O., & Sivrikaya, P. (2021). Dentist-patient communication on dental anxiety using the social media: A randomized controlled trial. *Scandinavian Journal of Psychology*, *62*(6), 780–786. DOI: 10.1111/sjop.12769 PMID: 34333783

Slack-Smith, L., Arena, G., & See, L. (2023). Rapid Oral Health Deterioration in Older People-A Narrative Review from a Socio-Economic Perspective. *Journal of Clinical Medicine*, *12*(6), 2396. DOI: 10.3390/jcm12062396 PMID: 36983395

Soltani, Z., Zareie, B., Milani, F. S., & Navimipour, N. J. (2018). The impact of the customer relationship management on the organization performance. *The Journal of High Technology Management Research*, *29*(2), 237–246. DOI: 10.1016/j.hitech.2018.10.001

Sørensen, K., Van den Broucke, S., Fullam, J., Doyle, G., Pelikan, J., Slonska, Z., & Brand, H. (2012). Health literacy and public health: A systematic review. *BMC Public Health*, *12*(1), 80. DOI: 10.1186/1471-2458-12-80 PMID: 22276600

Sousa, B. M., & Alves, G. M. (2019). The role of relationship marketing in behavioural intentions of medical tourism services and guest experiences. *Journal of Hospitality and Tourism Insights*, *2*(3), 224–240. DOI: 10.1108/JHTI-05-2018-0032

Sravya, K., Movva, J. B., Sinha, R., Sharma, S., Patel, B. R., Thanneeru, D., & Tiwari, H. D. (2024). Electronic Health Records in Dentristry: A Systematic Review. *Journal of Contemporary Clinical Practice*, *10*(1), 71–79. DOI: 10.18683/jccp.2024.1091

Srijaroen, W., Chuenjaichon, W., Tosasukul, J., Yamchuen, P., & Jongjitvimol, T. (2025). Factors associated with dental health care behaviors among elderly patients in lower northern Thailand: A case study of Mueang Phitsanulok Health Center. *Journal of Public Health Research*, *14*(4), 22799036251388588. DOI: 10.1177/22799036251388588 PMID: 41211227

Srinivasan, M., Kalberer, N., Fankhauser, N., Naharro, M., Maniewicz, S., & Müller, F. (2021). CAD-CAM complete removable dental prostheses: A double-blind, randomized, crossover clinical trial evaluating milled and 3D-printed dentures. *Journal of Dentistry, 115*, 103842. DOI: 10.1016/j.jdent.2021.103842 PMID: 34637889

Srivastava, R., Tangade, P., & Priyadarshi, S. (2023). Transforming public health dentistry: Exploring the digital foothold for improved oral healthcare. *International Dental Journal of Student's Research, 11*(2), 61–67. Advance online publication. DOI: 10.18231/j.idjsr.2023.013

Stamate, A., Marzan, M. D., Velciu, M., Paul, C., & Spiru, L. (2024). Advancing user-centric design and technology adoption for aging populations: A multifaceted approach. *Frontiers in Public Health, 12*, 1469815. DOI: 10.3389/fpubh.2024.1469815 PMID: 39712308

Stark, A. L., Geukes, C., & Dockweiler, C. (2022). Digital health promotion and prevention in settings: Scoping review. *Journal of Medical Internet Research, 24*(1), e21063. DOI: 10.2196/21063 PMID: 35089140

Stoumpos, A. I., Kitsios, F., & Talias, M. A. (2023). Digital Transformation in Healthcare: Technology Acceptance and Its Applications. *International Journal of Environmental Research and Public Health, 20*(4), 3407. DOI: 10.3390/ijerph20043407 PMID: 36834105

Stuck, A. K., & Schimmel, M. (2022). A model for a geriatric teaching programme and its impact on self-rated and tested competencies of undergraduate dental students. *European Journal of Dental Education : Official Journal of the Association for Dental Education in Europe, 26*(1), 21–27. DOI: 10.1111/eje.12668 PMID: 33512016

Sun, Y. (2022). Consumers' evaluation of web-based health information quality: Ameta-analysis. *Journal of Medical Internet Research, 24*(4), 1–20. https://www.jmir.org/2022/4/e36463/

Sun, Y., Wang, X., Hoegg, J., & Dahl, D. W. (2023). How consumers respond to embarrassing service encounters: A dehumanization perspective. *JMR, Journal of Marketing Research, 60*(4), 646–664. DOI: 10.1177/00222437221130721

Surdu, A., Foia, C. I., Luchian, I., Trifan, D., Budala, D. G., Scutariu, M. M., Ciupilan, C., Puha, B., & Tatarciuc, D. (2025). Telemedicine and Digital Tools in Dentistry: Enhancing Diagnosis and Remote Patient Care. *Medicina (Kaunas, Lithuania), 61*(5), 826. DOI: 10.3390/medicina61050826 PMID: 40428784

Surve, K. S., Padawe, D., & Takate, V. (2025). Digital Dilemma: The Intersection of Social Media Influencers and Pediatric Dental Health. *Journal of Clinical Insights and Research in Dentistry*, *1*(2), 82–88. DOI: 10.5005/jcird-11034-0015

Swenson, E. R., Bastian, N. D., & Nembhard, H. B. (2018). Healthcare market segmentation and data mining: A systematic review. *Health Marketing Quarterly*, *35*(3), 186–208. DOI: 10.1080/07359683.2018.1514734 PMID: 30470165

Tadjoedin, F. M., Adiatman, M., Lee, Y. Y. A., Banu, U. S., Tan, S. S. L., & Garg, V. (2025). Oral health and healthy aging: A multiregional review. *JAR Life*, *15*, 100057. DOI: 10.1016/j.jarlif.2025.100057 PMID: 41536749

Tapuria, A., Porat, T., Kalra, D., Dsouza, G., Xiaohui, S., & Curcin, V. (2021). Impact of patient access to their electronic health record: Systematic review. *Informatics for Health & Social Care*, *46*(2), 194–206. DOI: 10.1080/17538157.2021.1879810 PMID: 33840342

Tarazona-Montoya, R., Devece, C., Llopis-Albert, C., & García-Agreda, S. (2024). Effectiveness of digital marketing and its value in new ventures. *The International Entrepreneurship and Management Journal*, *20*(4), 2839–2862. DOI: 10.1007/s11365-024-00959-5

Teymourifar, A. (2026). Defining an integrative multidimensional framework for patient complaint management systems. *Frontiers in Health Services*, *6*, 1767605. DOI: 10.3389/frhs.2026.1767605 PMID: 41982510

Thai, N. V., Trang, B. T. Q., Quy, N. L. D., Huong, N. T. Q., & Huyen, V. T. T. (2024). Factors affecting the successful implementation of customer relationship management in 3-to-5-star hotels in Viet Nam. *Cogent Social Sciences*, *10*(1), 2316062. DOI: 10.1080/23311886.2024.2316062

The Bangkok Charter for Health Promotion in a Globalized World (2005). Bangkok: World Health Organization. Available at: https://www.who.int/healthpromotion/conferences/6gchp/hpr_050829_%20BCHP.pdf?ua=1

Theriault, H., & Bridge, G. (2023). Oral health equity for rural communities: Where are we now and where can we go from here? *British Dental Journal*, *235*(2), 99–102. DOI: 10.1038/s41415-023-6058-4 PMID: 37500855

Thomas, J., & Harden, A. (2008). Methods for the thematic synthesis of qualitative research in systematic reviews. *BMC Medical Research Methodology*, *8*(1), 45. DOI: 10.1186/1471-2288-8-45 PMID: 18616818

Thompson, L. A., Kaplish, S., Park, S. E., & Chamut, S. (2022). Is dental education meeting the oral health needs of older adults? *Journal of Dental Education, 86*(9), 1233–1241. DOI: 10.1002/jdd.13026 PMID: 36165248

Thonburi Health Report. (2024). AI and patient compliance in urban Thailand. *Bangkok Metropolitan Administration*. https://ir.thg.co.id

Thorat, V., Rao, P., Joshi, N., Talreja, P., & Shetty, A. R. (2024, May 07). Role of Artificial Intelligence (AI) in Patient Education and Communication in Dentistry. *Cureus, 16*(5), e59799. DOI: 10.7759/cureus.59799 PMID: 38846249

Tiffany, B., Blasi, P., Catz, S. L., & McClure, J. B. (2018). Mobile apps for oral health promotion: Content review and heuristic usability analysis. *JMIR mHealth and uHealth, 6*(9), e11432. DOI: 10.2196/11432 PMID: 30181114

Tımarcıoğlu, G., Kargu, E. C., Çerçi Akçay, H., & Tımarcıoğlu, B. (2026). Evaluating the reliability and educational quality of YouTube™ and TikTok™ videos on custom subperiosteal implants: a cross-sectional methodological analysis. *BMC Oral Health*. https://link.springer.com/article/10.1186/s12903-026-08290-x

Timlin, D., McCormack, J. M., & Simpson, E. E. (2021). Using the COM-B model to identify barriers and facilitators towards adoption of a diet associated with cognitive function. *Public Health Nutrition, 24*(7), 1657–1670. DOI: 10.1017/S1368980020001445 PMID: 32799963

Trivium Packaging. (2024). 2024 Global buying green report. https://buyinggreen.triviumpackaging.com/

Tsai, I. C., Wei, H. C., & Chen, P. T. (2024). User Preferences for Medical Digital Transformation: A Case Study of Orthodontic Services. *Human Behavior and Emerging Technologies, 2024*(1), 7476097. DOI: 10.1155/2024/7476097

Tubaishat, A. (2019). The effect of electronic health records on patient safety: A qualitative exploratory study. *Informatics for Health & Social Care, 44*(1), 79–91. DOI: 10.1080/17538157.2017.1398753 PMID: 29239662

Tuncer, I., Unusan, C., & Cobanoglu, C. (2021). Service quality, perceived value and customer satisfaction on behavioral intention in restaurants: An integrated structural model. *Journal of Quality Assurance in Hospitality & Tourism, 22*(4), 447–475. DOI: 10.1080/1528008X.2020.1802390

Uddin, K. S., Bhuiyan, M. R. I., & Hamid, M. (2024). Perception towards the acceptance of digital health services among the people of Bangladesh. *WSEAS Transactions on Business and Economics, 21*, 1557–1570. DOI: 10.37394/23207.2024.21.127

Ugargol, A. P., & D'Souza, P. M. (2025). Addressing Ageism in Healthcare: Insights for an Age-Inclusive Longevity Society. In Rajan, S. I. (Ed.), *Handbook of Aging, Health and Public Policy*. Springer., DOI: 10.1007/978-981-99-7842-7_234

UNICEF. (n.d.). *Digital health.* UNICEF. Available at: https://www.unicef.org/health/digital-health

Upadhyay, S., Tuli, N., & Kumar, H. (2024). Crafting inclusive marketing campaigns: Insights and influential factors in the Indian context. *Australasian Marketing Journal, 32*(3), 223–238. DOI: 10.1177/14413582241247328

Usuemerai, P., Ibikunle, O., Abass, L., Alemede, V., Nwankwo, E., & Mbata, A. (2024). *A conceptual framework for integrating digital transformation in healthcare marketing to boost patient engagement and compliance.* World Journal of Advanced Pharmaceutical and Medical Research., DOI: 10.53346/wjapmr.2024.7.2.0045

Vafeiadis, M. (2023). Message interactivity and source credibility in online dental practice reviews: Responding to reviews triggers positive consumer reactions regardless of review valence. *Health Communication, 38*(1), 80–90. DOI: 10.1080/10410236.2021.1935538

Valenza, G., Citi, L., Gentili, C., Lanata, A., Scilingo, E. P., & Barbieri, R. (2015). Characterization of depressive states in bipolar patients using wearable textile technology and instantaneous heart rate variability assessment. *IEEE Journal of Biomedical and Health Informatics, 19*(1), 263–274. DOI: 10.1109/JBHI.2014.2307584 PMID: 25561449

Valmohammadi, C. (2017). Customer relationship management: Innovation and performance. *International Journal of Innovation Science, 9*(4), 374–395. DOI: 10.1108/IJIS-02-2017-0011

Van Dijk, J. (2020). *The Digital Divide.* Polity Press.

van Veen, S., Binz, S., Muminovic, M., Chaudhry, K., Rose, S., Calo, S., Rammal, J., France, J., & Miller, J. B. (2019). Potential of mobile health technology to reduce health disparities in underserved communities. *The Western Journal of Emergency Medicine, 20*(5), 799–802. DOI: 10.5811/westjem.2019.6.41911 PMID: 31539337

Vashishth, T. K., Sharma, V., Sharma, K. K., Kumar, B., Chaudhary, S., & Panwar, R. (2024). Industry 4.0 Trends and Strategies: A Modern Approach with Focus on Knowledge Management. *Knowledge Management and Industry Revolution, 4*(0), 111–158. DOI: 10.1002/9781394242641.ch5

Väyrynen, E., Hakola, S., Keski-Salmi, A., Jämsä, H., Vainionpää, R., & Karki, S. (2023). The Use of Patient-Oriented Mobile Phone Apps in Oral Health: Scoping Review. *JMIR mHealth and uHealth, 11*, e46143. Advance online publication. DOI: 10.2196/46143 PMID: 37672331

Velmurugan, R., Bhuvaneswari, R., & Thirumalaisamy, R. (2026). Dental Tourism Marketing: Attracting International Patient Strategies for Dental Clinics and Health Tourism Operators. In Şarkbay, Ö., & Kaya, A. (Eds.), *Next-Generation Treatment Methods and Destinations in Dental Health Tourism* (pp. 97–118). IGI Global., DOI: 10.4018/979-8-3373-4114-9.ch005

Verbytska, A., Lysenko, I., Babachenko, L., & Kraskivska, N. (2023). Inclusive social marketing: Representation and diversity in brand campaigns. *Marketing and Branding Research, 10*, 45–58. DOI: 10.32038/mbr.2023.10.01.04

Verdejo, A. V., & Gutiérrez-Santiuste, E. (2019). Service-dominant logic in public services: Value co-creation in e-government. *Public Management Review, 21*(7), 1011–1031. DOI: 10.1080/14719037.2018.1529878

Veseli, E., & Bencharit, S. (2026). FDI guidelines for AI in dental education: FDI guidelines for AI in dental education. *British Dental Journal, 240*(5), 317–317. DOI: 10.1038/s41415-026-9690-y PMID: 41826442

Vieira, A. R. R., Meurer, M. I., da Cruz, G. S., & Reses, M. de L. N., Castilhos, E. D. de, & Mello, A. L. S. F. de. (2025). Older adults' oral health follow-up in primary care: A teledentistry feasibility exploratory study. *Saúde em Debate*, 49(spe1). DOI: 10.1590/2358-28982025e19901i

Vrančić, A., Zadravec, H., & Orehovački, T. (2024). The Role of Smart Homes in Providing Care for Older Adults: A Systematic Literature Review from 2010 to 2023. *Smart Cities, 7*(4), 1502–1550. DOI: 10.3390/smartcities7040062

Wallace, B. B., & MacEntee, M. I. (2012). Access to dental care for low-income adults: Perceptions of affordability, availability and acceptability. *Journal of Community Health, 37*(1), 32–39. DOI: 10.1007/s10900-011-9412-4 PMID: 21590434

Walsh, K., Joseph, P., Herbert, A., O'Neill, M., & Vogel, C. (2025). Digital technology design in ageing and engaged societies: Challenges in inclusion and context. *Behaviour & Information Technology*, •••, 1–19. DOI: 10.1080/0144929X.2025.2584205

Wang, X., & Xie, F. (2026). Global artificial intelligence governance research in the digital and intelligent era: Advances, trends and countermeasures. *Journal of Knowledge Management, 30*(1), 30–68. DOI: 10.1108/JKM-01-2025-0006

Wang, Z., & Kim, H. G. (2017). Can Social Media Marketing Improve Customer Relationship Capabilities and Firm Performance? Dynamic Capability Perspective. *Journal of Interactive Marketing*, *39*(1), 15–26. DOI: 10.1016/j.intmar.2017.02.004

Watt, R. G., & Sheiham, A. (2012). Integrating the common risk factor approach into a social determinants framework. *Community Dentistry and Oral Epidemiology*, *40*(6), 473–481. DOI: 10.1111/j.1600-0528.2012.00680.x PMID: 22429083

Wells, C., & Spry, C. (2022). *An Overview of Smartphone Apps: CADTH Horizon Scan*. Canadian Agency for Drugs and Technologies in Health., Available at https://www.ncbi.nlm.nih.gov/books/NBK595384/ DOI: 10.51731/cjht.2022.269

WHO. (World Health Organization), (2023). *Hypertension: Fact sheet*. Available at: https://www.who.int/news-room/fact-sheets/detail/hypertension

WHO. (World Health Organization), (2024a). *Nearly 1.8 billion adults at risk of disease from not doing enough physical activity*. Available at: https://www.who.int/news/item/26-06-2024-nearly-1-8-billion-adults-at-risk-of-disease-from-not-doing-enough-physical-activity

WHO. (World Health Organization), (2024b). *Noncommunicable diseases: Fact sheet*. Available at: https://www.who.int/news-room/fact-sheets/detail/noncommunicable-diseases

WHO. (World Health Organization), (2024c). *Obesity and overweight: Fact sheet*. Available at: https://www.who.int/news-room/fact-sheets/detail/obesity-and-overweight

Willis, V. C., Thomas Craig, K. J., Jabbarpour, Y., Scheufele, E. L., Arriaga, Y. E., Ajinkya, M., Rhee, K. B., & Bazemore, A. (2022). Digital health interventions to enhance prevention in primary care: Scoping review. *JMIR Medical Informatics*, *10*(1), e33518. DOI: 10.2196/33518 PMID: 35060909

Wintz, D., Wright, K., & Schaffer, K. B. (2024). Medical influence: What does success look like? *Palliative Care and Social Practice*, *18*, 26323524241297695. Advance online publication. DOI: 10.1177/26323524241297695 PMID: 39539771

Wong, E., Mavondo, F., & Fisher, J. (2020). Patient feedback to improve quality of patient-centred care in public hospitals: A systematic review of the evidence. *BMC Health Services Research*, *20*(1), 530. DOI: 10.1186/s12913-020-05383-3 PMID: 32527314

Wood, N. H. (2024). From Trends to Trust: Harnessing Social Media for the Future of Dentistry. *South African Dental Journal*, *79*(10), 521–524. https://www.scielo.org.za/scielo.php?pid=S0011-85162024001000001&script=sci_arttext

World Health Organisation. (2021). *Improving oral health through the use of digital technology*. https://www.who.int/publications/i/item/9789240035225.https://www.who.int/publications/i/item/9789240061484

World Health Organization. (2021). *Global strategy on digital health 2020–2025*. WHO.

World Health Organization. (2022). *Global oral health status report: Towards universal health coverage for oral health by 2030*. World Health Organization. https://www.who.int/publications/i/item/9789240061484

World Health Organization. WHO. (2020). Decade of Healthy Ageing; WHO: Geneva, Switzerland. Available online: https://www.who.int/initiatives/decadeof-healthy-ageing (accessed on 16 March 2026).

World Health Organization. WHO. (2021). Global strategy on digital health 2020-2025, 1–44. https://www.who.int/publications/i/item/9789240020924 (accessed March 2026).

World Health Organization. WHO. (2022). WHO highlights oral health neglect affecting nearly half of the world's population. 18 November 2022. Available at: https://www.who.int/news/item/18-11-2022-who-highlights-oral-health-neglect-affecting-nearly-half-of-the-world-s-population (accessed March 2026).

Xi, J. Y., Liang, B. H., Zhang, W. J., Yan, B., Dong, H., Chen, Y.-Y., Lin, X., Gu, J., & Hao, Y.-T. (2025). Effects of population aging on quality of life and disease burden: A population-based study. *Global Health Research and Policy*, *10*(2), 2. Advance online publication. DOI: 10.1186/s41256-024-00393-8 PMID: 39810282

Xu, T., Zheng, Y. H., Zhang, J., & Wang, Z. (2025). "They" threaten my work: How AI service robots negatively impact frontline hotel employees through organizational dehumanization. *International Journal of Hospitality Management*, *128*, 104162. DOI: 10.1016/j.ijhm.2025.104162

Yang, R., Gao, S., & Jiang, Y. (2024). Digital divide as a determinant of health in the U.S. older adults: Prevalence, trends, and risk factors. *BMC Geriatrics*, *24*(1), 1027. DOI: 10.1186/s12877-024-05612-y PMID: 39709341

Yap, S. F., Lim, W. M., Gaur, S. S., & Lim, P. Y. (2023). A framework for preventive health marketing. *Journal of Strategic Marketing*, *31*(4), 894–917. DOI: 10.1080/0965254X.2021.2013933

Yeoh, C. W., & Oh, Z. J. (2025). Integrating AI-Powered Digital Marketing Strategies for Enhancing Educational Communication and Technopreneurship. *International Journal of Academic Research in Business & Social Sciences*, *15*(2), 1159–1176. DOI: 10.6007/IJARBSS/v15-i2/24835

Yetisen, A. K., Martinez-Hurtado, J. L., Ünal, B., Khademhosseini, A., & Butt, H. (2018). Wearables in Medicine. *Advanced Materials*, *30*(33), 1–17. DOI: 10.1002/adma.201706910 PMID: 29893068

Yin, Q., Chai, Z., Tao, B., Liu, P., Luo, Y., Zhao, Q., & Yang, B. (2025). The Impact of Online Interactive Platform Services on Oral Health Behaviors in Older Adults with Mild Cognitive Impairment: Protocol for a Randomized Controlled Trial. *Journal of Multidisciplinary Healthcare*, *18*, 663–674. DOI: 10.2147/JMDH.S508247 PMID: 39935432

Yu, P., & Qian, S. (2018). Developing a theoretical model and questionnaire survey instrument to measure the success of electronic health records in residential aged care. *PLoS One*, *13*(1), e0190749. DOI: 10.1371/journal.pone.0190749 PMID: 29315323

Yu, S., Huang, S., Song, S., Lin, J., & Liu, F. (2024). Impact of oral health literacy on oral health behaviors and outcomes among the older adults: A scoping review. *BMC Geriatrics*, *24*(1), 858. Advance online publication. DOI: 10.1186/s12877-024-05469-1 PMID: 39438807

Zainal, H., Xiaohui, X., Thumboo, J., Seah, S. J., Leng, L. L., & Kok Yong, F. (2025). Exploring caregiver challenges, digital health technologies, and healthcare support: A qualitative study. *Frontiers in Digital Health*, *7*, 1587162. DOI: 10.3389/fdgth.2025.1587162 PMID: 40547053

Zare, J., & Persaud, A. (2024). Digital transformation and business model innovation: A bibliometric analysis of existing research and future perspectives. *Management Review Quarterly*, *75*(3), 1999–2032. DOI: 10.1007/s11301-024-00426-z

Zeng, H., Yao, G., & Ma, X. (2025). The impact of short videos on young people's willingness to engage in martial arts: Establishing and testing a conditional process model. *Humanities & Social Sciences Communications*, *12*(1), 624. DOI: 10.1057/s41599-025-04963-0

Zhang, K., Cheng, X., Li, D., & Meng, X. (2025). The digital divide of older people in communities: Urban-rural, gender, and health disparities and inequities. *Health & Social Care in the Community*, 2025(1). DOI: 10.1155/hsc/1361214

Zhang, C., Mohamad, E., Azlan, A., Wu, A. Y., & Qi, Y. (2024). Social Media and eHealth Literacy Among Older Adults: Systematic Literature Review. *Journal of Medical Internet Research, 27*, e66058. Advance online publication. DOI: 10.2196/66058 PMID: 40138684

Zhang, Y., & Kim, Y. (2022). Consumers' Evaluation of Web-Based Health Information Quality: Meta-analysis. *Journal of Medical Internet Research, 24*(4), 1–20. DOI: 10.2196/36463 PMID: 35482390

Zhao, F., Huang, X., Huang, L., Gong, Y., Wang, Z., & Liu, H. (2026). Health communication on Chinese social media: A case study of stress urinary incontinence-related videos on TikTok and Bilibili. *Journal of Consumer Health on the Internet*, •••, 1–13. DOI: 10.1080/15398285.2026.2658036

Zheng, C. (2023). Research on the flow experience and social influences of users of short online videos. A case study of DouYin. *Scientific Reports, 13*(1), 3312. DOI: 10.1038/s41598-023-30525-y PMID: 36849531

Zhu, C., Xu, X., Zhang, W., Chen, J., & Evans, R. (2020). How health communication via TikTok makes a difference: A content analysis of TikTok accounts run by Chinese provincial health committees. *International Journal of Environmental Research and Public Health, 17*(1), 192. https://www.mdpi.com/1660-4601/17/1/192. DOI: 10.3390/ijerph17010192 PMID: 31892122

Ziebland, S., & Wyke, S. (2012). Health and illness in a connected world: How might sharing experiences on the internet affect people's health? *The Milbank Quarterly, 90*(2), 219–249. DOI: 10.1111/j.1468-0009.2012.00662.x PMID: 22709387

Zohriah, A., Muin, A., Rohimat, S., & Faqih, S. (2025). The Dynamics of Educational Services Marketing in the Digital Era. International *Journal of Education, Social Studies, and Management*. .DOI: 10.52121/ijessm.v5i3.871

Zwack, C. C., Haghani, M., Hollings, M., Zhang, L., Gauci, S., Gallagher, R., & Redfern, J. (2023). The evolution of digital health technologies in cardiovascular disease research. *NPJ Digital Medicine, 6*(1), 1. DOI: 10.1038/s41746-022-00734-2 PMID: 36596833

About the Contributors

Martínez-Asanza is first and second degree specialist in Comprehensive Dentistry. She is PhD in Medical Education Sciences at Havana Medical Sciences University, Cuba. Dr. Martínez-Asanza holds a master's degree in dental emergencies care and other in geriatric dentistry. She is a Senior Researcher and Full Professor at the department of Scientific-Technical Results Management of the National School of Public Health (ENSAP), Cuba. Additionally, Dr. Martínez-Asanza is a professor of geriatric dentistry master's degree at Havana Dental School. She is a member of the Cuban Society of Dentistry and the Cuban Society of Geriatric and Gerontology. She has over 26 participations in national and international scientific conferences.

***

Sarah Ali Saeed Alameri is a Lecturer at the College of Administration and Economics, University of Baghdad, specializing in Marketing Management within the broader field of Business Administration. She earned her Bachelor's degree in Administration and Economics from the University of Baghdad in 2006, followed by a Master's degree from the same institution in 2012, and holds a Ph.D. in 2017. Her academic and professional expertise encompasses financial management, strategic planning, and international administration. Dr. Alameri has conducted research on topics including customer voice and competitive advantage in the mobile phone industry, the interrelationship between financing and investment in infrastructure development, and innovative approaches to creativity and self-marketing, contributing valuable insights to both theoretical and practical aspects of marketing and business strategy.

layla laftah Ali Basrah management technical college Southern technical University

Alaa Abdulkareem Ghaleb Almado is a faculty member at the College of Administration and Economics, University of Baghdad, Iraq, specializing in Business Administration with a focus on Human Resources and Industrial Organization. Her expertise spans management, organizational theory, strategic management, human resource management, business management, change management, innovation, organizational development, and innovation management. Almado has conducted research on topics including proactive marketing and its impact on customer satisfaction, the role of banks in promoting financial literacy and the adoption of financial technologies, and the contribution of strategic information systems to sustainable development, reflecting his commitment to both theoretical and practical advancements in business administration.

Najat Dakhil Oufi Alnaemat holds a Master's in Management from the University of Basrah, Iraq. Since 2023, she has been serving as an assistant lecturer at the University of Basrah, Iraq. Dr. Alnaemat's research interests cover a broad range of contemporary topics in management, including digital marketing, entrepreneurship, human resource management, marketing management, and organizational behavior. Her work focuses on exploring innovative strategies and practices that support organizational growth and adaptation in dynamic business environments. She has published several research papers in reputable journals and has participated in various academic conferences, contributing to the development of knowledge and exchange of ideas within the management and business fields. As an emerging scholar and dedicated educator, Dr. Alnaemat is passionate about guiding students and fostering a research-driven learning environment. Her commitment to both teaching and research supports the advancement of academic excellence and practical management solutions in Iraq and beyond.

Sarab Jawad Mohammed Al-Obaidi is a professor and researcher in the Department of Industrial Management at the College of Administration and Economics, University of Baghdad. She earned her Master's degree in Industrial Management from the University of Baghdad, Iraq, in 2024. Her academic and research activities focus on a wide range of contemporary topics, including entrepreneurial performance, digitalization, industrial technology, artificial intelligence, digital marketing, and green marketing. Throughout her academic career, she has contributed to scientific research through the publication of several scholarly articles and active participation in numerous national and international academic conferences.

|**Sarab Al-Obaidi** is a faculty member in the Department of Industrial Management, College of Administration and Economics, University of Baghdad,

she has published numerous local and international research papers and possesses administrative and teaching experience.

Arafat Alyousuf's academic and research interests are diverse and interdisciplinary, spanning project management, entrepreneurship, strategic information systems, human resource management, marketing management, and organizational behavior. Her work reflects a deep commitment to advancing theoretical and practical knowledge in these fields, particularly in the context of modern organizational challenges and technological transformation. She has authored and co-authored numerous research papers published in reputable national and international journals, and has actively participated in a variety of scientific conferences and symposiums, both in Iraq and abroad. Her contributions aim to support the development of management practices and enhance academic discourse on strategic and technological advancements in business administration. Dr. Alyousuf is dedicated to mentoring students and emerging scholars, encouraging them to engage in innovative research and critical thinking. Her work continues to contribute significantly to the academic community and the development of managerial practices in Iraq and the wider region.

Astri Dwi Andriani is a distinguished academic leader and communication strategist currently serving as the Rector of Universitas Putra Indonesia. As an Associate Professor in Communication Science with over a decade of expertise, she has published 15 books and nearly 100 scholarly works, focusing on the intersection of digital innovation and social impact. In this publication, she applies her extensive background in health communication and digital literacy to the field of Dental Public Health, exploring how TikTok can be leveraged as a strategic marketing tool to bridge the gap between clinical expertise and community engagement. By integrating inclusive leadership with empathetic digital narratives, she provides a visionary framework for using short-form video content to drive public health awareness and foster sustainable global communication partnerships in the healthcare sector.

Muralidhar L B is a professionally qualified dental surgeon. He holds Ph.D. from Canara Bank School of Management Studies, Bangalore University after his MBA from Christ University. He has 22 years of total teaching experience spanning across dental education, healthcare management and general management and 4 years of corporate experience. He has worked as research associate in Institute for Social and Economic Change, Bangalore in a project entitled as "Management By and For Common Man: An Exploration of the Concept and Direction for Future"post Ph.D. He had secured 28th rank 10th Standard examination for Karnataka State in 1993. He has been the co-facilitator of a MOOC course on "Social Entrepreneurship and Sustainability",offered through SWAYAM portal, jointly sponsored by GoI and IIMB. His 32 patents have been published and 2 design patents have been granted. He has 41 research publications to his credit out of which 36 are Scopus-indexed and 5 are ABDC indexed. He has co-authored 13 books. He is currently working as Assistant Professor (Grade-3) in Department of Business Management Studies, School of Commerce, Jain Deemed to be University, Bangalore.

Snehal Baviskar holds a Master of Public Health from Southern Connecticut State University, United States. Her research interests include epidemiology, public health research, and chronic disease prevention. She is engaged in evidence-based public health practice with a focus on improving population health outcomes and strengthening health systems through research and data-informed decision-making.

Mohammad Rakibul Islam Bhuiyan is now working as Assistant Professor at Management Information Systems department in the Begum Rokeya University, Rangpur since September 2025. He completed his BBA and MBA from the University of Dhaka in Management Information Systems Department. He was working as Lecturer at Khaja Yunus Ali University in Sirajgonj for 1.5 years. He has also worked as Lecturer in MIS at School of Business at Uttara University in Bangladesh. He also worked as a research assistant, project research associate, teaching assistant and has many notable contributions in different research aspects. His research interest topic is including Digital Economy, Cashless Society, Cashless Economy, Digital Transformation, Emerging Technologies, E-wallet and so on. I have been reviewed more than 280 peer reviews and published more than 45 publications including article,conference paper, book chapter, technical paper, reports in national and international level.

Yasmin Doori is a lecturer in the Department of Industrial Management at the College of Administration and Economics, University of Baghdad. She has published numerous local and international research papers, provides consultations both within and outside educational institutions, and possesses extensive teaching experience.

Eshaq Hamdan is an Assistant Professor specializing in Business Administration, Organization Theory, and Organizational Behavior. I have taught over 10 courses across various academic levels in the Departments of Business Administration, Economics, and Tourism. I have more than 10 scientific research papers published in local and international journals. I served as Head of Department for three years and also as Director of a Consultancy Office

Ahmed Abbas Hammadi is a professor of business administration at the University of Fallujah, affiliated with the Ministry of Higher Education and Scientific

Research. He received his PhD from Tikrit University (2021), his master's degree from Voronezh State University (2014), and his bachelor's degree from Anbar University. He has served as Head of the Business Administration Department, Assistant Dean, and Editor-in-Chief of the Journal of Business Economics. His research interests include marketing, consumer behavior, strategy, governance, and information technology. He has published over 40 research papers and is the author of four books.

Mariam Jabbar is a lecturer at the Department of Management Information Systems, College of Administration and Economics, University of Basrah, Iraq. Mariam holds a Master's degree in Business Administration from the University of Basrah. Prof. Jabbar's research interests include Business Administration, E-commerce, and E- Marketing.

Ferdi Kamberi holds a PhD in Sociological Sciences, serves as an Assistant Professor, and is currently the Dean of the Faculty of Social Sciences at the University "Fehmi Agani"in Gjakova - Kosovo. He has also served as Vice-Rector for Budget, Finance, and Infrastructure at the same university. Previously, he worked as a lecturer in various university colleges and served as Acting Head of the Division for Policy Coordination and Head of the Division for Public Communication at the Ministry of Local Government Administration. He is certified by USAID and AUK – RIT in the Public Policy and Leadership Development program, a certified trainer by IKAP & GIZ in designing and managing public policies within the framework of European integration and licensed to provide professional social services by the Ministry of Justice in Kosovo. Trainer for Trainer -ToT -WB EDU4MIGRATION - Project for capacity development in higher education at University College UCL (Danmark), 2025. Ferdi Kamberi has published numerous impactful scientific works in reputable journals in the region and globally. His interests include sociology, social work and welfare, scientific research methodologies, deviant behaviors, social psychology, gender equality, the sociology of religion, family, media, social issues, community development, and other social fields. Ferdi Kamberi - Holds a PhD in Sociological Sciences, serves as an Assistant Professor, and is currently the Dean of the Faculty of Social Sciences at the University "Fehmi Agani"in Gjakova - Kosovo. He has also served as Vice-Rector for Budget, Finance, and Infrastructure at the same university. Previously, he worked as a lecturer in various university colleges and served as Acting Head of the Division for Policy Coordination and Head of the Division for Public Communication at the Ministry of Local Government Administration. He is certified by USAID and AUK – RIT in the Public Policy and Leadership Development program, a certified trainer by IKAP & GIZ in designing and managing public policies within the framework of European integration and licensed to provide professional social services by the Ministry of Justice in Kosovo. Trainer for Trainer -ToT -WB EDU4MIGRATION - Project for capacity development in higher education at University College UCL (Danmark), 2025. Ferdi Kamberi has published numerous impactful scientific works in reputable journals in the region and globally. His interests include sociology, social work and welfare, scientific research methodologies, deviant behaviors, social psychology, gender equality, the sociology of religion, family, media, social issues, community development, and other social fields.

Zaid Khawam Mahmood is a faculty member at the College of Administration and Economics, University of Fallujah, Iraq. He specializes in public administration, focusing on organizational theory, organizational behavior, and management. His expertise encompasses management, organizational theory, strategic management, human resource management, international organization management, change management, innovation, organizational development, and innovation management. Dr. Mahmood has conducted research on diverse topics, including the benefits of magnetic leadership and its impact on organizational stability, as well as research on authentic leadership and creative and enlightened leadership behaviors, reflecting his commitment to theoretical and practical developments in management in general.

Farida Mouloudj is an Assistant Professor in the Faculty of Letters and Languages at University of Medea, Algeria. Her academic and research have focused primarily on contrastive studies between Arabic and English. She earned her Bachelor and Master in Arabic literature from University of Medea, and Doctor of comparative linguistics from University of Blida 2, Algeria. She has over 6 years of teaching experience. She has 15 publications.

Kamel Mouloudj is a Professor in the College of Economics at the University of Medea, Algeria. His research primarily focuses on predicting individual behavior across various contexts, including customer interactions, tourism, employee dynamics, student engagement, and intentions to use online food delivery services, as well as waste management, green entrepreneurship, and ethical behavior. He earned a Bachelor of Science in Commercial Sciences and a Master's in Marketing from the University of Blida, followed by a Doctorate in Marketing from the University of Algiers 3. With over 20 years of teaching experience, he has published more than 75 research papers. Prof. Mouloudj has also participated in three major research projects at the University of Medea, focusing on industrial marketing, energy, and green start-ups. Since 2019, he has served as Chair of the Doctoral Training Committee in the Department of Commercial Sciences and will continue in this role through 2027.

Anuli Njoku is a Professor in the Department of Public Health at Southern Connecticut State University. She received her Bachelor of Science in Public Health from Rutgers University, Master of Public Health from Boston University, Doctor of Public Health from Drexel University, and postdoctoral training from Fox Chase Cancer Center. In 2023, she was selected as a Fulbright Specialist of Global/Public Health and completed a project in Brazil. Her research interests include social determinants of health, health disparities, environmental health, rural health, and culturally responsive pedagogy.

Supaprawat Siripipatthanakul is working as an Adjunct Professor at Manipal GlobalNxt University, Malaysia, and a Faculty Member at the Faculty of Education at Bangkok Thonburi University, Thailand. He is also a Visiting Professor at the Faculty of Economics and Business at Universitas Terbuka, Indonesia. He has published more than 90 papers and books on Google Scholar. He has a CEFR Level 5 (C1), an English Teacher certificate from AAARYA Business College in Singapore, TEFL & TESOL certificates. 9 certificates in research (Scopus & WOS), and 8 certificates of Ethics in Research. He lectures on research methodology (business/ education/ healthcare) for international universities. He has been invited to review the manuscripts of Q1 and Q2-Scopus, WOS journals/Scopus, and Springer books (240 verified reviews by WOS/ 393 verified reviews by ORCID) since 2022. He is an Editor of IGI Global Scopus Books and PLoS One, Scopus & WOS, SJR Q1 USA.

Hasime (Arif Bacaj) Terziqi, a medical doctor, specialist in Plastic, Reconstructive, and Aesthetic Surgery, and Assistant Professor at the Faculty of Medicine, "Fehmi Agani" University in Gjakovë, Kosovo. I hold a PhD in Medical Sciences from UMHATEM "N. I. Pirogov" EAD, Department of Burns and Plastic Surgery, Sofia, Bulgaria; a Master of Medical Sciences from the Medical Faculty of "Hasan Prishtina" University in Prishtina; and an MD degree from the same institution. I completed my specialization in Plastic, Reconstructive, and Aesthetic Surgery at "Hasan Prishtina" University in Prishtina and the "Nëna Terezë" Medical Faculty in Tirana, Albania. My academic and professional experience includes serving as Vice Dean of the Faculty of Medicine at "Fehmi Agani" University in Gjakovë and as Advisor to the National Preventive Mechanism at the Institution of the Ombudsperson in Prishtina. My teaching, research, and professional interests focus on plastic and reconstructive surgery, burn care, diabetic foot reconstruction, public health, nursing care, nursing education, medical education, digital transformation in healthcare, sustainable healthcare practices, and the integration of artificial intelligence in healthcare education. I am the author of the monograph Burn Care, published by the Faculty of Medicine, UFAGJ, in 2023. I have also contributed chapters to academic publications, with title" Soft Tissue Reconstruction of the

Diabetic Foot in Diabetes Mellitus Type 2". Chapter with "Prevention and Treatment through Nursing Care, Opportunities and Challenges of AI-Driven Transformation in Medical Education in Teaching in the Age of Medical Technology" published by IGI Global in 2025, and a 2026 chapter in Waste Reduction in Public Hospitals: Integrating Digital Solutions and Sustainable Practices. I have published multiple scientific papers in Scopus and Web of Science indexed journals, reviewed medical monographs and textbooks, and participated as a speaker in international congresses and symposia. My professional engagement also includes healthcare projects, student training, public health initiatives, and community health promotion.

Index

A

B

C

D

E

F

G

H

I

O

P

S

T

www.ingramcontent.com/pod-product-compliance
Lightning Source LLC
LaVergne TN
LVHW080904300926
849162LV00003B/541